Medieval

Studies

Library

OLD ENGLISH

Language and Literature

OLD ENGLISH
Language and Literature

Albert H. Marckwardt
PRINCETON UNIVERSITY

James L. Rosier
UNIVERSITY OF PENNSYLVANIA

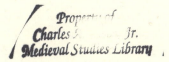

W · W · NORTON & COMPANY · INC ·
NEW YORK

Contents

Foreword

The Committee on Research Activities of the Modern Language Association welcomes the publication of this handbook. For some time the Committee has been attempting to encourage the production of excellent introductory handbooks for older languages. The Marckwardt-Rosier introduction to Old English illustrates the aims of the Committee.

Its texts are well chosen and carefully edited. The grammar is clear and concise, designed to help students understand texts rather than as an end in itself. The vocabulary is comprehensive and so arranged that students can devote their energies to understanding the texts rather than to deciphering them laboriously. Moreover, the introductions to the texts and the discussions of manuscripts with the illustrations give students information to interpret these texts, and other Old English literature, in this culture.

Students of English and medievalists no longer have time to take courses in all the fields they may need to master. Accordingly they need handbooks which will introduce them to a subject without the aid of a teacher. Such handbooks will permit rapid progress when used with a class. The Committee hopes that the Marckwardt-Rosier *Old English*: *Language and Literature* will encourage the publication of similar handbooks in other earlier languages, and in

this way lead to better knowledge of the languages in which much
early literature of great importance has been handed down to us.

W. P. Lehmann
Chairman, Committee on Research Activities
Modern Language Association

Preface

Basically there are two ways in which the grammar of an early stage of a language may be organized and presented. One of them is essentially logical, proceeding from the sounds to the inflections and other word-forming elements, then in turn to the syntax and lexicon. Each of these is internally structured, the section on phonology treating in turn the vowels, long and short, the diphthongs, and the consonants, the morphology proceeding through the catalogue of the parts of speech, and so on. This has been the conventional pattern for everything from Old Church Slavonic to Nahuatl. Properly speaking, these are reference grammars.

The other organizing principle may be termed psychological or pedagogical. It consists of ordering the elements of the language in a sequential and cumulative manner with the primary aim of a gradual development of language competence, simultaneously, however, with respect to the various facets of the language— phonology, morphology, syntax, and lexicon. This is the way in which most elementary textbooks of the commonly taught foreign languages are put together. In terms of the purpose of this text-book—namely, to provide an effective learning program for the corpus of written English extending from the seventh through the eleventh centuries—the pedagogical order will unquestionably best serve this end.

In keeping with this general aim, the presentation of grammatical items is reinforced in each chapter by reading selections which illustrate, insofar as possible, the features of morphology and syntax which have been introduced. In the earlier chapters the readings have been drawn for the most part from the Old English translation of the Gospels, thus employing a content which will be familiar to many students and for which at least an approximate aid in translation is readily available. The readings in the second portion of the grammatical introduction constitute a continued narrative, the story of Apollonius of Tyre, the sole example in Old English of Greek romance.

There are several additional features of our presentation which the instructor who uses this book should understand. They represent either departures from the general mode of a teaching grammar or adaptations to the special situation confronting the student of Old English. For example, the recognition of cognate words is an important aid to someone who is learning Spanish or German. The counterpart here, for the student of Old English, is the ability to see the relationship between words in Old English and their reflexes in the current language. From such equivalences as OE **stān** MnE *stone*, OE **fōd** MnE *food*, we hope that he will learn to generalize these phonological relationships and develop immediate recognition and understanding of a considerable portion of the Old English lexicon. The sooner he does, the more quickly he will build up confidence in his ability to cope with the language. In order to facilitate this, all words in the reading exercises in the first five chapters which have a clearly recognizable Modern English reflex are in boldface type.

Certain other features of the grammatical presentation merit brief mention. The emphasis throughout has been on the development of a sense of pattern, proceeding on the assumption that this will be more productive than mechanical memorization of paradigm after paradigm and conjugation after conjugation. Thus, an attempt has been made to point out distinctive features which run through the declensions of the definite article, the third personal pronoun, the strong adjective, and the demonstrative pronoun, those which are common to the weak noun and the weak adjective, and so on.

In this same connection, it will be observed that many of the chapters conclude with exercises. They have been devised for the purpose of reinforcing the inflectional patterns and phonological rules presented in the text. Some teachers of Old English have found them helpful; others consider such devices too elementary or inconsequential for students of advanced or graduate status. Those who fall into the second category are free to ignore them.

Traditionally, grammars of Old English have dealt with syntax in a somewhat perfunctory manner. With the conviction that the recognition of syntactic habits and relationships is as important to the learning of an early language as the understanding of morphology and lexicon, we have included selected topics in syntax at various intervals in the progressive presentation of the grammar. These syntactic discussions are reinforced and supplemented in the Glossary and Structural Notes for each chapter. The glossarial entries in these are, moreover, progressively phased, with the aim of training the student to use the conventional dictionaries of Old English. At the outset, forms are given in the glossary just as they occur in the reading passages. Later the entries shift to the nominative singular forms of the noun and the infinitive forms of the verb.

The presentation here gives more than ordinary attention to the various devices of word formation and combination which the language employed, again with the aim of giving the student a sense of pattern and a feeling for the language as a productive mechanism. In brief, the aim in presenting the grammar of Old English has been to include as many of the aspects of the language as possible, collectively and cumulatively, chapter by chapter. It would be fair to characterize this work as linguistically oriented rather than as a linguistic grammar of Old English.

The selection of reading texts has been made primarily in terms of intrinsic literary interest and value. But in selecting the texts an effort was also made to avoid, in part, duplication of poems and prose passages which have appeared as the traditional fare of many Old English grammars and readers. This effort seemed to us justifiable not merely on the grounds of providing "new" selections, but chiefly because many of the well-known, most frequently read poetic and prose texts are now readily available in inexpensive anthologies and single editions which can be used to supplement the readings in this volume. The Bibliography lists several such collections and editions. There is obviously still much to be learned about Old English texts from manuscripts, and we believe it important to give the student some idea of what is involved in the procedures of editing. To this end we include two transcriptions and five manuscript plates, in the hope that some students may wish to apply their acquired knowledge of the language to basic tasks in textual scholarship.

The preparation of different parts of this book has benefited from the expert advice generously given by several Old English teachers and scholars. We wish to thank Professor John C. Pope for suggestions of texts, Professor Sherman Kuhn for counsel on the Glossary, Mr. Neil R. Ker for help in selecting manuscript plates, Professors Edward B. Irving, Jr., Robert M. Lumiansky, and Helen Cohen for their exacting criticisms of textual apparatus, and Professors Harold B. Allen and W. Nelson Francis for their helpful comments on the grammatical portion of the book. We are also grateful to Mr. Peter Phelps of W. W. Norton & Company, Inc., for the painstaking and imaginative care he has given to the presentation of our work.

For kind permission to reproduce plates from manuscripts in their possession, we are grateful to the Dean and Chapter of Exeter Cathedral for the plates on pages 280–281; to the Keeper of Western Manuscripts of the Bodleian Library for the plate on page 282; and to the Trustees of the British Museum for the plates on pages 283–284.

Albert H. Marckwardt

James L. Rosier

OLD ENGLISH
LANGUAGE

Chapter 1

1. The Importance of Pronunciation

The immediate purpose of studying Old English is to be able to read and comprehend the literary, historical, and miscellaneous materials which have survived from that period. For this reason, learning Old English differs from learning a modern foreign language. The student is not concerned with acquiring a speaking knowledge or the ability to compose written sentences and paragraphs. His primary aim is a facile reading comprehension.[1]

Nevertheless, it is important to develop an adeptness in pronouncing the language. Properly employed, it can be a useful aid in learning. There are times when the vagaries of spelling will conceal the relationship between an Old English word and its modern counterpart—as in **yfel** *evil*, **Þegen** *thane*, **hrycg** *ridge*. In such instances the ability and readiness to pronounce the word make for quick recognition, which in turn may help to clarify not only the individual word but an entire construction. Pronunciation provides a basis for understanding the historical develop-

1. One must distinguish here between the immediate purpose of acquiring a familiarity with Old English and the various uses to which such a knowledge may be put. In addition to making possible a much more immediate experience of the literature of the period than modernizations can possibly afford, it provides a necessary base for the study of the subsequent history of the language, in terms of its structure as well as of an important segment of its word stock. It rounds out the preparation of the student of Germanic linguistics by giving him a further point of comparison with other Germanic languages.

ment of the language as well as for recognizing Old English words and constructions which are related to Modern English. It is an important element in an appreciation of the literature of the period, especially the poetry.

As a consequence, not only is this first chapter devoted to an account of the sound system of Old English, but it is expected that a good share of the subsequent class activities and the time spent by the student in class preparation will consist of oral work. To study Old English in silence is to fail to take advantage of the aid to learning and comprehension which comes from oral reinforcement.

2.   *The Extent and Limitations of Our Knowledge*

Nothing would be more foolhardy than to pretend that the pronunciations given in this or any other Old English textbook are an absolutely accurate reproduction of the sounds of the language during the reign of Alfred or of Athelstan. There is much that we do not know, the pitch levels and intonation patterns in particular. Several sounds were in the process of development, and the precise stage which they had reached in the tenth century, for example, must remain a matter of conjecture.

At the same time, we do know a great deal in a general way. There is a fair amount of agreement on the number of distinctive sounds or phonemes in the language, both vowels and consonants. We know that long and short vowel sounds were paired in a manner somewhat resembling the language today. The gross features of the stress system are matters of common agreement and an important factor in understanding the system of versification. An alphabet considerably more consistent and regular than ours measurably shortens the task of learning an adequate pronunciation.

3.   *Practical Phonetics and Practical Pedagogy*

Any understanding of the sound system of Old English, in terms of its relationship either to Modern English or to the earlier stages of other Germanic languages, requires from the student at least a rudimentary but nevertheless firmly based knowledge of articulatory phonetics. He should, for example, recognize the vowel sound of *feet* as a high front unround tense vowel and know what each of these terms means with respect to the position and movements of the vocal folds, the jaws, the tongue, and the lips. He should known that [f] is a fricative, produced in a manner distinct from such other fricatives as [s] on the one hand and [v] on the other; that [t] is a stop, with its own distinctive phonetic features. This kind of knowledge provides a proper context for understanding the development of English sounds and for interpreting their status in Old English.

Yet there is a point of diminishing returns in the pursuit of phonetic virtuosity. It has already been pointed out that to a degree our knowledge is limited. We know that there were significant (or phonemic) distinctions between one class of sounds and another, but we do not always know how these distinctions were realized in actual speech. Moreover, certain sounds or sound combinations were pronounced in a manner which many students would find difficult to reproduce. For example, it is likely that about the year 900 the initial sound of the Old English word **scip** (Modern English *ship*) was a combination of [s] and a sound not unlike Modern German *ch* in *ich*. In a case of this kind, it seems preferable for all practical purposes to assign to the sound the value of Modern English *sh* rather than to insist on a closer approximation to what we believe to have been the actual state of affairs. Some of the sounds indicated by the Old English letters **c**, **g**, and **r** call for a similar adjustment to practicality.

4. *The Old English Alphabet*

The Old English alphabet regularly employed twenty-three letters. The vowel characters were seven in number: **a**, **æ**, **e**, **i**, **o**, **u**, **y**. The second of these is usually referred to as *ash*.[2] The consonant

---

2. Each of the characters of the runic alphabet, which had a limited use in England prior to the adoption of the Latin alphabet, had a mnemonic name, consisting of a common word for which it was the initial letter. Thus **æ** was called *ash* (**æsc**), referring to the ash tree; **þ** was known as *thorn* (**þorn**). The name *eth* (pronounced as in *wether*) follows the pattern of the names given to some of the fricatives in the modern version of the Latin alphabet, as in *eff* for *f*, *ess* for *s*. **Eth** was the Icelandic name of the letter **ð**, as adopted from Old English.

characters included **b**, **c**, **d**, **f**, **g**, **h**, **l**, **m**, **n**, **p**, **r**, **s**, **t**, **w**, **þ**, and **ð**. The last two are called *thorn* and *eth* respectively. (See page 5, note 2.) The letters **k** and **x** appear only infrequently. Certain of the characters, notably **g**, **r**, and **w**, were written quite differently from their modern counterparts, as a glance at the manuscript reproductions in this book (pages 278–282) will indicate.

5. *Vowels*

Old English has fourteen distinctive vowel sounds, grouped into seven long and short pairs. Whether the difference in so-called length was solely one of duration or whether it involved the quality of the sound as well is debatable. We know that there was a recognizable and systematic difference because of the subsequent history of the words involved. Thus: OE **bāt** MnE *boat*; OE **batt** MnE *bat*; OE **fūl** MnE *foul*; OE **full** MnE *full*.[3] Old English scribes were not consistent in indicating vowel length. In this book long vowels are regularly marked with a macron, as in the preceding examples.

The Old English long vowels had the following values:[4]

ā,	as in MnE *calm*;	OE **bāt**
ǣ,	as in MnE *band*;	OE **bǣd**
ē,	as in MnE *fate*;	OE **fēt**
ī,	as in MnE *feet*;	OE **tīm**
ō,	as in MnE *coat*;	OE **bōt**
ū,	as in MnE *food*;	OE **hūs**
ȳ,	as in Modern German *grün*;	OE **fȳr**[5]

---

3. The abbreviations OE for Old English and MnE for Modern English will be used throughout the text.

4. In MnE the vowels employed here as key words quite regularly are followed by a rising off-glide, e.g., [ei], [ou], more noticeable in some phonetic environments than in others. Listen closely to the way in which you pronounce *fate*, *fade*, *fame*; *coat*, *code*, *cold*, *know*. According to one school of thought, this was true in Old English as well. Some scholars are content to say that the off-glide was an auxiliary or concomitant feature of vowel length. Others prefer to consider the Old English long vowel phonemes as consisting of a vowel plus semivowel nucleus, and thus analyze the vowels **ē** and **ō** as /ey/, /ow/. The subsequent development of English

The Old English short vowels had the following values:

a,	as in MnE (U.S.) *cot*;	OE **batt**
æ,	as in MnE *bat*;	OE **fæst**
e,	as in MnE *bet*;	OE **bedd**
i,	as in MnE *bit*; ·	OE **rib**
o,	as in MnE *bought*;	OE **post**
u,	as in MnE *full*;	OE **pund**
y,	as in Modern German *fülle*;	OE **syll**[6]

6. *Diphthongs*

It is important to recognize that a diphthong is a combination of two vowel *sounds*, irrespective of spelling. Thus in MnE the word *tide* contains the diphthong [ai], but the two-letter spellings *oa* in *coat* and *ea* in *peak* indicate merely a single vowel.

Standardized or "classical" Old English, namely that of the last half of the tenth century and the first half of the eleventh, had four spellings representing diphthongs: **ēa, ea, ēo, eo**. The first pair, **ēa, ea**, had the vowel of **ǣ̆**, that is long and short, initially and the neutral vowel [ə] as a second element: **bēam, rēad, hēaþ, beard, hearm, mealt**.

The second pair, **ēo, eo**, had the vowel of **ē** initially and the neutral vowel [ə] as a second element: **bēor, tēon, fēol, feorm, weorpan, heort**.

Some of the early West Saxon texts also have **īe, ie**, with the vowel **ĭ** initially and the neutral vowel [ə] as a second element: **hīe, fierd**.[7] In later West Saxon the **ĭe** spellings usually appear as **ĭ** or **y̆**, and it is assumed that at that time they were pronounced as

sounds leaves this matter in some doubt; consequently the simpler presentation is employed here.

5. Described in phonetic terms, OE **ȳ** is a high front rounded tense vowel. It is made by placing the jaw and tongue in position for the vowel of *tree* and simultaneously rounding the lips as in pronouncing *true*.

6. Described in phonetic terms, OE **y** is a high front rounded lax vowel. It is made by placing the jaw and tongue in the position they have when pronouncing the vowel of *fill* and simultaneously rounding the lips as in pronouncing *full*.

7. For information on the dialects of Old English, see Chapter 25, section 135, and the accompanying map.

single vowels. Certain non-West Saxon texts have the diphthongal spellings **ïo** and **io**. These would have the normal values for the first letter and those of the neutral vowel for the second.

7. *Vowels of Unstressed Syllables*

Although Old English pronunciation was characterized by heavy stress on the root syllable, vowels in unstressed syllables were articulated clearly, with little or no tendency toward the neutralization which became a regular feature of later periods of the language. Preservation of vowel contrast in lightly stressed syllables had the effect of distinguishing otherwise identical inflectional forms: **stānas** was a nominative-accusative plural, **stānes** a genitive singular; **stāne** was a dative singular, **stāna** a genitive plural; **lime** was dative singular, **lima** genitive plural, **limu** nominative-accusative plural; **drifen** was past subjunctive, **drifon** past indicative. Once these distinctions were no longer maintained, the entire grammatical system underwent a radical change.

8. *Consonants*

The characters **b**, **d**, **l**, **m**, **n**, **p**, **r**, **t**, and **w** have approximately their ordinary values: **bād**, **dūn**, **lǣdan**, **man**, **pīl**, **rūn**, **tūn**, **wēnan**.

The consonant letters **f** and **s** are pronounced as [v] and [z] respectively when they occur singly between voiced sounds: **drīfan**, **hæfde**, **wīse**, **hæslen**. In all other situations they have the values of [f] and [s]: **fæt**, **stæf**, **swift**, **Offa**, **sunu**, **wæs**, **hæsp**, **wisse**.

The characters **þ** and **ð** were used interchangeably for the final sounds of *cloth* (voiceless) and of *clothe* (voiced). Both characters have the value of *th* in *clothe* when they occur between voiced sounds: **ōðer**, **sūþern**, **lāðra**, **lāþlēas**. In all other situations these characters have the value of *th* in *cloth*: **þunor**, **sūð**, **oððe**, **sōþfæst**.

It is important to recognize the difference between Old and Modern English with respect to the status of the [f] and [v], [s] and [z] pairs as well as the two values of the sounds currently spelled *th*. Each of the pairs consists of a voiceless and the corresponding voiced fricative. In Modern English the two sounds constitute different phonemes: an identical sequence of sounds except for the presence of one or the other members of the pair will result in two different words. Note *feel* as compared with *veal*, *ice* as compared with *eyes*, *ether* as compared with *either*. In Old English such minimal contrasts could not have occurred, since only the voiceless varieties could have been pronounced in initial and final position (*veal* and *eyes* would have been impossible), and only the voiced sound could have occurred intervocalically (*ether* would have been impossible). Under these circumstances, where [f] and [v], [s] and [a], [θ] and [ə] are in complementary distribution, they are in each instance allophones of the same phoneme.

Just as the consonant sounds [k] and [g] shift their points of contact in Modern English according to the nature of the sound which follows (compare *keep* and *cool*, *give* and *good*), so did they in Old English as well. Initially before a front vowel or diphthong (ī, i ē, e ēo, eo, ēa, ea) or finally after ī or i, the letter **c** had a value approximating Modern English *ch* in *cheap*: **cīdan, ċild, ċēosan, ċeorl, ċēap, ċeaster, dīċ, iċ.** (As a help to the student, a dot will be placed over the palatalized **c** in the early chapters of this book.) Under all other circumstances, namely before original back vowels and consonants, **c** had the value of Modern English [k]: **camp, cost, cuman, cū, cȳf, cynd, climban, cnapa, crūse, cwēn.**[8]

The front value of the letter **g** was like that of MnE *y*, pronounced either with the glide quality which we give to it or, especially in final position, as a fricative with the tongue remaining at what is normally the starting point for MnE *y*. Palatalization

8. In all probability the palatalized sound of **c** was not so far forward as the MnE equivalent would suggest. It may have been a palatal stop or palatal affricate, made with the mid-portion of the tongue in contact with the palate rather than the tongue-blade alveolo-palatal affricate which we now have in *cheap*. The modern sound is reasonably close, however, and pedagogically more feasible.

Although on the surface the front and back values of the letters **c** and **g** would appear to have been in complementary distribution, this was true only at a very early period of Old English, antedating any of the written records. At the stage of development represented here, the two sounds indicated by each of the characters were phonemically distinct, just as they are in MnE, where *kin* contrasts with *chin*, *yes* with *guess*.

occurred rather more readily with **g** than with **c**. Final **g** after any front vowel, **g** between any two front vowels, and initial **g** followed by a front vowel became palatalized. As with **c**, the superimposed dot indicates palatalization. Examples are: **ġītsian, ġift, ġeond, ġēotan, ġēar, ġearu, læġ, swēġ, hāliġ, dæġes, swiġe**.

Elsewhere, **g** was pronounced like Modern English *g* in *good*, except that the contact between the back of the tongue and the roof of the mouth was fairly loose: **galan, gold, gōs, gūþ, grāf, gǣd, gnīdan, lōg, fāg**.⁹

The character **h** was pronounced as in Modern English when it occurred before vowels or diphthongs: **hāt, heofon, heals, hēr, him, holt, hōf, hūs, hund**. When it occurred before consonants or in final position it had the value of German *ch*: **seah, feoh, lēoht, nāht, hwǣr, hlēapan, hnǣst, hrīs, hlōh**. The phonetic symbol for this sound is [x]; it should not be confused with the letter **x**, which had a totally different phonetic value. Thus the phoneme /h/ had two allophones, [h] and [x], which were in complementary distribution.¹⁰

The letter combinations **sc** and **cg** were pronounced as in Modern English *ship* and *edge* respectively: **scīr, scot, æsc, ecg, licgan, brycg**. The customary phonemic symbols for these are /š/ and /ǰ/. The character **x**, used only rarely, had the value of [ks]: **axian** is sometimes written for **acsian**.

In most situations the letter **n** was pronounced as in MnE *new, pen*. It had the value of Modern English *ng* as in *sing* when followed by *c* or *g*, but in such combinations the second of the two letters was also pronounced, as they are in Modern English *sink* and *hunger*: **sinc, lengra, drincan, cyning**. This again is in contrast to Modern English, where [n] and [ŋ] are phonemically distinct: *thin* vs. *thing*; *lawn* vs. *long*. In Old English [n] and [ŋ] were allophones of the phoneme /n/.

---

9. There is some reason for believing that /g/ in final position was devoiced and pronounced as [x].

10. In all subsequent discussions of OE phonology, spelling characters will be in boldface type. The characters of the International Phonetic Alphabet, used to refer to phones or sounds irrespective of phonemic status, will be enclosed in square brackets. Phonemic symbols will be placed between slash lines.

There are no "silent letters" in Old English, either vowels or consonants. All consonant characters are pronounced, even though the combinations of sounds they indicate do not occur in Modern English: **wrītan**, **cweorn**, **wlite**, **fnæst**, **cniht**, **gnīdan**.

Just as there were phonemically distinct short and long vowels in Old English, so were there short and long consonants: **hopian** *to hope*, **hoppian** *to hop*; **swelan** *to burn*, **swellan** *to swell*; **freme** *vigorous*, **fremme** (*I*) *make, do, perform*; **cȳðe** (*I*) *make known*, **cȳððe** *kinship* (dative singular). All consonants could occur with length except /ġ/, /ǰ/, /š/, and /w/. The lengthened quality of the consonant was undoubtedly something like the MnE combinations *ripe pear, head dress, pen knife, half fed*, where the closure either is maintained for a longer period of time than for a single consonant, as with *head dress* vs. *head rest*, or is given a second breath impulse as in *pen knife* vs. *penny*. Double consonant spellings at the end of a word were pronounced as single consonants.

Stress is normally placed on the root syllable. Prefixes are generally unstressed. Compounds are stressed on the first element: **nácod**, **púrpure**, **ġefýrn**, **begáng**, **forlǽtan**, **wiðstándan**, **lífdæġ**, **ċíldisc**, **bíterness**.

9. *The Phonemes of Old English*

Although because of practical considerations it has been necessary to proceed from the spellings to the sounds which they were intended to convey, the latter are primary in importance in terms of the phonological structure of the language. Just as every language maintains, in the structure of its sounds, a symmetry peculiar to itself, or perhaps more accurately a near-symmetry, so too does every stage of a language. The following tables illustrate the phonemic structure of Old English.

	VOWELS		DIPHTHONGS
	front	back	front first element
high	/i/ /y/ (rounded)	/u/	/iə/
mid	/e/	/o/	/eə/
low	/æ/	/a/ (unrounded)	/æə/

Length is phonemic, occurring with all vowels and diphthongs.

CONSONANTS

Stops:	/p/, /b/, /t/, /d/, /k/, /g/	Voiced and voiceless pairs.
Fricatives:	/f/, /θ/, /s/, /š/, /h/	
Affricates:	/č/, /ǰ/	Voiced and voiceless pairs.
Nasals:	/m/, /n/	
Liquids:	/l/, /r/	
Glides:	/ġ/, /w/	

Length is phonemic, occurring with all consonants except /ġ/, /ǰ/, /š/, /w/.

Reading

From the Old English translation of the Gospels, Matthew 6: 9–13

The following passage provides practice in reading aloud in a context which is generally familiar.

9. ... **Fæder, ūre**, **þū** þe **eart on heofonum**; sī þ**ïn nama** ġehālgod.
10. **Tō** becume þ**ïn** rīċe; ġewurþe **ðïn willa on eorðan** swā swā **on heofonum**.
11. **Ūrne** ġedæġhwǣmlīcan **hlāf, sele ūs tōdæġ**,
12. **And forġyf ūs ūre gyltas** swā swā **wē forġyfað ūre** gyltendum,
13. **And** ne **ġelǣd þū ūs on** costnunge, āc ālȳs **ūs of yfele** . . .

Chapter 2

10. *Grammatical Gender*

Gender, as a grammatical device, places few demands upon the speaker of Modern English. It requires merely that when he employs a singular personal pronoun to refer to any member of one set of nouns, it must be *he* or one of its case forms; another set demands one form or another of *she*, and a third group calls for *it*. The three groups are easily distinguishable on the basis of sex or the absence of sex-defining characteristics: *boy* is masculine, *daughter* is feminine; words like *table* and *book*, which fall outside these two categories, are neuter. Such a structural arrangement is called natural gender.

The situation in Old English differed in two important ways. On the one hand, a word like **wīf** (MnE *wife*) was neuter, not feminine, as one might expect. But **stān** (*stone*) was masculine, and **scofl** (*shovel*) was feminine. In short, the classification of nouns into genders was quite arbitrary, totally unrelated to biological or metaphorical factors. An arbitrary classification like this is called grammatical gender.

A further difference is to be found in the extent of correspondence or concord which the language demanded. Not only did personal pronouns agree in gender with their antecedents but so did the demonstratives and the relative pronouns, and articles and adjectives matched the nouns which they modified.

Although a system such as this seems arbitrary and cumbersome to speakers of Modern English, it prevails in many languages of the world. Moreover, native speakers master these languages with ease. German children are not conscious of gender and scarcely ever hear the term until they go to school. English children in the tenth century were not conscious of gender, and the great majority of them never heard the term at all. For the present-day student of Old English there is only one avenue open: namely, to learn each noun, together with its appropriate article, as he encounters it in the paradigms which follow.

11. *The Strong Masculine Declension*

Numerically this is the most important Old English declension, comprising more than 30 percent of the nouns that anyone is likely to encounter in his reading. Historically it is equally important in that it is from this declension that we derive the regular pattern for noun plurals in Modern English, and along with the strong neuter declension, it constitutes the basis for our genitive or possessive singular form.

Old English had five inflected case forms: nominative, accusative, instrumental, and genitive. In the noun declensions not every case ending was distinct from all the others. Very often, however, when two case forms for the noun were identical, they were differentiated by the forms of the accompanying article. Compare the nominative-accusative singular and dative-instrumental singular case forms as given below.

The paradigms of **bāt** *boat*, **mūð** *mouth*, **bæcere** *baker*, and **dēofol** *devil* are as follows:

SINGULAR

	DEFINITE ARTICLE				
NOM	sē	bāt	mūð	bæcere	dēofol
ACC.	þone	bāt	mūð	bæcere	dēofol
DAT.	þæm	bāte	mūðe	bæcere	dēofle
INST.	þȳ	bāte	mūðe	bæcere	dēofle
GEN.	þæs	bātes	mūðes	bæceres	dēofles

PLURAL

NOM., ACC.	þā	bātas	mūðas	bæceras	dēoflas
DAT., INST.	þǣm	bātum	mūðum	bæcerum	dēoflum
GEN.	þāra	bāta	mūða	bæcera	dēofla

In disyllabic nouns in which the first syllable is long, the second vowel is syncopated in the inflected case forms: **dēofol**, **dēoflas**. Disyllabic nouns with an initial short syllable generally retain their second vowel when inflected: **bæcere**, **bæceres**.

One feature of this declension accounts for certain irregularities in the plural forms of certain Modern English nouns. Note that **mūð**, singular, ends in a voiceless consonant sound, whereas in **mūðas** the same consonant is voiced because the inflection places it in an intervocalic position. This is reflected in the present-day singular and plural forms of nouns like *calf, knife, house, mouth, wreath.*[1]

12. *Case Functions: The Nominative*

The use of the various cases in Old English is much like that of Latin or Modern German. Any word acting as the subject of a verb is in the nominative case. Words in the predicate serving as the complement of verbs like *be, seem,* etc., are also nominative. The nominative is also the case of direct address.

Subject:
1. Eft clypode **sē engel** Abraham.
   The angel again called Abraham.
2. On þissum ġēare cōm **micel sciphere**.
   In this year a great fleet came.

Predicate Complement:
3. Ælfrēd wæs **cyning** ofer eall Angelcynn.
   Alfred was king over all the English people.
4. Sum sēoc man wæs ġenemned **Lazarus**.
   A certain sick man was called Lazarus.

---

1. Note, however, that a form such as the MnE genitive *mouth's* has been reconstructed by analogy. Had it developed directly from the OE **mūðes**, it would be pronounced like the plural *mouths*.

5. Hē wearð **wǣdla**.
   He became a poor man.

Direct Address:

6. Hwæt seġst þū, **bæcere**?
   What do you say, baker?

Note that the position of words in the nominative case is more flexible than in Modern English. This especially true of subjects, which may occur either before the verb (**Ælfrēd** in 3 and **man** in 4) or after the verb (**engel**, **sciphere**, and **þū** in 1, 2, and 6).

13. *Case Functions: The Accusative*

The direct object of a verb is in the accusative case. Certain prepositions, particularly those expressing movement or direction toward, also govern the accusative. As in Latin, it is used adverbially to indicate extent of time or space.

Direct Object:

1. Berað **þā stānas** to sǣstrande.
   Bear the stones to the seashore.
2. Hie ġefliemdon **þone here**.
   They defeated the army.

Object of Preposition:

3. Hwæt māre dēst þū **on dæġ**?
   What more do you do during the day?
4. Hē myċel þurh **bōceras** ġeleornode.
   He learned much through (from) scholars.
5. Þǣr sint micle mere fersce ġeond **þa mōras**.
   There are large fresh lakes throughout the highlands.
6. his ūp āstiġness in **heofonas** . . .
   his ascension into the heavens . . .
7. . . . oð **þone fyrst** . . .
   . . . until the time . . .

Extent of Time or Space:

8. Hē seglode fīf **dagas**.
   He sailed for five days.

9. **Ealne weġ wæs þæt wēste lond on þæt stēorbord**.
   There was waste land on the starboard the entire way.

As the detailed treatment of word-order patterns in Chapter 5, section 32, indicates, the direct object usually follows both verb and subject. Instances of pre-verbal position for the direct object may be found in the discussion of transposed word order, section 37.

For further discussion of case functions, see sections 18, 24, and 27.

14. *The Agentive Suffix*

One of the nouns in the foregoing paradigm is **bæcere**, formed from the verb **bacan** *to bake*. As is the case with Modern English *-er*, OE **-ere** was added to many verbs and nouns to indicate the agent or doer of the action: **fisc**, *fish*, **fiscere**, *fisher*; **wrītan** *to write*; **wrītere** *writer*. Nouns formed by adding the agentive suffix **-ere** are always masculine.

Reading

From the Old English translation of the Gospels, Luke 9: 14–17

The Authorized Version of the Bible, if used with care, can be helpful in determining the meaning of unfamiliar words. It does not necessarily reflect the constructions which are employed in the Old English version. Words which have followed a regular pattern of development into Modern English are indicated in boldface type, as are certain other easily recognizable forms, e.g., OE **fif**, MnE *five*. In a case such as this, *five* is called the modern reflex of OE **fif**. As you read this passage, be able to identify the case and number of every noun in the passage and to explain the case function of those in the nominative and accusative cases.

14. **Þær wæron** nēah **fīf þūsenda** wera. Ðā cwæþ **hē tō his** leorningcnihtum, "**Dōþ þæt** hī **sitton**, þurh ġebēorscipes **fīftigum**.

15. **And** hī swā **dydon**, and hī **ealle sǣton**.

16. Ðā nam **hē** þā **fīf hlāfas and** þā twēġen **fiscas, and** on þone

heofon beseah, **and** blētsode hī, **and** bræc, **and dælde** his leorningcnihtum þæt hī **āsetton** hī **beforan** þǣm menegum.
    17. Ðā **ǣton** hī **ealle** and wurdon **ġefyllede** . . .

Glossary and Structural Notes

beseah	3rd sing. past of **besēon** *to look.*
blētsode	3rd sing. past of **blētsian** *to bless.*
dælde	3rd sing. past of **dǣlan** *to deal, distribute.*
dōþ	Imperative pl. of **dōn** *to do,* here used in a causative function.
ġebēorscipas	Noun, m.; Usually means *banquet, feast,* from **bēor** *beer,* but here means *in companies.*
hī	Pron., *they, them.*
hlāf	Noun, m., *loaf, bread.*
leorningcnihtum	Noun, m., *disciples.*
menegum	Noun, f., *multitudes,* from **monig** *many.*
nām	3rd sing. past of **niman** *to take.*
nēah	Adv., *nearly;* literally, *nigh.*
swā	Adv., *so.*
twēġen	Number, *two;* cf. MnE *twain.*
þūsenda	Number, gen. pl., *thousands.* Note the double gen. construction, literally, *five of thousands of men.*
wer	Noun, m., *man.* The word survives in MnE *werewolf.*
wurdon	3rd pl. past of **weorðan** *to become.*

Modern English Reflexes

Find and pronounce aloud the words in the above passage which
have as their Modern English reflexes the following:

all	did	he	sit
and	do	heaven	that
ate	fifty	his	there

before	fill	loaf	thousand
broke	fish	sat	to
dealt	five		

Practice Exercise

Using the paradigms given in section 11 as a basis, give the declensions of the following article-noun combinations: **sē stān** *stone*; **sē ende** *end*; **sē æcer** *acre, field*; **sē helm** *helmet*; **sē brēmel** *bramble*.

Chapter 3

15. Syllabic Length

In some Old English declensions and conjugations the length of the root syllable influences the form of the inflectional ending. Accordingly, it is important to know under what circumstances a syllable is considered long. In general, Old English rules of syllabic length and of syllabic division are similar to those of Latin. Naturally, any syllable containing a long vowel or diphthong is a long syllable, but if a short vowel or diphthong is followed by two consonants, the syllable is also considered long. Note the following:

> long-stemmed monosyllables: **wā**, **lār**, **nēah**, **word**
> long-stemmed disyllables: **hēafod**, **norðan**
> short-stemmed monosyllables: **scip**, **glæd**, **scead**
> short-stemmed disyllables: **cyme**, **æcer**, **cleofa**

16. The Strong Neuter Declension

In the nominative-accusative plural of this declension, syllabic length determines the nature of the inflectional ending. Monosyllabic nouns with short stem-syllables end in **-u**. Monosyllabic nouns with long stem-syllables have no ending. Disyllabic nouns ending in **-e** replace it with a **-u** in the nominative-accusative plural. Disyllabic nouns ending in a consonant are inconsistent in their behavior, appearing sometimes with **-u** and sometimes without ending.

A distinguishing feature of the neuter declension is the identity of nominative and accusative, in both article and noun, not only in the plural but in the singular as well. This is a feature of the neuter declension in a number of Indo-European languages.

The paradigms of **scip** *ship*, **swīn** *swine*, **hors** *horse*, **spere** *spear*, and **wǣpen** *weapon* are as follows:

SINGULAR

	DEFINITE ARTICLE					
NOM., ACC.	þæt	scip	swīn	hors	spere	wǣpen
DAT., INST.	þǣm, þȳ	scipe	swīne	horse	spere	wǣpne
GEN.	þæs	scipes	swīnes	horses	speres	wǣpnes

PLURAL

NOM., ACC.	þā	scipu	swīn	hors	speru	wǣpen, wǣpnu
DAT., INST.	þǣm	scipum	swīnum	horsum	sperum	wǣpnum
GEN.	þāra	scipa	swīna	horsa	spera	wǣpna

It is this declension to which Modern English owes its unchanged plurals for the names of such animals as *sheep, swine, deer*, etc. Actually, the number of nouns conforming to this pattern has increased considerably over the past thousand years. Currently such words as *antelope, caribou, rhinoceros* behave in this fashion, particularly when they are spoken of as game animals. On the other hand, some originally neuter nouns such as *horse* have developed the regular plural *horses*, though the old uninflected plural appears in the military expression *a troop of horse*.

17. *The Personal Pronoun*

By the beginning of the tenth century the distinction between dative and accusative in the first and second persons of the pronoun had disappeared, the dative form having prevailed.[1] In

1. In earlier Old English the accusative of the first and second personal pronouns were differentiated from the dative. These were: **mec**, **þec**, **ūsic**, and **ēowic**. They occurred infrequently, however, even in the prose of the ninth century. For a treatment of the dual number in the pronoun, see section 131.

the second person, the distinction between singular and plural was rigidly maintained; there was as yet no evidence of the use of the plural as a polite or formal singular. The dual number of the first and second persons is treated in section 131.

SINGULAR	FIRST PERSON	SECOND PERSON
NOM.	ic	þū
ACC., DAT., INST.	mē	þē
GEN.	mīn	þīn
PLURAL		
NOM.	wē	ġē
ACC., DAT., INST.	ūs	ēow
GEN.	ūre	ēower

18. Case Functions: The Dative

The dative is the indirect object case, as in Latin and Modern German. Unlike Modern English, where the indirect object regularly precedes the direct in the absence of a preposition (John gave Mary the book), Old English word order was not absolutely fixed. The accusative object could precede the dative, as in 2 and 3 below.

The dative is also the principal case used with prepositions. The prepositions listed below regularly occur with, or in grammatical terminology are said to "govern," the dative:

æfter	*after*	**betwēonan**	*between*	**mid**	*with*
ǣr	*before*	**būtan**	*without*	**of**	*from*
ǣt	*at*	**for**	*before*	**tō**	*to, for*
be	*beside*	**fram**	*from, by*		

In most of these the idea of location is paramount, in contrast to those which were shown in Chapter 2, section 13, to govern the accusative, where the main idea was that of motion or direction.

At times the dative served as the quasi-object of certain verbs, the equivalents of which in Modern English are regarded as transitive and are also likely to require a preposition as well: **ætbregdan** *to snatch from*, **æthlēapan** *to run away from*, **bedrēosan** *to deprive of*, **betǣċan** *to entrust to, to commit.*

Indirect Object:

1. þā dǣlde hē **him** his ǣhta.
   Then he gave (dealt) him his goods.
2. Þū scealt Īsaac **me** onsecgan.
   You shall offer Isaac to me.
3. Wē foddor **ūrum horsum** habbað.
   We have fodder for our horses.

Object of Preposition:

4. Augustinus mid **his ġefērum** fērde **tō** þisum iġlande.
   Augustine with his companions went to this island.
5. Hēr wæs tōbrocen Rōmānaburh from **Gotum**.
   Here Rome was destroyed by the Goths.
6. And Columba mæssepreost cōm tō **Pihtum**.
   And the priest Columba came to the Picts.
7. þā cōmon þā menn of **þrym mǣgðum** Germānie, of **Seaxum**, **of Anglum, of Iotum**.
   Then the men came from three Germanic tribes, from the Saxons, from the Angles, from the Jutes.
8. On Þǣm **dagum** rixode Æþelbryht cyning.
   In those days King Aethelbryht ruled.

Use with verbs:

9. He betǣhte hine sylfne **Gode**.
   He committed himself to God.
10. Nū is þēos ġifu **ēow** ætbroden.
    Now is this gift snatched from you.
11. Þēah þrǣl hwylc **hlāforde** æthlēape . . .
    Though a serf may run away from his lord . . .
12. Sē apostol þā bebēad **ðǣm twām ġebrōðrum** . . .
    The apostle then commanded the two brothers . . .

19. *Noun Derivatives in* **-nd**

The Old English inflection for the present particle was **-ende**, added to the base form of the verb. Thus: **hǣlan** *to heal*, **hǣlende** *healing*; **helpan** *to help*, **helpende** *helping*; **līðan** *to sail, journey*, **līðende** *sailing, journeying*. These present-participle forms gave rise to a noun declension indicating the doer or the agent of the action: **Hǣlend** *Healer, Savior*; **helpend** *helper*; **līðend** *traveler*.

20.   *The Verbal Prefixes* **to-** *and* **for-**

It is important to understand the ways in which prefixes modified the meanings of the verbs to which they were attached. The prefix **for-** denoted loss or destruction: **ġieldan** *to yield, pay*, **forġieldan** *to forfeit, give up*; **dōn** *to do, make*, **fordōn** *to destroy*; **weorðan** *to become*, **forweorðan** *to perish*.

The prefix **tō** occasionally had the meaning of adverbial **tō** *to* in such combinations as **tōcuman** *to approach, come toward*, but more often had the meaning of *asunder, apart*: **feallan** *to fall*, **tōfeallan** *to fall apart*; **scufan** *to shove*, **toscufan** *to push apart*. When the prefix **tō** had the latter meaning, the primary stress was on the root syllable of the verb.

Reading
From the Old English translation of the Gospels, Mark 11:15–18

15. þā **cōmon** hī eft **tō** Hierusalem, and þā hē on þæt templ ēode, hē **ongann** drīfan of þǣm **temple sellendas and** bicgendas **and** mynetera þrocu. **And** hēahsetlu þe þā culfran cȳpton, **hē** tōbræc.

16. **And hē** ne geþafode **þæt ǣniġ man** ǣniġ fæt **ðurh þæt templ** bǣre.

17. **And hē** þā lǣrende **ðus** cwæð tō him, "Nis **hit āwriten þæt mīn hūs fram eallum** þēodum bið ġenemned ġebedhūs? Sōðlīċe **ġé dydon þæt** tō sceaðena scræfe.

18. Ðā **þāra** sacerda ealdras and þā bōceras **ðis gehȳrdon,** hī **þōhton hū** hī hine forspilden . . .

Glossary and Structural Notes

bǣre	Verb, 3rd sing. past subjunctive of **beran** *to bear*. The verb is in the past tense because the verb of the main clause is in the past.
(ġe)bedhūs	Noun, n., *chapel, oratory*, literally *prayer house*.

bicgendas	Noun, m., formed from the pres. participle of **bycgan** *to buy.*
bōceras	Noun, m., *scribe, scholar*, from **bōc** *book.*
culfran	Noun, f., acc. pl. of **culfre** *dove.*
cȳpton	Verb, 3rd pl. past of **cȳpan** *to buy*; cf. MnE *cheap, chapman.*
dydon	Verb, 3rd pl. past of **dōn** *to do*. Used in verse 17 in a factitive sense, *made it into a den of thieves.*
ealdras	Noun, m., *chief, chief priest*. Nom. sing., **ealdor**, from **eald** *old.*
eft	Adv., *again.*
ēode	Verb, 3rd sing. past of **gān** *to go.*
fæt	Noun, n., *vessel*; cf. MnE *vat.*
forspilden	Verb, 3rd pl. past subjunctive of **forspillan** *to destroy.*
hēahsetlu	Noun, n., *high seat*; cf. MnE *settle.*
lǣrende	Verb, pres. participle of **lǣran** *to teach.*
mynetera	Noun, m., *money changer, coiner*, from **mynet** *coin, money*; cf. MnE *mint.*
(ġe)nemned	Verb, past participle of **nemnan** *to name.*
of	Prep., *from.*
ongann	Verb, 3rd sing. past of **onginnan** *to begin.*
sacerda	Noun, m., *priest.*
sceaðena	Noun, m., gen. pl. of **sceaða** *thief, criminal*; cf. MnE *scathe.*
scræf	Noun, n. *den.*
sellendas	Noun, m., formed from the pres. participle of **sellan** *to give, sell.*
tō	Prep. For the use of this word in verse 17, see the explanation given under **dȳdon.**
tōbræc	Verb, 3rd sing. past of **tōbrecan** *to break into pieces.*
(ġe)þafode	Verb, 3rd sing. past of **þafian** *to permit.*
þe	As used in verse 15, it is an indeclinable relative pron., to be construed as a gen. pl.

þēodum   Noun, f., dat. pl., *people, nation.*
þrocu   Noun, n., acc. pl. of þroc *table.*

The prefix ġe- appears somewhat inconsistently with certain nouns and a great many verbs, with little or no perceptible modification of meaning. Those words which occur consistently with the prefix are listed under the letter **g** in the Glossary and Structural Notes which follow the reading passages in each chapter of the grammar section of this book. Words which occur both with and without the prefix are entered in the glossary under the letter following the prefix, the prefix being enclosed in brackets.

Modern English Reflexes

Find the words in the passage which have as their Modern English reflexes the following:

all	drive	my	this
and	from	of	thought
any	heard	sell	through
be	house	spill	thus
began	how	temple	to
come	Jerusalem	that	written
did	man		

Practice Exercise

Using the paradigms given in section 16 as a basis, give the declension of the following article-noun combinations: þæt **corn** *corn, grain*; þæt **hēafod** *head*; þæt **rīce** *kingdom*; þæt **hof** *court*; þæt **dūst** *dust*; þæt **wundor** *wonder*.

Chapter 4

21. *The Strong Feminine Declension*

In this declension monosyllabic nouns with short stem-syllables have the ending **-u** in the nominative singular. Monosyllabic nouns with long stem-syllables and disyllabic nouns have no ending. Remember that a syllable is counted as long if it contains a long vowel or a short vowel followed by two consonants.

Disyllabic nouns retain the second vowel in all cases other than the nominative singular if the stem-syllable is short. The second vowel is syncopated when the stem-syllable is long: **sēo netel**, **ðǣre netele; sēo sāwol, ðǣre sāwle**.

A distinguishing feature of the feminine declension is to be found in the agreement in form of the accusative singular with the singular dative and genitive, whereas in the masculine and neuter genders the agreement is between accusative and nominative.

The paradigms of **scinu** *shin*, **glōf** *glove*, **scofl** *shovel*, **netel** *nettle*, and **sāwol** *soul* are as follows:

SINGULAR

	DEFINITE ARTICLE					
NOM.	sēo	scinu	glōf	scofl	netel	sāwol
ACC.	þā	scine	glōfe	scofle	netele	sāwle
DAT., INST.	þǣre	scine	glōfe	scofle	netele	sāwle
GEN.	þǣre	scine	glōfe	scofle	netele	sāwle

27

PLURAL

NOM., ACC.	þā	scina	glōfa	scofla	netela	sāwla
DAT., INST.	þǣm	scinum	glōfum	scoflum	netelum	sāwlum
GEN.	þāra	scina	glōfa	scofla	netela	sāwla

Two irregularities occur at times in this declension. The nominative-accusative plural of all types of nouns may end in **-e** instead of **-a**, **þā scine**, **þā glōfe**. The genitive plural, especially of the short-stemmed nouns, may have **-ena** instead of **-a**: **þāra scinena**.

Two important groups of derived nouns are regularly feminine: abstract nouns ending in **-ness**, e.g., **biterness**, **blindness**, and verbal nouns ending in **-ung** and **-ing**: e.g., **leornung** *learning*, **rǣding** *reading*. These nouns never syncopate the vowel of the second syllable, regardless of the length of the stem.

22. *The Definite Article: Complete Declension*

The declension of the definite article for all genders and cases, and for both singular and plural, is as follows:

		MASCULINE	NEUTER	FEMININE
SINGULAR	NOM.	sē	þæt	sēo
	ACC.	þone	þæt	þā
	DAT.	þǣm	þǣm	þǣre
	INST.	þȳ	þȳ	þǣre
	GEN.	þæs	þæs	þǣre

		ALL GENDERS
PLURAL	NOM., ACC.	þā
	DAT., INST.	þǣm
	GEN.	þāra

23. *Uses of the Definite Article*

Modern English employs three forms with a specifying or determining function: *the, that,* and *this*. Old English had only two: the various forms of **sē**, for which the paradigm has just been given, and a demonstrative, **þēs**, the ancestor of the current form *this*. In general **þēs** is used to indicate the more specific and near at hand; **sē** is used to identify the known and expected rather than to point out, and to suggest the remote rather than the near at hand. In this sense, it combined the functions of MnE *the* and *that*. Nouns were used without the article in many situations where *a/an* occur today. Note the following instances from the reading in Chapter 3: **bið genemned gebedhūs** *is called a house of prayer*; **tō sceaðena scræfe** *into a den of thieves*. The MnE indefinite article represents one of two developments of OE **ān** *one*.

24. *Case Functions: The Instrumental*

Just as the locative case was approaching extinction in classical Latin, so was the instrumental in Old English. It was indistinguishable in form from the dative in the plural of nouns, pronouns, articles, and adjectives, and in the feminine singular as well. Its distinctiveness in form was virtually confined to the masculine and neuter singular of the article and strong adjective.

	INSTRUMENTAL	DATIVE
MASCULINE	**þȳ stāne**	**þǣm stāne**
NEUTER	**þȳ worde**	**þǣm worde**
MASCULINE	**hearde stāne**	**heardum stāne**
NEUTER	**scearpe worde**	**scearpum worde**

As its name indicates, this case was used to indicate the instrument, means, or manner by which something is accomplished. It was also used to indicate accompaniment, cause (often with the subsequent result), and in certain expressions of time. It appears in such set phrases as **for þȳ** *because, therefore*; **þȳ lǣs þe** *unless, lest*. The instrumental generally appears without an accompanying preposition. When a preposition is used, the construction is normally in the dative.

Instrumental:

Ðā beseah Arcestrates **blīðe andwlitan** to Apolloniō.   *Then Arcestrates looked at Apollonius with a happy countenance.*

Dative:

Ðēs ġeonga mann sitt onġēan þē **mid sārlicum andwlītan**.   *This young man sits opposite you with a sorrowful countenance.*

Instrumental:

And **þȳ ġēare** nāmon Westseaxe friþ . . .   *And in that year the West Saxons made peace . . .*

Dative:

Hēr **on þisum ġēare** fór sē micla here . . .   *Here in this year the great army went . . .*

The following examples illustrate the various uses of the instrumental case:

Means or Instrument:

1. Hē swā **smylte dēaðe** middangeard wæs forlǣtende.
   He left the world with (by means of) a gentle death.
2. Þā ġit . . . **earmum** þehton, **mundum** bregdon.
   Then the two of you enfolded with your arms, moved swiftly with your hands.
3. **golde** ġegyrwed
   adorned with gold
4. **Þȳ betstan lēoðe** ġeglenged
   embellished with the best song

Accompaniment:

5. Tryddode tirfæst **ġetrume micle**.
   The glorious one trod with a great troop.
6. Reste he þǣr **mǣte weorode**.
   He remained there with a small host.
7. Ġefeaht Ælfrēd cyning wiþ alne þone here **lȳtle werede** æt Wiltūne.
   King Alfred with a little band fought against all the Danish army at Wilton.

Causal relationships:

8. Þā cōmon for **þȳ** on weġ.
   Therefore those came away.
9. Þæt wæs for **þȳ** hīe wǣron benumene . . .
   That was because they were deprived . . .
10. and **þȳ** þǣr licgað þā deadan men swā lange . . .
    . . . and therefore the dead men lie there so long . . .

11. **Dȳ** māra wīsdom on lande wǣre, **þȳ** we mā ġeðeoda cūðon.
    *The more languages we know, the more wisdom there will be in the
    land.*

25. *The Verb* **bēon**: *Indicative Mood*

In many languages the verb *to be* is highly irregular. It
often represents a composite of several conjugations. This was the
case in Old English, where the conjugation contained elements
of at least three earlier verbs. There are two paradigms for the
present indicative, the first of which, related to Latin *esse*, generally
expresses present time, and the second, cognate with Latin *fui*,
is often used with a suggestion of the future. The past tense is a
development of **wesan**, originally a strong verb. The indicative
forms of the verb are:

			PRESENT		PAST
SINGULAR	1	(iċ)	**eom**	or **bēo**	**wæs**
	2	(þū)	**eart**	or **bist**	**wǣre**
	3	(hē)	**is**	or **bið**	**wæs**
PLURAL	1	(wē)	**sind(on)** or **bēoð**		**wǣron**
	2	(ġē)	**sind(on)** or **bēoð**		**wǣron**
	3	(hīe)	**sind(on)** or **bēoð**		**wǣron**

Reading

From Ælfric's translation of the Heptateuch, Genesis 3 : 1–5

The Authorized Version of the Bible, if used with due caution,
can be helpful in determining the meaning of unfamiliar words.
It does not necessarily reflect or reproduce the constructions which
are employed in Ælfric's version.

Sēo næddre **wæs** ġeapre **þonne ealle** **þā ōðre** nytenu þe **God**
ġeworhte **ofer eorðan**. **And** sēo næddre cwæð tō þām **wife**, "**Hwȳ**
forbēad God ēow, þæt **ġē** ne **ǣton** of ǣlcum **trēowe** binnan **para-**
disum?" þæt **wīf** andwyrde, "**Of** þǣre wæstme þe synd **on para-**
disum, **wē** **etað**; ac **of** þæs **trēowes** wæstme, þe **is on middan**

neorxnawange, **God** bebēad **ūs** þæt **wē** ne **ǣton**, ne **wē** þæt **trēow** ne hrepodon, þȳ lǣs **wē** swulton."

Ðā cwæð sēo næddre eft **tō** þǣm **wīfe**, "Ne bēo ġe nāteshwon **dēade**, þēah þe **ġe** of þǣm **trēowe** eton. Ac **God** wāt sōðlīċe **þæt** ēowre ēagan **bēoð** ġeopenode **on** swā hwylcum **dæġe** swā **ġe** etað **of** þǣm **trēowe**, and **ġe** bēoð þonne **englum** ġelīce, witende **ǣgðer** ġe **gōd** ġe **yfel**."

Glossary and Structural Notes

ac	Conj., *but.*
ǣgðer ġe . . . ġe.	*Both . . . and; as well as.*
ǣlcum	Dat. sing. of **ǣlc** *each.*
ǣton	A past subjunctive form of the verb **etan**, ending in **-on** instead of the more usual **-en** This applies also to **hrepodon** and **swulton** later in the passage. The pres. subjunctive form of the verb occurs later as **eton**.
andwyrde	Verb, 3rd sing. past indicative of **andwyrdan** *to answer.*
bebēad	Verb, 3rd sing. past of **bebēodan** *to command.*
bēo	The regular form of the verb here would be **bēoð**. The form without ending occurs when the verb is followed immediately by either of the pl. pronominal subjects **wē** or **ġē**.
binnan	Prep., *within.*
cwæð	Verb, 3rd sing. past of **cweðan** *to say.*
ēagan	Noun, nom. pl. of **ēaġe** *eye.*
eft	Adv., *again.*
forbēad	Verb, 3rd sing. past of **forbēodan** *to forbid.* Although this verb in itself is negative in meaning, it introduces a clause containing the negative particle **ne**; literally, *forbade that you should not eat.* Multiple negation was wholly permissible in Old English.

ġēapre	Adj. A comparative form of **ġēap** *deceitful, cunning*.
hrepodon	Verb, 1st pl. past of **hrepian** *to touch*.
næddre	Noun, f., *adder, snake, serpent*.
nāteshwon	Adv., *not at all*.
neorxnawange	Noun, m., dat. sing., *paradise*.
nytenu	Noun, n., nom. pl. of **nyten**, **nieten**.
paradisum	The **-um** inflection here is in all probability a Latin acc. sing. The Late Latin form was **paradisus** in the nom.
sōðlīċe	Adv., *truly*.
swā hwylcum	*Whatsoever, whichever*.
swulton	Verb, 1st pl. past of **sweltan** *to die*.
þēah þe	Conj., *even though*.
þȳ læs	Conj., *lest*.
wæstme	Noun, m., dat. sing. of **wæstm** *fruit*.
wāt	Verb, 3rd sing. pres. of **witan** *to know*. This is one of approximately a dozen verbs in which the past-tense form came to be used with reference to present time. These verbs are known as preteritive presents.
wīf	Noun, n., *wife, woman*.
witende	Verb, pres. participle of **witan** *knowing*.
(ġe)worhte	Verb, 3rd sing. past of **ġewyrcan** *to make, create*.

Modern English Reflexes

Find the words in the passage which have as their Modern English reflexes the following:

was	earth	that	on	opened
than	and	ye	amid	day
all	to	eat, ate	us	angel
other	wife	tree	we	like
God	why	paradise	be	either
over	forbade	of	dead	good
				evil

Practice Exercise

Using the paradigms given in section 21 as a model, provide the nominative singular of each noun from the form given and complete the declension: þǣre lēode people, þǣre dene *valley*, þǣre linde *linden*, þǣre fetere *fetter*.

Chapter 5

26. *The Weak Noun or* **-n** *Declension*

In descriptions of the various Germanic languages, the words *weak* and *strong* are frequently used to indicate regular and irregular inflectional patterns respectively. Jacob Grimm, the Germanic philologist, adopted these terms to suggest that highly regularized endings tended to weaken or destroy formal distinctions of case and tense, whereas more irregular patterns strengthened or preserved them.

The paradigms of **mōna** *moon*, **ēare** *ear*, and **sunne** *sun*, masculine, neuter, and feminine, are as follows:

SINGULAR

	MASCULINE		NEUTER		FEMININE	
NOM.	(sē)	mōna	(þæt)	ēare	(sēo)	sunne
ACC.	(þone)	mōnan	(þæt)	ēare	(þā)	sunnan
DAT.,	(þǣm)	mōnan	(þǣre)	ēaran	(þǣm)	sunnan
INST.	(þȳ)	mōnan	(þǣre)	ēaran	(þȳ)	sunnan
GEN.	(þæs)	mōnan	(þǣre)	ēaran	(þæs)	sunnan

PLURAL

NOM., ACC.	(þā)	mōnan	ēaran	sunnan
DAT., INST.	(þǣm)	mōnum	ēarum	sunnum
GEN.	(þāra)	mōnena	ēarena	sunnena

Masculine nouns ending in **-a** belong to the weak or **-n** declension, as do feminine nouns ending in **-e**. Other than **ēare** the only weak neuter nouns are **ēage** *eye* and **wange** *cheek*. Note that the neuter declension preserves the customary identity of nominative and accusative in the singular. Quite often, when nouns were formed from other parts of speech — as **ēaca** *addition* from **ēac**, adverb, *also* — they were declined as weak nouns.

27. *Case Functions: The Genitive*

The genitive is the one inflected case form remaining in Modern English; its functions are many and they are not easily classified. This observation applies equally to the genitive case in Old English. Some of the functions of the Old English genitive correspond fairly closely to those of the Modern English noun. Others have been more or less completely taken over by the modern constructions with *of*. As in Modern English, the Old English genitive was used to indicate possession, measure or quantity, and subjective and objective relationships, as well as for descriptive and adverbial uses. In addition the genitive was used in partitive constructions (especially after **fela**) and as the sole or the second object of certain verbs.

In contrast to Modern English, however, where the genitive always precedes the noun with which it is construed, the Old English genitive might either precede or follow the governing noun: **folces weard** *guardian of the people*, **wine Scyldinga** *lord of the Scyldings*.

The following examples illustrate various uses of the genitive case:

Possession:

1. **þæs cyninges** þeġnas
   The king's followers.
2. Hunta ic eom. **Hwæs? Cinges.**
   I am a hunter. Whose? The king's.
3. **Æþelrēdes** eard
   Aethelred's territory.

Subjective:[1]
  4. Swutol sang **scopes**
     Clear song of the minstrel.
  5. On **þæs wīfes** ġebǣrum
     From the woman's behavior.

Objective:
  6. Hiere āgenne dōm **fēos** ond **londes**
     Their own choice of property and land.
  7. **Godes** lōf
     Praise of the Lord.
  8. **Oþres līfes** ingong
     Entrance into another life.

Descriptive
  9. He wæs **ġelȳfdre ylde**
     He was of advanced age.
  10. **Mǣres līfes** man
     A man of glorious life.
  11. Wōd þā **wiġes** heard.
     Then the hardy one in battle advanced.

Material or Composition:
  12. on ðǣm scennum **scīran goldes**
      on that handle of bright gold
  13. **senepes** sǣd
      seed of the mustard plant
  14. sēo lār **Lǣdenġeðīodes**
      the knowledge of the Latin language
  15. fætels full **ealað**[2] oððe **wæteres**
      vessels full of ale or water

1. The following transformations will help to clarify the distinction between the subjective and objective genitive:
   Subjective:
   swutol sang scopes *clear song of the minstrel* ← **Sē scop sang swutollice** *The minstrel sang clearly.*
   Objective:
   Godes lōf *praise of the Lord* ← **Man lōfiaþ God** *One praises the Lord.*
2. **Ealað** is an irregular genitive singular form.

Adverbial:

16. Hīe fōron **dæġes** ond **nihtes**
    They went by day and by night

17. þā woldon ferian **norþweardes**
    and wished to transport that northward

Measure

18. þrēo hīda **bōclondes**
    three hides of private land

19. þrēo wǣga **spices** ond *īeses*
    three measures of bacon and cheese

Partitive:

20. þrēo **hida** bōclondes
    three hides of private land

21. þǣr wæs **māðma** fela
    there were many treasures

22. **heora** ān
    one of them

23. **þāra scipa** tū.
    two of the ships

Use with Verbs:

24. Fandiaþ **þises goldes** and **ðissera ġymstāna**
    Test this gold and these gems.

25. Hie wǣron benumene ǣġðer ġe **þæs ċeapes** ġe **þæs cornes**.
    They were robbed of both cattle and grain

26. Maurīcius **þæs** Gode þancode
    Mauricius thanked God for that.

27. þā Deniscan him ne mehton **þæs rīpes** forwiernan
    The Danes could not deprive them of the harvest.

28. *Nouns in Apposition*

A noun in apposition agrees in case and number with the noun which it describes.

Nominative:

Gregorius **sē hālga pāpa** Engliscre ðēode **Apostol.**   *Gregorius,*
    the holy Pope, Apostle to the English people.

Accusative:

Ælfrēd kyning hāteð grētan **Wæferð biscep**   *King Alfred*
commands to greet Bishop Waerferth.

Genitive:

We syndon discipuli **Drihtnes Hǣlendes Cristes**   *We are disciples*
of the Lord Savior Christ.

Dative:

Ohtere sǣde his hlāforde, **Ælfrēde cyninge**   *Ohtere told his lord,*
King Alfred

29.   *The Weak Verb Conjugation*

Verbs which form the past tense and past participle by
means of a suffix containing **d** or **t**, followed by endings for the
person and number, are called weak verbs. The use of this dental
suffix[3] is one of the features which distinguish the Germanic languages from the rest of the Indo-European family. A high proportion, possibly 80 percent, of the verbs one is likely to encounter in
one's reading of Old English are weak. This was by far the most
productive conjugation of the period, and the vast majority of
verbs added to the language since that time belong to it.

30.   *Principal Parts of Weak Verbs*

The principal parts of a weak verb are: (1) the infinitive,
(2) the first-person singular of the past tense, and (3) the past
participle. With some verbs the suffix is added directly to the stem;
in others there is a vowel **e** or **o** between the stem and the suffix.
The principal parts of **hǣlan** *to heal,* **wȳscan** *to wish,* **lǣdan** *to lead,*
dynnan *to make a noise, din,* **ferian** *to carry,* and **lufian** *to love* are:

hǣl-an	**hǣl-de**	**hǣl-ed**
wȳsc-an	**wȳsc-te**	**wȳsc-ed**

---

3. In MnE the consonants [t] and [d] are usually described as voiceless and
voiced alveolar stops, respectively. The term *alveolar* implies that the tip of the
tongue makes contact with the alveolar or gum ridge, above the front teeth. In
OE the point of contact is assumed to have been dental, that is, against the back
of the front teeth.

lǣd-an	**lǣd-de**	**lǣd-ed**
dynn-an	**dyn-e-de**	**dyn-ed**
fer-ian	**fer-e-de**	**fer-ed**
luf-ian	**luf-o-de**	**luf-od**
habb-an	**hæf-de**	**hæf-d**

31. *Personal Endings of Weak Verbs, Past Tense*

Weak verbs take the following personal endings in the past indicative:

SINGULAR	1	**-e**	PLURAL 1, 2, 3	**-on**
	2	**-est**		
	3	**-e**		

By observing the conjunction of the two verbs given below with their pronominal subjects, apply the pattern to the remaining verbs for which the principal parts have been listed in the preceding section.

SINGULAR	1	**(ic)**	**hǣlde**	**dynede**	**wȳscte**
	2	**(þū)**	**hǣldest**	**dynedest**	**wȳsctest**
	3	**(hē)**	**hǣlde**	**dynede**	**wȳscte**
PLURAL	1	**(wē)**	**hǣldon**	**dynedon**	**wȳscton**
	2	**(ġē)**	**hǣldon**	**dynedon**	**wȳscton**
	3	**(hī)**	**hǣldon**	**dynedon**	**wȳscton**

32. *Word Order: Direct and Inverted*

The most common word order within clauses and sentences in Old English prose consists of the subject with its modifiers, then the verb and its modifying elements, and finally the object or complement, if there is one. This may be symbolized as **S V (O/C)**, and is called the direct word order. The direct word order is normal in affirmative statements occurring in independent clauses but is used elsewhere as well. Examples: **Sēo sunne gǣð betwēonan heofone and eorðan**. *The sun goes between heaven and earth.* **Ic eom fiscere**. *I am a fisherman.*

When the verb precedes the subject, the word order is called inverted. It may be symbolized as **V S (O/C)**. The inverted word order is likely to occur under the following circumstances:

a. In questions:

Hæfst þū hafoc?

Have you a hawk? (See also Chapter 12, section 65.)

b. In negative statements and questions:

Ne cōm sē here.

The army did not come.

Ne drincst þū wīn?

Don't you drink wine? (See also Chapter 13, section 70.)

c. In clauses introduced by question words:

Hwæt sæġð hē?

What does he say?

Hū ġefēhst þū fiscas?

How do you catch fish?

d. In clauses introduced by certain adverbs:

þā sæġde hē ...

Then he said ...

þǣr bið myċel ġewinn on þǣm lande.

There was great strife in the land.

Reading

From Bede's De Temporibus Anni, *a practical treatise on astronomy and related matters, translated into Old English by Ælfric. (Ælfric's version has been somewhat simplified.)*

Sēo **sunne gǣð betwēonan heofonan and eorðan: on dæġ bufon eorðan and on niht under ðysse eorðan.** Ǣfre hēo byþ yrnende ymbe þās **eorþan, and** ealswā **leohte scīnð under** þǣre **eorðan on niht,** swā swā hēo **on dæġ** dēð **bufan ūrum** hēafdum.

On ðā **healfe** þe hēo **scīnð,** þǣr byð **dæġ; and on** þā **healfe** þe hēo ne **scīnð,** ðǣr byð **niht.** Wē hātaþ **ānne dæġ fram sunnan** upgange oð **ǣfen.**

Dæġhwǣmlīċe ðæs **mōnan leoht** byþ **weaxende** oððe **waniende.** Simle **hē went his hrycg tō** ðǣre **sunnan. Hwonne hē weaxeð is hē full.** Sōðlīċe ðæs **mōnan ġēar hæfð seofon and twentiġ daga**

and eahta tīda. On ðam fyrste **hē** underyrnð **ealle** þā **twelf** tācna þe sēo **sunne** undergæð **twelf mōnað**.

On ðām **ġēare** sind ġetealde **twelf mōnðas, and twā and fīftiġ** wucena, **þrēo hund daga and fīf and syxtiġ daga and** ðǣr tō ēacan **syx tīda**.

Glossary and Structural Notes

daga	Gen. pl. of the noun **dæġ**, used in a partitive construction. The nouns **tīda**, **tācna**, **wucena** are also partitive gen. pl.
dēð	3rd sing. pres. indicative of **dōn** *to do*.
ēaca	Noun, m. weak, *addition*, from **ēac**, adv., *also*.
ealswā	*Just as*.
fyrst	Noun, m., *period, space of time*.
hātaþ	1st pl. pres. indicative of **hātan**, *name, call*.
hēafdum	Noun, n., dat. pl. of **hēafod** *head*.
heofonan	Here used as a weak noun, dat. pl.
leohte	Adv. *brightly*.
oð	Prep., *until*.
oððe	Conj., *or*.
simle	Adv., *ever*.
tācna	Noun, gen. pl., *token, sign (of the zodiac)*.
(ġe)tealde	Past participle of the verb **tellan**. *tell, reckon*.
twelf mōnað	Acc. of extent of time.
ðās	Acc. sing. f. of **ðēs** *this*.
undergǣð	3rd sing. pres. indicative of **undergān** *to go through, complete; under + go*.
underyrnð	3rd sing. pres. indicative of **underyrnan** *to run through, progress; to under-run*.
weaxende, waniende	Pres. participles with the inflection **-ende, -iende**.
went	A shortened form of the 3rd sing. pres. indicative of **wendan** *turn*. The full form would be **wendeþ**.
wucena	Noun, gen. pl., *week*.
ymb	Prep., *about, around*. It governs the acc. here.

Modern English Reflexes

Find the words in the reading passage which have as their Modern English reflexes the following:

sun	shines	ridge	all
between	our	when	twelve
heaven	half	is	month
earth	there	he	two
on	we	full	fifty
day	one	year	three
and	even(ing)	has	hundred
night	daily	seven	five
under	moon	twenty	sixty
this	waxing	eight	six
ever	waning	tide	
light	wends	first	

Practice Exercises

1. Note the following complex words. Of what elements are they composed?

dæġhwǣmliċe   mōnað   sōðliċe   upgange

2. Explain the changes in meaning which have occurred in the modern reflexes of the following Old English words compared with those which they have in the foregoing reading selection:

ġēar   tīda

healfa   went

hrycg

Chapter 6

33. The Personal Pronoun, Third Person

The declension of the first and second persons of the personal pronoun has already been given in Chapter 3, section 17. It was evident there that the distinctions in form between the dative and accusative singular had generally disappeared; they were maintained only in early texts. In the third person, however, this leveling had not yet occurred. Observe the following paradigm:

		MASCULINE	NEUTER	FEMININE
SINGULAR	NOM.	**hē**	**hit**	**hēo**
	ACC.	**hine**	**hit**	**hī**
	DAT., INST.	**him**	**him**	**hire**
	GEN.	**his**	**his**	**hire**

		ALL GENDERS
PLURAL	NOM., ACC.	**hī**
	DAT., INST.	**him**
	GEN.	**hira**

Certain of these pronouns occur in a variety of forms: for **hī**, **hire**, **hira** we often encounter **hīe**, **hiere**, **heora**; **heom** is found at times for the dative-instrumental plural. At a late stage of Old English, **hine**, **hit**, and **him** may be spelled with a **y**.

34. The Pronoun-Article Pattern

In learning any inflected language it is often helpful to compare paradigms for the purpose of trying to detect recurring elements or patterns. If this can be done, the sheer memory burden can be considerably eased. The definite article (see section 22) and the third personal pronoun offer an opportunity for such a comparison. Even though the words are short, there are a number of corresponding elements in them. Note such pairs as **hēo-sēo**; **hine-þone**. A paradigm of the common elements follows:

		MASCULINE	NEUTER	FEMININE
SINGULAR	NOM.	**-ē**	**-t**	**-ēo**
	ACC.	**-ne**	**-t**	= nom. -acc. Pl.
	DAT., INST.	**-m**	**-m**	**-re**
	GEN.	**-s**	**-s**	**-re**

		ALL GENDERS
PLURAL	NOM., ACC.	= f. acc. sing.
	DAT., INST.	**-m**
	GEN.	**-ra**

Note that at every place in the paradigm save two there is a correspondence in vowel, consonant, or consonant plus vowel. Phonetically **hī** and **þā** have little in common, but it is significant that both of them occur as identical forms for the accusative singular feminine and the nominative-accusative plural.

35. *Principal Parts of Strong Verbs*

Verbs which form the past tense and past participle by changing their stem vowel are called strong verbs. Whereas in Modern English the forms of all verbs are arranged on the basis of three so-called principal parts, it is necessary to cite four in order to display the variations in OE strong verbs: (1) the infinitive, (2) the past indicative first-person singular, (3) the past plural, and (4) the past participle. Each of the verbs, for which the principal parts are given below, is representative of a number of others. In this manner the strong verbs are grouped into seven classes, each of which will be taken up in detail later. Although the principal parts are four in number, not all four parts necessarily had different vowels. Some verbs differentiated the vowel for three of the four, others for only two. In every instance, however, the vowel or vowels of the past tense were distinct from that of the present.

INFINITIVE	PAST SINGULAR	PAST PLURAL	PAST PARTICIPLE	MODERN ENGLISH
crēopan	crēap	crupon	cropen	creep
rīsan	rās	rison	risen	rise
springan	sprang	sprungon	sprungen	spring
teran	tær	tǣron	toren	tear
wefan	wæf	wǣfon	wefen	weave
bacan	bōc	bōcon	bacen	bake
blāwan	blēow	blēowon	blawen	blow
slǣpan	slēp	slēpon	slǣpen	sleep

The last of these verbs, **slǣpan**, which has become regular in Modern English, already had an alternate weak past-tense form in Old English.

36. *Personal Endings of Strong Verbs, Past Tense*

Strong verbs take the following endings in the past indicative:

SINGULAR	1	-			
	2	-e	PLURAL	1, 2, 3	-on
	3	-			

By observing the conjugation of the two verbs given below, with their pronominal subjects, be able to apply the pattern to the remaining verbs for which the principal parts have been listed in the preceding section. Note that the second-person singular is based on the *third* principal part.

SINGULAR	1	(iċ)	crēap	rās
	2	(þū)	crupe	rise
	3	(hē)	crēap	rās
PLURAL	1	(wē)	crupon	rison
	2	(ġē)	crupon	rison
	3	(hī)	crupon	rison

37. *Word Order: Transposed*

A third type of word order in Old English consists of the subject, followed by the object or complement, with the verb coming last. This may be symbolized as **S**, **O/C**, **V**, and is called the transposed word order. It occurs chiefly in subordinate clauses.

God bebēad us þæt **wē þæt trēow ne hrepodon**.   *God commanded us that we should not touch the tree.*

Ic bycge þing **þā on þisum lande ne bēoþ ācennede**.   *I will buy things which are not known in this land.*

Sē micle here **þe wē ġefyrn ymbe spræcon*. . .   *The great army which we spoke about before . . .*

On occasion the positions of subject and object are reversed, resulting in the order **O/C S V**. Swā ge wyllað, **þæt ēow men dōn**. *As you desire, so will men do to you.*

Reading
From the Old English translation of the Gospels, Luke 6 : 31–35

At this point the lists of Modern English reflexes which have hitherto accompanied the readings will be discontinued, as well as the practice of setting in boldface type Old English words with Modern English reflexes. It is expected, however, that the student will continue to recognize the correspondences between Old English and Modern English words. In addition, the practice of marking the palatalized **c**'s and **g**'s will be given up, on the assumption that the student will be able to modify his pronunciation appropriately without the orthographic clues.

To repeat the observation made in Chapter 4, the Authorized Version of the Bible, if used with due caution, can be helpful in determining the general sense of the passage and the meaning of unfamiliar words. It does not necessarily reproduce or reflect the constructions employed in the Old English version.

31. And swā ge wyllað þæt ēow men dōn, dōþ him gelīce.

32. And hwylc þanc is ēow, gif ge lufiað þā þe ēow lufiað? Sōðlīce synfulle lufiað þā þe hī lufiað.

33. And gif gē wel dōð þām ðe ēow wel dōð, hwylc þanc is ēow? Witodlīce þæt dōð synfulle.

34. And gif gē lǣnaþ þām ðe gē eft æt onfōð, hwylc þanc is ēow? Sōðlīce synfulle synfullum lǣnað, þæt hī gelīce onfōn.

35. Þēah hwæðere lufiað ēowre fynd and him wel dōð, and lǣne syllað, nān þing þanun eft gehihtende; and ēower mēd byþ mycel on heofone, and gē bēoþ þæs Hēhstan bearn: for þām hē is God ofer unþancfulle and ofer yfele.

Glossary and Structural Notes

æt	Used in the sense of *from*.
dōþ	In verse 31, imperative pl. of **dōn** to do.
eft	Adv., *again*.
for þām þe	Literally, *for that which; because*.
fȳnd	An irregular m. noun, often appearing as **fēond**, which sometimes had no inflection in the nom.-acc. pl.; *enemy*.
gehihtende	Pres. participle; *hoping for*.
hēhstan	A substantive use of the adj. *highest*, declined as a gen. sing. weak noun.
lǣne	As used in verse 35, a f. acc. noun. The corresponding verb appears in verse 34.
mēd	Noun, f., *meed, reward*.
onfōð, onfōn	Verb, *to take, receive*.
syllað	A late form of the verb **sellan** *to give*.
þā þe	The full form of the relative construction *those who*, as is **þām þe** in verse 34.
þanun	Adv., *thence*. The more usual form is **þanon**.
þēah hwæðere	A conjunctive construction, *yet, nevertheless, however*.
witodlīce	Adv., *truly, indeed*.

Chapter 7

38. *Strong and Weak Adjective Declensions*

We have already encountered the terms *strong* and *weak* in connection with noun declensions and verb conjugations. In both instances the term *strong* indicated a fairly high degree of inflectional diversification, in contrast to the greater regularity of whatever is termed *weak*. The same differentiation applies to the adjective declension as well.

At the same time, we must recognize one important difference between adjectives on the one hand and nouns and verbs on the other. A noun or verb is strong or weak for historical reasons; it may be thought of as "belonging" to a particular declension or conjugation. As speakers of Modern English we simply accept the fact that *to ride* forms its past tense and past participle by means of internal change, and that *to glide* adds the weak *-ed* inflection. Occasionally, to be sure, a particular verb may transfer from one conjugation to another, as *to help* did a few centuries ago, and as *to strive* is in the process of doing now, but this is a matter of gradual development.

With the Old English adjectives the situation was substantially different: the same adjective might employ either the strong or weak inflectional suffixes, depending upon the situation in which it occurred.

a. When the adjective occurred after any form of the definite article, after the demonstrative **þēs**, or after a possessive pronoun, the adjective took the appropriate ending of the weak declension.

b. Adjectives used predicatively and those which did not appear in accompaniment with an article, demonstrative, or possessive pronoun took the appropriate endings of the strong declension.

Unquestionably, it is more important to comprehend the principle governing this pattern of distribution than the details of its operation. We may begin with the understanding that it is the function of any system of inflectional endings to identify the ways in which a particular word is being used. With respect to the articles and pronouns, for example, we have already seen that the **-ne** of **þone** and **hine** signals masculine gender, singular number, and accusative case, and that the **-s** of **þæs** and **his** indicates singular number, genitive case, and masculine or neuter gender.

Accordingly, in constructions such as **Hē wearp þone stān** or **Hē wæs þæs cnihtes fæder** the constructions of **stān** and **cniht** are already being shown by the article. It was scarcely necessary, therefore, for an adjective used with **stān** or **fæder** to repeat this information; it appeared with the weak or non-distinctive series of endings under these circumstances. **Hē wearp þone heardan stān. Hē wæs þæs geongan cnihtes fæder**.

On the other hand, when there was no article, demonstrative pronoun, or possessive to identify the use and construction, the adjective itself took on a much more highly distinctive set of endings: **Hē wearp heardne stān. Hē wæs geonges cnihtes fæder**. The principle may be termed one of the economy of distinctive form. We may see a further demonstration of it in Modern German by comparing *alter Mann* with *der alte Mann*, in which the *-er* element, tagging the construction as masculine, nominative, and singular, occurs in the article if there is one, but failing that, is transferred to the adjective.

39. *Masculine Strong and Weak Adjectives*

Adjectives agree with the nouns they modify in case, number, and gender. The strong and weak inflections of adjectives modifying masculine nouns are:

SINGULAR

	STRONG	WEAK
NOM.	heard stān	sē hearda stan
ACC.	heardne stān	þone heardan stān
DAT.	heardum stāne	þæm heardan stāne
INST	hearde stāne	þȳ heardan stāne
GEN.	heardes stānes	þæs heardan stānes

PLURAL

	STRONG	WEAK
NOM., ACC.	hearde stānas	þā heardan stānas
DAT., INST.	heardum stānum	þæm heardum stānum
GEN.	heardra stāna	þāra heardena stāna

It should be evident immediately that the weak adjective has precisely the same inflectional pattern as the weak noun. In most details, the strong adjective endings conform to the article and third personal pronoun pattern. Note that because the choice of adjective inflection is governed by the presence or absence of an article, demonstrative, or possessive, a strong adjective may accompany a weak noun on occasion, and a weak adjective may accompany a strong noun. **Hē seah ealdne huntan. Hē wearp þone heardan stān**.

40. *Sound Changes in Prehistoric Old English*

As any language develops throughout the centuries, its pronunciation changes. This has already become apparent from the comparison of Old English words and their Modern English reflexes listed in the first five chapters. Moreover, these changes occur in a systematic rather than in a chaotic manner, in that words having the same sound appear to be affected in a similar fashion. It is not only OE **hūs** in which the pronunciation of the vowel has shifted from [u] to [au]; the vast majority of words in that category behaved in a similar fashion. Thus: OE **mūs** MnE *mouse*, OE **cū** MnE *cow*, OE **tūn** MnE *town*, OE **būr** MnE *bower*. In short, sound changes tend to apply to an entire class of words, not to individual items here and there.

We must not, however, make the mistake of considering the Old

English values as a starting point. The phonological system of Old English was the product of a series of changes which had taken place prior to the invasion of Britain and prior to the development of a writing system[1] Some of these changes help to account for certain irregularities in the declensions of Old English nouns and adjectives.

41. *Fronting of West Germanic* **a**

West Germanic **a** became OE **æ** in closed syllables, in open syllables when followed by **i** or **e** (*i.e.*, front vowels), or when followed by **h**. It remained **a** in open syllables when followed by a back vowel (**a**, **ō**, or **u**) or by **w**. When followed by a nasal it was written either **a** or **o** in Early West Saxon, but in Late West Saxon it was consistently spelled **a**. In short, a fronting of the vowel occurred unless it was hindered by a back vowel or consonant in the immediate vicinity. Thus WGmc **dag** > OE **dæg**;[2] WGmc **dagas** > OE **dagas**; WGmc **gladra** > OE **glædra**; WGmc **gladum** > OE **gladum**.

This change serves to explain the variation in stem vowel of nouns such as OE **stæf** (m.) and **fæt** (n.) and adjectives such as OE **sæd**. Note the following:

SINGULAR

NOM., ACC.	**stæf**	**fæt**
DAT., INST.	**stæfe**	**fæte**
GEN.	**stæfes**	**fætes**

PLURAL

NOM., ACC.	**stafas**	**fatu**
DAT., INST.	**stafum**	**fatum**
GEN.	**stafa**	**fata**

1. For a more detailed discussion of earlier periods of the language, see sections 132–135.

2. Certain conventional symbols are used in treating the historical development of sounds, words, or forms. The direction sign > signifies *became* or *changed to*; the sign < means *developed from* or *was derived from*. Conventionally, all hypothetical or reconstructed forms are preceded by an asterisk (WGmc* *craft* > OE **cræft**), but in the interests of simplicity, they have been omitted here.

With respect to such adjectives as **sad**, the change of *a* to **æ** explains the forms **sæd, sædne, sæde, sædra, sædena** as opposed to **sada, sadan, sadum**.

42. *Derivatives in* **-līc, -līce**.

In Modern English one way of converting a noun into an adjective is to add the suffix- *-ly*: *man, manly*; *friend, friendly*. The same suffix also serves to change an adjective into an adverb: *bitter, bitterly*; *earnest, earnestly*. Both suffixes have their roots in OE **-līc, -līce**.

In Old English adjectives were formed from nouns by the addition of **-līc**: **heofon** *heaven*, **heofonlīc** *heavenly*; **wīf** *woman*, **wīflic** *womanly*. On occasion, adjectives thus formed were converted into adverbs by the addition of **-e**: **cræft** *skill*, **cræftlīc** *skillful*, **cræftlīce** *skillfully*; **gēar** *year*, **gēarlīc** *yearly* (adj.), **gēarlīce** *yearly* (adv.). Once this pattern was established, other adjectives were converted to adverbs by the addition of **-līce**: **heard** *severe*, **heardlīce** *severely*; **hold** *loyal*, **holdlīce** *loyally*; **læt** *slow*, **lætlīce** *slowly*.

Reading
From the Old English translation of the Gospels, Luke 7:1–10

1. Sōþlīce ðā hē ealle his word gefylde on þæs folces hlyste, he eode intō Cafarnaum.

2. Þā wæs sumes hundredmannes þēowa untrum, sē wæs sweltendlīc, sē wæs him dēore.

3. And þā hē gehȳrde be þām Hælende, hē sende tō him Iūdēa ealdras, and bæd þæt hē cōme and hys þēow gehælde.

4. Þā hī tō þām Hælende cōmon, hī bædon hyne geornlīce and þus cwædon, "Hē is wyrðe þæt ðū him tilie.

5. Witodlīce hē lufað ūre þēode, and hē ūs ūre samnunge getimbrode."

6. Þā fērde sē Hælend mid him. And þā hē wæs unfeor þām hūse, sē hundredmann sende hys frēondas tō him and cwæþ, "Drihten, nelle þū bēon gedreht; ne eom ic wyrðe þæt ðū ga under mīne þecene;

7. For þām ic ne tealde mē sylfne þæt ic ðē cōme; ac cweð þīn word, and mīn cniht byð gehǣled.

8. Ic eom ān man under anwealde gesett, cempan under mē hæbbende; and ic secge þissum, 'Gā,' and hē gǣð; and ic secge þissum, 'Cum,' þonne cymð hē; and ic secge mīnum þēowe, 'Dō þis,' and hē dēð."

9. Ðā wundrode sē Hǣlend, þām gehȳredum, and cwæþ tō þǣre menigeo bewend, "Sōþlīce ic secge ēow, ne funde ic on Israhēl swā mycelne gelēafan."

10. And þā ðā hām cōmon ðe āsende wǣron, hī gemētton hālne þone þe ǣr untrum wæs.

Glossary and Structural Notes

anwealde	Noun, m., *power, authority*.
be	Prep., *concerning, about*.
bewend	Verb, past participle of **bewendan** *to turn around or about*.
cempan	Noun, m. weak, *soldier, warrior*.
(ge)dreht	Verb, past participle of **(ge)dreccan** *to trouble, vex*.
(ge)fylde	Verb, 3rd sing. past of **(ge)fyllan** *to fill, fulfill, complete*.
geornlice	Adv., *eagerly*.
(ge)hælde	Verb, 3rd sing. past subjunctive of **(ge)hǣlan** *to heal*.
hlyste	Noun, m., *hearing*.
hundredesmannes	Noun, m., gen. sing. of **hundredmann** *centurion*.
(ge)hȳredum	From the past participle of **(ge)hȳran** *to hear*. This is a dat. absolute construction similar to the Latin ablative absolute *Those things having been heard*.
menigeo	Noun, f., *multitude*.
nelle	Verb, 2nd sing. pres. subjunctive of **willan** *to desire* preceded by the negative particle **ne**

	and contracted with it. Cp. Modern English *willy nilly*.
samnunge	Noun, f., *assembly, synagogue*. From **samnian** *to gather, collect*.
sweltendlīc	Adj., formed from the pres. participle of **sweltan** *to die*.
tilie	Verb, 2nd sing. pres. subjunctive of **tilian** *to try, endeavor, tend, cherish*.
(ge)timbrode	Verb, 3rd sing. past of **(ge)timbrian** *to build*.
þe	Indeclinable particle, functioning as a relative pronoun, subject of **āsende wǣron**. See Section 45.
þecene	Noun, f., *thatch, roof*.
þēowa	Noun, m. weak, *servant*. This is often declined as a strong noun, **þēow**.
untrum	Adj., *weak, infirm*.
witodlīce	Conj., *truly, indeed*.
wyrðe	Adj., *worthy*.

Practice Exercises

1. Decline the following combinations of adjectives with masculine nouns in both the strong and weak forms, prefixing the definite article for the weak form: **wīd æcer** *wide field*, **beorht mōna** *bright moon*, **lang stæf** *long staff*, **eald æðeling** *old nobleman*, **geong cempa** *young warrior*.

2. Convert the following West Germanic forms into Old English: **land, bacern, cwað, hala, fareld, raca, gafol, dage, fast, gang, maðel, clawu, gamol, hat, nafu, rasc, manu, las, fala, daftu.**

Chapter 8

43. *Neuter Strong and Weak Adjectives*

The strong and weak inflections of adjectives modifying neuter nouns are:

SINGULAR

	STRONG	STRONG	WEAK
NOM.	wīs word	til word	þæt wīse word
ACC.	wīs word	til word	þæt wīse word
DAT.	wīsum worde	tilum worde	þǣm wīsan worde
INST.	wīse worde	tile worde	þȳ wīsan worde
GEN.	wīses wordes	tiles wordes	þæs wīsan wordes

PLURAL

	STRONG	STRONG	WEAK
NOM., ACC.	wīs word	tilu word	þā wīsan word
DAT., INST.	wīsum wordum	tilum wordum	þǣm wīsum wordum
GEN.	wīsra worda	tilra worda	þāra wīsena worda

It should be evident immediately that the weak declension of the adjective follows point for point the declension of the few weak neuter nouns which were present in Old English, the distinguishing mark being the **-e** inflection in both nominative and accusative singular.

With respect to the strong adjective, it should be noted that **wīs**, with a long stem-syllable, has no inflection in the nominative-accusative plural, whereas **til**, with a short stem-syllable, has the inflection **-u**. This follows the pattern of the strong neuter noun declension. Syllabic length again serves as the criterion: **heard, fæst, lēof, gōd, hāl, stearc, dēad, dēop** were declined like **wīs; trum, grim, cwic, bliþe, æðele, grēne** were declined like **til**.[1]

Disyllabic adjectives ending in a consonant often appeared without the **-u** in the nominative-accusative plural and without syncopation: **manig, swutol, maniges, swutoles**. Those with long stem-syllables tended to have **-u** in the nominative-accusative plural and to syncopate the second vowel in all inflected forms: **lȳtel, lȳtlu, lȳtles; hālig, hālgu, hālges**.

44. *The Interrogative Pronoun*

The interrogative pronoun had only masculine and neuter forms and was declined only in the singular.

	MASCULINE	NEUTER
NOM.	**hwā**	**hwæt**
ACC.	**hwone**	**hwæt**
DAT.	**hwǣm**	**hwǣm**
INST.	**hwȳ**	**hwȳ, hwon**
GEN.	**hwæs**	**hwæs**

The similarity of pattern between the interrogative pronoun and such other declensions as the third personal pronoun, the definite article, and the strong adjective declension is immediately apparent. The neuter instrumental form **hwon** appears chiefly in the phrases **tō hwon, for hwon**, roughly equivalent to **hwȳ** *why*. For the most part, **hwā** was used with an anticipated personal antecedent; **hwæt** with an impersonal. To a degree, however, there was already present the current distinction between *who* as an interrogative calling for identification and *what* as an interrogative calling for classification: *Who is Mr. Jones? What is Mr. Jones?* Note the following: **Hwā mæg synna forgyfan būton God āna?** *Who can forgive sins but God alone?* **Nāt ic hwæt hē is ne hwanon hē is.** *I don't know what he is or whence he is.*

1. Disyllabic adjectives ending in **-e, bliþe, grēne**, etc., are inflected like the corresponding nouns. See section 15.

45. The Relative Pronoun

There were three ways of indicating the relationship between clauses requiring a pronoun of reference.

a. The most frequently used relative was the indeclinable particle **þe. Ælc þāra þe mīn word gehyrþ**. *Each of them who hears my words.* **Sīo scīr hātte Hālgoland þe hē on būde**. *The district in which he lived was called Halgoland.*

b. The definite article was sometimes used with a relative function. **Æþelswīþ cwēn, sēo was Ælfrēdes sweostor cyninges, forþfērde**. *Queen Athelswith, who was the sister of King Alfred, died.* **Gode þancode, mihtigan Drihtne þæs sē man gespræc**. *He thanked God, the mighty Lord, for that which the man spoke.*

c. The definite article and indeclinable particle could occur in combination. **Eart þū sē Bēowulf, sē þe wið Brecan wunne?** *Are you that Beowulf who contended against Breca?* **þǣm þe ūte synt, ealle þing on bigspellum gewurþað**. *To them that are without, all things shall be clarified in parables.*

46. The Reflexive Pronoun

As in many other languages, the accusative case of the personal pronoun served a reflexive function in Old English, when its antecedent was the subject of the clause or its equivalent. **Hē wæs hine trymmende**. *He was preparing himself.* **Ne ondrǣd þū ðē**. *Do not fear for yourself.* Certain intransitive verbs which regularly took a dative quasi-object also required the dative in reflexive constructions. **Gewāt him þā to waroðe, þegn Hrōðgāres**. *Hrothgar's thane departed (took himself off) to the shore.*

The intensive **self** also appeared with the personal pronoun in a reflexive function, inflected to agree with the pronoun which it accompanied. **Ic ne tealde mē sylfne þæt ic tō ðē cōme**. *I did not reckon myself (worthy) that I should come to you.* **Hē wæs hine seolfne segniende**. *He was crossing himself.* **Ic mē selfum andwyrde**. *I answered myself.*

47. Breaking

In prehistoric Old English, front vowels developed a transitional glide before certain consonants or consonant groups, which resulted in their being written as diphthongs. The development of this transitional glide is known as *breaking*. It occurred under the following circumstances:

a. æ became **ea** before **l** plus a consonant, **r** plus a consonant, **h** occurring alone or followed by a consonant. **æld** > **eald**, **wærm** > **wearm**, **sæh** > **seah**.

b. **e** became **eo** and **i** became **io** before **l** followed by **c** or **h**, **r** plus a consonant, **h** occurring alone or followed by a consonant. **melcan** > **meolcan**, **erþe** > **eorþe**, **feh** > **feoh**, **mihs** > **miohs**, **lirnōjan** > **liornian**.

The æ affected by this change was the vowel which had developed from an earlier **a**, as described in section 41. Thus, for the words treated under a above, three stages of development can be supplied, *e.g.*, **warm** > **wærm** > **wearm**. The vowel æ broke before **l** plus a consonant only in the West Saxon and Kentish dialects. West Saxon and Kentish **eald** appears in Mercian and Northumbrian as **ald**. (See section 135.)

There is often some uncertainty over the precise interpretation of "**l** plus consonant," and "**r** plus a consonant." The glide **j** is not considered a consonant but rather a semi-vowel. A doubled **l** (**ll**) which is etymological in nature is considered as **l** plus a consonant, but the **ll** which developed as the result of gemination — that is, West Germanic consonant lengthening (see section 77) — did not cause breaking. Thus **fællan** > **feallan**, but **sælljan** remained unchanged (but later became **sellan** by palatal umlaut[2] and loss of **j**).

Reading
From the Old English translation of the Gospels, Luke 7:11–21

11. Þā wæs syððan geworden þæt hē ferde on þā ceastre þe is genemned Nāim, and mid him ferdon hys leorningcnihtas and mycel menego.

12. Þā hē geneālæhte þære ceastre geate, þā wæs þær ān dēad

2. See section 81.

man geboren, ānre wudewan sunu þe nānne ōðerne næfde; and
sēo wudewe wæs þǣr, and mycel menegu þǣre burhware mid hyre.

13. Þā sē Hǣlend hī geseah, þā wæs hē mid mildheortnesse
ofer hī gefylled, and cwæþ tō hyre, "Ne wēp þū nā."

14. Ðā genēalǣhte hē and þā cyste æthrān. Þā ætstōdon þā þe
hyne bǣron. Þā cwæþ sē Hǣlend, "Ealā geonga, þē ic secge,
'Ārīs.'"

15. Ðā ārās sē þe dēad wæs and ongan sprecan. Ðā āgeaf hē
hine hys mēder.

16. Þā oferēode ege hī ealle, and hī God mǣrsodon, and cwǣdon
þæt mǣre wītega on ūs ārās, and þæt God his folc geneosode.

17. Ðā fērde þēos spǣc be him on ealle Iūdēa and embe eall
þæt rīce.

18. Ðā cȳðdon Iōhannes leorningcnihtas him be eallum þysum
þingum.

19. Þā clypode Iōhannes twēgen of his leorningcnihtum and
sende tō þǣm Hǣlende, and þus cwæð, "Eart þū þe tō cumenne
eart, hwæðer þe wē ōðres sculon onbīdan?"

20. Ðā hī tō him cōmon, þus hī cwǣdon, "Iōhannes sē fulluht-
ere ūs sende to þē, and þus cwæð, 'Eart þū ðe tō cumenne eart,
hwæðer þe wē ōðres sculon onbīdan?'"

21. Sōðlīce on ðǣre tīde hē gehǣlde manega of ādlum, ge of
wītum and of yfelum gāstum; and manegum blindum hē gesihþe
forgeaf.

Glossary and Structural Notes

ādlum	Noun, f., **ādl** *disease*.
æthrān	Verb, 3rd sing. past of **æthrīnan** *to touch*.
ætstōdon	Verb, 3rd pl. past of **ætstandan** *to halt, stand by*.
burhware	Noun, f., *citizen*.
ceastre	Noun, f., **ceaster** *city*. Cp. Lat. *castra*.
clypode	Verb, 3rd pl. past of **clypian** *to call, summon*.
cyste	Noun, f., **cyst** *chest, cofin*.
cȳðdon	Verb, 3rd pl. past of **cȳðan** *to inform, make known*.

ege	Noun, m., *fear, terror.*
embe	Prep., *around, about.* The usual form of this word is **ymbe**.
fērde	Verb, 3rd sing. past of **fēran** *to go.*
fulluhtere	Noun, m., *Baptist,* from **fulluht** *baptism.*
gāstum	Noun, m., **gāst** *spirit.*
hwæðer þe	Conj., *or.*
leorningcnihtas	Noun, m., *disciple.*
mǣre	Adj., *famous, illustrious.*
mǣrsodon	Verb, 3rd pl. past of **mǣrsian** *to glorify, praise.*
mēder	Noun, f., dat. sing. of **mōdor** *mother.*
mildheortnesse	Noun, f., *compassion.*
(ge)nēalǣhte	Verb, 3rd sing. past of **(ge)nēalǣcan** *to approach, draw near.*
(ge)nēosode	Verb, 3rd sing. past of **(ge)nēosian** *to visit.*
oferēode	Verb, 3rd sing. past of **ofergān** *to overtake, come upon.*
ōðres	Pron., gen. sing. of **ōðer** *other, another.* The verb **onbīdan** *to await* takes a gen. object.
spǣc	Noun, f., *speech, word.*
syððan	Adv., *afterward.*
wītega	Noun, m., *prophet.*
wītum	Noun, n., **wīte** *punishment, torture.*
wudewan	Noun, f., **wudewe** *widow.*

Practice Exercise

1. Decline the following combinations of adjectives with neuter nouns in both the strong and weak forms, prefixing the definite article for the weak form: **scearp ēare** *sharp ear,* **lang scip** *long ship,* **wilde dēor** *wild animal,* **smæl fæt** *small vessel,* **blind ēage** *blind eye.*

2. Convert the following West Germanic forms into Old English: **fehtan, harpe, ferm, sihiþ, bald, selh, fahs, barc, feld, rerd, hals, cild, derc, scarp, seh, elh, flahs, gard, hert, stelan.**

Chapter 9

48. *Feminine Strong and Weak Adjectives*

The strong and weak inflections of adjectives modifying feminine nouns are:

SINGULAR

	STRONG	WEAK
NOM.	gōd (tilu) lār	sēo gōde lār
ACC.	gōde lāre	þā gōdan lāre
DAT., INST.	gōdre lāre	þǣre gōdan lāre
GEN.	gōdre lāre	þǣre gōdan lāre

PLURAL

	STRONG	WEAK
NOM., ACC.	gōda lāra	þā gōdan lāra
DAT., INST.	gōdum lārum	þǣm gōdum lārum
GEN.	gōdra lāra	þāra gōdena lāra

Again the weak declension of the adjective follows the pattern of the weak feminine nouns, the distinguishing feature being the **-e** inflection in the nominative singular.

In the nominative singular of the strong declension, the presence or absence of **-u** depends upon syllabic length, just as it does in the noun declension. Short-stemmed adjectives retain the **-u**; those with long stems have no inflection. Disyllabic adjectives follow the general pattern of behavior outlined in connection with the nominative-accusative plural of neuter nouns (see section 16).

49. *The Demonstrative* þēs

The demonstrative pronoun þēs has the following forms:

SINGULAR

	MASCULINE	NEUTER	FEMININE
NOM.	þēs	þis	þēos
ACC.	þisne	þis	þās
DAT.	þissum	þissum	þisse
INST.	þȳs	þȳs	þisse
GEN.	þisses	þisses	þisse

PLURAL

	ALL GENDERS
NOM., ACC.	þās
DAT., INST.	þissum
GEN.	þissa

Those forms of the demonstrative with **-ss-** medially often simplified the doubled consonant in Late Old English: þisum. The oblique cases of the feminine singular and the genitive plural sometimes substituted **-re** and **ra** respectively, by analogy with the noun declension: þisre, þissere; þisra, þissera. For the distinction in use and function between the article **sē** and the demonstrative þēs, see section 23.

50. *The Possessive Adjective*

When the genitive case forms of the first and second personal pronouns are used in an adjectival function, they are declined like strong adjectives. For example, the first person **mīn** has the following forms:

SINGULAR

	MASCULINE	NEUTER	FEMININE
NOM.	mīn	mīn	mīn
ACC.	mīnne	mīn	mīne
DAT.	mīnum	mīnum	mīnre
INST.	mīne	mīne	mīnre
GEN.	mīnes	mīnes	mīnre

PLURAL

	MASCULINE	NEUTER	FEMININE
NOM., ACC.	**mīne**	**mīn**	**mīne**
DAT., INST.	**mīnum**	**mīnum**	**mīnum**
GEN.	**mīnra**	**mīnra**	**mīnra**

The second-person singular **þīn** is declined in identical fashion. **Ūre**, the first-person plural, behaves as any other disyllabic adjective ending in **-e**: the nominative singular feminine and the nominative-accusative plural neuter appear as **ūru**. The second-person plural, **ēower**, shows syncopation in the inflected forms: **ēowre**, **ēowres**, **ēowrum**, but **ēowerne**.

It is this general adherence to the inflectional pattern of the article and demonstrative on the part of the possessive adjective which explains the use of the weak declension in such a construction as **þīnre gōdan gife**, *of your (sing.) good gift*. The older third-person possessive **sīn** *his, her, their* was also inflected in the same fashion, but the later and more current forms, **his**, **hire**, **hira**, were not declined. Despite this, the weak inflection of the adjective was used with them: **his langa bāt**.

51. *The Inflectional Pattern for Words of Secondary Rank*

It will have been observed by this time that the inflections of the article, the demonstrative, the third personal pronoun, the interrogative pronoun, and the strong adjective adhere quite consistently to a pattern which has a number of common elements. These may be represented as follows:

SINGULAR

	MASCULINE	NEUTER	FEMININE
NOM.	**ē/φ**	**-t,/φ**	**ēo/φ, -u**
ACC.	**-ne**	**-t,/φ**	**ā/-e**
DAT.	**-(u)m**	**-(u)m**	**-re**
INST.	**ȳ/-e**	**ȳ/-e**	**-re**
GEN.	**-(e)s**	**-(e)s**	**-re**

PLURAL

	ALL GENDERS
NOM., ACC.	**ā/-e**, **φ**, **-u**
DAT., INST.	**-(u)m**
GEN.	**-ra**

Boldface type is used to indicate base vowels or diphthongs or final elements characteristic of two or more forms. The symbol **φ** represents zero or no inflection. For example, the chart entry for feminine nominative singular conveys the information that some forms have **ēo** as a typical stressed vowel, namely **sēo, þēos, hēo**. The second portion of the entry tells us that the ending of some feminine forms may alternate between **-u** and no inflection.

52. *Diphthongization by Initial Palatals*

That the velar stops [k] and [g] developed into palatal glides or affricates when they were followed by front vowels has already been noted (see section 8). This occurred not only before **i** and **e** but also before the **æ** which reflected the fronting of an earlier **a**. Some time later, when a palatal **c**, **g**, or **sc** preceded **ǣ** or **ē**, these vowels came to be written **ēa** and **ie** respectively, and subsequently the **ie** was written as **i** or **ȳ**. Thus, **cǣw > cēaw**; **gǣr > gēar**, **sceran > scieran > sciran**, **scyran**; **gēt > giet > gīt, gȳt**.

This change occurred chiefly in the West Saxon dialect. Whether the diphthongs which resulted from this change were pronounced in a fashion identical to others spelled in the same way, for example those resulting from breaking, is open to question. It is fairly clear that a transition glide developed between the palatal consonant and the vowel. Whether or not the rising diphthong so produced (e.g., **ié**) then became converted into a falling diphthong is much less certain.

Reading
From the Old English translation of the Gospels, Luke 19:1–10

1. Đā ēode hē geond Iericho.
2. Þā wæs þǣr sum man, on naman Zacheus, sē wæs welig.

3. And hē wolde gesēon hwylc sē Hǣlend wǣre. Da hē ne mihte for ðǣre menegu, for þām þe hē wæs lytel on wæstmum.

4. Þā arn hē beforan and stāh up on ān trēow sicomōrum, þæt he hine gesāwe, for þām þe hē wolde þanon faran.

5. Þā hē cōm tō þǣre stōwe, þā geseah se Hǣlend hine, and cwæð tō him, "Zacheus, efst tō þīnum huse, for þām þe ic wylle tōdæg on þīnum hūse wunian."

6. Ðā efste hē, and hine blīþelīce onfēng.

7. Da hī þæt gesāwon þā murcnodon hī ealle, and cwǣdon þæt hē tō synfullum men gecyrde.

8. Ðā stōd Zacheus and cwæð tō Drihtne, "Nū, ic sylle ðearfum healfe mīne ǣhta; and gif ic ǣnigne berēafode, ic hit be fēower-fealdum āgyfe."

9. Ðā cwæð sē Hǣlend tō him, "Tōdæg þisse hīwrǣdene is hæl geworden, for þām þe hē wæs Abrāhāmes bearn.

10. Mannes Sunu cōm sēcan and hāl dōn þæt forwearð."

Glossary and Structural Notes

ǣhta	Noun, f., **ǣht** *possession, goods.*
arn	Verb, 3rd sing. past of **irnan** *to run.* The Modern English form *ran* represents a sound change known as metathesis, that is, a reversal of position of two successive sounds.
bearn	Noun, n., *child, son, descendant.*
cōm sēcan	A complementary infinitive construction, literally, *came to seek.*
(ge)cyrde	Verb, 3rd sing. past of **(ge)cyrran** *to turn to. Consorted with* best fits this particular context.
dōn	Verb infinitive, used here in a causative sense, *to make whole.* It is part of the complementary infinitive construction dependent upon **cōm.**
efst	Verb, imperative sing. of **efstan** *to hasten.* **Efste** is 3rd sing. past.
forwearð	Verb, 3rd sing. past of **forweorðan** *to perish, be lost.*

hǣl   Noun, f., *health, salvation*.

hīwrǣdene   Noun, f., dat. sing., *household*. Literally the clause means, *Today salvation has come upon this household*.

hwylc   Pron., *which, who*.

murcnodon   Verb, 3rd pl. past of **murcnian** *to murmur, complain*.

onfēng   Verb, 3rd sing. past of **onfōn** *to receive*.

(ge)sāwe   Verb, 3rd sing. past subjunctive of **(ge)sēon** *to see*.

sicomōrum   Noun, *sycamore*. The Latin form of the word has been retained here.

stāh   Verb, 3rd sing. past of **stīgan** *to ascend, climb*.

stōwe   Noun, f., **stōw** *place*. The word is retained in such English place-names as *Barstow, Chepstow, Stow-on-the-Wold*, and in the MnE verb *bestow*.

sylle   Verb. A variant form of **selle** *give*.

þanon   Adv., *thence*.

þearfum   Noun, m., **þearfa** *pauper, poor*.

wǣre   Verb, 3rd sing. past subjunctive of **bēon** *to be*.

wæstmum   Noun, m., **wæstm**. Generally *fruit, offspring*, but used here in the special sense of *stature*.

wunian   Verb, infinitive, *to dwell*.

Practice Exercises

1. Decline the following combinations of adjective and feminine nouns in both the strong and weak forms, prefixing the demonstrative **þēos** for the weak form: **eald wuduwe** *old widow*, **smalu scofl** *small shovel*, **gōd talu** *good tale*, **lang þrāg** *long while*, **brād swaþu** *broad path*.

2. Convert the following West Germanic forms into Old English: **scaft**, **gelpan**, **cǣce**, **gēna**, **cafer**, **gǣton**, **gest**, **caster**, **scǣron**, **getan**.

Chapter 10

53. Personal Endings, Present Tense, Indicative Mood

Old English verbs take the following endings in the present indicative:

a. When the infinitive ends in **-an**.

SINGULAR	1	**-e**		
	2	**-est**	PLURAL	1, 2, 3 **-aþ**
	3	**-eþ**		

b. When the infinitive ends in **-ian**.

SINGULAR	1	**-ie**		
	2	**-ast**	PLURAL	1, 2, 3 **-iaþ**
	3	**-aþ**		

In general, all strong verbs and weak verbs of the first class have infinitives ending in **-an** and are conjugated with the personal endings given under a above. But for a few exceptions like **ferian**, **nerian** (see section 94), verbs with infinitives ending in **-ian** are classified as weak verbs of the second class. These are conjugated with the personal endings given under b above. The present forms of **hǣlan** *to heat* and **hopian** *to hope* are:

SINGULAR	1	(**ic**) **hǣle**	**hopie**
	2	(**þū**) **hǣlest**	**hopast**
	3	(**hē**) **hǣleþ**	**hopaþ**

PLURAL	1	(wē) **hǣlaþ**	**hopiaþ**
	2	(gē) **hǣlaþ**	**hopiaþ**
	3	(hī) **hǣlaþ**	**hopiaþ**

54. *Uses of the Indicative*

The present indicative expresses both present and future action and is also used to indicate a continuing state. It normally indicates factual and objective expression and is customarily found in grammatically independent constructions.

a. **Ūre blōd flōweð tō ūrum fōtum ādūne.**
Our blood is flowing to our feet.

b. **Ic ārīse and ic fare to mīnum fæder.**
I shall arise and I shall go to my father.

c. **Sē munt byrneþ ǣfre.**
The mountain burns always.

There was no special construction in Old English to indicate future time. The present tense was normally used for this purpose, and any differentiation between present and future was inferred from the context, as it still is in Modern English in such constructions as *I leave for Boston tomorrow afternoon. He is working all of next week.* Periphrastic constructions like *shall leave, will work* were beginning to develop just at the close of the Old English period. Actually, the most precise labels for the Old English tense forms are *past* and *non-past*.

55. *Personal Endings, Present Tense, Subjunctive Mood*

Old English verbs take the following endings in the subjunctive mood:

a. When the infinitive ends in **-an**.

SINGULAR	1, 2, 3	**-e**	(ic, þū, hē) **hǣle**
PLURAL	1, 2, 3	**-en**	(wē, gē, hī) **hǣlen**

   b. When the infinitive ends in **-ian**.

SINGULAR	1, 2, 3	**-ie**	(**ic, þū, hē**) **hopie**
PLURAL	1, 2, 3	**-ien**	(**wē, gē, hī**) **hopien**

56. *Subjunctive Forms of the Verb* to be

     As with the indicative, there were two conjugations of the verb *to be* in the present tense and one in the past, and as with other verbs, the characteristic features of the subjunctive were the **-e(n)** inflection and the lack of differentiation in form among the three persons.

		PRESENT		PAST
SINGULAR	1, 2, 3	**sī, sȳ**	**beō**	**wǣre**
PLURAL	1, 2, 3	**sīn, sȳn**	**bēon**	**wǣren**

57. *Uses of the Subjunctive*

     In general, the subjunctive expresses the non-factual, whether it be that which is desired, hypothetical, or conceded, or that which is dependent upon the contingency of one factor or another. Rather than compiling a long list of specific uses, many of which overlap with one another, we have chosen to present the subjunctive in terms of paired contrasts with the indicative. In each of the pairs below, the subjunctive construction is given first, followed by a corresponding or similar use of the indicative.

   a. **Sī þīn nama gehalgod.**
      Hallowed be thy name.
      þīn nama is gemǣrsod.
      Thy name is exalted.
   b. **Ic bidde þē þæt þū hine sende tō mīnes fæder hūse.**
      I ask that you send him to my father's house.
      Þū sendest hine to mīnes fæder hūse.
      You are sending him to my father's house.
   c. **þū wēnest þæt ic sȳ stīð man.**
      You suppose that I may be a stern man.
      Þū wast þæt ic eom stīð man.
      You know that I am a stern man.

d. **Gif hit næbbe lēafe þæs Ælmihtigan . . .**
   If it should not have the Almighty's permission . . .
   For þām þe hit næfþ lēafe þæs Ælmihtigan . . .
   Because it has not the Almighty's permission . . .

e. **Gif þū wille witan hwæt hē sȳ . . .**
   If you should wish to know what he may be . . .
   Gif þū wilt witan hwæt hē is . . .
   If you wish to know what he is . . .

f. **Þēah menn swā ne wēnen . . .**
   Although men may not think so . . .
   Menn swā ne wēnaþ.
   Men do not think so.

g. **Gehwelc man hæfþ āgenum cyre ǣr ðǣm ðe hē syngie.**
   Every man has his own choice before he sins.
   Gehwelc man dōþ yfel þā he syngaþ.
   Each man does evil when he sins.

h. **Sē prēost segeþ þæt ān mann fare on Engla land.**
   The priest says that a man is going to England.
   Sē prēost segeþ, "An mann fareþ on Engla land."
   The priest says, "A man is going to England."

58. *Grimm's Law*

One of the features characteristic of all the Germanic languages is the consonant system. Where words appear with certain consonants in most of the other Indo-European languages (represented say by Latin or Greek), the cognate or related words in Germanic appear with different consonants, always however with a certain set of equivalents. Latin *decem*, English *ten*: Latin *dentis*, Greek *odont-*, English *tooth*. Since the Germanic languages generally agree with each other as against the other Indo-European languages, it has been concluded that a systematic series of changes occurred in Germanic, not long after the speakers of this parent language were separated from the speakers of the other Indo-European tongues.

A partial statement of these correspondences was formulated in 1822 by the German scholar Jakob Wilhelm Grimm and is still referred to as Grimm's Law. The details may be summarized as follows:

a. The Indo-European voiceless stops **p**, **t**, and **k** became the corresponding voiceless fricatives **f**, **þ**, and **h** in the Germanic languages: Latin *piscis*, English *fish*, German *fisch*; Latin *tenuis* English *thin*; Latin *cornus*, English *horn*.

b. The Indo-European voiced stops **b**, **d**, **g** became the corresponding voiceless stops **p**, **t**, **k**, in the Germanic languages: Latin *cannabis*, English *hemp*; Latin *decem*, English *ten*; Latin *genu*, German *cnie*, Old English **cnēow**.

c. The Indo-European aspirates **bh**, **dh**, **gh**, became the corresponding voiced fricatives **ƀ**, **ð**, **ʒ**, which later on in English developed into voiced stops: Sanskrit *bharāmi*, English *bear*; Sanskrit *rudhiras*, English *red*; Indo-European *ghostis*, English *guest*.

Reading

From the Old English translation of the Gospels, Luke 14: 16–24

16. Ðā sǣde hē him, "Sum man worhte mycele feorme and manega gelaðode.

17. Þā sende hē his þēowan tō þǣre feorme tīman, þæt hē sǣde þǣm gelaðedum þæt hig cōmon, for þām þe ealle þing gearwe wǣron.

18. Þā ongunnon hig ealle hig belādian. Se fōrmā hīm sǣde, 'Ic bohte ānne tūn. Ic hæbbe nēode þæt ic fare and hine gesēo. Ic bidde þē þæt ðū mē belādige.'

19. Ðā cwæþ se ōðer, 'Ic bohte ān getȳme oxena; nū wille ic faran and fandian hyra. Nu bidde ic þē, belāda mē.'

20. Ðā cwæð sum, 'Ic lǣdde wīf hām, for þǣm þe ic ne mæg cuman.'

21. Þā cyrde se þēowa and cȳdde his hlāforde þæt. Ðā cwæð sē hlāford mid yrre tō þǣm þēowan, 'Gā hraþe on þā strǣta and on wīc þisse ceastre, and þearfan and wanhāle and blinde and healte lǣd hider in.'

22. Ðā cwæð sē þēowa, 'Hlaford, hit ys gedōn swā þū bude, and nū gȳt hēr is æmtig stōw.'

23. Þā cwæð sē hlāford þā gyt tō þām þēowan, 'Gā geond þās wegas and hegas, and nȳd hig þæt hig gān in, þæt mīn hus sī gefylled.

24. Sōðlīce ic ēow secge, þæt nān þāra manna þe geclypode synt ne onbyrigiað mīnre feorme.''

Glossary and Structural Notes

æmtig	Adj., *empty, vacant*.
belādian	Verb, infinitive, *to excuse*. The construction in verse 18 is reflexive. **Belāda** is the imperative form.
bude	Verb, 2nd sing. past of **bēodan** *to command, order*.
ceastre	Noun, f., gen. sing. of **ceaster** *city*.
(ge) clypode	Verb, past participle of **(ge)clypian** *to call*, here inflected as a strong adj.
cȳdde	Verb, 3rd sing. past of **cȳþan** *to make known*. The regular form would be **cȳðde**; here the **ð** has become assimilated to the **d** of the past inflection.
cyrde	Verb, 3rd sing. of **cyrran** *to turn, return*.
fandian	Verb, infinitive, *to test, try out*.
feorme	noun, f., *sustenance, feast*.
gān	Verb, 3rd pl. subjunctive of **gān** *to go*.
gearwe	Adjective, *ready*.
hegas	Noun, m., of **hege** *hedge*.
hig	A late writing for **hī**, **hȳ**.
hraþe	Adv., *quickly*.
lǣd	Verb, imperative sing. of **lǣdan** *to lead*.
(ge)laðode	Verb, 3rd sing. past of **(ge)laðian** *to invite*. **Gelāðedum**, verse 17, is a past participle used substantively.
nȳd	Verb, imperative sing. of **nȳdan** *to compel, urge*.

onbyrigiað	Verb, 3rd pl. pres. of **onbyrigian** *to taste.* Used with a gen. object.
tīman	Noun, m., **tima** *time.*
tūn	Noun, m., *enclosure, homestead, villa.*
wanhāle	Adj., *weak.* Composed of **wan** *lacking* and **hāl** *hale, healthy.*
wīc	Noun, n., *place.* Widely used as a place-name element.
worhte	Verb, 3rd sing. past of **wyrcan** *to work, make, prepare.*

Chapter 11

59. *The Strong Verb Conjugation*

The distinguishing feature of the Old English strong verb conjugation has already been discussed (section 35), namely, that the shifts from present to past tense and past participle were made by changing the stem vowel rather than by adding a suffix. The series of vowel alternations which occur in such verbs as Modern English *drive, drove, driven* and *sing, sang, sung,* observable also in Old English **drīfan, drāf, drifon, drifen** and **singan, sang, sungon, sungen,** resulted from differences in stress upon the same stem vowel at a much earlier period, probably before the diversification of a common Indo-European language. This was not unlike the development of the Old English adverb-preposition **of** [ɔf] into Modern English *off* [ɔf] and *of* [əv], the first, regularly having full stress and the second, ordinarily a reduced grade. Such variations in stress are called *gradation* in English, *ablaut* in German. The latter word is now used as a general term for the various types of strong verb alternation in all the Germanic languages.

There are seven ablaut series which form the basis of classification for Germanic strong verbs. Actually, this conventional division is not the most economical way of describing the situation in Old English, but it has been retained here in the interest of uniformity with the classification used in the grammars of other Germanic languages.

60. *Strong Verbs, Classes 1 and 2*

The ablaut or gradation series for the first and second classes of the Old English strong verbs are:

	PRESENT	PAST SINGULAR	PAST PLURAL	PAST PARTICIPLE
1	ī	ā	i	i
2a	ēo	ēa	u	o
2b	ū	ēa	u	o

Thus, a typical verb of the strong first class would have as its principal parts **drīfan, drāf, drifon, drifen**. The two divisions of the second class may be illustrated by **drēopan** *to drip*, (**drēap, drupon, dropen**) and **slūpan** *to slip*, (**slēap, slupon, slopen**). The present stem of both classes of verbs consists of a long vowel followed by a single consonant, here symbolized by **-V̄C**. They are the only classes where this situation prevails throughout, although some seventh-class strong verbs also show the same long vowel–single consonant sequence. For Old English there is no way of differentiating those strong verbs of the second class which have **ēo** in the present from those which have **ū**; they developed from a different degree of vowel grade in the Indo-European present.

61. *The Complete Conjugation of the Strong Verb*

The tabulation below gives all forms of the strong verb, as they would have occurred with **drīfan, drēopan,** and **slūpan**. Note particularly the principal part upon which each of the forms is based.

CLASS 1

Principal Parts: **drīfan, drāf, drifon, drifen**

		PRESENT INDICATIVE	PAST INDICATIVE
SINGULAR	(ic)	drīfe	drāf
	(þū)	drīfest	drife
	(hē)	drīfeþ	drāf
PLURAL	(wē, gē, hī)	drīfaþ	drifon

		PRESENT SUBJUNCTIVE	PAST SUBJUNCTIVE
SINGULAR	(ic, þū, hē)	**drīfe**	**drife**
PLURAL	(wē, gē, hī)	**drīfen**	**drifen**

IMPERATIVE: Singular, **drīf**   Plural, **drīfaþ**
PARTICIPLES: Present, **drīfende**   Past, **drīfen**
INFINITIVE: **drīfan**   GERUND: **tō drīfenne**

CLASS 2

Principal Parts: **drēopan, drēap, drupon, dropen**
                   slūpan, slēap, slupon, slopen

		PRESENT INDICATIVE		PAST INDICATIVE	
SINGULAR	(ic)	**drēope**	**slūpe**	**drēap**	**slēap**
	(þū)	**drēopest**	**slūpest**	**drupe**	**slupe**
	(hē)	**drēopeþ**	**slūpeþ**	**drēap**	**slēap**
PLURAL	(wē, gē, hī)	**drēopaþ**	**slūpaþ**	**drupon**	**slupon**

		PRESENT SUBJUNCTIVE		PAST SUBJUNCTIVE	
SINGULAR	(ic, þū, hē)	**drēope**	**slūpe**	**drupe**	**slupe**
PLURAL	(wē, gē, hī)	**drēopen**	**slūpen**	**drupen**	**slupen**

IMPERATIVE: Singular, **drēop, slūp**   Plural, **drēopaþ, slūpaþ**
PARTICIPLES: Present, **drēopende, slūpende**   Past, **dropen, slopen**
INFINITIVE: **drēopan, slūpan**   GERUND: **tō drēopenne, tō slūpenne**

The number of Old English strong verbs in all seven classes has been placed at 312. Currently, 66 of these remain in the standard language as strong verbs. Of the others, 129 have become weak, as for example OE **bacan** *to bake* and **helpan** *to help*. The remaining 117 have become obsolete or archaic or are confined to dialect use, as OE **drēogan**, MnE dialect *dree*.

Frequently in the West Saxon dialect the second and third persons, present indicative singular, underwent a further sound change which would have resulted in such forms as **drīpst, drīpþ**,

slȳpst, slȳpþ. These will be taken up in sections 87, 88; for the present only the regular full forms are given.

It should also be noted that the past subjunctive is based on the third principal part of the verb. Consequently there is no distinction in form between indicative and subjunctive in the second-person singular of the past tense. Another point of identity between indicative and subjunctive is in the first-person singular of the present.

62. *Tense Sequence in the Subjunctive*

In Old English somewhat more frequently than in Modern English, the tense of a subjunctive verb in a dependent clause was governed by or agreed with the tense of the verb in the main clause. Thus: **Hēo hine ... lǣrde þæt hē woroldhād forlēte** (*past*). *She advised him that he give up secular life.* **On eallum þǣm hē geornlīce gīemde þæt hē menn ātuge** (*past*) **fram synna lufan and māndǣda**. *In all those matters he earnestly took care to draw men away from the love of sins and evil deeds.*

63. *Consonant Alternation: Verner's Law*

Certain strong verbs show an irregularity in the consonants for the third and fourth principal parts. Thus:

snīðan *to cut*	**snāþ**	**snidon**	**sniden**
cēosan *to choose*	**cēas**	**curon**	**coren**
tēon (earlier **tēohan**) *to draw*	**tēah**	**tugon**	**togen**

These irregularities may be accounted for on the basis of Verner's Law. In essence this consists of a series of statements explaining certain instances where the Germanic consonant shift operated in a manner other than that which Grimm had described. It dealt primarily with the relationship between voicing and the placement of stress. We can see a similar phenomenon in Modern English by comparing:

díssolute *ss* = [s]   dissólve *ss* = [z]
éxercise *x* = [ks]   exért *x* = [gz]

From such pairs it is evident that when the stress precedes the fricative, it is voiceless; when it follows, the fricative is voiced. In precisely the same fashion, such originally voiceless consonants as the þ, **s**, and **h** of the verbs cited above became voiced in the past plural and past participle, for originally the stress in these came after the consonants in question. Shortly afterward the stress did shift to the first syllable, but not until the consonant change had taken place. Subsequently West Germanic *sniðon, sniðen* became **snidon** and **sniden** in Old English, and similarly, West Germanic *cuzon, cozen* became **curon** and **coren**. There will be some strong verbs affected by this change in every class except the fourth. This accounts for the divergence in Modern English of *lose* and *forlorn*, the latter being based upon **loren**, the past participle of **lēosan**.

64. *The Verbal Prefixes* **be-** *and* **on-**

The prefix **be-**, though sometimes merely an intensive, as in **swelgan** *to swallow*, **beswelgan** *to swallow up*, often adds the sense of *round, over, about* to the meaning of the stem to which it is added: **standan** *to stand*, **bestandan** *to stand round or about*; **sēon** *to see*, **besēon** *to look around, behold*; **rīdan** *to ride*, **berīdan** *to ride around, surround*; **sprecan** *to speak*, **besprecan** *to speak about*. In some instances it has privitive force: **dǣlan** *to deal, distribute*, **bedǣlan** *to deprive*; **hādian** *to ordain*, **behādian** *to unfrock*. Finally, it may perform a transitivizing function as in þencan *to think*, beþencan *to consider*; **wēpan** *to weep*, **bewēpan** *to lament*.

At times the prefix **-on** has the meaning of the preposition **on**: **blāwan** *to blow*, **onblāwan** *to blow on or into*; **clifian** *to adhere*, **onclifian** *to stick to*. On other occasions it has inceptive or subjective force: **bærnan** *to burn*, **onbærnan** *to kindle, to excite*; **gytan** *to get*, **ongytan** *to understand, perceive*. In such verbs as **onbindan** *to unbind*, **onwindan** *to unwind*, **onsǣlan** *to untie*, the prefix has negative meaning and is here an unstressed form of **un-**.

Reading
From the Old English translation of the Gospels, Luke 9: 37–45

37. Ōðrum dæge, him of þām munte farendum, him agēn arn mycel menego.

38. Þā clypode ān wer of þǣre menego and cwæð, "Lāreow, ic hālsie þē, geseoh mīnne sunu, forþām hē is mīn ānlīca sunu.

39. And nū se unclǣna gāst hine æthrīnð, and hē fǣrlīce hrȳmð; and fornimð hyne and fǣmð, and hyne tyrð and slīt.

40. And ic bæd þīne leorningcnihtas þæt hīg hine ūt ādrifen, and hīg ne mihton."

41. Þā cwæð se Hǣlend him tō andsware, "Ealā, ungelēafulle and þwure cnēores, swā lange swā ic beo mid ēow and ēow þolie? Lǣd hider þīnne sunu."

42. And þā hē hyne lǣdde him to, se dēofol hine fornam and fordyde. Ðā nȳdde se Hǣlend þone unclǣnan gāst ūt, and gehǣlde þone cnapan, and āgeaf hine his fæder.

43. Þā wundredon hīg ealle be Godes mǣrðe. And eallum wundriendum be þām þingum þe gewurdon, hē cwæð to his leorningcnihtum.

44. "Asettað þās spǣca on eowrum heortum: hit ys tōweard þæt mannes Sunu sī geseald on manna handa."

45. Ðā beþōhton hī þis word, and hit wæs bewrigen beforan him þæt hī hit ne ongēaton, and hī ne dorston hine be þām worde ācsian.

Glossary and Structural Notes

From this point on in the glossary, verbs will be identified as to conjugation (weak or strong) and class. Weak verbs of the first or second class will be indicated by the appropriate Roman numerals; strong verb classes will be shown in Arabic numbers.

æthrīnð	Verb, 3rd sing. pres. of **æthrīnan** (1) *to touch, seize.*
agēn	Prep., *toward.* A late spelling of **ongēan**.
ānlīca	Adj., *only.*

arn Verb, 3rd sing. past of **irnan** (3) *to run.*

beþōhton Verb, 3rd pl. past of **beþencan** (I) *to consider.* This appears to have been a mistranslation of *ignorabant* in the Latin Vulgate.

bewrigen Verb, past participle of **bewrēon** (1) *to conceal.* The infinitive form of this verb is irregular.

cnēores Noun, f., *generation, race.*

dorston Verb, 3rd pl. past of **durran** *to dare.* Usually employed as an auxiliary, this verb is historically strong, but by the Old English period it had become part of a special conjugation.

ēalā Interjection, *O, alas!*

fǣmð Verb, 3rd sing. pres. of **fǣman** (I) *to foam, froth.*

fǣrlīce Adv., *suddenly.*

farendum Verb, pres. participle of **faran** (6) *to go,* used in a dat. absolute construction.

fordyde Verb, 3rd sing. past of **fordōn.** The meaning here is *to harass.* The verb **dōn** is too irregular to be classified as either weak or strong. It is usually placed in a so-called anomalous category with three other highly irregular verbs.

fornimð Verb, 3rd sing. pres. of **forniman** (4) *to take away, overcome.* **Fornām** is the 3rd sing. past.

hālsie Verb, 1st sing. pres. of **hālsian** (II) *to entreat, beseech.*

him Pron., here an alternate form for the dat. pl.

hrȳmð Verb, 3rd pl. pres. of **hrȳman** (I) *to cry out, exclaim.*

mǣrðe Noun, f., dat. sing. of **mǣrð** *fame, glory, magnitude.*

nȳdde Verb, 3rd sing. past of **nȳdan** (I) *to force, compel, urge.*

ongēaton Verb, 3rd pl. past of **ongitan** (5) *to perceive, understand.*

ōðrum	Adj., dat. sing. of **ōðer** *second, following.* This is an adverbial use of the dat. case.
(ge)seald	Verb, past participle of **(ge)sellan** (I) *to give, sell.* Combined with the subjunctive **sī**, it forms a perfect passive construction.
slīt	Verb, 3rd sing. pres. of **slītan** (1) *to slit, rend.* The full form would be **slīteþ**: **slīt** represents a syncopation of the vowel **e** and assimilation of the consonants **t** and **þ**.
sunu	Noun, m., nom. sing. of *son.* **Sunu** belongs to a minor noun declension which had **-u** in the nom. sing., if the stem syllable was short.
swā lange swā	A somewhat clumsy rendering of **uscue cuo**, better translated in other versions as **hū lange** *how long.*
tōweard	Adj., *approaching, in the future.*
tyrð	Verb, 3rd sing. pres. of **teran** (4) *to tear.*
þolie	Verb, 1st sing. pres. of **þolian** (II) *to suffer, endure.*
þwure	Adj., nom. pl. strong of **þweorh** *crooked, perverse.*
wundriendum	Verb, pres. participle of **wundrian** (II) *to wonder, marvel,* used adjectivally in the dat. pl.
(ge)wurdon	Verb, 3rd pl. past of **(ge)weorþan** (3) *to become, happen.*

Practice Exercise

Identify the following verb forms as to person, number, tense, mood, and class. Be able to give the principal parts of each verb: **hē strād, wē smucon, þū hlēotest, hī nipaþ, ic strice, hē þēat, wē þwīten, hit þwineþ, hē scupe, hē scūpe.**

Chapter 12

65. Strong Verbs, Class 3

The strong verbs of the third class offer a striking illustration of the importance of sound change in accounting for what was historically a uniform pattern. This is the one strong verb class in which originally the stem consisted of a short vowel followed by two consonants (**-VCC**) in all four principal parts. At the outset, the ablaut series was: **e a u u**.

By the time of the Old English period, five subgroups had developed within this single conjugation. These may be illustrated by the following types:

a.	**bregdan** *to shake*	**brægd**	**brugdon**	**brogden**
b.	**helpan** *to help*	**healp**	**hulpon**	**holpen**
c.	**beorcan** *to bark*	**bearc**	**burcon**	**burcen**
d.	**gielpan** *to boast*	**gealp**	**gulpon**	**golpen**
e.	**drincan** *to drink*	**dranc**	**druncon**	**druncen**

Type a shows the least change. The first and third principal parts retain the vowels which they had at an earlier period. The second principal part illustrates the fronting of West Germanic **a**, discussed in section 41. The vowel of the past participle reflects an early lowering of **u** to **o** when the following syllable contained the still lower vowel **a**. The Primitive Germanic form of the past was **brugdanaz**, hence the change to **brogden**. The form of the past plural was **brugdun**; accordingly the lowering of **u** to **o** did not occur.

Type b, illustrated by **helpan**, differs from the preceding type only in that it reflects the subsequent breaking of the past singular before **l** plus a consonant: **halp** > **hælp** > **healp**. The **e** of the present stem did not break since the **l** was not followed by **h** (see Section 47). The past participle reflects the same change of **u** to **o** which was explained in connection with Type a.

Type c, consisting of stems containing **r** followed by a consonant, shows breaking both in the infinitive or present stem and in the past singular. The present stem developed from **bercan** to **beorcan**. The past singular, like the preceding type, went through the stages **barc** > **bærc** > **bearc**.

Type d consists of verbs beginning with a palatal consonant, which diphthongized the vowels of both the first and second principal parts (see Section 52). The present stem **gelpan** became **gielpan** (LOE **gilpan**, **glypan**). In the past tense the progression was **galp** > **gælp** > **gealp**.

Type e consists of stems which end in a nasal followed by another consonant (nasal or otherwise). As with the other types, the Primitive Germanic present stem had the vowel **e** (**drencanan**), but Primitive Germanic **e**, followed by a nasal plus another consonant or a double nasal, became **i**. The **a** of the past singular, because it was followed by a nasal, did not front to **æ** but remained unchanged or was spelled with **o** (**dranc**, **dronc**). The **u** of the past participle, because of the following nasal, did not lower to **o**, as did the other types, but remained unchanged.

The third-class verbs were the most numerous of the seven Old English strong verb classes, including no less than eighty-one different verbs, nineteen more than the first class, the closest competitor. Of these, twenty-two retain their strong forms in Modern English, again more than any other class, and thirty-one others have become adjusted to the regular or weak pattern.

66. *Interrogative Verb Structure*

That the inverted word order is regularly used in questions was pointed out in Chapter 5, section 32. So-called yes or no questions normally have the active verb in initial position and the subject following it. If the verb structure is expanded, the infinitive or participle generally follows the subject. **Hæfst þū hafoc?** *Have you a hawk?* **Slēa wē mid swurde?** *Shall we strike with the sword?* **Wæs ēow ǣnig þing wana?** *Was anything lacking to you?* **Canst þū temian hīe?** *Do you know how to tame them?* **Mæg ǣnig þing gōdes bēon of Nazareth?** *Can there be any good thing from Nazareth?*

As in Modern English, questions calling for information rather than simple affirmation or negation begin with an interrogative word, followed in turn by the active verb and the subject. **Hwæt is ēcnes?** *What is eternity?* **Hwæt wille gē sprecan?** *What do you want to say?* **Hwī dēst þū swā?** *Why do you act in this manner?* **Hū beswīcst þu fugelas?** *How do you snare birds?* **Hwylcne cræft canst þū?** *What skill do you know?* **Hwæðer lufode him swīðor?** *Which one loved him the more?* **Hwā mæg synna forgyfan?** *Who can forgive sins?* Note that in the last two sentences the interrogative word also functions as the subject.

67. *Impersonal Verb Construction*

Certain Old English verbs occurred only in the third-person singular, either present or past, with no expressed subject and with an accusative or dative object usually preceding the verb. **Forþon mē þynceð wīslīc.** *Therefore (it) seems wise to me.* **Þē gebyrede gewistfullian and geblissian.** *It was fitting for you to feast and rejoice.* Other verbs were used both personally and impersonally. **Gif ēow swā licige ...** *If it so please you ....* **þæt wē þurh þæt ealle Gode līcien. ...** *that through that we may all please God.* In Late Old English the subject **hit** began to appear as the overtly expressed subject: **And þā eall þæt folc þæt gehīerde, hit him līcode.** *And when all the people heard that, it pleased them.*

It is especially important to note that in Old English the verb **þencan** *to think*, with **þōhte** as its past-tense form, always had a personal subject, whereas **þyncan** *to appear, seem*, with **þūhte** as the past-tense form, was used impersonally. **Hē hī nǣfre forlǣtan ne þenceð.** *He never thinks to forsake them.* **For þon him þūhte þæt his forðfōr swā nēah ne wǣre.** *For it seemed to them that his departure was not so near.* It is the verb **þyncan**, with its meaning of *appear* or *seem*, which is preserved in the Middle and Early Modern English **me thinketh, methinks.**

68. *Uses of the Past Tense*

Just as the present tense covered a broader range of time in Old English than it does today, so too did the past. The past tense had the following uses:

a. To indicate a single act occurring in the past:

Þā cyrde sē þēowa and cȳdde his hlāforde þæt.

Then the servant returned and made that known to his lord.

b. To indicate an act continuing in the past:

Hit gelamp on sumne sǣl þæt hī sǣton ætgædere, Oswold and Aidan.

It happened on a certain occasion that Oswold and Aidan were sitting together.

c. To indicate the equivalent of the present perfect in Modern English:

Gif ic ǣnigne berēafode, ic hit be fēowerfealdum āgyfe.

If I have robbed anyone, I shall return it fourfold.

d. To indicate the equivalent of the past perfect in Modern English:

Sōþlīce ðā hē ealle his word gefylde on þæs folces hlyste, hē ēode intō Cafarnaum.

Truly when he had completed his words in the hearing of the people, he went into Capernaum.

69. *The Verbal Prefix* **a-**

In origin **ā-** was the unstressed form of the Germanic prefix **or-**, implying movement onward, outward, or away from a position. Thus: **scūfan** *to shove,* **āscūfan** *to shove away;* **gēotan** *to pour,* **āgēotan** *to pour out;* **beran** *to bear, to carry,* **āberan** *to remove.* When the notion of outward motion was already implicit to some degree in the meaning of the verb itself, the **ā-** served primarily as an intensive, as in **āsendan** *to dispatch,* **ālecgan** *to lay down.* The prefix appeared also with some nouns and adjectives derived from verbs: **ācennedness** *birth,* **ārǣd** *resolute,* **āblǣcung** *pallor.*

Reading

From the Old English translation of the Gospels, Luke 13 : 6–17.

6. Ðā sǣde hē him þis bigspel: Sum man hæfde ān fīctrēow geplantod on his wīngearde. Þā cōm hē and sōhte his wæstmas on him, þā ne funde hē nānne.

7. Þā cwæð hē tō þǣm hyrde, "Nū synt þrēo gēar syðþan ic cōm wæstm sēcende on þissum fīctrēowe, and ic ne funde. Forceorf hine. Hwī ofþricð hē þæt land?"

8. Ðā cwæð hē, "Hlāford, lǣt hine gȳt þis gēar, oð ic hine bedelfe and ic hine beweorpe mid meoxe.

9. And witodlīce hē wæstmas bringð. Gif hit elles hwæt byð, ceorf hine syððan."

10. Ðā wæs hē restedagum on hyra gesamnunge lǣrende.

11. Þā wæs þār sum wīf, sēo hæfde untrumnesse gāst ehtatȳne gēar; and hēo wæs ābogen, nē hēo eallunga ne mihte ūp besēon.

12. Þā sē Hǣlend hig geseah, hē clypode hig tō him and sǣde hyre, "Wīf, þū eart forlǣten of þīnre untrumnesse."

13. And his hand hyre on sette. Þā wæs hēo sōna ūp ārǣred, and hēo God wuldrode.

14. Ðā gebealh sē duguðe ealdor hine, for þām þe sē Hǣlend on restedæge hǣlde, and sǣde þām menegum, "Syx dagas synt on þām gebyrað þæt man wyrce: cumaþ on þām and bēoð gehǣlede, and nā on restedæge."

15. Ðā andswarode sē Hǣlend and cwæð, "Lā, līceteras, ne untīgð ēower ǣlc on restedæge his oxan oððe assan fram þǣre binne and lǣt to wætere?

16. Þēos Abrahāmes dohtor, þe Sātanas geband nū eahtatȳne gēar, ne gebyrede hyre bēon unbunden of þissum bende on restedæge?"

17. Þā hē þis sǣde, þā scamode ealle his wiðerwinnan; and eall folc geblissode on eallum þām ðe wuldorfullīce fram him gewurdon.

Glossary and Structural Notes

ābogen   Verb, past participle of **ābugan** (2) *to bow, bend.*

ārǣred   Verb, past participle of **ārǣran** (I) *to raise, make straight.*

(ge)bealh   Verb, 3rd sing. past of **(ge)belgan** (3) *to become enraged*, reflexive.

bedelfe   Verb, 1st sing. pres. of **bedelfan** (3) *to dig about.*

beweorpe   Verb, 3rd sing. pres. of **beweorpan** (3) *to throw about, bestrew.*

(ge)byrað   Verb, 3rd sing. pres. of **(ge)byrian** (II) *to befit, pertain*, impersonal.

duguðe   Noun, f., **duguð** *people, elders*, collective.

eallunga   Adv., *entirely, at all.*

forceorf   Verb, imperative of **forceorfan** (3) *to carve away, cut down.*

forlǣten   Verb, past participle of **forlǣtan** (7) *to let go, set free.*

funde   Verb, 3rd sing. past of **findan** (3) *to find.* An irregular form, historically a second-person sing. used for the first and third persons.

gēar   Noun, n., *year.* The instances in verses 7 and 16 are both accusatives of extent of time.

hæfde   Verb, 3rd sing. past, used here in a past perfect sense.

hig   Pron., a late spelling for **hī**, **hīe**.

hyrde   Noun, m., **hyrd** *herd, keeper.*

lǣt   Verb, 3rd sing. present of **lǣdan** (I) *to lead.* This is a syncopated and assimilated form of **lǣdeþ**.

līceteras   Noun, m., **līcetere** *dissembler, hypocrite.*

meoxe   Noun, n., **meox** *dung, muck.*

ofþricð   Verb, 3rd sing. pres. of **ofþriccan** *to encumber, oppress.*

(ge)samnunge   Noun, f., **gesamnung** *assembly, congregation, synagogue.*

untrumnesse   Noun, f., **untrumness** *weakness, affliction, infirmity.*

wiðerwinnan   Noun, m. weak, *adversary.*
wuldorfullīce   Adv., *gloriously.*
wuldrode   Verb, 3rd sing. past of **wuldrian** (II) *to glorify.*

Practice Exercises

1. Give the principal parts of the following strong verbs of the third class: **grimman** *to rage,* **swellan** *to swell,* **deorfan** *to labor,* **stregdan** *to strew,* **beorcan** *to bark,* **sweltan** *to die,* **clingan** *to cling,* **beteldan** *to cover,* **steorfan** *to die.*

2. Identify the following forms, giving the person, number, tense, mood, and class: **hē swāf, wē durfon, þū clingest, hit nipe, wē flēotaþ, hī swulton, gē gruton, þū stīge, hī burcen, þū þrunte.**

Chapter 13

70. Strong Verbs Classes 4 and 5

The ablaut or gradation series for the fourth and fifth classes of the Old English strong verbs are:

	PRESENT	PAST SINGULAR	PAST PLURAL	PAST PARTICIPLE
4	e	æ	$\bar{æ}$	o
5	e	æ	$\bar{æ}$	e

In one sense these two classes could be considered subgroups of a single category. Basically, verbs of the fourth class have infinitives in **e** followed by a single so-called liquid consonant, **r** or **l**. Those of the fifth class also have **e** as the stem vowel of the infinitive, followed by a consonant other than **r** or **l**. The only difference in the ablaut series occurs in the past participle. Thus, we have:

4	**stelan**	**stæl**	**stǣlon**	**stolen**
5	**sprecan**	**spræc**	**sprǣcon**	**sprecen**

A few verbs in both classes had stems beginning with an initial palatal consonant or consonant combination. This resulted in diphthongization in three of the four principal parts of the fourth-class verbs and in all of the principal parts of the fifth. Note the following:

scieran	scear	scēaron	scoren
giefan	geaf	gēafon	giefen
gietan	geat	gēaton	gieten

For a variety of reasons, two verbs of the fourth class, **cuman** *to come* and **niman** *to take*, were highly irregular. These appear as:

cuman	cōm, cam	cōmon	cumen
niman	nōm, nam	nōmon, nāmon	numen

Even in Old English there were relatively few verbs in these two classes, fourteen in the fourth and twenty-six in the fifth. Moreover, in the intervening centuries the mortality has been high. Only five verbs of the fourth class retain their strong forms in Modern English: *bear, break, come, steal,* and *tear*. Of the fifth-class verbs, *get, speak, tread,* and *weave* have gone over in some measure to the fourth-class pattern through the adoption of a long or short *o* in the past tense and past particle. They had been anticipated in this by the verb **brecan** *to break*, which even in Old English had **brocen** as its past participle and must therefore be counted as a fourth-class verb. Another type of irregularty is seen in **etan** *to eat* and **fretan** *to devour*, which had ǣ instead of æ in the past singular. The operation of Verner's Law may be seen in the past plural **wǣron** (originally a form of **wesan**) and in the forms **cwǣdon** and **cweden** from **cweðan** *to speak*.

71. *Patterns of Negation*

The particle **ne** was the simplest and most frequently employed device for indicating negation in Old English. It usually came immediately before the active verb: **Wē ne reccaþ bi þinum cræft**. *We don't care about your occupation*. **Ure God ūs ne forlǣteþ**. *Our God will not forsake us*. **Hīe ne mehton þā scipu ūt bringan**. *They could not bring out the ships*. Frequently in negative statements the inverted word order was employed, with **ne** preceding the verb: **Ne habbað wē færsceat**. *We do not have passage money*. **Ne cann ic ēow**. *I do not know you*. **Ne stel þū**. *Thou shalt not steal*.

With a number of verbs of high incidence (principally forms of **bēon** *to be*, **habban** *to have*, **willan** *to desire*, and **witan** *to know*), the vowel of the particle was elided when the verb form began with a vowel, **h**, or **w**: ne is > nis, ne wæs > næs, ne hæfde > næfde, **ne habban > nabban, ne wille > nylle, ne wolde > nolde, ne wiste > nyste, ne wāt > nāt**, etc. **Hē nolde in gān**. *He did not want to go in*. **Næs ðēah mīnes ðonces**. *It was not, however, my intent*. **Nāt ic hwæt hē is**. *I do not know what he is*.

The modern objection to multiple negation did not apply in Old English. Structures such as the following were not unusual: **Nān heort ne onscunede nænne līon**. *No hart avoided any lion*. **Andreas, þū ne gefīrenodest nānwuht**. *Andreas, you did not sin in any manner*. **Ne con ic nōht singan**. *I can't sing anything*. **Næfre sīo tīd næs þæt hē nære, nē næfre ne wyrð**. *Never was there a time when He was not, nor ever a time when He will not be*.

The negative-interrogative employed the inverted word order preceded by the negative particle **ne**: **Ne canst þū huntian buton mid nettum?** *Can't you hunt except with snares?* **For hwī ne fixast þū on sæ?** *Why don't you fish in the sea?* **Nyton gē þis bigspell?** *Do you not know this parable?* **Hū ne sēowe þū gōd sæd on þīnum æcere?** *Why did you not sow good seed in your field?*

72. *Compound Tenses in Old English*

Although the simple present and past tenses were used in Old English in many situations where Modern English would employ composite constructions, nevertheless Old English did make some use of compound tense forms. In the use of **habban** as an auxiliary with transitive verbs and of **bēon** with intransitive verbs there is a partial similarity to the present practice of many European languages, though the distinction has not been maintained in English.

a. **Þās þing wē habbað be him gesægde**.

These things we have said concerning him.

Þā þā hīe ealle hæfdon bisne ræd betwux him gefæstnod...

Then, when they had all agreed upon this plan among themselves...

b. **Nū is sē dæg cumen**...

Now the day has come . . .

Sē hālga fæder wæs inn āgān.

The holy father had gone in.

At times the participles were inflected. When used with the auxiliary **bēon**, the inflected participle agreed with the subject; when a form of **habban** was the auxiliary, the inflected participle agreed with the direct object. Thus: **Siþþan hīe āfarene wǣron.** *After they had gone.* **Hī hæfdon hiora meta genotudne.** *They had consumed their food.*

Somewhat less frequently the verbs **sculan** *shall* and **willan** *will* were employed to indicate future time, especially in Late Old English, though almost invariably with overtones of the ideas of obligation or volition which these verbs regularly conveyed. Nevertheless, Byrhtnoth's stout-hearted reply to the messenger of the Vikings at the outset of the Battle of Maldon, **Hī willað ēow tō gafole gāras syllan**, *They will give you spears as tribute*, is not entirely without its suggestion of future time, nor are occasional instances of **sculan**.

73. *Uses of the Gerund*

Historically the gerund is an inflected form of the infinitive, the preposition **tō** with which it regularly appeared taking the dative case. The term itself is derived from the Latin *gerere to carry on*, and as the etymology implies, its function is primarily completive (indicating the end of an action) or catenative (indicating a link in the expression of an action). It was used with:

a. Substantives:

   And bindaþ scēafmǣlum tō forbærnenne.

   And bind them into sheaves to be burned.

b. Adjectives:

   Hit bið swīðe gedwolsum tō rǣdenne.

   It is very misleading to read.

c. Verbs:

   Crīst . . . began tō bodienne his hālige godspell.

   Christ began to preach his holy Gospel.

When used with the verb *to be* the gerund indicates obligation or necessity.

Is ēac tō witanne.
It must also be known

74. *The Development of West Germanic* ā

Just as the short vowel **a** moved forward to æ at the outset of the Old English period, or just before, so the corresponding long vowel showed an even greater propensity to become the front vowel **ǣ**. It was prevented from developing in this direction only when it was followed by the velar consonants **w**, **p**, **g**, or **k**, and only if they in turn were followed by a back vowel. WGmc **rādan** > OE **rǣdan**, **hār** > **hǣr**, **wāpen** > **wǣpen**, **stālon** > **stǣlon**. But WGmc **blāwan** remained OE **blāwan**, as did **māgas**, **hrāca**, **slāpol**. Before nasals, West Germanic **ā** became Old English **ō**: **nāmon** > **nōmon**, OHG **getān**, OE **gedōn**.

The **ǣ** which developed from West Germanic **ā** was subject to breaking, but only before **h**: WGmc **nāh** *near* > OE **nāh** > **nēah**; **þāh** *throve* > **þǣh** > **þēah**. It was also diphthongized by a preceding palatal consonant (see section 52).

Reading
From the Old English translation of the Gospels, Luke 21:1–19

1. Ðā hē hine beseah, hē geseah þā welegan hyra lāc sendan on þone sceoppan.

2. Þā geseah hē sume earme wudewan bringan twēgen fēorðlingas.

3. Ðā cwæð hē, "Sōð ic ēow secge þæt ðēos earme wudewe ealra mǣst brōhte.

4. Sōðes ealle þās brōhton Gode lāc of hyra mycelan welan; þēos wudewe brōhte of þām þe hēo hæfde ealle hyra andlyfene."

5. And þā cwæð hē tō þām þe sǣdon be þām temple, þæt hit wǣre geglenged mid gōdum stānum and gōdum gifum,

6. "Þās þing þe gē gesēoð, þā dagas cumað on þām ne bið stān lǣfed ofer stān þe ne bēo tōworpen."

7. Þā ahsodon hig hine, "Lā Bebēodend, hwænne bēoð þās þing, and hwylce tācna bēoð þonne þās þing geweorðaþ?"

8. Ðā cwæþ he, "Warniað þæt gē ne sȳn beswicene: manege cumað on mīnum naman and cweðað, 'Ic hit eom,' and 'Tīd genēalǣcð.' Ne fare gē æfter him.

9. Ne bēo gē brēgede þonne gē gesēoð gefeoht and twȳrǣdnessa. Ðās þing gebyriað ǣrest, ac nys þonne gȳt ende."

10. Ðā cwæð hē tō him, "Þēod arīst agēn þēode, and rīce agēn rīce.

11. And bēoð mycele eorþan styrunga geond stōwa, and cwealmas, and hungor, and egsan of heofone, and mycele tācna bēoð.

12. Ac tōforan eallum þissum hig nimað ēow and ēhtað, and syllað ēow on gesamnunga and on hyrdnyssa, and lǣdaþ ēow tō cyningum and tō dēmum for mīnum naman.

13. Þis ēow gebyrað on gewitnesse.

14. Ne sceole gē on ēowrum heortum foresmēagan, hū gē andswarian.

15. Ic sylle ēow mūð and wīsdōm, þām ne magon ealle ēower wiðerwinnan wiðstandan and wiðcweðan.

16. Gē bēoð gesealde fram māgum, and gebrōðrum, and cūðum, and frēondum; and hig ēow tō dēaðe geswencað.

17. And gē bēoð eallum on hatunga for mīnum naman.

18. And ne forwyrð ān locc of eowrum hēafde.

19. On ēowrum geþylde gē gehealdað ēowre sāwla."

Glossary and Structural Notes

andlyfene	Noun, f., **andlyfen** *food, wages, living.*
ārīst	Verb, 3rd sing. pres. of **ārīsan** (1). This is an alternate form, syncopated and assimilated, of **ārīseþ**.
Bebēodend	Noun, m., *commander, master.* From the verb **bebēodan** (2).
brēgede	Verb, past participle of **brēgan** (I) *to frighten, alarm.*
(ge)byriað	Verb, 3rd pl. pres. of **(ge)byrian** (I) *to happen, occur, pertain to, befit.*

cūðum   Noun, m., **cūða** *acquaintance*.

cwealmas   Noun, m., **cwealm** *pestilence*.

dēmum   Noun, m., **dēma**, literally *judge*, but here *ruler*.

egsan   Noun, m., **egsa** *fear, terror*, from **ege** *awe, fear, terror*.

ēhtað   Verb, 3rd pl. pres. of **ēhtan** (I) *to attack, persecute*.

fēorðlingas   Noun, m., **fēorðling** *a farthing, a fourth part*.

foresmēgan   Verb, infinitive (I), *to premeditate, think beforehand*.

forwyrð   Verb, 3rd sing. present of **forweorþan** (3) *to perish*. An alternate form of **forweorðeð**.

(ge)glenged   Verb, past participle of **(ge)glengan** (I) *to adorn*.

geþylde   Noun, f., **geþyld** *patience*.

hatunga   Noun, f., **hatung** *hatred*: *You will be in a state of being hated*.

hyrdnyssa   Noun, f., **hyrdness** *custody*.

lāc   Noun, n., *gift, offering*.

læfed   Verb, past participle of **læfan** (I) *to leave, remain*.

māgum   Noun, m., **mæg** *kinsman*.

(ge)nēalæcð   Verb, 3rd sing. pres. of **(ge)nēalæcan** (I) *to approach*. From **nēah**, adj., *near* and **læcan** *to join with*.

(ge)samnunga   Noun, f., used here in the special sense of *synagogue*.

sceoppan   Noun, m., **sceoppa** *booth*. This is the only occurrence of the word in Old English. It is a rendering of **gazophylacium** *treasury of the temple*, in the Latin Vulgate.

sōðes   Noun, n., **sōð** *truth*. In verse 4, an adverbial use of the gen.

(ge)swencað   Verb, 3rd pl. pres. of **(ge)swencan** (I) *to harass, oppress*.

tācna   Noun, n., gen. pl. of **tācen** *sign, token.*

twȳrǣdnessa   Noun, f., **twȳrǣdness** *discord, sedition.* From **twȳ** *two* and **rǣd** *counsel.*

warniað   Verb, imperative pl. of **warnian** (II) *to take heed, beware.*

wiðcweðan   Verb, infinitive, *to gainsay, contradict.*

Practice Exercises

1. Identify the following forms, giving the person, number, tense, mood, and class: **wē stelaþ, gē rīsen, hē wearð, hēo tredeþ hī curfon, wē sprǣcen, ic crupe, gē gietaþ, hē mealc, wē scēaron, hit scān, ic dranc, hēo bær þū scūfest hī hǣlon.**

2. Convert the following West Germanic forms into their Old English equivalents: **āþm, lāgon, brām, lāh, tāl, tāla, gāfon, spān, nādl, crāwan.**

Chapter 14

75. *Strong Verb Classes 6 and 7*

The verbs in these two classes differ from those of the preceding five in that they have the same vowel in the past singular and past plural, and for the most part the same vowel in the present stem and past participle. The seventh class divides into two sub-groups in that some of the verbs have **ē** in the past tense, and a rather larger number have **ēo**. Typical verbs are:

PRESENT		PAST SINGULAR	PAST PLURAL	PAST PARTICIPLE
6	**wascan** *wash*	**wōsc**	**wōscon**	**wascen**
7a	**lǣtan** *let*	**lēt**	**lēton**	**lǣten**
7b	**feallan** *fall*	**fēoll**	**fēollon**	**feallen**
	blāwan *blow*	**blēow**	**blēowon**	**blāwen**

According to the regular rule for the fronting of WGmc **a**, most verbs of the sixth class should have had **æ** in the past participle, since the **a** was followed by a single consonant plus a front vowel. However, analogy with the present stem often restored the **a**. Thus we have **faren** *gone* alongside **færen**, similarly **grafen** *graven*, **bacen** *baked*, **slagen** *slain*.

Verbs of Class 7 have no single typical stem vowel for the present stem and past participle. They include such varied examples as: **hātan** *command*, **lǣtan** *leave*, **blandan** *mix*, and **fōn** *take* with **ē** past-tense forms, and **blāwan** *blow*, **bēatan** *beat*, **bannan** *proclaim*, **fealdan** *fold*, and **flōwan** *flow* with **ēo**. All that can be said about them is that this class includes no verbs which have the present stem vowel of any of the other six classes, and that typically the present-stem vowels of seventh-class verbs are those which occur in the past-tense forms of the other strong verb classes.

Moreover, there is no certain way of predicting from the present stem whether the past tense will have **ē** or **ēo** as its vowel. It is true, however, that many of the verbs with **ē** in the past tense have **ǣ** in the present stem: **ondrǣdan** *dread*, **rǣdan** *advise*, **slǣpan** *sleep* (all of which also had weak past-tense forms — **ond-rǣdde**, etc.). Verbs with **ā** and **ō** in the present stem might have either **ē** or **ēo** in the past: **hātan**, **hēt**; **cnāwan**, **cnēow**; **blandan**, **blēnd**; **spannan**, **spēon**; **fōn**, **fēng**; **grōwan**, **grēow**. As for the rest, verbs like **bēatan**, **fealdan** have only **ēo** in the past.

The seventh-class strong verbs are sometimes called reduplicating, but this term refers to a process which had taken place considerably earlier than the Old English period, namely, a doubling of the initial syllable of a word to produce an inflectional form. Gothic did have reduplicated past forms such as **haihald**, from the infinitive **haldan** *to hold*, and **lailaik**, from **laikan** *to leap*, but the only remnants of this in Old English are the forms **heht** *called*, from **hātan**, and **leolc** *played*, from **lācan**, where the recurrence of the consonant is all that remains of the reduplicated form.

There were, in Old English, more sixth- and seventh-class verbs than fourth and fifth, but they were fewer in number than the first three classes. They have shown a strong tendency to adjust to the regular weak pattern. In present-day English only seven representatives of each class have remained strong, as against eighteen sixth-class and twenty-six seventh-class verbs having become weak.

76. *The Passive Voice*

The verb **hātan** is also the source of the one remaining inflected passive in Old English, namely the form **hātte** *am called*, *is called*: **Sēo scīr hātte Halgoland.** *The shire is called Halgoland.* Except for this one petrified form, the passive was indicated by means of the auxiliaries **bēon** or **weorþan** with the past participle, or by means of an impersonal construction. To some degree Old English maintained the distinction between a statal passive and an actional passive, a feature which is characteristic of Modern German. In Old English the passives constructed with some form of **bēon** indicated a state and those formed with **weorþan** indicated the result of an action. The distinction was far from clear-cut, however, especially since **weorþan** came to be used less and less, and ultimately it disappeared from the language altogether.

a. Passive constructions with **bēon**:

Ealle þing sȳn gefyllede þe āwritene synt.

All those things which are written may be fulfilled.

Nacode wē wǣron ācennede.

Naked we were brought forth.

Þæs gēares wǣrun of slægene viii eorlas ond ān cyning.

In that year eight earls and one king were slain.

b. Passive constructions with **weorþan**:

Ond hāt wyrcean twēgen stengas of ðǣm trēowe ... ðæt ne wyrð nǣfre forrotod.

And command that two shafts be made of that tree which is never decayed.

Æþelwulf aldormon wearþ ofslægen.

Magistrate Aethelwulf was killed.

Note that the last instance under *b* refers to a specific action or incident, whereas that under *a* summarizes the battle fatalities for the entire year.

c. Impersonal constructions with passive meaning:

Þonne is ān port ... þone man hǣt Sciringeshēal.   *Then there is a port which is called Sciringesheal.*

Ond Hæstenes wīf ond his suna twēgen mon brōhte tō þǣm cyninge.   *One brought Hæsten's wife and two of his sons to the king,* i.e. *Hæsten's wife and two of his sons were brought to the king.*

It should be observed that in Old English there was no formal distinction between the active and the passive infinitive. The first citation under *b* above shows the active infinitive employed in a passive sense. So, too, does a sentence like: **Hine hēt his hlāford gesellan, and his wīf and his cild, and eall ꝥæt hē āhte.** *His lord commanded him to be sold, and his wife, and his child, and all that he possessed.*

77. *Gemination*

At a time considerably later than the operation of Grimm's Law and Verner's Law, but prior to the fronting of West Germanic **a**, a sweeping change in the West Germanic consonant system occurred. During this period all single consonants except **r** were lengthened after short vowels when they were followed by **j**. Thus: **latjan** > **lattjan, gramjan** > **grammjan, cwaljan** > **cwalljan**; but **narjan, bōtjan, dōmjan, hāljan,** and **bandjan** would have remained unchanged.

Although the result of the development was a lengthened rather than a doubled consonant, the spelling system of Old English could indicate this only by writing the consonant character twice. Accordingly the term **gemination** (from Latin **gemini** *twins*) came to be applied to the change. It should be recognized, however, that certain Old English words had doubled consonants which were not the result of gemination, notably strong verbs of the third and seventh classes: **swimman, winnan, bannan, feallan**.

78. *The Development of West Germanic Diphthongs*

Up to this point only the Old English developments of West Germanic **ā** and **a** have been considered in detail. It is helpful, however, for the recognition of many Old English vocabulary items to consider some of the other changes which took place at nearly the same time.

Two that are particularly important in this connection are the development of West Germanic **ai** to Old English **ā** and that of West Germanic **au** to Old English **ēa**. Thus, WGmc **haim** > **hām**, **claiþ** > **clāþ, bain** > **bān, stain** > **stān**; and WGmc **dauf** > *OE* **dēaf, draum** > **drēam, hlaupan** > **hlēapan**. Note that the Modern German cognates of these words preserve the quality of the West

Germanic diphthongs: *heim, kleid, bein, stein, taub, traum, laufen.*
Another group of words which had **au** in West Germanic and
developed into **ēa** in Old English have long *o* in their Modern
German form: WGmc **daud** > OE **dēad** (Ger. *tot*); WGmc **aura** >
OE **ēare** (Ger. *ohr*), WGmc **straum** > OE **strēam** (Ger. *strom*).

Clearly the change of WGmc **ai** to OE **ā** must have taken place
after the fronting of WGmc **ā** to OE **ǣ**, or else the two groups of
words would have merged. This did not occur.

Reading
From the Old English translation of the Gospels, Luke 21:20–38

20. "Þonne gē gesēoð Hierusalem mid here betrymede, witað
þæt hyre tōworpennes genēalǣcð.

21. Þonne flēoð on muntas þā ðe on Iūdēa synt; and nyðer ne
āstīgað þā ðe on hyre middele synt; and intō hyre ne magon þā
ðe þār ute synt.

22. For þām ðe þis synt wrace dagas, þæt ealle þing sȳn gefyllede
þe āwritene synt.

23. Sōðlīce wā ēacniendum wīfum and fēdendum on þām dagum! Þonne bið mycel ofþriccednys ofer eorðan and yrre þissum
folce.

24. And hig feallað on sweordes ecge and bēoð hæftlingas on
ealla þēoda; Hierusalem bið fram þēodum fortreden, oð mǣgða
tīda sȳn gefyllede.

25. And bēoð tācna on sunnan, and on mōnan, and on steorran;
and on eorðan þēoda forþriccednys, for gedrēfednesse sǣs swēges
and ȳða;

26. Bifiendum mannum for ege and anbide þe eallum ymbe
hwyrfte tō becumað; ðonne bēoð heofones myhta āstyrede.

27. And þonne hig gesēoð mannes Sunu on lyfte cumende mid
mycelum anwealde and mægenþrymme.

28. Ðonne þās þing agynnað, besēoð and ēowre hēafdu ūp
āhebbaþ, for þām ðe ēower ālȳsednes genēalǣcð."

29. Ðā sǣde hē him sum bigspel: "Behealdað þone fīcbēam and
ealle trēowu.

30. Þonne hig wæstm bringað, gē witon þæt sumor ys gehende.

31. And þonne gē þās þing gesēoð, witað þæt Godes rīce is ge-hende.

32. Sōðlīce ic ēow secge þæt þēos cnēores ne gewīt ǣr þām þe ealle þās ðing geweorþen.

33. Heofen and eorðe gewītaþ; sōðlīce mīne word ne gewītað.

34. Warniaþ ēow, þe lǣs ēower heortan gehefegode sȳn on ofer-fylle, and on druncennesse, and þises līfes carum, and on ēow sē fǣrlīca dæg become.

35. Swā swā grīn hē becymþ on ealle þā ðe sittað ofer eorðan ansȳne.

36. Waciað on ǣlcere tīde, and biddað þæt gē wyrðe sȳn þæt gē þās tōweardan þing forflēon and standan beforan mannes Suna."

37. Sōðlīce hē wæs on dæg on þām temple lǣrende; and on niht hē ēode and wunode on þām munte þe ys gecweden Oliuēti.

38. And eall folc on morgen cōm tō him tō þām temple, þæt hī hine gehȳrdon.

Glossary and Structural Notes

āhebbað	Verb, imperative pl. of **āhebban** (6) *to raise*.
ālȳsednes	Noun, f., *redemption*.
anbid	Noun, n., *expectation*.
ansȳne	Noun, f., **ansȳn** *face*.
anwealde	Noun, m., **anweald** *power*.
āstigað	Verb, 3rd pl. pres. of **āstīgan** (1). Basically, **stīgan** meant *to change altitude*; whether in an upward or downward direction was usually indicated by the accompanying adverb. Here, because of **nyðer** *nether*, the meaning is *to descend*.
betrymede	Verb, past participle of **betrymman** (1) *to surround*, used adjectivally with f. acc. sing. strong inflection. That **Hierusalem** was construed as feminine is shown by the pronoun **hyre**.

bifiendum   Verb, past participle of **bifian** (II) *to tremble*, used here adjectivally in a dat. absolute construction.

carum   Noun, f., **caru** *care*.

cnēores   Noun, f., *generation, race*.

ēacniendum   Verb, pres. participle of **ēacnian** (II) *to become pregnant*, used adjectivally as a dat. pl.

fǣrlīca   Adj., *sudden, unexpected*.

fēdendum   Verb, pres. participle of **fēdan** (I) *to feed*, used adjectivally here in the special sense of *nursing*.

forþriccednys   See **ofþriccednys**.

gedrēfednesse   Noun, f., **gedrēfedness** *confusion, disturbance*.

grīn   Noun, n., *snare*.

hæftlingas   Noun, m., **hæftling** *captive*.

hēafdu   Noun, n., **hēafod** *head*.

(ge)hefegode   Verb, past participle of **(ge)hefegian** (II) *to burden, make heavy*, with pl. adj. inflection.

here   Noun, m., **here** *army*.

mægenþrymme   Noun, m., **mægenþrymm** *majesty*. Compounded of **mægen** *strength* plus **þrymm** *glory, splendor*.

ofþriccednys   Noun, f., *oppression, distress, trouble*. From **þryccan** (I) *to trample, crush*.

swēges   Noun, m., **swēg** *sound, noise, melody*.

tōweardan   Adj., *future*.

tōworpennes   Noun, f., *destruction, desolation*. Formed from **tō** plus the past participle of **weorpan** (3) *to throw*.

trēowu   Noun, n., **trēow** *tree*. Sometimes long-stemmed neuter nouns of this type retained **-u** in the nominative-accusative pl., possibly because of the influence of the final **w**.

þis   The demonstrative which occurs in verse 22 is in the sing. despite the pl. verb and complement.

(ge)wīt	Verb, 3rd sing. pres. of **(ge)wītan** (1) *to go, depart*. This is a syncopated and assimilated form of **(ge)wīteþ**.
wrace	Noun, f., **wracu** *vengeance*. **Wræce** would be the regular form; the **a** has been retained by analogy with the nom.
ymbehwyrfte	Noun, m., **ymbehwyrft** *circuit, orbit, world*.
ȳða	Noun, f., **ȳð** *wave*.

Practice Exercises

1. Identify the following verb forms as to person, number, tense, mood, and class: **gē gōlon, ic feaht, þū healdest, hēo bere, ic strād, hit crēoseþ, þū cnāwest, hē hæle, wē swefaþ, hī spēonon, hē cēaw, hī scafaþ, wē hulpen, wē slēpon, gē þigen.**

2. Indicate how gemination would have operated upon the following forms: **hlahjan, þridja farjan, tūnjan, bidjan, satjan, bōtjan, harjan, fastjan, trumjan.**

3. Give the Modern German cognates of the following Old English words: **hāt** *hot*, **hēafod** *head*, **brād** *broad*, **dāg** *dough*, **hēah** *high*, **æfen** *evening*, **ēac** *also*, **hlāf** *loaf*, **ræd** *advice*, **ēast** *east*, **sæton** *sat*.

Chapter 15

79. *Umlaut or Mutation*

The term *umlaut* is German in origin, a combination of the preposition **um** *around, about* and the noun **laut** *sound*. It was used by Grimm as a term for the change from one vowel to another through the influence of a vowel or semivowel in the syllable immediately following. Some historians of the language, notably the British, prefer to speak of *mutation* rather than *umlaut*, but since the latter term is more precise in its application, it will be used here. The only other use of *umlaut* is in connection with German spelling, where the term refers to a diacritical mark (¨) placed over a vowel character to indicate a quality of sound different from the un-modified letter. Incidentally, in the situations where these occur, the sound change or process we speak of as *umlaut* has taken place.

80. *Common Germanic Palatal Umlaut*

Early in the common Germanic period, the vowel **e** became **i** if an **ī, i,** or **j** occurred in the next syllable. This change affected especially the second- and third-person singular, present indicative, of third-, fourth-, and fifth-class strong verbs, since at that time the personal endings were **-is** for the second person and **-iþ** for the third. Thus: **helpis > hilpst, helpiþ > hilpþ, beris > birst, beriþ > birþ, sprecis > spricst, spreciþ > spricþ.** This change was shared by other Germanic languages; note German *ich helfe, du hilfst, er hilft.*

81. *Palatal Umlaut in Old English*

Early in the Old English period, but after the fronting of **a**, breaking, and diphthongization by initial palatals (presumably in the first half of the sixth century), a further series of vowel changes occurred in response to the presence of an **ī**, **i** or **j** in the syllable following. They were as follows:

ū became **ȳ**	**tūnjan > tȳnan**
u became **y**	**trummjan > trymman**
ō became **ē**	**dōmjan > dēman**
o became **e**	**morgin > mergen**
a (or **o**) before a nasal became **e**	**frammjan > fremman**
ā became **ǣ**	**lārjan > lǣran**
a became **æ**	**ladin > lædin**
æ became **e**	**ægi > ege**
io (**ēo**) became **ie**, later **ī** or **ȳ̌**	**strīonjan > strīenan (strȳnan, strīnan)**
io (**eo**) became **ie**, later **i** or **y**	**hiordi > hierde (hyrde, hirde)**
ēa became **īe**, later **ī** or **ȳ**	**gēlēafjan > gelīefan (gelȳfan, gelīfan)**
ea became **ie**, later **i** or **y**	**ealdira > ieldra (yldra ildra)**

Certain of these changes require a word of explanation:

a. The umlaut of **ō̆** (i.e., long or short) progressed through the intermediate stage **œ̆** (a mid front rounded vowel) before it became **ē̆** and in some parts of England, notably in the central-west, remained at mid-stage for a long period of time.

b. The **ā** which underwent palatal umlaut was not West Germanic **ā**, which by this time had already become **ǣ**, but rather the early Old English **ā**, which had developed from WGmc **ai**.

c. Words with **a** which underwent palatal umlaut consisted largely of Latin words borrowed after the fronting of WGmc **a** to **æ**, and some others which had remained at the **a** stage as the result of some analogical process.

d. The umlaut of the diphthongs **ĭo** and **ĕa** occurred only in West Saxon and not in the other dialects. Moreover, the resulting diphthong became a simple vowel within a relatively short time.

82. *Phonetic Interpretation of Palatal Umlaut*

As in many other instances, the details involving a dozen or so vowel and diphthong changes may be reduced to a few phonetic generalizations. First of all, it is apparent that the sounds which brought about palatal umlaut (**ī, i, j**) are all made with the jaw raised and the tongue thrust forward. They are high front. Second, it is equally evident from the accompanying diagram that the direction of change in the vowels affected is chiefly from the back to a corresponding position in the front. The front vowels which were subject to change, including the Primitive Germanic **e**, simply move one level higher. The diphthongs also move upward from a mid or low front to a high front position.

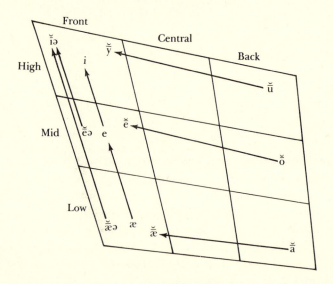

Whether these changes were due to anticipation of the high front sound in the next syllable or to assimilation to the following consonant, which had previously been palatalized by the following high front vowel, cannot be precisely determined. There are proponents of each point of view. The essential thing is to grasp the systematic nature of this series of changes and to understand how their operation affected a number of grammatical categories.

83. *Development of* ĭ, i, *and* j *after Umlaut*

The vowel or semivowel causing palatal umlaut was final in some instances, medial in others. The subsequent development of these sounds was as follows:

a. Final unstressed ĭ disappeared if preceded by a long syllable. It became **e** if preceded by a short syllable. Thus **dāli** > **dǣli** > **dǣl**; **slægi** > **slegi** > **slege**.

b. Medial **i** became **e** except when followed by **c**, **g**, **sc**, or **ng**, in which case it remained **i**. Thus: **morgin** > **mergin** > **mergen**; **hæfig** > **hefig**.

c. Medial **j** disappeared after all consonants except single **r** preceded by a short vowel. When retained, it was written **i**. Thus: **frammjan** > **fremmjan** > **fremman**;   **lārjan** > **lǣrjan** > **lǣran**; **nærjan** > **nerjan** > **nerian**.

84. *Germanic Stems*

Many grammars of the early Germanic languages, and those of some other Indo-European branches as well, classify the major parts of speech according to stem. Up to now this terminology has not been employed here, principally because the form of most Old English nouns and verbs does not indicate the stem. Because of its frequent use elsewhere, it is helpful to be aware of this scheme of classification and to understand the concept implicit in the use of the term.

Originally a stem consisted of a base or root element plus a suffix which consisted of a syllable (usually a vowel, or a consonant plus a vowel) to which the inflectional endings were added. For this very reason, classification on the basis of the syllables juxtaposed to the root came to be a convenient device. Accordingly, stems such as **daga** (**dag** + **a**), **barwa** (**bar** + **wa**), **sagja** (**sag** + **ja**) came to be known as **a**-stems, **wa**-stems, and **ja**-stems respectively. It is important to distinguish between the roots or base forms **dag**-, **bar**-, etc., and the stems **daga**, **barwa**, etc.

From the sound changes which have already been considered, it is clear that the **ja**-stems would have been subject to gemination in some instances and to palatal umlaut in every case, whereas the **a**-stems and **wa**-stems were not so affected, and that a **wa**-stem under certain conditions (when preceded directly by **l** or **r**) would have been subject to breaking. This is one reason for certain irregularities in the base forms of the various Old English declensions and conjugations.

85.   *Root-Consonant Stems: The* **man** *Declension*

This declension consisted of a small number of nouns which, however, were used with such frequency that remnants of its irregularity are still present in Modern English. In this particular instance, the inflectional endings were added directly to the final consonant of the root—hence the name *root-consonant stem*. The Germanic inflection for the dative singular was **-i**, for the nominative plural **-iz**, both of which gave rise to palatal umlaut. Feminine nouns sometimes reflected it in the genitive singular as well. Thus in nouns like **fōt** *foot* (m.) and **hnutu** *nut* (f.), the following declensional forms developed:

		MASCULINE	FEMININE
SINGULAR	NOM., ACC.	**fōt**	**hnutu**
	DAT., INST.	**fēt**	**hnyte**
	GEN.	**fōtes**	**hnute, hnyte**
PLURAL	NOM., ACC.	**fēt**	**hnyte**
	DAT., INST.	**fōtum**	**hnutum**
	GEN.	**fōta**	**hnuta**

The Modern English nouns *man, goose, tooth, mouth,* and *louse* owe their current irregularity to their having belonged to this declension. Subsequent to the Old English period all the cases of the plural were generalized with the umlauted form of the vowel, and those of the singular with the non-umlauted form. OE **bōc** *book* was also a root-consonant stem, with **bēc** as the dative-instrumental singular and nominative-accusative plural form, but it became regular early in the Middle English period.

86.   *Derivatives in* **-iþu**

One Germanic device for converting adjectives into feminine abstract nouns was adding the suffix **-iþu**, which caused palatal umlaut of the base vowel, after which the **i** of the suffix disappeared. Thus, we find such pairs as **fūl** *foul,* **fȳlþ** *filth;* **lang** *long,* **lengþu** *length.* This accounts for such differences as are found today between pairs like *strong, strength* and *whole, health,* in addition to those cited previously.

Reading

From Apollonius of Tyre

The reading selections in the remaining chapters of the grammatical section of this book will be drawn from the Old English version of *Apollonius of Tyre,* one of the more entertaining specimens of Old English prose and the earliest tale of romantic adventure in English literature. The story of Apollonius, drawn from a no-longer-extant third-century Greek source and then translated into Latin, was a favorite romance of the Middle Ages, familiar to all the people of Europe. Versions exist in more than a dozen vernacular languages, and it was also included in the popular *Gesta Romanorum.*

The Old English version, consisting of two fragments of the tale, survives in an eleventh-century manuscript. The language is classical Old English, of the late West Saxon period. The text will be given here as it occurs in the manuscript, with no attempt at normalization except for the indication of vowel length. The best edition is by Peter Goolden, *The Old English Apollonius of Tyre* (New York: Oxford University Press, 1958), to which the present version is heavily indebted; another edition, by J. Raith (Munich, 1956) contains a critical text of the Latin version as well as the Old English paraphrase of it.

Hēr onginneð sēo gerecednes by Antioche þām ungesǣligan cingce and be Apollonige þām Tiriscan.

An Antiochia þāre ceastre wæs sum cyninge Antiochus gehāten; æfter þæs cyninges naman wæs sēo ceaster Antiochia gecīged. Þises cyninges cwēn wearð of līfe gewiten, be ðāre hē hæfde āne swīðe wlītige dohter ungelīfedlīcre fægernesse. Mid þī þe hēo becōm tō giftelīcre yldo, þā gyrnde hyre mænig mǣre man micele mǣrða bēodende. Ðā gelamp hit sārlīcum gelimpe: þā ðā sē fæder þōhte hwām hē hī mihte hēalīcost forgifan, þā gefēol his āgen mōd

on hyre lufe mid unrihtre gewilnunge, tō ðām swīðe þæt he forgeat
þā fæderlīcan ārfæstnesse and gewilnode his āgenre dohtor him
tō gemæccan, and þā gewilnunge nāht lange ne ylde, ac sume dæge
on ǣrnemergen þā hē of slǣpe āwōc, hē ābræc intō ðām būre
þǣr hēo inne læg and hēt his hȳredmen ealle him āweg gān, swilce
hē wið his dohtor sume dīgle spǣce sprecan wolde. Hwæt, hē
ðā on ðāre mānfullan scilde ābisgode and þā ongēanwinnendan
fǣmnan mid micelre strengðe earfoðlīce ofercōm, and þæt gefremede mān gewilnode tō bedīglianne.

Glossary and Structural Notes

From this point on, nouns listed in the Glossary and Structural
Notes will be entered in their nominative singular forms, verbs in
the infinitive, and adjectives without inflection. This will prepare
the student to use general glossaries and dictionaries of Old English.

ābisigian	Verb II, *to engage, occupy oneself.* **bisig**, adj., *busy.*
an	Prep., **on** *in.* A late spelling of WGmc **a** before a nasal, usually **o** in earlier texts.
ārfæstnes	Noun, f., *virtue.* Cp. **ār**, noun, *honor.*
bedīglian	Verb II *to conceal.* Cp. **dīgol**, adj., *secret.*
bēodan	Verb 2, *to offer.*
būr	Noun, n., *bower, chamber.*
(ge)cīgan	Verb I, *to call, summon.*
cyning	Noun, m., *king.* Frequently in this text uninflected forms of the noun are spelled **cingc**. This may indicate a devoicing of the final stop after a nasal.
dīgol	Adj., *secret.* Acc. sing. fem., **dīgle**, line 15.
(ge)fremman	Verb I, *to perform.* On line 17; *gefremede* is a past participle used as adj., n. acc. sing. weak, modifying **mān**.
gelimp	Noun, n., *occurrence, misfortune.*
gemæcce	Noun, f., *mate.*
giftelīc	Adj., *marriageable,* from **gift**, noun, *marriage.*

gyrnan   Verb I, *to yearn, desire*. Cp. **georn**, adj., *eager*.

hēalīce   Adv., *nobly, in an exalted manner*. From **hēah**, adj., *high* + **-līce**. **h** disappeared in Late Old English when it occurred between voiced sounds. **hēalīcost**, superlative.

(ge)limpan   Verb 3, *to happen, occur*.

mænig   Adj, *many*. The usual form is **menig**, which developed by palatal umlaut from **manig**. The spelling **mænig**, common in this text, appears to have been an intermediate stage characteristic of Essex. In OE **menig** with a sing. noun is a distributive construction, equivalent to *many a . . .*

mǣre   Adj., *famous*. **mǣrþ**, noun, f., usually *glory, fame*, but in this instance it means *wonderful things*.

mān   Noun, n., *crime*. **mānful**, adj., *criminal, wicked*.

mōd   Noun, n., *heart, mind, spirit*. **þā gefēol his āgen mōd on hyre lufe**. *Then his own heart fell into love of her*.

nāht   Adv., *not, not at all*. From **nān** *no* and **wiht** *whit, creature*.

ongēanwinnan   Verb 3, *to resist, struggle against*. Cp. **winnan** *to contend*.

(ge)recednes   Noun, f., *narrative*. From **reccan** *to tell, relate*.

scild   Noun, f., *crime, guilt*. Often appears as **scyld**.

swiþe   Adv., *very*. **tō ðām swīðe** *to the extent*.

Tirisc   Adj., *Tyrian, of Tyre*.

ungelīfedlīc   Adj., *incredible*. Cf. **gelīfan** *to believe*, **lēafa** *belief*.

ungesǣlig   Adj., *unfortunate, unhappy*.

wlitig   Adj., *beautiful, radiant*. Cp. **wlītan** *to look*, and **wlita**, noun, *countenance*.

yldo   Noun, f., *age*. From **eald**, adj., *old*. The earlier form **ieldo** shows that palatal umlaut has occurred.

Practice Exercises

1. Apply the rules for the operation of palatal umlaut and for the development of the vowel or semivowel which caused the umlaut to the following forms: **hāljan, duni, geasti, geþuldig, bōtjan, oli, guldin, gōsi, dearni, līohtjan.**

2. Trace the development of the Primitive Germanic forms listed below through the stages of each of the following sound changes to the extent to which they are applicable: gemination, fronting of WGmc **ā**, development of the diphthongs **ai** and **au**, breaking, diphthongization by initial palatal, palatal umlaut.

hlahjan	**hailjan**	**satjan**	**haurjan**	**bidjan**
brūciþ	**taljan**	**bugjan**	**sōcjan**	**girnjan**

Chapter 16

87. *Syncopation in the Present-Tense Forms of Strong Verbs*

The occurrence of palatal umlaut in the second and third persons present indicative of the strong verb classes has already been discussed (section 81). After this sound change took place, the vowels of the **-is** (second-person singular) and **-iþ** (third-person singular) became **e**, according to rule b, section 83. In the case of these particular strong verb inflections, however, the **e** tended to syncopate or disappear, placing the consonants of the inflectional endings immediately adjacent to the final consonant of the stem. The **-s** of the second person had by this time acquired a final **-t** as well. Thus, for the verbs **beran** *to bear* and **lūcan** *to lock* the following developments occurred: **beris > bires > birest > birst; beriþ > bireþ > birþ; lūcis > lȳces > lȳcest > lȳcst; lūciþ > lȳceþ > lȳcþ**.

This syncopation of an unstressed vowel was not unlike that which takes place in Modern English in such a word as *interesting*, which tends to become *int'resting*, or *secretary*, often heard in British English as *secret'ry*. Syncopation of the verb inflections was particularly marked in the West Saxon and Kentish dialects. In the central and northern portions of the country the vowels of the inflectional syllables were often retained.

88. *Assimilation in the Present-Tense Forms of Strong Verbs*

Syncopation of the vowels of the second- and third-person singular inflectional endings often brought together combinations of two, three, or even four consonants which tended to alter or influence each other. Thus, in the second person:

a. **-sst > st: rīsst > rīst (rīsan** *to rise*)

b. **-þst > sst > st: wierþest > wiersst > wiersst > wierst** (**weorþan** *to become*)

c. **-dst > tst: drǣdest > drǣtst, findest > fintst** (**drǣdan** *to dread*, **findan** *to find*)

At a later period **drǣst** and **finst** also occur, as was the case with stems ending in **-t: lǣtest > lǣtst > lǣst** (**lǣtan** *to leave*).

In the third-person singular present indicative of strong verbs the following developments occurred after syncope of the vowel:

d. **-þþ > þ: wierþþ > wierþ** (**weorþan** *to become*)

e. **-sþ > st: cīesþ > cīest** (**cēosan** *to choose*)

f. **-tþ > tt > t: miltþ > miltt > milt** (**meltan** *to melt*)

g. **-dþ > tt > t: bindþ > bintt > bint** (**bindan** *to bind*)[1]

---

1. A more compact and economical way of expressing these assimilative developments in syncopated verb forms is in terms of four ordered rules, which may be formulated as follows:

$$1 \quad a \quad d \rightarrow t / - \left\{ \begin{matrix} s \\ \overline{þ} \end{matrix} \right\}$$

$$b \quad þ \rightarrow s / - s$$

$$2 \quad þ \rightarrow t / - \left\{ \begin{matrix} s \\ t \end{matrix} \right\}$$

$$3 \quad C: \rightarrow C$$

According to the first rule, any final **d** in a base form becomes **t** when followed by **s** or **þ**; any **þ** becomes **s** when followed by **s**. These two observations account for the examples under *b*, *c*, and *g* above. According to the second rule, **þ** becomes **t** when it follows **s** or **t**, as in the examples under *e* and *f*. The third rule provides for the instances where doubled or lengthened consonants become single, as in *a* and *d*. Thus according to rule in this note, **wierþst** is converted to **wiersst**, which on the basis of *c* then simplifies to **wierst**.

Assimilation may be defined as the process through which a sound takes on one or more characteristics of a neighboring sound. Turning again to Modern English for a parallel, we note that in a plural form such as *moths*, the final interdental consonant of the stem is assimilated to an alveolar position by the *s* of the plural inflection. In a combination such as *oldster*, especially when spoken rapidly, the final *d* of *old* is first unvoiced as a consequence of the two consonants following, and next, the ensuing stop tends to become fricative, a process virtually identical with that occurring in OE **findst** > **fintst** > **finst**.

89. *Derivatives in* **-isc** *and* **-ig**

These suffixes were used primarily to convert nouns to adjectives denoting the quality indicated by the simplex or base form. Thus: **cild** *child*, **cildisc** *childish*; **mann** *man*, **mennisc** *human*; **þurst** *thirst*, **þyrstig** *thirsty*; **stān** *stone*, **stǣnig** *stony*. The suffix **-ig** seems not to have been added to nouns denoting humans; the suffix **-isc** is usually but not invariably so applied. Generally the vowel of the derivative suffix caused palatal umlaut of the vowel of the base form, as evidenced by **mennisc**, **stǣnig**, and **þyrstig**, but in some instances the vowel of the base form was restored by analogy, resulting in forms like **stānig** and **þurstig**. The suffixes survive in such Modern English words as *childish*, *stony*, etc. The use of *ish* as a qualitative diminutive—i.e., *bluish* (approaching the quality of blue), *wettish*, etc.—did not develop until later.

90. *Derivatives in* **-ing**, **-ling**

By the addition of **-ing**, concrete nouns masculine in gender were formed from adjectives or from other nouns, often with the sense of *proceeding from*, *associated with*, or *having the quality of*. Thus: **brant** *high* **brenting** *ship*, i.e., *high one*; **earm** *poor*, *miserable*, **ierming** *wretch*; **æþele** *noble*, **æþeling** *nobleman*. This suffix was also the basis of the patronymic naming system employed in England prior to the Norman Conquest: **Ælfrēd Æþelwulfing**, *Alfred, son of Aethelwulf*; **Ēadweard Ælfrēding**, *Edward, son of Alfred*. It is possible that from forms like **æþeling** *nobleman*, **lȳtling** *child*, the suffix became extended to **-ling**, also employed, often with palatal mutation of the vowel of the base form, to produce concrete nouns, masculine in gender: **rāp** *rope, fetter*, **rǣpling** *captive*; **dēor** *dear*, **dēorling** *favorite*; **cnapa** *youth*, **cnæpling** *youth*, probably in a diminutive sense; **eorþe** *earth*, **ierþling** *husbandman, plowman*.

Reading
From Apollonius of Tyre

Đā gewearð hit þæt þæs mǣdenes fōstormōdor intō ðām būre ēode and geseah hī ðār sittan on micelre gedrēfednesse and hire cwæð tō, "Hwīg eart þū, hlǣfdige, swā gedrēfedes mōdes?" Þæt mǣden hyre andswerode, "Lēofe fōstormōdor, nū tōdæg forwurdon twēgen æðele naman on þisum būre." Sēo fōstormōdor cwæð, "Hlǣfdige, be hwām cwist þū þæt?" Hēo hyre andwirde and cwæð, "Ǣr ðām dæge mīnra brīdgifta ic eom mid mānfulre scilde besmited." Đā cwæð sēo fōstormōdor, "Hwā wæs ǣfre swā dirstiges mōdes þæt dorste cynges dohtor gewæmman ǣr ðām dæge hyre brȳdgifta and him ne ondrēde þæs cyninges irre?" Đæt mægden cwæð, "Ārlēasnes þā scilde on mē gefremode." Sēo fōstormōdor cwæð, "Hwī ne segst þū hit þīnum fæder?" Đæt mǣden cwæð, "Hwār is sē fæder? Sōðlīce on mē earmre is mīnes fæder nama rēowlīce forworden and mē nū forðām dēað þearle gelīcað." Sēo fōstormōdor sōðlīce þā ðā hēo gehȳrde þæt þæt mǣden hire dēaðes girnde, ðā cliopode hēo hī hire tō mid līðere sprǣce and bæd þæt hēo fram þāre gewilnunge hyre mōd gewǣnde and tō hire fæder willan gebuge, þēah ðe hēo tō genēadod wǣre.

Glossary and Structural Notes

ārlēasnes	Noun, f., *impiety, wickedness*. Cp. **ār** *honor, dignity, reference*.
besmītan	Verb 1, *to defile, pollute*.
(ge)būgan	Verb 2, *to submit, bow*. In line 18, **gebuge** is past subjunctive, maintaining the past-tense sequence throughout the clause.

dirstig   Adj., *bold, presumptuous.* Cp. **durran**, verb, *to dare.*

drēfan   Verb I, *to afflict, trouble.* **(Ge)drēfednes**, noun, f., *tribulation, distress.*

earm   Adj., *poor, wretched.* In line 13, dat. sing. f. strong, modifying **mē**.

fōstormōdor   Noun, f., *nurse.*

(ge)fremman   Verb I, *to do, to perform.* The past-tense form **gefremode** in line 11 is irregular; **gefremede** would normally be expected here.

girnan   Verb I, *to desire, yearn.* Note that the verb takes a gen. object in line 16.

hwīg   Adv., *why.* **Hwīg** is a late spelling for earlier **hwȳ** or **hwī**.

irre   Noun, n., *anger, ire.* Often **ierre** in earlier texts.

(ge)līcian   Verb II, *to please.* Used with dat. object.

liðre   Adj., *wicked, corrupt.*

mǣden   Noun, n., *maiden.* The earlier form of this word was **mægden**. In Late Old English, palatalized **g** between a short vowel and a dental or alveolar consonant was frequently dropped and the preceding vowel was lengthened.

(ge)nēadian   Verb II, *to compel, force.*

ondrǣdan   Verb 7, *to dread, fear.* The **him** preceding the verb is a dat. reflexive; the form in line 11 is past subjunctive.

rēowlīce   Adv., *miserably, grievously.* Earlier **hrēowlīce**.

þēah   Conj., *even though*, with subjunctive of the verb following.

þearle   Adv., *very much.*

(ge)wæmman   Verb I, *to defile, besmirch.* From **wamm** *blot, stain, scar*. The usual form of this verb is **(ge)wemman**.

Practice Exercise

Give the umlauted, syncopated, and assimilated forms of the second- and third-persons singular present indicative of the following verbs: **fealdan** *to fold,* **hwōpan** *to threaten,* **lācan** *to leap,* **grafan** *to dig,* **cnedan** *to knead,* **cuman** *to come,* **feohtan** *to fight,* **meltan** *to melt,* **weorþan** *to become,* **scūfan** *to shove,* **frēosan** *to freeze,* **snīþan** *to cut,* **gēotan** *to pour,* **strūdan** *to ravage,* **cweþan** *to say.*

Chapter 17

91. *Weak Verbs, Class I*

It has already been pointed out (section 29) that the device of indicating the past tense and past participle of verbs by means of a suffix containing the consonants **d** or **t** was a feature peculiar to the Germanic languages. Furthermore, the rationale of the term *weak* in connection with such verbs has already been explained.

Even so, the application of the dental suffix was not wholly uniform. There were two major patterns of weak verb inflection and one minor pattern as well. The two major patterns may be differentiated by the ending of the infinitive: usually **-an** (with one notable exception) for the first class, as opposed to **-ian** for the second. Likewise, when a vowel does appear in the past-tense and past-participle inflections of verbs of the first class, it is **e**; the second-class verbs uniformly have **o**. Thus, **fremman**, **fremede** for Class I as opposed to **lufian**, **lufode** for Class II.

92. *The Form of the Infinitive*

For the most part, the weak verbs in Old English were derivative in origin, that is, formed from other parts of speech. Whereas in later English this end could be achieved simply by using a noun as verb without change in form (*model* noun becomes *to model* verb, and so with *service, loan, host*), in Germanic the conversion was brought about by adding a stem containing **-j-**, which appeared in the infinitive as **-jan**. Thus, **dōm** *judgment*, **dōmjan** *to judge*, i.e. *to make a judgment*; **gern** *eager*, **gernjan** *to desire, be eager*;

tam *tame*, **tamjan** *to make tame, to tame*; **daru** *injury*, **darjan** *to injure, cause an injury.*

Although the **-jan** suffix was uniformly applied in Germanic, the subsequent sound changes of gemination and palatal umlaut gave rise to differences in form in Old English:

a. **dōmjan**, with a long vowel in the base form, did not undergo gemination, but the vowel was fronted as a result of palatal umlaut, resulting in the Old English form **dēman**. Similarly **gernjan**, with a long root syllable despite the short vowel, shows only breaking and umlaut but not gemination in the Old English form **giernan**, later **gyrnan**. In both instances the **j** was lost after palatal umlaut occurred.

b. **tamjan**, with a short vowel followed by a single consonant in the base form, underwent both gemination and umlaut, and again the **j** disappeared after umlaut: **tamjan** > **tammjan** > **temman**.

c. **darjan**, with a base form ending in **r** preceded by a short vowel, did not geminate the consonant. It did undergo palatal umlaut, but because of the short vowel plus **r** combination, the **j** of the stem subsequently became **i**: **darjan** > **dærjan** > **derian**.

93.   *Sources of the Weak I Conjugation*

The **-jan** suffix could be affixed to nouns, to adjectives, or to strong verbs. In the case of the last, it was usually attached to the past singular form. The following examples will illustrate the relationship between the meaning of the verb and the part of speech from which it was derived.

a. Nouns

scrūd *garment*	**scrȳdan** *to clothe*
fōd *food*	**fēdan** *to feed*
þurst *thirst*	**þyrstan** *to thirst*
wamm *blot, stain*	**wemman** *to defile*

b. Adjectives

cōl *cool*	**cēlan** *to make cool*
hāl *whole, hale*	**hǣlan** *to heal*
hwīt *white*	**hwītan** *to whiten*
wōd *mad*	**wēdan** *to rage*

c. Verbs

hwearf *turned* (**hweorfan** 3)	**hwyrfan** *to convert*
sanc *sank* (**sincan** 3)	**sencan** *to submerge*
sprang *jumped* (**springan** 3)	**sprengan** *to scatter*

For the most part the relationship between the **-jan** verbs and their sources is either causative or factitive. The latter term, as its etymology indicates, refers to performance (Latin *facere, factus — to do, done*).

94. *The Present Tense of Weak I Verbs*

The Germanic personal endings in the present tense, from which the Old English forms of the Weak I verbs were derived, were:

SINGULAR	1	**-jō**
	2	**-īs**
	3	**-iþ**
PLURAL	3	**-janþ**

Originally the forms for the first- and second-person plural were distinct from that for the third, but these disappeared early in the Germanic period, and their place was taken by the form for the third person. This accounts for the identity of form for all three persons in the indicative plural in Old English.

Just as the **-j** of the infinitive affected groups of these verbs differently with respect to gemination, so the alternation between **j** and **i** in the present indicative resulted in a differentiation in form in Old English, depending upon the length of the syllable of the base form and whether or not that syllable ended in **r**.

The greatest regularity in Old English is to be found in the verbs with a long syllable in the base form. They were not subject to gemination and were affected uniformly by palatal umlaut. To show how they developed, the Germanic and the resultant Old English forms are given below.

		GERMANIC	OLD ENGLISH
SINGULAR	1	**dōmjō**	**dēme**
	2	**dōmis**	**dēmst**
	3	**dōmiþ**	**dēmþ**
		dōmjanþ	**dēmaþ**

SINGULAR	1	**gernjō**	**gyrne**[1]
	2	**gernis**	**gyrnst**
	3	**gerniþ**	**gyrnþ**
PLURAL		**gernjanþ**	**gyrnaþ**

Those verbs which in their base form had a short vowel followed by a single consonant other than **r** developed as follows:

		GERMANIC	OLD ENGLISH
SINGULAR	1	**tamjō**	**temme**
	2	**tamis**	**temest**
	3	**tamiþ**	**temeþ**
PLURAL		**tamjanþ**	**temmaþ**

Whereas in the strong verbs the **i** of the second- and third-person singular inflections generally syncopated after causing palatal umlaut, in the weak I verbs it tended to disappear only after long stems. Thus: **dēmst**, **dēmþ**, **gyrnst**, **gyrnþ**, but **temest**, **temeþ**. For verbs like **temman**, the present subjunctive shows gemination in all persons of the present tense: **ic, þū, hē temme**; **wē, gē, hī temmen**.

Verbs which had in their base form a short vowel followed by **r** alone did not undergo gemination. They derive their characteristic features from the change of **j** to **i** after palatal umlaut.

		GERMANIC	OLD ENGLISH
SINGULAR	1	**darjō**	**derie**
	2	**daris**	**derest**
	3	**dariþ**	**dereþ**
PLURAL		**darjanþ**	**deriaþ**

Verbs of this type have **-ie** in the subjunctive: **derie** (singular), **derien** (plural).

95. *The Comparative and Superlative of Adjectives*

For the majority of Old English adjectives, the comparative degree was formed by adding **-ra** to the base form, the superlative

---

1. The OE form **gyrne** reflects the development **gernjō** > **geornjō** > **gierne** > **gyrne**.

CHAPTER 17: SECTIONS 95–96

by adding **-ost(a)**. The comparative was invariably declined as a weak adjective; the **-ra**, characteristic of the masculine nominative singular, became **-re** for the feminine and neuter. For the superlative, which could be declined either strong or weak, **-ost** was the invariable form of the nominative singular, strong, of all genders; **-osta** and **-oste** were the weak declension forms. Adjectives ending in **-e** lost the final vowel when the inflections for comparative and superlative were added. The specimen forms below omit the optional **-a** in the superlative.

wīd *wide*	**wīdra**	**wīdost**
lāþ *hostile*	**lāþra**	**lāþost**
scearp *sharp*	**scearpra**	**scearpost**
wearm *warm*	**wearmra**	**wearmost**
smæl *small*	**smealra**	**smalost**

96. *Irregular Comparison*

There were two types of irregular comparison. The first arose as a result of palatal umlaut, stemming from the prehistoric Old English suffixes **-ira** and **-ist**, which were used with a few adjectives. In the comparative the **i** was lost after the period of umlaut; in the superlative it usually became **e**.

eald *old*	**yldra**	**yldest**
feorr *far*	**fyrra**	**fyrrest**
geong *young*	**gingra**	**gingest**
grēat *large*	**grȳtra**	**grȳtest**
hēah *high*	**hȳrra**	**hȳhst**
lang *long*	**lengra**	**lengest**
sceort *short*	**scyrtra**	**scyrtest**
strang *strong*	**strengra**	**strengest**

Certain other adjectives formed their comparative and superlative from a root other than that which was the basis for the positive degree. Chief among them are:

gōd *good*	**betra, sēlra**	**betst, sēlest**
lȳtel *little*	**lāssa**	**lǣst**
micel *much, many*	**māra**	**mǣst**
yfel *bad*	**wyrsa**	**wyrst**

Reading
From Apollonius of Tyre

On þisum þingum sōðlīce þurhwunode sē ārlēasesta cyngc Antiochus and mid gehȳwedan mōde hine sylfne atȳwde his ceastergewarum swilce hē ārfæst fæder wǣre his dohtor, and betwux
his hīwcūðum mannum hē blissode on ðām þæt hē his āgenre
dohtor wer wæs, and tō ðām þæt hē þe lengc brūcan mihte his
dohtor ārlēasan brīdbeddes and him fram ādrȳfan þā ðe hyre
girndon tō rihtum gesynscipum, hē āsette ðā rǣdels þus cweðende,
"Swā hwilc man swā mīnne rǣdels riht arǣde, onfō sē mȳnre
dohtor tō wīfe, and sē ðe hine misrǣde, sȳ hē behēafdod." Hwæt
is nū māre ymbe þæt tō sprecanne būton þæt cyningas ǣghwanon
coman and ealdormen for ðam ungelīfedlican wlite þæs mǣdenes,
and þone dēað hī oferhogodon and þone rǣdels understōdon tō
arǣdenne. Ac gif heora hwilc þonne þurh āsmēagunge bōclīcre
snotornesse þone rǣdels āriht rǣdde, þonne wearð sē tō behēafdunge gelǣd swā same swā sē ðe hine āriht ne rǣdde. And þā
hēafda ealle wurdon gesette on ūfeweardan þām geate.

Glossary and Structural Notes

ādrȳfan	A late spelling for **ādrīfan** (1).
ǣghwanon	Adv., *from all parts, everywhere.* From **ǣg** *each, every* and **hwanon** *whence.*
ætȳwan	Verb I, *to show, reveal.* This verb is often reflexive, as it is here.
ārǣdan	Verb I, used here in the sense of *to interpret.*
āsmēagung	Noun, f., *application, consideration.* From **āsmēagan** (I), *to consider, examine, investigate.*
bōclīc	Adj., *scholarly, literary.*
brūcan	Verb 2, *to use, enjoy, possess.*
ceastergewaru	Noun, f., *townsfolk, citizens.*
hīwcūþ	Adj., *domestic, familiar.*
(ge)hȳwian	Verb II, *to dissemble, feign.* The past participle, in which **e** appears in place of **o**, is used adjectivally in line 2.

lengc	Adv., *longer*. The form in line 5 is the comparative degree of **lange**, showing palatal umlaut and loss of final **e**.
misrǣdan	Verb I, used here in the sense of *to misinterpret*.
oferhogian	Verb II, *to despise, scorn*.
onfōn	Verb 7, *to receive*. The form in line 8 is 3rd sing. pres. subjunctive.
rǣdels	Noun, n., *riddle*. From **rǣdan**. The **ðā** preceding the noun in line 7 is an adv. rather than an article.
snotorness	Noun, f., *wisdom*. From **snotor**, adj., *wise*.
swā hwilc . . . swā	*Whatsoever*.
(ge)synscipe	Noun, m., *marriage*.
tō ðām þæt	*In order that*.
þurhwunian	Verb II, *to continue, persist*.
ūfewearda	Noun, m., *upper part*. From **ūfeweard**, adv., *above*.
understandan	Verb 6, used here in the sense of *to undertake*.
wer	Noun, m., *man*, husband.
wlite	Noun, m., *beauty*.

Practice Exercises

1. What would be the infinitive form of the first-class weak verbs corresponding to and derived from the following: **lār** *lore*; **heorte** *heart*; **cēap** *bargain*; **sand** *message, deputation*; **lād** *journey*; **trum** *strong, firm*; **hēan** *lowly, despised*; **ēac** *also*; **sceort** *short*; **rūm** *spacious*; **grom** *angry*.

2. Conjugate the following first-class weak verbs in the present tense, making allowance for the possibility of syncopation and assimilation in the second- and third-person singular: **cnyssan** *to strike*, **snyrian** *to hasten*, **dǣlan** *to distribute*, **scyrpan** *to sharpen*, **spildan** *to destroy*, **þennan** *to extend*, **werian** *to defend*, **spǣtan** *to spit*, **wreþþan** *to support*, **lǣfan** *to leave*.

Chapter 18

97. *The Past Tense of Weak I Verbs*

The stem and personal endings in the past tense from which the Old English forms of the weak I verbs were derived were:

SINGULAR	1	**-ide**
	2	**-ides**
	3	**-ide**
PLURAL	3	**-idun**

Because the stem of the past tense contained an **i** rather than a **j**, there is no evidence of gemination in the past-tense forms of any of the Class I weak verbs, but palatal umlaut did occur. As with the second- and third-person singular of the present tense, the medial **i** was syncopated after causing umlaut when the base form consisted of a long syllable; it became **e** when the base form consisted of a short syllable. Thus: **dōmide > dēmde**; **girnide > giornide > giernde > gyrnde**; **tamide > tæmide > temede**; **daride > dæride > derede**.

98. *The Complete Conjugation of Weak I Verbs*

The full conjugation of **dēman** *to judge*, **temman** *to tame*, and **derian** *to injure* will serve as models for this class.

PRESENT INDICATIVE

INGULAR	(ic)	dēme	temme	derie
	(þū)	dēmst	temest	derest
	(hē)	dēmþ	temeþ	dereþ
LURAL	(wē, gē, hī)	dēmaþ	temmaþ	deriaþ

PRESENT SUBJUNCTIVE

INGULAR	(ic, þū, hē)	dēme	temme	derie
LURAL	(wē, gē, hī)	dēmen	temmen	derien

PAST INDICATIVE

INGULAR	(ic)	dēmde	temede	derede
	(þū)	dēmdest	temedest	deredest
	(hē)	dēmde	temede	derede
LURAL	(wē, gē, hī)	dēmdon	temedon	deredon

PAST SUBJUNCTIVE

INGULAR	(ic, þū, hē)	dēmde	temede	derede
LURAL	(wē, gē, hī)	dēmden	temeden	dereden

MPERATIVE,	Sing.:	dēm	teme	dere
	Pl.:	dēmaþ	temmaþ	deriaþ
ARTICLES,	Pres.:	dēmende	temmende	deriende
	Past:	dēmed	temed	dered
NFINITIVE		dēman	temman	derian
GERUND		tō dēmenne	tō temmenne	tō derienne

99. *Assimilation in Class I Weak Verbs*

Since the stem vowel which caused palatal umlaut was so frequently lost in this conjugation, and since the consonant **d** figured so prominently in the inflectional endings, it is not surprising that, as with certain of the inflections of the strong verbs, some consonant changes should have occurred as a result of assimilation. In general the assimilations were of two types:

a. Devoicing of **d** to **t**. When the final consonant of a base form with a long syllable was voiceless, the **d** of the past inflection also became voiceless after syncopation of the vowel, appearing as **t**.

Thus: **wūscide** > **wȳscte** *wished*; **scearpide** > **scierpte** > **scyrpte** *sharpened.*

b. Syncopation and coalescence of **d** and **t** inflections. When the final consonant of the base form was a **d** or **t** preceded by a vowel, syncopation occurred irrespective of the length of the syllable. The vowel of the past participle inflection was also syncopated at times and in Late Old English was often simplified to a single final consonant. When the final consonant of the base form was a **d** or **t** preceded by another consonant, the syncopation was accompanied by coalescence of the **d** of the inflectional ending, or the **t** which had developed according to *a* above, to the **d** or **t** of the stem.

The principal parts of verbs with base forms ending in **d** and **t** are as follows:

INFINITIVE	PAST TENSE	PAST PARTICIPLE
fēdan *to feed*	**fēdde**	**fēded, fēdd, fēd**
treddan *to tread on*	**tredde**	**treded, tredd, tred**
grētan *to greet*	**grētte**	**grēted, grētt, grēt**
cnyttan *to bind*	**cnytte**	**cnyted, cnytt, cnyt**
bendan *to bend*	**bende**	**bended, bend**
restan *to rest*	**reste**	**rested, rest**

100.   *The Formation of Adverbs in* -e

The use of the suffix **-līce** in forming adverbs from adjectives was discussed in section 42. This was by no means the only way in which such a conversion could be made in Old English. Another common method was to add **-e** to the base form of the adjective. Thus: **heard**, adj., **heardlīce**, adv., **hearde**, adv. Similarly, **fæst**, adj., **fæste**, adv.; **gearu**, adj., **gearwe**, adv. In the case of adjectives ending in **-e**, such as **clǣne**, **nīwe**, the adjectival and adverbial forms were identical.

It is this pattern of formation which gave rise to the so-called 'flat' adverbs in Modern English: **fast, hard**, etc. During the Middle English period the final **-e** which had distinguished them from the adjectives in Old English ceased to be pronounced and finally dropped from the spelling as well, leaving the adjectives and adverbs identical in form. This development also accounts for the use of *slow* as an adverb alongside the more approved form *slowly*.

101. *The Adverbial Functions of Noun Cases*

The genitive singular, masculine and neuter, was often used to indicate an adverbial relationship. Thus, **dæges ond nihtes** *by day and by night*, **nȳdes** *of necessity*, **ealles** *entirely*, **innanbordes** *internally*, **singales** *always*. With certain words the dative also acquired an adverbial function, especially **hwīlum** *at times*, **firenum** *criminally*, and with compounds ending in **mǣl** *time, point of time*; **stæpmǣlum** *gradually*, **stundmǣlum** *at intervals*. The use of the accusative to indicate extent of time and space has already been mentioned (section 13).

102. *The Comparison of Adverbs*

Most adverbs added **-or** to form the comparative degree and **-ost** for the superlative, the vowel of the ending coalescing with the final **-e** of the adverbial form.

oft *often*	**oftor**	**oftost**
swīþe *very*	**swīþor**	**swīþost**
hearde *firmly*	**heardor**	**heardost**
bealdlīce *boldly*	**bealdlīcor**	**bealdlīcost**

As was the case with the adjectives (section 96), a few adverbs show palatal umlaut in their comparative and superlative forms.

ēaþe *easily*	**īþ**	**ēaþost**
feorr *far*	**fyrr**	**fyrrest**
lange *long*	**leng**	**lengest**
nēah *near*	**nēarra**	**nȳhst**
sōfte *softly*	**sēft**	**sōftost**

Those adjectives which built their comparative and superlative degrees upon different base forms from the positive have corresponding adverbial forms.

wel *well*	**bet, sēl**	**betst, sēlest**
lȳtle, lȳt *little*	**læs**	**læst**
micle *much*	**mā**	**mǣst**
yfle *evilly*	**wyrs**	**wyrst**

Reading
From Apollonius of Tyre

Mid þī sōðlīce Antiōchus sē wælrēowa cyningc on þysse wælrēownesse þurhwunode, ðā wæs Appolonius gehāten sum iung man sē wæs swīðe welig and snotor and wæs ealdorman on Tīro þāre mǣgðe, sē getrūwode on his snotornesse and on ðā bōclīcan lāre and āgan rōwan oð þæt hē becōm tō Antiochian. Eode þā intō ðām cyninge and cwæð, "Wes gesund, cyningc. Hwæt ic becōm nū tō ðē swā swā tō gōdum fæder and ārfæstum. Ic eom sōðlīce of cynelīcum cynne cumen and ic bidde þīnre dohtor mē tō gemæccan." Ðā ðā sē cyngc þæt gehȳrde þæt hē his willes gehȳran nolde, hē swīðe irlīcum andwlitan beseah tō ðām iungan ealdormen and cwæð, "Þū iunga mann, canst ðū þone dōm mȳnra dohtor gifta?" Apollonius cwæð, "Ic can þone dōm and ic hine æt þām geate geseah." Ðā cwæð sē cyningc mid æbilignesse, "Gehīr nū þone rædels, 'Scelere vereor, materna carne vescor.'" Þæt is on englisc, "Scylde ic þolige, mōddrenum flǣsce ic brūce." Eft hē cwæð, "Quaero patrem meum, meae matris virum, uxoris meae filiam nec invenio." Þæt is on englisc, "Ic sēce mīnne fæder, mȳnre mōdor wer, mīnes wīfes dohtor and ic ne finde." Appolonius þā sōðlīce onfangenum rædelse hine bewænde hwōn fram ðām cyninge, and mid þȳ þe hē smēade ymbe þæt ingehyd, hē hit gewan mid wīsdome and mid Godes fultume hē þæt sōð ārǣdde. Bewænde hine þā tō ðām cynincge and cwæð, "Þū gōda cyningc, þū āsettest rædels; gehȳr ðū þā onfundennesse. Ymbe þæt þū cwǣde þæt þū scilde þolodest, ne eart ðū leogende on ðām— besēoh tō ðē silfum; and þæt þū cwǣde 'mōddrenum flǣsce ic brūce,' ne eart ðū on ðām lēogende—besēoh tō þīnre dohtor.'"

Glossary and Structural Notes

æbilignes Noun, f., *anger, offense.*

āginnan Verb, equivalent to **onginnan** (3) *to begin.* The prefix shows neutralization of the initial vowel and loss of **n**.

andwlita Noun, m., *face, countenance.*

ārǣdan Verb I, used in line 22 in the sense of *to perceive, discover.*

besēon Verb 5, *to look at, behold.* The form **besēoh** is imperative.

bewændan Verb I, *to turn.* Usually **bewendan**.

dōm Noun, m. Used here in the sense of *condition* rather than its more usual meaning of *judgment.*

fultum Noun, m., *help, assistance.*

gemæcce Noun, f., *mate.*

gesund Adj., *well, healthy, prosperous.*

hwæt Interjection, *lo.*

hwōn Adv., *a little.*

ingehygd Noun, n., *meaning.*

irlīc Adj., *angry.*

lēogan Verb 2, *to lie, deceive.*

mǣgð Noun, f., *people, country.*

mōddren Adj., *maternal.*

mōdor Noun, f., *mother.* This noun belongs to an irregular declension and appears in the acc. and gen. sing. without inflection.

nolde Verb, a contracted form of **ne wolde** *would not, did not wish.*

onfangenum Past participle of **onfōn**, verb 7, *to receive.* The form in line 19 has a dative-instrumental inflection, used with **rǣdelse** in an absolute construction.

onfundennes Noun, f., *solution.* From **onfindan**, verb 3, *to learn, discover.*

rōwan Verb 7, *to row.*

scild	Noun, f., *guilt.*
snotor	Adj., *wise, prudent.*
Tiro	Noun, *Tyre.* The inflection here is a Latin dat.
(ge)trūwian	Verb II, *to trust.*
þolian	Verb II, *to suffer, endure.*
þurhwunian	Verb II, *to continue, persist.*
wælrēow	Adj., *cruel.*
welig	Adj., *wealthy.*
wes	Verb, imperative, *be.*
will	Noun, n., *will, desire.*
(ge)winnan	Verb 3, used in line 21 in the sense of *to obtain, gain.*

Practice Exercise

Be able to give the complete conjugation of the following weak I verbs: **āgyltan** *to sin,* **wēnan** *to suppose,* **herian** *to praise,* **hyspan** *to scorn,* **dynnan** *to resound,* **rȳman** *to make room,* **scendan** *to injure,* **bǣtan** *to beat,* **byrian** *to befit,* **hwettan** *to incite.*

Chapter 19

---

103. *Irregular Weak I Verbs*

Although the inflectional pattern of the different groups
of first-class weak verbs presented in the preceding chapter was
far from uniform, all the variations in pattern were capable of
explanation on the basis of sound change. That is to say, they are
historically regular.

Among the verbs of this class, however, there is one group which
shows irregular behavior not capable of immediate historical
explanation. A typical instance is to be found in the verb **sellan**
to give, sell, which has **sealde** as a past-tense form and **seald** as the
past participle.

The infinitive and present-tense forms are wholly regular. The
former must represent the development **saljan** > **salljan** >
sælljan > **sellan**. The forms of the present tense are **selle**, **selest**,
seleþ, **sellaþ**, reflecting the normal operation of gemination and
palatal umlaut.

We can account for the irregularity of the past tense and the past
participle only by proceeding backward in time from the Old
English form. From **sealde** and **seald** we can only conclude that
breaking occurred, but not palatal umlaut. If this was the case,
there must have been nothing in the form which could have
caused palatal umlaut. In short, the medial -**i**- must not have been
present. The development of the first-person singular of the past
tense may therefore be indicated as follows: **salda** > **sælde** >

sealde The other forms of the past tense and the past participle had a similar development.

Other verbs which had a broken vowel in the past tense and past participle are:

cwellan *to kill*	**cwealde**	**cweald**
dwellan *to hinder*	**dwealde**	**dweald**
stellan *to place*	**stealde**	**steald**
tellan *to count, recount*	**tealde**	**teald**
cweccan *to shake*	**cweahte**	**cweaht**
dreccan *to afflict*	**dreahte**	**dreaht**
leccan *to moisten*	**leahte**	**leaht**
reccan *to narrate*	**reahte**	**reaht**
streccan *to stretch*	**streahte**	**streaht**
þeccan *to cover*	**þeahte**	**þeaht**
weccan *to awake*	**weahte**	**weaht**

In verbs like **cweccan** the medial consonant was originally **k**. The **cc** represents gemination and palatalization. The **h** of the past tense reflects an early change of **kt** to **ht**, prior to the time when breaking occurred.

In a second group of irregular weak I verbs the vowels of the base form were not liable to breaking in the past tense and past participle. In these the vowel of the present is the result of palatal umlaut, but the past tense and past participle, because of the absence of the middle vowel, give no evidence of this sound change.

bringan *to bring*	**brōhte**	**brōht**
bycgan *to buy*	**bohte**	**boht**
rǣcan *to reach*	**rāhte, rǣhte**	**rāht**
sēcan *to seek*	**sōhte**	**sōht**
tǣcan *to teach*	**tāhte**	**tāht**
þencan *to think*	**þōhte**	**þōht**
þyncan *to seem*	**þūhte**	**þūht**
wyrcan *to make*	**worhte**	**worht**

The long vowels in **brōhte**, **þōhte**, **þūhte** represent compensatory lengthening resulting from the early (Germanic) loss of the **n** preceding the **h** in the past tense and past participle. The loss of **n** did not occur in the infinitive.

104. *Strong Verbs with Weak Present-Tense Forms*

Certain strong verbs, chiefly of the fifth and sixth classes, conform to pattern throughout their entire conjugation except for the infinitive, the imperative, and the indicative and sub-junctive forms of the present tense. The Old English equivalent of Modern English *step* may be taken as an example. It has **stōp**, **stōpon** as past singular and plural forms, and the appropriate marked and unmarked personal endings for them. The past participle is **stapen**. Thus far its behavior is that of a regular sixth-class strong verb. But its infinitive is **steppan**, and in the present tense it is conjugated as follows:

			PRESENT INDICATIVE	PRESENT SUBJUNCTIVE
SINGULAR	1	(ic)	**steppe**	**steppe**
	2	(þū)	**stepest**	**steppe**
	3	(hē)	**stepeþ**	**steppe**
PLURAL, all persons			**steppaþ**	**steppen**

The imperative forms for the singular and plural are **stepe** and **steppaþ** respectively.

To account for this series of developments we must assume that at an earlier period of the language, **i** and **j** were distributed among the present endings in exactly the same manner as was the case with the weak I verbs, the **j** giving rise to gemination and umlaut in the infinitive, the first-person indicative singular, and all of the subjunctive singular forms in the present tense; the plural of the present indicative and subjunctive; and the imperative plural. The **i** caused palatal umlaut but not gemination in the second- and third-person indicative singular and the imperative singular.

We may thus begin with the base form **stap-**, the first principal part of the sixth-class gradation series, and assume for the infinitive a **-jan** ending. Such a form would progress through the following stages: **stapjan** > **stappjan** > **stæppjan** > **steppan**. In the third-person singular present indicative, however, the development would have been **stapiþ** > **stæpiþ** > **stepeþ**.

Class 5	biddan *to ask*	bæd	bǣdon	beden
	sittan *to sit*	sæt	sǣton	seten
	licgan *to lie*	læg	lǣgon	legen
	þicgan *to partake*	þeah	þǣgon	þegen
Class 6	hebban *to raise*	hōf	hōfon	hafen
	swerian *to swear*	swōr	swōron	swaren, sworen
	sceþþan *to injure*	scōd	scōden	sceaþen
	hlihhan *to laugh*	hlōh	hlōgon	
	scieppan *to create*	scōp	scōpon	scapen
Class 7	wēpan *to weep*	wōp	wōpon	wōpen

We can now understand the relationship between **sittan** and **settan**, **licgan** and **lecgan** and their unstable progeny in Modern English, *sit* and *set, lie* and *lay*. In each instance the intransitive verb belonged to this group of strong verbs with weak present-tense forms: **sittan, licgan**. In each instance also the transitive verb, that is, the forerunner of *set* and *lay*, was a weak I verb, actually a causative, formed by adding the suffix **-jan** to the past singular form. Thus, **satjan** developed into the weak I **settan**; **lagjan** into the weak I **lecgan**.

105. *Old English Sound Changes*

a. Loss of intervocalic **h**. About the year 700, **h** between a diphthong and a vowel, or between a diphthong and **l** or **r**, disappeared. When this occurred, the preceding diphthong was lengthened if it was not already long, and the second vowel was contracted. Thus: **tēohan** > **tēon** *to draw*, **seohan** > **sēon** *to see*, **seolhes** > **sēoles** *seal's*, **feorhes** > **fēores** *life's*.

b. In Late Old English (i.e., sometime after 900), when **ġ** occurred between a front vowel and **d** or **n** it disappeared and at the same time caused lengthening of the preceding vowel: **sǣgde** > **sǣde** *said*; **frignan** > **frīnan** *asked*.

c. In Late Old English, **eo** when preceded by **w** and followed by **r** was often spelled **u**: **weorþan** > **wurþan** *to become*.

d. In Late Old English, **o** preceded by **sc** was spelled **eo**: **scolde** > **sceolde** *should*. This may or may not have represented a change in sound. The **e** is interpreted by some as a spelling device to indicate the fricative quality of the **sc** combination.

106. *Adjective Suffixes*

Old English formed adjectives from nouns by means of the following suffixes:

a. **-en** was used in forming adjectives indicating the material from which something was made or suggesting a characteristic quality: **æsc** *ash wood*, **æscen** *made of ash wood*; **fell** *skin*, **fellen** *made of skins*; **stān** *stone*, **stǣnen** *stony, made of stone*. Sometimes, but not invariably, the principal vowel of the derived form shows palatal umlaut.

b. **-erne** was used chiefly in adjectives indicating direction: **norþ**, **norþerne**; **west**, **westerne**.

c. **-iht** was used to indicate characteristic quality or material of composition; **þorniht** *thorny*, **wudiht** *woody*.

Reading
From Apollonius of Tyre

Mid þȳ þe sē cynincg gehīrde þæt Apollonius þone rǣdels swā rihte ārǣdde, þā ondrēd hē þæt hit tō wīdcūð wǣre. Beseah ðā mid irlīcum andwlitan tō him and cwæð: "Ðū iunga man, þū eart feor fram rihte; þū dwelast and nis nāht þæt þū segst; ac þū hæfst behēafdunge geearnad. Nū lǣte ic ðē tō þrittigradaga fæce þæt þū beþence ðone rǣdels āriht and ðū siððan onfōh mīnre dohtor to wīfe, and gīf ðū þæt ne dēst þū scealt oncnāwan þone gesettan dōm." Ðā wearð Apollonius swīðe gedrēfed and mid his gefērum on scip āstāh and rēow oð þæt hē becōm tō Tīrum.

Sōðlīce æfter þām þe Apollonius āfaren wæs, Antiochus sē cyningc him tō gecīgde his dihtnere sē wæs Thaliarcus gehaten. "Thaliarce, ealra mȳnra dīgolnessa mȳn sē getrȳwesta þegn, wīte þū þæt Apollonius āriht arædde mȳnne rædels. Astīh nū rædlīce on scip and far æfter him, and þonne þū him tō becume, þonne ācwel ðū hine mid īsene oððe mid āttre, þæt þū mage frēodōm onfōn þonne þū ongēan cymst." Thaliarcus sōna swā hē þæt gehȳrde, hē genām mid him ge fēoh ge attor and on scip āstāh and fōr æfter þām unscæððian Apollonie oð ðæt hē tō his eðle becōm. Ac Apollonius þēahhwæðre ær becōm tō his ægenan and intō his hūse ēode and his bōcciste untynde and āsmēade þone rædels after ealra ūðwitena and Chaldea wīsdōme. Mid þī þe nāht elles ne onfunde būton þæt hē ær geþōhte, hē cwæð þā tō him silfum, "Hwæt dēst þū nū, Apolloni? Ðæs cynges rædels þū ās-meadest and þū his dohtor ne onfēnge; forðām þū eart nū for-dēmed þæt þū ācweald wurðe." And hē þā ūt ēode and hēt his scip mid hwæte gehlæstan and mid micclum gewihte goldes and seolfres and mid mænifealdum and genihtsumum rēafum, and swā mid fēawum þam getrȳwestum mannum on scip āstāh on ðāre þriddan tīde þāre nihte and slōh ūt on ðā sæ.

Glossary and Structural Notes

ācwellan	Verb I, *to kill*.
andwlita	Noun, f., *face, countenance*.
āttor	Noun, n., *poison*. More often spelled **ātor**.
bōccist	Noun, f., *book chest, bookcase*.
Chaldea	Noun, m., *Chaldeans*. The form occurring in the text is gen. pl.
(ge)cīgan	Verb I, *to call*.
dīgolness	Noun, f., *secret*.
dihtnere	Noun, m., *steward*.
dwelian	Verb II, *to err, be mistaken*.
ēþel	Noun, m., *native land, country*.
fæc	Noun, n., *interval, period (of time)*.
fēoh	Noun, n., *money, property*.
ge . . . ge	Conj., *both . . . and*.

gefēra	Noun, m., *companion*.
gehlæstan	Verb I, *to load*
genihtsum	Adj., *abundant*.
gewiht	Noun, f., *weight*. The form in line 27 is inst. sing.: *with much of gold and silver by weight*.
irlīc	Adj., *angry*.
īsen	Noun, n., *iron*. Also functions as an adj.
oncnāwan	Verb 7, *to acknowledge, know by experience*.
ondrǣdan	Verb 7, *to fear*.
onfōn	Verb 7, *to receive*. The form here is in error; **onfēhst** would be the normal form, the pres. tense used with future meaning.
ongēan	Adv., *again*.
rǣdlīce	Adv., *quickly*, *immediately*. Older forms of this word were **hrædlīce**, **hræðlīce**.
rēaf	Noun, n., *clothing, garment*.
rōwan	Verb 7, *to row*.
(ge)sett	Adj., *established*, *appointed*. The form here is acc. sing. m. weak, based on the past participle of the verb **(ge)settan**, I.
slēan	Verb 6, *to strike*.
tīd	Noun, f., used here in the sense of *hour*.
þēahhwæðre	Adv., *nevertheless*. Formed from **þēah** *though* and **hwæðere** *whether*.
unscæþþig	Adj., *innocent, guiltless*.
untȳnan	Verb I, *to open, unlock*.
ūþwita	Noun, m., *philosopher, sage*.
weorðan	Verb 3, *to become*. The form **wurðe** is 2nd sing., pres. subj. In earlier OE this would have been **weorðe**.
wīdcūþ	Adj., *widely known*.

Chapter 20

107. *Contract Verbs: Conjugation*

The disappearance of **h** between voiced sounds and the resulting lengthening and elision of the adjacent vowels has already been explained in the preceding chapter (section 105). These changes, though operating on a purely phonetic basis, did affect the conjugation of a sufficient number of strong verbs to create what is in essence a subclass known as contract verbs.

It will be instructive to follow the development of a single verb in order to see how and in what ways the loss of intervocalic **h** affected the conjugation. The second-class verb **flēon** *to flee* will serve as an example. The following forms resulted from this sound change:

a. The infinitive reflects the change **flēohan** > **flēon**. Since the diphthong **ēo** was already long, lengthening did not occur, but the vowel of the infinitive ending **-an** was absorbed. The gerund and present participle lost the **h** in the same manner: **tō flēohenne** > **tō flēonne**; **flēohende** > **flēonde**.

b. The first-person singular present indicative and subjunctive reflect the change **flēohe** > **flēo**, again with absorption of the vowel of the personal ending.

c. The second- and third-person singular present indicative retain the **h** because after the occurrence of palatal umlaut, the vowel of the inflectional endings **-ist** and **-iþ** disappeared. As a consequence of this, the **h** was no longer intervocalic and accord-

142

ingly was retained: **flēohist** > **flīehst** > **flīhst**; **flēohiþ** > **flīehþ** > **flīhþ**.

d. The present plural indicative and subjunctive and the imperative plural had the **h** between vowels. It disappeared, and in all these forms the vowel of the inflectional ending was absorbed: **flēohaþ** > **flēoþ**; **flēohen** > **flēon**.

e. The imperative singular, **flēoh**, and the first- and third-person singular of the past tense, **flēah**, had the **h** in final position and hence retained it.

f. The past plural and past participle have **g** instead of **h** because of the operation of Verner's Law: **flugon, flogen** (see Chapter 11, section 63).

The complete conjugation of **flēon**, showing the results of the changes detailed above, follows:

		INDICATIVE		SUBJUNCTIVE
Present Singular	1	**flēo**		**flēo**
	2	**flīhst**		**flēo**
	3	**flīhþ**		**flēo**
Present Plural 1, 2, 3		**flēoþ**		**flēon**
Past Singular	1	**flēah**		**fluge**
	2	**fluge**		**fluge**
	3	**flēah**		**fluge**
Past Plural 1, 2, 3		**flugon**		**flugen**
Imperative Singular		**flēoh**	Imperative Plural	**flēoþ**
Infinitive		**flēon**	Gerund	**tō flēonne**
Present Participle		**flēonde**	Past Participle	**flogen**

108. *Contract Verbs: Classes*

There are contract verbs in six of the seven classes of the strong conjugation. Those which occur most commonly are:

Class 1. **lēon** *to lend*, **lēah**, **ligon**, **ligen**. Also **strēon** *to strain*, **tēon** *to accuse*, **þēon** *to thrive*, **wrēon** *to cover*.

Class 2. **tēon** *to draw, pull.*

Class 3. **fēolan** *to resist*, **fealh**, **fulgon**, **folgen**.

Class 5. **sēon** *to see*, **seah**, **sǣgon**, **segen**. Also **fēon** *to rejoice*, **scēon** *to happen*.

Class 6 **slēan** *to strike*, **slōh**, **slōgon**, **slǣgen**, or **slagen**. Also **flēan** *to flay*, **lēan** *to blame*, **þwēan** *to wash*.

Class 7. **fōn** *to seize*, **fēng**, **fēngon**, **fangen**.

Certain forms of the verbs listed above require further explanation:

a. The infinitive forms of the first-class verbs reflect a late change of **io**, caused by breaking of **ī** before **h** to **ēo**: **līhan** > **līohan** > **līon** > **lēon**.

b. The infinitive and present-tense forms of fifth- and sixth-class verbs show vowel lengthening as a consequence of the loss of intervocalic **h** and absorption of the following vowel: **sehan** > **seohan** > **sēon**.

c. In the case of the third-class verb **feolhan**, the **h** was intervocalic by virtue of its occurrence between a voiced consonant and a vowel.

d. The verb **sēon** also has past-plural and past-participle forms in **w**: **sāwon**, **sewen**.

109. *Strong Masculine Nouns Ending in* **h**

The loss of intervocalic **h** also had its effect upon the noun declension. A noun such as **mearh** *horse* retained the **h** only in the nominative-accusative singular, as the following paradigm shows:

	SINGULAR	PLURAL
NOM.	mearh	mēaras
ACC.	mearh	mēaras
DAT., INST.	mēare	mēarum
GEN.	mēares	mēara

Other nouns which behaved in a similar fashion were: **ealh** *temple*, **eolh** *elk*, **fearh** *pig*, **healh** *corner*, **sealh** *willow*, **seolh** *seal*, **wealh** *foreigner*, **scōh** *shoe*, **slōh** *slough, mire*, **eoh** *horse*, **horh** *dirt*.

110. *Adjectives Ending in* **h**

The loss of intervocalic **h** affected all inflected forms of the adjective, that is to say everything except the nominative singular masculine and neuter of the strong declension, the accusative singular masculine strong, and long-stemmed nominative and accusative neuter plurals and feminine singulars, also in the strong declension. Thus, the following developments occurred in connection with the adjective **hēah** *high*: **hēahne** > **hēane**, **hēahes** > **hēas**, **hēahe** > **hēa**, **hēahre** > **hēare**, etc. Inflections ending in **-um** retained the **u**: thus **hēahum** > **hēaum**.

The other adjectives most commonly affected by this change were: **fāh** *hostile*, **flāh** *deceitful*, **hrēoh** *rough, violent*, **nēah** *near*, **rūh** *rough, not smooth*, **scēoh** *shy*, **tōh** *tough*, **wōh** *crooked*, **sceolh** *awry*, and **þweorh** *cross, perverse*. In the last two the diphthong was lengthened as a consequence of the loss of **h**: **scēolre**, **þwēores**, etc.

111. *Noun Derivatives in* **-hād**

The suffix **-hād** was used to form masculine abstract nouns from concrete nouns of all genders. Thus: **abbud** m., *abbot*, **abbudhād** *rank or position of an abbot*; **mægþ** f., *maiden*, **mægþhād** *virginity*; **cild** n., *child*, **cildhād** *childhood*. Other examples are **camphād** *warfare*, **cnihthād** *boyhood*, **fulwihthād** *baptismal vow*, **munuchād** *monastic state*, **prēosthād** *priesthood*, **woruldhād** *secular life*.

112. *Noun Derivatives in* **-dōm**

The suffix **-dōm** was attached to both nouns and adjectives to indicate state, condition, or office. The resulting nouns were masculine. Thus, **cynedōm** *kingdom*, **ealddōm** *age*, **frēodōm** *freedom*, **lǣcedōm** *medicine*, **lāreowdōm** *office of teacher*, **swicdōm** *deceit*, **þēowdom** *slavery*, **wīsdōm** *wisdom*.

Reading
From Apollonius of Tyre

Þā ðȳ æftran dæge wæs Apollonius gesōht and geācsod, ac hē ne wæs nāhwǣr funden. Ðǣr wearð ðā micel morcnung and ormǣte wōp, swā þæt sē hēaf swēgde geond ealle þā ceastre. Sōðlīce swā micele lufe hæfde eal sēo ceasterware tō him, þæt hī lange tīd ēodon ealle unscorene and sīdfeaxe and heora wāforlīcan plegan forlēton and heora baða belucon. Þā ðā þās þingc ðus gedōne wǣron on Tiron, ðā becōm sē foresǣda Thaliarcus sē wæs fram Antiocho þām cynincge āsænd tō ðām þæt hē scolde Apollonium ācwellan. Þā hē geseah þæt ealle þās þingc belocene wǣron, þā cwæþ hē tō ānum cnapan: "Swā ðū gesund sȳ, sege mē for hwilcum intingum þēos ceaster wunige on swā micclum hēafe and wōpe?" Him andswerode sē cnapa and þus cwæð: "Ēala hū mānful man þū eart, ðū þe wāst þæt þū æfter āxsast! Oððe hwæt is manne þe nyte þæt þēos ceasterwaru on hēafe wunað, forðǣm ðe Apollonius sē ealdorman fǣringa nāhwǣr ne ætȳwde siððan hē ongēan cōm fram Antiocho þǣm cyninge?" Ðā þā Thaliarcus þæt gehȳrde, hē mid micclan gefēan tō scipe gewǣnde and mid gewīsre seglunge binnon anum dæge cōm tō Antiochian and ēode intō þām cynge and cwæð: "Hlāford cyngc, glada nū and blissa, forðām þe Apollonius him ondrǣt þīnes rīces mæg na swā þæt hē ne dear nāhwār gewunian." Ðā cwæð sē cyningc: "Flēon hē mæg, ac hē ætflēon ne mæg." Hē þā Antiochus sē cyningc gesette þis geban þus cweðende: "Swā hwilc man swā mē Apollonium lifigendne tō gebringð, ic him gife fīfti punda goldes, and þām ðe mē his hēafod tō gebringð, ic gife him C punda goldes." Þā ðā þis geban þus geset wæs, þā wǣron mid gitsunge beswicene nā þæt ān his fīnd ac ēac swilce his frīnd, and him æfter fōran and hine geond ealle eorðan sōhton ge on dūnlandum ge on wudalandum ge on dīglum stōwum, ac hē ne wearð nāhwǣr funden.

Glossary and Structural Notes

(ge)ācsian Verb II, used here in the sense of *to ask after, inquire about.*

æfterra Adj., *second, following, next.*

ætflēon Verb 2, *to escape.*

ætwȳwan Verb I, *to appear.*

faran	Verb 6. The form **fōran** which appears in this selection is past pl., a Late Old English writing of the earlier **fōron**.
(ge)fēa	Noun, m., *joy*.
fēond	Noun, m., *enemy*. The form **find** is nom. pl., showing palatal umlaut of the diphthong. *Not only his enemies but his friends likewise were overcome with covetousness.*
frēond	Noun, m., *friend*. See the explanation of **fīnd**, which applies equally to **frīnd**.
gebann	Noun, n., *proclamation, edict*. The form here shows simplification of the final double consonant.
gesund	Adj., *sound, healthy*.
gewiss	Adj., *certain, sure*. The form here shows simplification of the double consonant.
gītsung	Noun, f., *avarice, covetousness*. Formed from **gītisan**, II, *to be greedy*.
hēaf	Noun, m., *lamentation, grief*.
intinga	Noun, m., *cause, reason*.
mānful	Adj., *wicked, evil*. From **mān** *crime, evil deed*.
micel	The form **micclan**, used with **gefēan**, is a late writing for **miclum**.
morcnung	Noun, f., *sorrow, mourning*. The usual form was **murcning**, from **murcnian**, Verb II, *to mourn*.
nyte	A collapsed form of **ne wite**, negative particle and pres. subjunctive of **witan** *to know*.
ormǣte	Adj., *boundless, excessive*. The suffix **or-** meant *without*. The adjective **mǣte** meant *suitable, moderate*. Compare Modern English *meets and bounds*.
sīdfēaxe	Adj., *long-haired*. From **sīd** *ample* and **fēax** *hair*.
stōw	Noun, f., *place*

swēgan   Verb I, *to sound, resound.* From **swēg** *sound, noise, clamor.*

wāforlīc   Adj., *theatrical.*

wāst   Second sing. pres. indicative of **witan** *to know.*

Chapter 21

113. *The Preteritive-Present Verbs: Characteristic Features*

There are about a dozen verbs in Old English and in the other Germanic languages which share a peculiarity in their conjugations. They were originally strong verbs in which, for a variety of reasons, the original present tense disappeared and the past tense acquired a present meaning. Thus, in effect, the original past-tense forms, with no personal endings in the first- and third-person indicative singular, and usually with a change of stem vowel in the past plural, functioned as the present tense—hence the name preteritive present. Accordingly we have Old English **ic, hē sceal**, Modern German *ich, er soll*, Modern English *I, you, he shall*. From the point of view of Modern English, these are the verbs which depart from the normal conjugational pattern by not admitting an **-s** inflection in the third-person singular present indicative.

From time to time, however, the common Germanic language did seem to need a past-tense form in these verbs. This developed on the basis of the weak verb pattern in that it had an inflectional ending with **-d-** or **-t-**, often occurring with the vowel of the third or fourth principal part (**scolde**). In some ways the form of the past tense and the past participle, when there was one, was reminiscent of the irregular weak verbs of the first class without a middle vowel. Thus, verbs with present stems ending in a palatal consonant had **-ht-** in the past tense (**mæg, mihte**—like **sēcan, sōhte**); those with an alveolar consonant had **-st-** (**wāt, wiste**); those with a labial had

-ft-(**þearf**, **þorfte**). Unlike most of the strong verbs, however, the vowel of the second-person indicative singular of the new present and original past was the same as the first and third persons, but generally added the consonants of the newly-formed past inflection: thus **wāst** (2nd singular present indicative), **wiste**, **wiston** (past singular and plural).

It is of some interest to consider why, in these instances, the present did replace the past tense. In some cases semantic considerations seem to account for the development. For example, **witan** is a cognate of the Latin perfect *videre*, Sanskrit *veda*, meaning *I have seen*, from which the meaning *I know* was apparently derived. In other instances the primarily modal meaning of the verb obscured the time relationship between present and past, resulting in the disappearance of the former. It is possible to get some notion of what happened by comparing the Modern English uses of *may* and *might*. Although these are the reflexes of the present and past tenses respectively of the Old English preteritive-present verb **magan**, the difference today between *it may rain* and *it might rain* is one of degree of probability rather than of time. That is to say, a mechanism originally designed to indicate remoteness in time has been converted to indicate what is remote in probability.

Nor is the disappearance of the present in favor of the past tense without parallel in later English. In two verbs the process has occurred twice. Old English **mōtan** *to be permitted, allowed* also developed its modal meaning as the result of a semantic process. The earlier meaning is illustrated by Gothic **ga-motan** *to find room*. When, in a figurative sense, room has been found, one may say that an action has been permitted. But more important than this, just as an earlier past tense **mōt** replaced whatever the present form may have been, so in the late thirteenth and early fourteenth centuries **must**, the new analogical past, began to be used with present meaning, with the result that for the second successive time in this verb, the present tense was displaced. A similar development occurred in the case of *ought*, the modern reflex of **āhte**, the past tense of **āgan** *to possess*. Our Modern English *have to* shows how easily verbs indicating possession slip into the sense of obligation.

114.   *The Preteritive-Present Verbs: Conjugation*

With verbs as idiosyncratic in behavior as these, little else can be done except to indicate the conjugation of each insofar as it is recorded in Old English. Some of them were defective, especially with respect to imperative and past-participial forms. The full conjugation of **witan** *to know* is given below; it is sufficiently full and regular to serve as a model for the rest.

		INDICATIVE	SUBJUNCTIVE
Present Singular	1	**wāt**	**wite**
	2	**wāst**	**wite**
	3	**wāt**	**wite**
Present Plural	1, 2, 3	**witon**	**witen**
Past Singular	1	**wiste, wisse**	**wiste, wisse**
	2	**wistest, wissest**	**wiste, wisse**
	3	**wiste, wisse**	**wiste, wisse**
Past Plural	1, 2, 3	**wiston, wisson**	**wisten, wissen**
Imperative Singular	**wite**	Imperative Plural	**witaþ**
Infinitive	**witan**	Gerund	**tō witenne**
Present Participle	**witende**	Past Participle	**witen**

115.   *Preteritive-Present Verbs: Principal Parts*

In order to conjugate other preteritive-present verbs according to the pattern given in the preceding section, it is necessary to know four forms: the first- and third-person singular present indicative; the second-person singular present indicative; the present indicative plural, and the first- and third-person past indicative singular. These give the necessary clues to the rest of the conjugation. In the following listing, the remaining preteritive-present verbs are arranged according to the strong verb classes to which they originally belonged.

CLASS			PRESENT SINGULAR FIRST AND THIRD PERSONS	PRESENT SINGULAR SECOND PERSON	PRESENT PLURAL	PAST SINGULAR
1	**āgan**	*to possess*	**āh**	**āhst**	**āgon**	**āhte**
2	**dugan**	*to avail*	**dēag**		**dugon**	**dohte**
3	**unnan**	*to grant*	**ann**		**unnon**	**ūþe**
3	**cunnan**	*to know*	**cann**	**canst**	**cunnon**	**cūþe**
3	**þurfan**	*to need*	**þearf**	**þearft**	**þurfon**	**þorfte**
3	**durran**	*to dare*	**dear(r)**	**dearst**	**durron**	**dorste**
4	**munan**	*to remember*	**man**	**manst**	**munon**	**munde**
4	**sculan**	*to be obliged*	**sceal**	**scealt**	**sculon**	**sceolde**
5	**magan**	*to be able*	**mæg**	**meaht**	**magon**	**meahte**
5	**(ge)nugan**	*to suffice*	**neah**		**nugon**	**nohte**
6	**mōtan**	*to be permitted*	**mōt**	**mōst**	**mōton**	**mōste**

The verbs **dugan, þurfan, munan, sculan** have alternate forms with **y** in the subjunctive. The second-person singular present of **magan** sometimes appears as **miht** and the past-tense forms as **mihte, mihton,** etc.

116. *Velar Umlaut*

About the year 700 the front vowels **i, e,** and **æ,** when followed by a single consonant, were diphthongized to **io, eo,** and **ea** respectively by a back vowel (**u, o,** or **a**) in the following syllable. Thus **hliþu > hlioþu** *slope,* **sidu > siodu** *custom,* **herot > heorot** *hart,* **hefon > heofon** *heaven,* **alu > ealu** *ale.*

Because the vowel **æ** did not occur in an open syllable in the West Saxon dialect, it could not undergo velar umlaut. At the time of this change, however, Mercian and Kentish had **æ** before back vowels as well as before front vowels, hence there are such Mercian and Kentish forms as **heafoc** and **featu,** where West Saxon has **hafoc** and **fatu.** The only instance of velar umlaut of **æ** in West Saxon is **ealu,** where the **æ** was either a dialect borrowing from Mercian or an analogical substitution from the dative singular **æleþe.**

117. *The Noun Suffix* -en

There were two such suffixes in Old English, alike in form but with different historical backgrounds. One was used to form neuter nouns, often with diminutive force, much as -*chen* is used in Modern German. Thus we have **gǣten** *little goat*, **mægden** *maiden*, **ticcen** *kid*.

Another use of **-en** was to form the feminine from nouns denoting male creatures: **fyxen** *she-fox*, **gyden** *goddess*, **þēowen** *female servant*, **wiergen** *she-wolf*. Note that the vowels show umlaut, thus indicating that this ending had **i** at the time of palatal umlaut (the equivalent in modern German is still -*in*, as in **kaiserin** *empress*. This suffix became extended in use to form such feminine abstract nouns as **hæften** *custody*, **scielden** *protection*, **gīman** *responsibility*, **tyhten** *enticement*.

118. *The Noun Suffix* -scipe

This suffix was used to form masculine abstract nouns from other nouns and adjectives: **dryhtscipe** *valor*, **gālscipe** *pride*, **hǣþenscipe** *paganism*, **þegenscipe** *service*, **hlāfordscipe** *lordship*, **fēondscipe** *enmity*, **wǣrscipe** *prudence*.

Reading
From Apollonius of Tyre

Ðā hēt sē cynge scipa gegearcian and him æfter faran, ac hit wæs lang ǣr ðām þe ðā scipa gegearcode wǣron, and Apollonius becōm ǣr tō Tharsum. Ðā sume dæge ēode hē be strande. Þā geseah hine sum his cūðra manna sē wæs Hellanicus genemnod, sē þe ǣrest þider cōm. Þā ēode hē tō Apollonium and cwæð: "Wes gesund, hlāford Apolloni." Ðā forseah hē Apollonius cyrlisces mannes grētinge æfter rīcra manna gewunan. Hellanicus hine eft sōne gegrētte and cwæð, "Wes gesund, Apolloni, and ne forseoh ðū cyrliscne man þe bið mid wurðfullum þēawum gefrætwod. Ac gehȳr nū fram mē þæt þū silfa nāst. Þē is sōðlīce micel þearf þæt þū ðē warnige, forðām þe ðū eart fordēmed." Ðā cwæð Apollonius: "Hwā mihte mē fordēman, mīnre āgenre þēode ealdorman?"

Hellanicus cwæð: "Antiochus sē cyngc." Apollonius cwæð: "For hwilcum intingum hæfð hē mē fordēmed?" Hellanicus sǣde: "Forðām þe þū girndest þæt þū wǣre þæt sē fæder is." Apollonius cwæð, "Micclum ic eom fordēmed?" Hellanicus sǣde, "Swā hwilc man swā ðē lifigende tō him bringð, onfō sē fīftig punda goldes. Sē ðe him bringe þīn hēafod, onfō sē hundtēontig punda goldes. Forðām ic ðē lǣre þæt þū flēo and beorge þīnum līfe." Æfter þysum Hellanicus fram him gewǣnde and Apollonius hēt hine eft tō him geclipian and cwæð tō him, "Þæt wyrreste þingc þū didest þæt þū mē warnodest. Nym nū hēr æt mē hundtēontig punda goldes, and far tō Antiocho þām cynge and sege him þæt mē sȳ þæt hēafod fram þām hneccan acorfen, and bring þæt word þām cynge tō blisse; þonne hafast þū mēde and ēac clǣne handa fram þæs unscæðþigan blōde." Ðā cwæð Hellanicus: "Ne gewurðe þæt, hlāford, þæt ic mēde nime æt ðē for þisum þingum, forðon þe mid gōdum mannum nis nāðer ne gold ne seolfor wið gōdes mannes frēondscipe wiðmeten." Hī tōēodon þā mid þisum wordum.

Glossary and Structural Notes

cūþ Adj., *known, familiar*. From the past tense of **cunnan** *to know*.

cyrlisc Adj., *common*. From **ceorl**, n., *churl*.

fordēman Verb I, *to condemn*.

forsēon Verb 5, *to overlook, reject*.

(ge)frætwian Verb II, *to adorn, clothe*.

(ge)gearcian Verb II, *to prepare*.

hundtēontig Adj., *one hundred*. **Hund**, when used independently, meant *one hundred*, but it also appeared as a prefix before the decades from 70 to 120. Consequently, the number 100 was often expressed by the full form as given here.

lifian Verb II, *to live*. This alternated with **libban**, one of the few weak verbs of the third class,

	and some forms of **libban** had **f** as an un-geminated consonant.
micel	The phrase **for micclum** is to be interpreted as *for how much.*
nāst	A collapsed form of **ne wāst** (*you*) *do not know.*
onfōn	Verb 7, *to receive.* The form **onfō** is the pres. sing. subjunctive of a contract verb.
sǣde	Verb III, *to say.* The preterit form listed here is a late development of the earlier **sægde**.
tōgān	Verb, *to separate,* having **tōēode** as a past tense.
þearf	Noun, f., *need, necessity.*
þēaw	Noun, m., *custom, behavior.*
unscæþþig	Adj., *innocent.*
wiþmeten	Verb 5, *to compare.*
(ge)wuna	Noun, m., *habit, custom, practice.*
wyrresta	Adj., *worst.* This word makes little sense in the context in which it appears. It seems to have resulted from a corruption in the Latin text which served as the basis for the translation. Other Latin texts have such words as *opti-mam, pîissimam.* Note, however, that *pessimam* would be an easy corruption of *pîissimam* in the Latin and might well account for the OE form.

Chapter 22

119. *Weak Verbs of the Second Class*

This class, a very large one, includes all verbs with infinitives in **-ian**, other than the majority of those with a base form in which a short vowel is followed by **r**. For the most part, the stem syllables were not affected by palatal umlaut. Many of the verbs in this conjugation developed from nouns, particularly those of the strong feminine declension. Thus, **lufu** *love*, **lufian** *to love*; **scamu** *shame*, **scamian** *to be ashamed*; **ār** *honor*, **ārian** *to honor*; **sealf** *salve*, **sealfian** *to anoint*.

The verbs of this class are conjugated as follows:

		INDICATIVE	SUBJUNCTIVE
Present Singular	1	**lufie**	**lufie**
	2	**lufast**	**lufie**
	3	**lufaþ**	**lufie**
Present Plural	1, 2, 3	**lufiaþ**	**lufien**
Past Singular	1	**lufode**	**lufode**
	2	**lufodest**	**lufode**
	3	**lufode**	**lufode**
Past Plural	1, 2, 3	**lufodon**	**lufoden**

Imperative Singular	**lufa**	Imperative Plural	**lufiaþ**
Infinitive	**lufian**	Gerund	**tō lufienne**
Present Participle	**lufiende**	Past Participle	**lufod**

120. *Weak Verbs of the Third Class*

In their Old English form, the four remaining verbs of this conjugation display some characteristics of the first-class weak verbs, some of the second, and a few which are almost idiosyncratic. At an earlier period in the development of the Germanic languages, the conjugation was well defined as to form and included a significantly larger number of verbs. Gothic had some twenty-five. By the sixth century, however, those which remained in Old English had largely become assimilated to either the first or second weak verb class, leaving only those which, by virtue of their high frequency of use, were not changed by analogy.

The four remaining Old English verbs—**habban** *to have*, **hycgan** *to think, resolve*, **libban** *to live*, and **secgan** *to say*—were conjugated as follows:

INDICATIVE

Present Singular	1	hæbbe	hycge	libbe	secge
	2	hafast	hogast	lifast	sægst
	3	hafaþ	hogaþ	lifaþ	sægþ
Present Plural	1, 2, 3	habbaþ[1]	hycgaþ	libbaþ	secgaþ[2]

SUBJUNCTIVE

Present Singular	1, 2, 3	hæbbe	hycge	libbe	secge
Present Plural	1, 2, 3	hæbben	hycgen	libben	secgen

INDICATIVE

Past Singular	1	hæfde	hogde	lifde	sǣde
	2	hæfdest	hogdest	lifdest	sǣdest
	3	hæfde	hogde	lifde	sǣde
Past Plural	1, 2, 3	hæfdon	hogdon	lifdon	sǣdon

1. The **bb** in the forms **habban**, **hæbbe**, **habbaþ**, **libban**, etc., resulted from the gemination of the Germanic voiced labial fricative **ƀ**. The ungeminated form became **f** in OE. Gemination occurred at precisely the same points in the conjugation of Class III weak verbs as in those of the first class.

2. The **cg** in the forms **secgan**, **secge**, **secgaþ**, **hycgan**, etc., resulted from the germination of Gmc **g**. The **e** in **secgan**, etc., and the **y** in **hycgan**, etc., reflect subsequent palatal umlaut.

SUBJUNCTIVE

Past Singular	1, 2, 3	**hæfde**	**hogde**	**lifde**	
Past Plural	1, 2, 3	**hæfden**	**hogden**	**lifden**	
Imperative Singular		**hafa**	**hoga**	**lifa**	**sæge**
Imperative Plural		**habbaþ**	**hogaþ**	**libbaþ**	**secgaþ**
Present Participle		**hæbbende**	**hycgende**	**libbende**	**secgen**
Past Participle		**hæfd**	**hogod**	**lifd**	**sæd**

In the second- and third-person singular present indicative, **hæfst** and **hæfþ** appear as alternate forms, as does **hæbbaþ** in the plural. The gerund appears as **tō hæbbenne** and **tō habbenne**.

The forms **lifast** and **lifaþ** sometimes were subject to velar umlaut, appearing as **liofast** and **liofaþ**.

Secgan has **sagast** and **sagaþ** as alternate forms in the second- and third-person singular of the present indicative, and **sege** or **saga** in the imperative singular. The forms **sǣde**, **sǣdon**, etc., resulted from disappearance of the **g** in **sægde** and compensatory lengthening of the vowel. Early texts generally have **sægde**, **sægdon**, etc.

121. *Cardinal Numbers*

The cardinal numbers from one to twelve were as follows:

ān	*one*	**seofon**	*seven*
twegen, twā, tū	*two*	**eahta**	*eight*
þrī, þrēo	*three*	**nigon**	*nine*
fēower	*four*	**tȳn, tien**	*ten*
fīf	*five*	**endleofan**	*eleven*
six, siex	*six*	**twelf**	*twelve*

Of these, only the first three were declined. **Ān** was generally declined as a strong adjective, except that the accusative singular masculine often appeared as **ǣnne**. **Āna** declined weak meant *alone*.

The numbers *two* and *three* were declined in the plural only.

	MASCULINE	NEUTER	FEMININE
Nominative, Accusative	twēgen	tū	twā
Dative, Instrumental, All Genders		twǣm, twām	
Genitive, All Genders		twēgra	
Nominative, Accusative	þrī, þrīe	þrēo	þrēo
Dative, Instrumental, All Genders		þrim	
Genitive, All Genders		þrēora	

The dual **bēgen** *both* followed the pattern of **twēgen**, with **bā** or **bū** as the neuter in the nominative-accusative and **bā** as the feminine. The dative-instrumental form was **bǣm** or **bām**; the genitive was **bēgra**.

The numbers from thirteen to nineteen were formed with -**tȳne** (earlier **tīene**): **þrēotȳne**, **fēowertȳne**, **sixtȳne**, etc.

The decades from twenty to 120 were formed with -**tig** suffixed to the numbers from two to twelve: **twēntig**, **þrītig**, **fēowertig**, etc. Those from seventy to 120 often have the prefix **hund-**: (**hund**)- **seofontig**, **hundtēontig**, **hundendlefantig**, **hundtwelftig**. In compound numerals, the units normally preceded the tens: **ān and twēntig**, **six and fēowertig**. The hundreds usually came first: **þrēo hund and seofon and fīftig**. *Hundred* could also be expressed by the nouns **hund, hundred**. **Þūsend** *thousand* is usually declined as a neuter noun.

122. *Noun Compounds*

All the Germanic languages frequently use compounding as a word-forming device. Old English was no exception. In the poetry of the period, compounding was the basis of much of the characteristic vocabulary—witness **hringsele** *ring hall*, **fȳrdraca** *fire drake*, **þēodcyning** *people king*. In the prose it was a convenient means of extending the vocabulary to meet the challenges posed by the introduction of Christianity and learning. This is clearly seen in such words as **efensacerd** *fellow priest*, **scriftscīr** *confessor's area of jurisdiction*, **efenniht** *equinox*, **tungolwitega** *astrologer*.

In Old English compound nouns, the second element was always a noun in origin, and it was that noun which determined the declension and number of the combination. The first element could be a noun, an adjective, or an adverb.[3]

a. Noun-plus-noun combinations: **campstede** *battlefield*, **drȳcræft** *witchcraft*, **gafolland** *leased land*, **nihthwīl** *space of a night*, **selegyst** *hall guest*, **rodorstōl** *heavenly throne*.

Sometimes the first element appears in its inflected form: **dægesēage** *daisy*, **hellebryne** *hellfire*, **sunnanniht** *Saturday evening*, **Englaland** *England*.

b. Adjective-plus-noun combinations: **blæcgimm** *jet*, **hēahfæder** *patriarch*, **wīdsǣ** *open sea*, **ealdgeriht** *ancient right*, **nēahbebūr** *neighbor*, **wācmōd** *fainthearted person*.

c. Adverb-plus-noun combinations: **gēosceaft** *destiny*, **forecwide** *prophecy*, **eftsīb** *return journey*, **ūtwaru** *foreign defence*, **innhere** *native army*, **ūpflōr** *upper chamber*.

Reading
From Apollonius of Tyre

And Apollonius sōna gemētte ōðerne cūðne man ongēan hine gān þæs nama wæs Stranguilio gehaten. "Hlāford geong Apolloni, hwæt dēst ðū þus gedrēfedum mōde on þisum lande?" Apollonius cwæð: 'Ic gehīrde secgan þæt ic wære fordēmed.' Stranguilio cwæð: "Hwā fordēmde þē?" Apollonius cwæð: "Antiochus sē cyngc." Stranguilio cwæð: "For hwilcum intingum?" Apollonius sǣde: "Forðām þe ic bæd his dohtor mē tō gemæccan, be þāre ic mæg tō sōðe secgan þæt hēo his āgen gemæcca wǣre. Forðām gif hit gewurðan mæg, ic wille mē bedīhlian on ēowrum ēðle." Ðā cwæð Stranguilio: "Hlāford Apolloni, ūre ceaster is þearfende and ne mæg þīne æðelborennesse ācuman, forðon ðe wē þoliaþ þone heardestan hungor and þone reðestan, and mīnre ceasterwaru nis nān hǣlo hiht, ac sē wælrēowesta dēað stent ætforan ūrum ēagan." Ðā cwæð Apollonius: "Mīn sē lēofesta frēond Stranguilio, þanca Gode þæt Hē mē flīman hider tō ēowrum gemǣran gelǣdde. Ic

---

3. As was noted earlier (section 8), compound nouns had the primary stress on the root syllable of the first element, a pattern which still prevails in such MnE combinations as *blackbird*, *windshield*, etc.

sille ēowrum ceastergewarum hundtēontig þūsenda mittan hwǣtes
gif gē mīnne flēam bedīgliað." Mid þī þe Stranguilio þæt gehīrde,
hē hine āstrehte tō his fōtum and cwæð: "Hlāford Apolloni, gif
ðū þissere hungregan ceasterwaru gehelpest, nā þæt ān þæt wē
willað þīnne flēam bedīglian, ac ēac swilce, gif þē nēod gebirað,
wē willað campian for ðīnre hǣlo."

Glossary and Structural Notes

ācuman	Verb 4, *to sustain, support*.
āstreccan	Verb I, without middle vowel, *to prostrate* (reflexive), *to stretch*.
bedīglian	Verb II, *to hide, conceal*. From **dīgol**, earlier **dīegol** *secret*. The consonant **g** alternates with **h** in this verb.
(ge)birian	Verb I, *to happen, pertain to*.
campian	Verb II, *to fight*. From **camp**, noun, *battle*.
cūþ	Adj., *known*. From the past participle of the preteritive present verb **cunnan**.
drēfan	Verb I, *to disturb*. **Gedrēfed** is a past participle used adjectivally.
ēþel	Noun, n., *country, native land*.
flēam	Noun, m., *flight*.
flīma	Noun, m., *fugitive*.
gemǣre	Noun, f., *border*.
hǣlu	Noun, f., *salvation, relief, safety*. The form here is gen. sing. In all cases of the sing. noun, **-u** and **-o** were alternate inflectional endings.
hiht	Noun, m., *hope*.
hwǣte	Noun, m., *wheat*.
intinga	Noun, m., *cause, reason*.
mitta	Noun, m., *measure, bushel*.
nā þæt ān . . . ac	not only that . . . but also
rēþe	Adj., *cruel*.
þearfende	Adj., *poor, destitute*.
þolian	Verb II, *to suffer*.
wælrēow	Adj., *cruel*.

Chapter 23

123. *Anomalous Verbs*

There were four verbs in Old English which, though they had some historical connection with one another, became so highly deviant and irregular throughout their conjugations that they cannot be assigned to any of the regular classifications and accordingly are characterized as anomalous. The verbs are **bēon (wesan)** *to be*, **don** *to do*, **gān** *to go*, and **willan** *to wish, desire*.

The conjugation of the verb **bēon** has already been given in earlier chapters (sections 25, 56) and need not be repeated here. The other verbs were conjugated as follows:

		INDICATIVE		
Present Singular	1	**dō**	**gā**	**wille**
	2	**dēst**[1]	**gǣst**	**wilt**
	3	**dēþ**	**gǣþ**	**wile**
Present Plural	1, 2, 3	**dōþ**	**gāþ**	**willaþ**

		SUBJUNCTIVE		
Present Singular	1, 2, 3	**dō**	**gā**	**wille, wile**
Present Plural	1, 2, 3	**dōn**	**gān**	**willan**

1. Both **dōn** and **gān** show evidences of palatal umlaut in the second- and third-person singular present indicative.

			INDICATIVE	
Past Singular	1	**dyde**	**ēode**[2]	**wolde**
	2	**dydest**	**ēodest**	**woldest**
	3	**dyde**	**ēode**	**wolde**
Past Plural	1, 2, 3	**dydon**	**ēodon**	**woldon**

			SUBJUNCTIVE	
Past Singular	1, 2, 3	**dyde**	**ēode**	**wolde**
Past Plural	1, 2, 3	**dyden**	**ēoden**	**wolden**
Imperative Singular		**dō**	**gā**	
Imperative Plural		**dōþ**	**gāþ**	
Present Participle		**dōnde**		**willende**
Past Participle		**dōn**	**gān**	

Forms not listed above have not been recorded. The verb **dōn** was frequently used as a causative and also as a factitive. Its use as a substitute verb seems to have begun during the Old English period.[3] **Gān** frequently meant *to proceed on foot*, in contrast to **rīdan**. **Willan** was not yet used as an auxiliary to indicate future time but was generally confined to the meanings *to desire* or *to exercise the will*.

124. *Ordinal Numbers*

The ordinals for the first six numbers do not conform to a pattern. The forms for *first* are in origin the superlatives of adverbs: **forma**, **formesta**, **fyrmest**, and **fyrst**, all related to **fore** *before*, and also **ǣrest**, from **ǣr** *before, early*. These are declined like weak adjectives.

Ōþer, which could mean either *second* or *other*, was regularly declined as a strong adjective, even after demonstratives. **Æfterra** was also used for *second*, especially when the sense of *following* or

2. A form such as **ēode**, wholly unrelated to the rest of the conjugation, is called a suppletive. The occurrence of unrelated forms within a single set or class, such as MnE *go, went* or *bad, worse* is called suppletion.

3. An example of **dōn** as a substitute verb occurs in the reading selection for Chapter 5: "Sēo sunne ... scīnþ under ðǣre eorðan on niht, swā swā hēo on dæg dēþ bufan ūrum hēafdum."

next was intended, just as **ǣrra** was sometimes used for *the first of two*.

A list of the ordinals through twelve follows:

þridda	*third*	**eahtoþa**	*eighth*
fēorþa	*fourth*	**nigoþa**	*ninth*
fīfta	*fifth*	**tēoþa**	*tenth*
sixta	*sixth*	**endlefta**	*eleventh*
seofoþa	*seventh*	**twelfta**	*twelfth*

The ordinals thirteen through nineteen are formed with **-tēoþa** (*tenth*) added to the cardinal units: **þrēotēoþa**, **fēowertēoþa**, **sixtēoþa**, etc.

The decades from twenty to 120 were formed by adding **-oþa** to the **-tig** of the cardinals, thus forming the dual or complex suffix **-tigoþa**: **twentigoþa**, **þrītigoþa**, **fēowertigoþa**. As with the cardinals, the numbers from seventy to 120 often had the prefix **hund-**: **(hund)seofontigoþa**, **hundtēontigoþa**, **hundendleftigoþa**, **hundtwelftigoþa**.

Compound ordinals were formed by placing an uninflected cardinal before the ordinal for the appropriate decade, the latter being inflected like a weak adjective: **ān and twentigoþa**, **six and fēowertigoþa**.

125. *Miscellaneous Numerals*

Multiplicatives were indicated by compounds of the cardinal numerals with **-feald**: **twifeald** *twofold* or *two times*, **þrēofeald**, **fēowerfeald**, etc. Repetitives, that is, answers to the questions *How many times?* or *Which time?* were expressed principally by phrases with **sīþ** *time, occasion*. Thus: **forman sīþe** *on the first occasion*, **fīf sīþum** *five times*. For the first three numbers, the genitive was also used: **ǣnes, tuwa, þrēowa**.

Certain other constructions occur frequently enough to merit listing:

Bēowulf, fīftyna sum

Beowulf, one of fifteen; in current terms, *Beowulf and fourteen others*

Ōþrum healfum lǣs þe xxx wintra
half of a second less than thirty winters, that is, *twenty-eight and one-half years*

Tēoþe healf hīd
half of a tenth hide, namely, *nine and one-half*

Eahtoþa healf þūsend
half of an eighth thousand — seventy-five hundred

126. *Compound Adjectives*

Compound adjectives were formed by means of the following types of combinations:

a. Noun plus adjective: **ǣhtspēdig** *wealthy,* **beadurōf** *bold in battle,* **brimceald** *sea-cold,* **dōmgeorn** *eager for glory,* **ecgheard** *hard of edge,* **snāhwīt** *snow-white,* **dryncwirig** *drunk.*

b. Adjective plus adjective: **hēaheald** *advanced in age,* **eallgōd** *perfectly good,* **geolohwīt** *pale yellow,* **wīsfæst** *discreet,* **seldcūþ** *unfamiliar.*

c. Noun or adjective plus participle, either present or past: **leohtberende** *luminous,* **goldhroden** *gold-adorned,* **sǣdberende** *seed-bearing,* **ǣrboren** *firstborn,* **glēawhycgende** *prudent.*

d. Adverb plus adjective: **ǣrwacol** *early awake,* **swīþstrang** *very strong,* **ūtfūs** *ready to start,* **ūphēah** *elevated,* **welwillende** *benevolent.*

e. Adjective plus noun: **drēorigmōd** *sad,* **rūmheort** *generous,* **mildheort** *merciful,* **brūnecg** *brown-edged,* **wīswyrde** *prudent in speech.* There were numerous combinations with **mōd** and **heort** in this group.

Reading
From Apollonius of Tyre

Ðā āstāh Apollonius on þæt dōmsetl on ðāre strǣte and cwæð tō ðām andweardan ceasterwarum: "Gē Tharsysce ceasterwaran, ic Apollonius sē Tirisca ealdorman ēow cȳðe þæt ic gelīfe þæt gē willan bēon gemindige þissere fremfulnesse and mīnne flēam bedīglian. Wite gē ēac þæt Antiochus sē cyngc mē āflīmed hæfð of mīnum earde, ac for ēowre gesǣlðe gefultumigendum Gode ic eom hider cumen. Ic sille ēow sōðlīce hundtēontig þūsenda mittan hwǣtes tō ðam wurðe þe ic hit gebohte on mīnum lande." Ðā ðā þæt folc þæt gehīrde, hī wǣron blīðe gewordene and him georne þancodon and tō geflites þone hwǣte ūp bǣron. Hwæt ðā Apollonius forlēt his þone wurðfullan cynedōm and mangeres naman þār genam mā þonne gifendes, and þæt wyrð þe hē mid þām hwǣte genam, hē āgeaf sōna agēan tō ðāre ceastre bōte. Þāt folc wearð ðā swā fagen his cystignessa and swā þancful þæt hīg worhton him āne ānlicnesse of āre, and on ðāre strǣte stōd and mid þāre swīðran hand þone hwǣte heold and mid þām winstran fēt þā mittan trǣd, and þāron þus āwriten: "Ðā gifu sealde sēo ceasterwaru on Tharsum Apollonio þām Tiriscan, forðām þe þæt folc of hungre ālēsde and heora ceastre gestaðolode."

Æfter þisum hit gelamp binnon fēawum mōnðum þæt Stranguilio and Dionisiade his wīf gelǣrdon Apollonium ðæt hē fērde on scipe tō Pentapolim þāre Ciriniscan birig, and cwǣdon þæt hē mihte þār bedīglad bēon and þār wunian. And þæt folc hine þa mid unasecgendlīcre wurðmynte tō scipe gelǣddon, and Apollonius hī bæd ealle grētan and on scip astah. Mid þī þe hīg ongunnon þā rōwan and hī forðweard wǣron on heora weg, þā wearð ðāre sǣ smiltnesse āwǣnd fǣringa betwux twām tīdum and wearð micel rēownes āweht, swā þæt sēo sǣ cnyste þā heofonlīcan tungla and þæt gewealc þāra ȳðe hwaðerode mid windum. Þārtōēacan cōman ēastnorðerne windas and sē angrislīca wūðwesterna wind him ongēan stōd and þæt scip eal tōbǣrst.

Glossary and Structural Notes

ālȳsan	Verb I, *to release, deliver*. The past-tense form **ālēsde** is non-West Saxon.
andweard	Adj., *present*.
angrislīc	Adj., *terrible*.
ār	Noun, n., *bronze*.
bōt	Noun, f., *assistance, relief*.
cirinisc	Adj., *Cyrenaican, of Cyrene*.
cnyssan	Verb I, *to beat against, strike*.
cystignes	Noun, f., *generosity, munificence*.

dōmsetl Noun, n., *judgment seat.*

fǣringa Adv., *suddenly.*

fēran Verb I, *to go, travel.* The form **fērde** in this selection is past subjunctive.

forþweard Adj., *advancing forward, progressing.*

fremfulnes Noun, f., *beneficence.*

(ge)fultumian Verb II, *to help, assist.* **Fultumiende** is part of a dat. absolute construction, *God assisting.*

geflit Noun, n., *strife, dispute.* **Tō geflites** is adverbial gen., *eagerly, zealously.*

gewealc Noun, n., *rolling, tossing motion.*

hwaþarian Verb II, *to roar.*

mangere Noun, m., *merchant.* Literally, *he took the name of a seller rather than a giver,* but the translation from the Latin is faulty at this point.

(ge)myndig Adj., *mindful.*

rēownes Noun, f., *rough weather, storm.* The earlier form of this noun was **hrēohnes**.

(ge)sǣlþ Noun, f., *prosperity, happiness.*

smiltnes Noun, f., *calm.*

(ge)staþolian Verb II, *to restore.*

swīþra Adj., *right.*

Tharsysc Adj., *of Tharsus.*

tīd Noun, f., *tide, time, hour.* It is used here to translate Latin *hora.*

tungol Noun, n., *star.* **Tungla** is acc. pl., a later development of **tunglu**.

unasecgendlīc Adj., *indescribable.*

winstre Adj., *left.*

wurþ Noun, n., *price, value.*

Chapter 24

127. *Irregular Noun Declensions*

The majority of Old English nouns belonged to one of the five declensions which were treated in the beginning chapters (sections 11, 16, 21, 26). The very fact that considerably more than 90 percent of all the nouns were distributed among these five indicates that many nouns which were originally declined according to other patterns had been drawn into them by some analogical process. Thus, with every such addition or accretion the five declensions advanced further toward becoming the major or regular noun patterns; the shrinking numbers in the remaining classes came more and more to merit the designation *minor* or *irregular*.

During the long-term course of a process of this kind, however, and we are speaking here of developments which ranged over the centuries, the words which were not affected by analogy were those which were used frequently, were learned as isolated phenomena early in life, and thus tended to retain their so-called irregularities or individualizing characteristics—much as the words *man* and *child* have retained their irregular plurals to the present day.

We have already considered the declension of one notable group of exceptional nouns, namely the root consonant stems (section 85), which include such nouns as **man**, **tōþ**, **gōs**, **mūs**. A treatment of the most important of the remaining minor declensions follows. They may be classified most conveniently in terms of the way in which they form their nominative-accusative plural: in **-a**, in **-ru**, or without inflection. In terms of such a classification, the nouns of the root-consonant declension might be considered palatal umlaut plurals, comprising a fourth group here.

128. *Nouns with Plurals in* **-a**

This is sometimes known as the **-u** declension, and in terms of its historical background corresponds to the fourth declension of nouns in Latin. The nouns remaining in this group were chiefly masculine, along with a very few feminines: **duru** *door*, **nosu** *nose*, **hand** *hand*, **cweorn** *hand mill*. The neuter nouns, by this time, had completely gone over to the strong neuter declension. The basic distinction among these nouns is the length of the base-form syllable rather than gender. They were declined as follows:

SINGULAR	SHORT BASE SYLLABLE	LONG BASE SYLLABLE
NOM., ACC.	**sunu**	**weald**
DAT., INST.	**suna**	**wealda**
GEN.	**suna**	**wealda**
PLURAL		
NOM., ACC.	**suna**	**wealda**
DAT., INST.	**sunum**	**wealdum**
GEN.	**suna**	**wealda**

Masculine nouns with short base syllables declined like **sunu** were **bregu** *prince*; **heoru** *sword*; **lagu** *sea, flood*; **medu** *mead*; **sidu** *custom*; and **wudu** *wood*. Nouns with long base syllables included **eard** *native country*, **feld** *field*, **flōr** *floor*, **ford** *ford*, **sēaþ** *pit*. The disyllabics **sumor** and **winter** generally followed the pattern of **weald**.

129. *Nouns with Plurals in* **-ru**

A few neuter nouns retained throughout the plural inflection an **-r** which did not appear in the singular. This declension, which is still strongly entrenched in Modern German, has only the noun *child* as its sole remaining representative in Modern English. In addition to Old English **cild**, the nouns **ǣg** *egg*, **cealf** *calf*, **lamb** *lamb*, and **brēadru** *crumbs* (in the plural only) were included in this declension.

SINGULAR		PLURAL	
NOM., ACC.	**cild**	NOM., ACC.	**cildru**
DAT., INST.	**cilde**	DAT., INST.	**cildrum**
GEN.	**cildes**	GEN.	**cildra**

130. *Uninflected Plurals*

There are two groups of nouns which have no inflectional suffix in the nominative-accusative plural, although historically they are not related to each other. The first group consists of a number of nouns of relationship: the masculines **fæder** and **brōþor**, and the feminines **dohtor** and **sweostor**.

The second group consists of a number of masculine agentive nouns ending in **-nd**, having been developed originally from the past participle inflection, as described in section 19. Typical nouns are **fēond** *enemy*, **wīgend** *warrior*, **frēond** *friend*, **wealdend** *ruler*. This group differs from the nouns of relationship, however, in that the genitive singular ends in **-es**.

Some, but not all, nouns in both subgroups have palatal umlaut in the dative singular, and a few nouns of the **-nd** declension also show an umlauted form in the nominative-accusative plural.

SINGULAR				
NOM., ACC.	**brōþor**	**sweostor**	**fēond**	**wīgend**
DAT., INST.	**brēþer**	**sweostor**	**fīnd**	**wīgend**
GEN.	**brōþor**	**sweostor**	**fēondes**	**wīgendes**

PLURAL				
NOM., ACC.	**brōþor**	**sweostor**	**fīnd**	**wīgend**
DAT., INST.	**brōþum**	**sweostrum**	**fēondum**	**wīgendum**
GEN.	**brōþra**	**sweostra**	**fēonda**	**wīgenda**

Remnants of another declension, consisting principally of **hæleþ** *hero*, **mōnaþ** *month* (masculine), and **mægþ** *maiden* (feminine) were also without ending in the nominative-accusative plural. In a fair number of instances the nouns **hæleþ** and **mōnaþ** did appear from time to time with the **-as** nominative-accusative inflection of the strong masculine declension.

131. *Personal Pronouns: Dual Number*

Certain languages throughout the world recognize a dual number (applying to two) in addition to the singular and plural. The Indo-European parent language presumably had distinct dual forms for nouns, verbs, and pronouns, and these survived in varying degrees in the derivative language families. Classical Greek furnishes an excellent illustration, with dual forms in all three parts of speech. In Old English the dual survived only in the first and second persons of the personal pronoun and was used chiefly, though not exclusively, in texts which reflected an early stage of the language—the Unferth-Breca episode in *Beowulf*, for example (ll. 506 ff.), where the reference throughout the passage, whether first or second person, is to Beowulf and Breca. The case forms of the dual number of the personal pronouns were as follows:

	FIRST PERSON	SECOND PERSON
NOM.	**wit**	**git**
ACC.	**uncit, unc**	**incit, inc**
DAT., INST.	**unc**	**inc**
GEN.	**uncer**	**incer**

Đā wit ætsomne on sæ wæron, fīf nihta fyrst. *Then the two of us were in the sea for a period of five nights.* **Git on wæteres æht seofon niht swuncon**. *The two of you toiled for seven nights in the water's power.*

Reading
From Apollonius of Tyre

On ðissere egeslīcan rēownesse Apollonius gefēran ealle forwurdon to dēaðe, and Apollonius āna becōm mid sunde tō Pentapolim

þǣm ciriniscan lande and þār ūp ēode on ðām strande. Þā stōd
hē nacod on þām strande and behēold þā sǣ and cwæð: "Ēala
þū sǣ Neptune, manna berēafigend and unscæððigra beswīcend,
þū eart wælrēowra þonne Antiochus sē cyngc. For mīnum þingum
þū gehēolde þās wælrēownesse þæt ic þurh ðē gewurde wǣdla
and þearfa, and þæt sē wælrēowesta cyngc mē þȳ ēaðe fordōn
mihte. Hwider mæg ic nū faran? Hwæs mæg ic biddan oððe hwā
gifð þām uncūðan līfes fultum.?" Mid þī þē hē þæs þingc wæs
sprecende tō him silfum, þā fǣringa geseah hē sumne fiscere gān,
tō þām hē beseah and þus sārlīce cwæð: "Gemiltsa mē, þū ealda
man, sȳ þæt þū sȳ; gemildsa mē nacodum, forlidenum, næs nā of
earmlīcum birdum geborenum, and ðæs ðe ðū gearo forwite
hwām ðū gemiltsige, ic eom Apollonius sē tirisca ealdorman."
Ðā sōna swā sē fiscere geseah þæt sē iunga man æt his fōtum læg,
hē mid mildheortnesse hine ūp āhōf and lǣdde hine mid him tō
his hūse and ðā ēstas him beforan legde þe hē him tō bēodenne
hæfde. Þā git hē wolde be his mihte māran ārfæstnesse him
gecȳðan, tōslāt his wǣfels on twā and sealde Apollonige þone
healfan dǣl þus cweðende: "Nim þæt ic þē tō sillenne habbe and
gā intō ðāre ceastre. Wēn is þæt þū gemēte sumne þe þē gemiltsige.
Gif ðū ne finde nǣnne þe þē gemiltsian wille, wǣnd þonne hider
ongēan and genihtsumige unc bām mīne litlan ǣhta and far ðē
on fisnoð mid mē. Þēahhwæðre ic mynegie þē, gif ðū fultumien-
dum Gode becymst tō ðīnum ǣrran wurðmynte, þæt ðū ne forgite
mīne þearfendlīcan gegirlan." Ðā cwæð Apollonius: "Gif ic þē
ne geþence þonne mē bet bið, ic wisce þæt ic eft forlidennesse ge-
fare and þīnne gelīcan eft ne gemēte."

Glossary and Structural Notes

ǣht	Noun, f., *possession, property*.
ārfæstnes	Noun, f., *honor, kindness*.
berēafigend	Noun, m., *robber, spoiler*. Cp. **rēaf** *booty, plun-der* and **berēafian** *to rob*.
beswīcend	Noun, m., *deceiver*. From **beswīcan** (1) *to deceive*.
egeslīc	Adj., *dreadful, terrible*. From **ege** *fear, terror*.

ēst   Noun, m., *delicacy.*

forwitan   Verb, pret. pres., *to know beforehand.*

gefēra   Noun, m., *companion.*

gegirla   Noun, m., *dress, garment.*

genihtsumian   Verb II, *to suffice.* In this selection the verb appears in the sing., but **ǣhta**, the subject, is pl.

hwæs   The interrogative pron. is in the gen. here, as the object of **biddan**.

(ge)miltsian   Verb II, *to pity.* The verb sometimes appears as **gemildsian**.

strand   Noun, n., *shore.*

sund   Noun, n., *swimming, the act of swimming.*

þēahhwæþre   Adv., *nevertheless.*

þearfa   Adj., *needy.* Often used as a noun. See note on **wǣdla**.

þing   Noun, n., **for mīnum þingum** *because of me, for my sake.*

unc   Pron., dual number.

wǣdla   Adj., *poor, destitute.* Often used as a noun. From the construction in this selection, **wǣdla** and **þearfa** could be interpreted as either noun or adj.

wēn   Noun, f., *expectation, hope;* **wēn is þæt** *perhaps.*

Chapter 25

132. *The Background of Old English*

Although the preceding chapters contain some casual references to stages of the language before the settlement of the Angles and Saxons in Britain, no systematic presentation has been given thus far. The reason is simple. This topic can be more easily comprehended after as full a presentation of the structure of Old English as the circumstances will permit.

At this point we are in a position to compare Old English and its modern counterpart. In so doing we cannot escape the awareness of an impressive array of systematic changes which have occurred over the past millenium: alterations in the sound pattern, the disappearance of some inflections, the increase in incidence of certain others, and the replacement of still others by periphrastic constructions. The word-order patterns of the language have also altered materially over the same period. Even in the shorter interval between the occupation of Britain in the mid-fifth century and the time at which most of the selections in this text were written, there are evidences of similar changes.

It takes but a moment's reflection to conclude that just as many changes must have occurred in the language of successive generations prior to the westward movement of the Angles and Saxons from their continental homeland as those we know to have taken place since that time. The study of these leads us into the domain of historical and comparative linguistics. From these disciplines we have learned not only that each of the languages of modern times is a historical product which developed slowly and regularly out of preceding stages but that many apparently dissimilar languages of the present day are really closely related and are the descendants of some original stock. Languages have thus been grouped into families, on the assumption that every individual language reflects in a manner peculiar to itself a process of progressive differentiation from a common original.

133. *The Indo-European Family*

One of the largest and most carefully studied groups of related languages is that known as the Indo-European family. As the name suggests, the group comprises certain of the languages of Asia and practically all those of Europe. There are no written records of the original unified Indo-European language. Its former existence and the details of its structure have been inferred from the comparative study of the languages which developed from it. No other theory serves so well to explain the many similarities which exist among them as that of a common origin.

There have been differences of opinion over the period and place in which this common original language was spoken, but there is considerable ground for believing that the place was south of the eastern extremity of the Baltic Sea, between the Vistula and the Dnieper rivers, and the time possibly as early as 3500 B.C. As successive tribal groups left the parent body and wandered eastward into Asia or westward toward the Atlantic, each of their dialects or languages developed an individual identity through continuity of change, and each in turn became the parent of a number of derivative languages.

The principal members of the Indo-European family, beginning with the languages now spoken farthest east in Asia and proceeding thence in order to the language families of western Europe are: Indo-Iranian, Tocharian, Armenian, Anatolian, Greek, Albanian, Balto-Slavonic, Italic, Celtic, and Germanic. The modern languages and their older counterparts which developed from these parent stocks are listed in the excellent chart which accompanies the treatment of the word *Indo-European* in *Webster's Third New International Dictionary*. Similar tabular presentations, differing only in minor detail, may be found in the endpapers of the Random House and American Heritage dictionaries. The names given to the various parent languages are generally self-explanatory except for Tocharian, an extinct language spoken in central Asia possibly as late as 1000 A.D., and Anatolian, a family of languages which included Hittite and its nearest relatives, spoken in Asia Minor before the beginning of the Christian era.

134. *The Germanic Languages*

It is the Germanic family which includes English and its nearest relatives. The hypothetical source language, in its turn derived from Indo-European, from which they developed, is called Proto-Germanic or simply Germanic. This parent language has not come down to us in written form, so its structure and lexicon must be inferred from its modern descendants and from the written records which we do have for the older stages of some of them, pieced together with some fragmentary historical information which is available from the first century onward, the time at which the Germanic tribes came into contact with the fringes of the Roman Empire. The progressive and divergent changes which eventually were to result in the various Germanic languages of today had begun to emerge just about that time.

In general, the parent Germanic language is supposed to have differentiated along the following lines, with each of the main divisions also representing a proto-language, which in turn gave rise to the derivative languages indicated.

a. East Germanic, the main representative of which is Gothic, known chiefly from fragments of a translation of the Bible made in the fourth century by Ulfilas, bishop of the West Goths. Vandalic was also a derivative of East Germanic.

b. North Germanic, including Swedish and Danish as an eastern subgroup, Norwegian and Icelandic as a western division.

c. West Germanic, which comprises the following subdivisions:

1. High German, in its three periods of Old High German, Middle High German, and New High German, the current

standard language of Germany and Austria. Yiddish, as well as the German spoken in Switzerland, belongs in this category.

2. Franconian. High Franconian was the source of some of the southern German and Rhenish dialects. The modern representatives of Low Franconian are the languages of Holland and Flanders.

3. Low German, in its two periods of Old Saxon and Modern Plattdeutsch.

4. Frisian, in the two periods of Old and Modern Frisian, the latter spoken today in the area near the mouth of the Rhine.

5. English, which developed through the respective stages of Old, Middle, and Modern English. Old English extends from 450 to 1050; Middle English from 1050 to 1475; and Modern English from 1475 to the present. The period from 1475 to 1700 is often referred to as Early Modern English.

Thus the line of descent which leads from Indo-European to Modern English includes these successive stages: Indo-European, Germanic, West Germanic, Old English, Middle English, Early Modern English, Modern English.

135. *Dialects of Old English*

It would be strange, indeed, for any language to be uniform in all respects over the entire area in which it is spoken. Normally one finds variations in pronunciation, vocabulary, inflections, and syntax distributed on a geographical basis. Such variant forms of a language are called regional (and sometimes local) dialects. The forces behind their development represent, to a degree at least, the same processes of differentiation which account for the break-up of a proto-language into its various component families, groups, and subgroups.

As the map on p. 178 shows, Old English had four dialect areas, corresponding in part to the patterns of settlement by the different Germanic tribes. The language of the Jutish settlements in Kent, in Surrey, and along the southern coast is called Kentish. For the rest of England south of the Thames, the dialect was West Saxon. The Anglian region was the most extensive. It included two dialects: Mercian, spoken in a broad belt across the center of the country, and Northumbrian, which covered the north of England as well as the Scottish lowlands.

According to the meager records which have come down to us, most of the dialect differences at this period seem to be concentrated in the sounds of the language. These can usually be explained in terms of the occurrence or nonoccurrence of certain sound changes, or the more extensive operation of a sound change in one dialect area as compared with another. For example, diphthongization by initial palatal occurred only in West Saxon. Thus the Kentish, Mercian, and Northumbrian equivalents of West Saxon **giefan** and **ceaster** were **gefan** and **cæster** (**cester** in Kentish and southwest Mercian, as the result of still another change).

Dialect Areas of Old English

Velar umlaut, confined to a very few words in West Saxon, operated extensively in the other dialects, especially Kentish and southwest Mercian, resulting in forms like **geatu** and **heafoc**, corresponding to West Saxon **gatu** and **hafoc**.

Certain sound changes had an impact upon the inflectional system as well. A loss of final **n** in Northumbrian affected the infinitive of verbs in particular. The syncopation of unstressed vowels in the third-person singular present indicative form of verbs, resulting in forms like **cymð**, was more frequent in West Saxon than elsewhere. Inflectional differences resulted from regionally distributed operation of analogical processes as well. In the north, feminine noun genitives show a tendency to adopt the **-es** inflection, on the pattern of the masculine and neuter nouns, much earlier than elsewhere.

It is partly an accident of history that most of the materials written in Old English have been preserved in the West Saxon dialect. There was a time, the seventh and early eighth centuries in particular, when the dominant language of literature and culture was Northumbrian. During the reign of two great Mercian kings, Aethelbald and Offa, somewhat after the beginning of the eighth century, the dialect of Mercia acquired considerable prestige. The Danish invasions and subsequent occupation of the northern part of England, combined with the extraordinary ability and resourcefulness of King Alfred, brought about a cultural and a political shift to the West Saxon kingdom in the ninth century. His court became the center of learning, and very often documents which had been originally written in other dialects were copied in West Saxon, and it is these later copies which have come down to us.

A detailed treatment of all the Old English dialect features would be far too extensive for inclusion here. Authoritative accounts may be found in Karl Luick's *Historische Grammatik der englischen Sprache* (Leipzig: Tauchnitz, 1914–40) and in Alois Brandl's *Zur Geographie der altenglischen Dialekte* (Berlin, 1915). A convenient summary is given in Chapter 3 of Samuel Moore's *Historical Outlines of English Sounds and Inflections*, revised by A. H. Marckwardt (Ann Arbor: George Wahr, 1957).

136.   *Summary of Sound Changes*

The phonological development from the Indo-European parent language through Germanic and West Germanic into Old English is a complex subject in its own right, one which merits careful study. It has not been the purpose in the foregoing chapters to present this aspect of linguistic history in full detail. The score or so of changes described here have been selected primarily because they were thought to be useful in explaining inflectional irregularities in Old English itself and in clarifying the relationship among words in various grammatical categories which developed from the same base form. From this point of view they constitute the most important and far-reaching changes. They are reviewed here and placed in chronological order. This should assist the student in tracing the development of words from earlier periods of the language into Old English, from which may be derived a concept of one important aspect of linguistic history as well as some understanding of the impact of phonological change upon grammatical structure.

For a detailed treatment of Germanic and Old English phonology, the student is advised to consult one or more of the following works: Joseph and Elizabeth Mary Wright, *Old English Grammar* (New York: Oxford University Press, 1925); Alistair Campbell, *Old English Grammar* (Oxford: Clarendon Press, 1959); E. Sievers, *Altenglische Grammatik*, revised by Karl Brunner (Halle: Niemeyer, 1951); and Karl Luick, *Historische Grammatik der englischen Sprache* (Leipzig: Tauchnitz, 1914–40).

There follows a chronological listing of the sound changes which have been described in the course of the preceding chapters.

    a. From Indo-European to Germanic.
        1. The first consonant shift; Grimm's Law: Chapter 10, section 58.
        2. The stress shift and its consequences; Verner's Law: Chapter 11, section 63.
    b. From Germanic to West Germanic.
        3. Common Germanic palatal umlaut: Chapter 15, section 80.

   4. Gemination: Chapter 14, section 77.

c. From West Germanic to Old English.
   5. Fronting of **ā** (with exceptions): Chapter 13, section 74.
   6. Fronting of **a** (with exceptions): Chapter 7, section 41.
   7. Development of West Germanic diphthongs: Chapter 14, section 78.
   8. Breaking: Chapter 8, section 47.
   9. Diphthongization by initial palatal: Chapter 9, section 52.

d. Early Old English changes, fifth to ninth centuries.
   10. Palatal umlaut: Chapter 15, section 81.
   11. Loss of final unstressed **-i** and **-u**; change or loss of medial unstressed **-i** and **-j**: Chapter 3, section 16; Chapter 15, section 83; Chapter 16, section 87.
   12. Velar umlaut: Chapter 21, section 116.
   13. Assimilation of final dental and alveolar consonant combinations: Chapter 16, section 88.
   14. Loss of intervocalic **h**: Chapter 19, section 105.

e. Late Old English changes, ninth to eleventh centuries.
   15. Simplification of **ie** to **i** or **ȳ**: Chapter 15, section 81.
   16. Earlier **o** plus nasal (from WGmc **a**) written as **a**: Chapter 7, section 41.
   17. **Sco** > **sceo**: Chapter 19, section 105.
   18. Disappearance of **ġ** between vowels and **d** or **n**: Chapter 19, section 105.
   19. **Weor-** > **wor**, **wur**: Chapter 19, section 105.

137. *Summary of Inflections*

   The chart on pages 182–185 presents in tabular form the essential facts of the Old English inflections of nouns, pronouns, adjectives, and verbs. It will be useful as a help in reviewing and as a ready reference chart in connection with reading assignments. Only a few of the minor noun declensions have been included; the minor verb conjugations are omitted.

OLD ENGLISH INFLECTIONS

NOUNS

	STRONG DECLENSION					WEAK DECLENSION			MINOR DECLENSIONS	
	Stems in **-a-**			Stems in **-ō-**		Stems in **-n**			Stems in **-u-**	Root Consonant
	Masculine	Neuter (short)	Neuter (long)	Feminine (short)	Feminine (long)	M.	N.	F.	M.F.	M.F.
Sing.										
Nom.	bāt	scip	horn	scinu	glōf	oxa	ēare	heorte	sunu	fōt
Acc.	bāt	scip	horn	scine	glōfe	oxan	ēaran	heartan	sunu	fōt
Dat.	bāte	scipe	horne	scine	glōfe	oxan	ēaran	heortan	suna	fēt
Gen.	bātes	scipes	hornes	scine	glōfe	oxan	ēare	heortan	suna	fōtes
Pl. Nom.-Acc.	bātas	scipu	horn	scina, -e	glōfa, -e	oxan	ēaran	heortan	suna	fēt
Dat.-Inst	bātum	scipum	hornum	scinum	glōfum	oxum	ēarum	heortum	sunum	fōtum
Gen.	bāta	scipa	horna	scina	glōfa	oxena	ēarena	heortena	suna	fōtes

ADJECTIVES

	STRONG DECLENSION						WEAK DECLENSION			DEFINITE ARTICLE		
	Short stem			Long stem								
	M.	N.	F.	M.	N.	F.	M.	N.	F.	M.	N.	F.
Sing.												
Nom.	til	til	tilu	wīs	wīs	wīs	wīsa	wīse	wīse	sē	ðæt	sēo
Acc.	tilne	til	tile	wīsne	wīs	wīse	wīsan	wīsan	wīsan	ðone	ðæt	ða
Dat.	tilum	tilum	tilre	wīsum	wīsum	wīsre	wīsan	wīsan	wīsan	ðǣm	ðǣm	ðǣre
Inst.	tile	tile	tilre	wīse	wīse	wīsre	wīsan	wīse	wīsan	ðȳ	ðȳ	ðǣre
Gen.	tiles	tiles	tilre	wīses	wīses	wīsre	wīsan	wīsan	wīsan	ðæs	ðæs	ðǣre
Pl. Nom.-Acc.	tile	tilu	tila, -e	wīse	wīs	wīsa, -e	wīsan	wīsan	wīsan	ðā	ðā	ðā
Dat.-Inst.	tilum	tilum	tilum	wīsum	wīsum	wīsum	wīsum	wīsum	wīsum	ðǣm	ðǣm	ðǣm
Gen.	tilra	tilra	tilra	wīsra	wīsra	wīsra	wīsena	wīsena	wīsena	ðāra	ðāra	ðāra

PRONOUNS

Personal — First and Second Person

		Sing.	Dual	Pl.
First Person	Nom.	ic	wit	wē
	Acc.	mē	une	ūs
	Dat.	mē	une	ūs
	Gen.	mīn	uncer	ūre
Second Person	Nom.	ðū	ġit	ġē
	Acc.	ðē	inc	ēow
	Dat.	ðē	inc	ēow
	Gen.	ðīn	incer	ēower

Personal (Third Person), Demonstrative, and Interrogative

	Personal — Third Person			Demonstrative			Interrogative	
	M.	N.	F.	M.	N.	F.	M.F.	N.
Sing. N.	hē	hit	hēo	ðes	ðis	ðēos	hwā	hwæt
A.	hine	hit	hīe	ðisne	ðis	ðās	hwane	hwæt
D.	him	him	hiere	ðis(s)um	ðis(s)um	ðisse	hwǣm	hwǣm
I.				ðȳs	ðȳs	ðisse	hwȳ	hwȳ
G.	his	his	his	ðis(s)es	ðis(s)es	ðisse	hwæs	hwæs
Pl. N.A.	hīe	hīe	hiere	ðǣs	ðǣs	ðǣs		
D.I.	him	him	him	ðis(s)um	ðis(s)um	ðis(s)um		
G.	hiera	hiera	hiera	ðissa	ðissa	ðissa		

OLD ENGLISH INFLECTIONS—(Continued)

		STRONG VERBS	WEAK I (short)	WEAK I (long)	WEAK II	PRETERITIVE PRESENT	TO BE	
VERBS Present Tense								
Ind.	Sing. 1	drife	fremme	hǣle	hopie	wāt	ēom	bēo
	2	drif(e)st	fremest	hǣl(e)st	hopast	wāst	eart	bist
	3	drif(e)ð	fremeð	hǣl(e)ð	hopað	wāt	is	bið
	Pl.	drifað	fremmað	hǣlað	hopiað	witon	sindon	bēoð
Subj.	Sing.	drife	fremme	hǣle	hopie	wite	sīe	bēo
	Pl.	drifen	fremmen	hǣlen	hopien	witen	sīen	bēon
Imp.	Sing.	drif	freme	hǣl	hopa	wite	wes	bēo
	Pl.	drifað	fremmað	hǣlað	hopiað	witað	wesað	beoð
	Infinitive	drifan	fremman	hǣlan	hopian	witan	wesan	bēon
	Gerund	tō drifenne	tō fremmenne	tō hǣlenne	tō hopienne	tō witenne		tō bēonne
	Participle	drifende	fremmende	hǣlende	hopiende	witende	wesende	bēonde
VERBS Past Tense								
Ind.	Sing. 1	drāf	fremede	hǣlde	hopode	wiste	wæs	
	2	drife	fremedest	hǣldest	hopodest		wǣre	
	3	drāf	fremede	hǣlde	hopode	wiste	wæs	
	Pl.	drifon	fremedon	hǣldon	hopodon	wiston	wǣron	
Subj.	Sing.	drife	fremede	hǣlde	hopode	wiste	wǣre	
	Pl.	drifen	fremeden	hǣlden	hopoden	wisten	wǣren	
	Participle	drifen	fremed	hǣled	hopod	witen		

CLASSES OF STRONG VERBS

Infinitive	Pres. 2nd Sing.	Pres. 3rd Sing.	Past 1st Sing.	Past Pl.	Past Participle
1 drīfan	drīfst	drīfð	drāf	drifon	drifen
2 crēopan	crīepst	crīepð	crēap	crupon	cropen
3 singan	singst	singð	sang	sungon	sungen
3 helpan	hilpst	hilpð	healp	hulpon	holpen
3 hweorfan	hwierfst	hwierfð	hwearf	hwurfon	hworfen
4 stelan	stilst	stilð	stæl	stǣlon	stolen
5 sprecan	spricst	spricð	spræc	sprǣcon	sprecen
6 bacan	bæcst	bæcð	bōc	bōcon	bacen
7 lācan	lǣcst	lǣcð	lēc	lēcon	lācen
7 flōwan	flēwst	flēwð	flēow	flēowon	flowen

VERBS

Practice Exercises

1. Convert the following West Germanic forms into Old English, applying to them when appropriate the sound changes indicated in 5 through 13 of section 136 above.

nādl	fader	gasti	brūciþ	blāwan
erþe	bain	stapol	stiorjan	cneht
dusig	warp	aust	brand	bāron
maltiþ	oli	þwah	salt	straum
acern	sihiþ	wōpjan	spōdi	caf
gaist	hana	plehan	limu	dīorling
scarp	faldan	flahaþ	spān	wandjan
morgin	scaft	stelan	felhan	hati
wirþiþ	daidi	gāfon	gelpan	flēohan
faht	flauh	strangira	spraidjan	bragd
help	māgas	herot	pleh	agi
sceran	derc	sād	craft	draumjan
gaumjaþ	wurti	selh	hlūdjan	lahist

2. Convert the following Germanic forms into Old English, applying to them when appropriate the sound changes indicated in 3 through 13 of section 136 above.

bedjan	cwaljan
hwaitjum	hlahjan
stapjan	ūþjum
swarjaþ	gramjan
tīohiþ	hlunjum

OLD ENGLISH
PROSE AND POETRY

Old English Prose and Poetry: Some Texts

The texts presented here are in most cases edited directly from the manuscripts in which they appear. The citation of previous editions in the headnotes is exhaustive only when the number of editions is relatively small; otherwise the citation is of preferred editions. In the textual commentary, manuscript readings and editorial emendations are signified by]; for the full record and bibliography of textual criticism pertinent to a given poetic text, see the notes in Krapp and Dobbie, *The Anglo-Saxon Poetic Records*, or those in a more recent edition, and for the prose see the editions cited in the headnote. Explanatory and interpretative comment is preceded by a colon. Abbreviations used are: cmpd(s). = compound(s); cp. = compare; MED = *Middle English Dictionary* (ed. Kurath and Kuhn); PL = *Patrologia Latina* (ed. Migne), cited by volume and column. References to BTD (Bosworth and Toller, *An Anglo-Saxon Dictionary*) signify both Dictionary and Supplement, except when the one (BTD) or the other (BTD, Supp.) is specified by page number or entry-word or both. Passages from poems used as supporting or illustrative evidence in the commentary are cited from *The Anglo-Saxon Poetic Records*; passages in Old English cited in the notes from both prose and poetry are glossed in the Glossary.

Towards Old English Poetic Meter

Printed on pp. 191–192 are thirty lines selected at random from the texts of poems edited in this volume. Spacing and a diagonal bar separate the half lines or verses, which are the basic metrical units of the poetry. The following problems, to be worked out in some or all of the examples, are suggested as a way of (1) establishing a habit of looking at verses and lines as arrangements of sounds, and (2) acquiring inductively an elementary knowledge of the principles which govern Old English versification. Discussions of scansion and classifications of verse-types will be found in the works cited in the Bibliography; especially useful introductions are provided by John C. Pope in *Seven Old English Poems* (pages 97–138), and C. L. Wrenn in *A Study of Old English Literature* (pages 37–45).

Begin each problem by reading aloud a half-line (for problems under I) or a whole line (for problems under II).

I. Syllabic Stress

Mark the linguistic emphasis or stress of each syllable in a verse, using an acute accent (´) for primary stress, a grave accent (`) for secondary stress, and an *x* over a syllable for weak (or tertiary) stress.

1. Each *verse* should have two principal (primary or secondary) stresses and at least two weak stresses; some verses may also contain a secondary stress together with two primary stresses.

2. The degree of stress given a syllable is commonly related to the grammatical and syntactic function of the syllable. The relative stress-value of the parts of speech and some affixes may be stated roughly as follows:

a. the root-syllables of nouns, adjectives, participles, and infinitives most frequently have a principal (primary or secondary) stress;

b. finite verbs and adverbs sometimes carry a principal stress;

c. articles, conjunctions, prepositions, and pronouns most frequently carry a weak stress;

d. prefixes (such as **ge-**, **be-**, **to-**, **on[d]**-) most frequently carry a weak stress; some prefixes, such as **for-** and **un-**, may have a principal stress, in cases in which their function is semantically or rhetorically significant;

e. suffixes, both grammatical (such as **-a**, **-um**, **-est**) and lexical (such as **-lic**, **-ing**, **-ig**), most frequently have weak stress.

3. The degree and position of stresses of a *verse* are related to the alliterating syllables of a *line*.

II. Syllabic Alliteration

Underline the alliterating sound in each *line*; circle each syllable in a line which has now been marked as having a principal stress *and* as beginning with an alliterating sound.

1. The alliteration of a line may be either consonantal or vocalic.

    a. Most alliterating consonant sounds are pure, that is, a consonant alliterates with itself alone (as **d** with **d**). However, the palatalized and unpalatalized (or guttural) sounds of **c**, and of **g**, may alliterate, and each of the clusters **sc**, **sp**, **st** alliterates with itself alone.

    b. In vocalic alliteration, any vowel or diphthong may alliterate with any other vowel or diphthong; in the practice of alliteration vowels and diphthongs are not distinguished.

2. Structurally, alliteration binds two verses to compose a poetic line.

Rhythmically, at least two of the syllables which carry a principal stress in a *line* (one in each *verse*) alliterate. In the initial verse of a line (the a-verse, or on-verse) alliteration may fall on one (usually the first) of the principally stressed syllables or on two such syllables, whereas in the second verse (the b-verse, or off-verse) alliteration occurs only on the first principally stressed syllable. Generally, then, the first principally stressed syllable of the second verse will show the alliterative sound which unites the line.

Sample Lines

1. Ða cwom wundorlicu wiht   /   ofer wealles hrof
2. geond þas wundorworuld   /   wide dreogan
3. geond þisne middangeard   /   mongum to frofre
4. wrætlicu wyrd   /   þa ic þæt wundor gefrægn
5. þeof in þystro,   /   þrymfæstne cwide
6. Ic þis giedd wrece   /   bi me ful geomorre
7. heardsæligne,   /   hygegeomorne
8. þonne ic on uhtan   /   ana gonge
9. under stanhliþe,   /   storme behrimed
10. Sittaþ æt symble,   /   soðgied wrecað

11. ungelice!   /   Sum on oferhygdo
12. eorl fore æfstum;   /   læteð inwitflan
13. gif þu þyslicne   /   þegn gemittest
14. on engla eard.   /   Ne bið þam oþrum swa
15. ond þonne in þæt eglond   /   up gewitað
16. wic weardiað   /   wedres on luste
17. eorlas ond yðmearas.   /   He hafað oþre gecynd
18. ut gewiteð.   /   Hi þær in farað
19. utsiþ æfre,   /   þa þær in cumað
20. wordum ond weorcum,   /   þæt we wuldorcyning
21. weorc Wuldorfæder,   /   swa he wundra gehwæs
22. ece Drihten,   /   or onstealde
23. þa middangeard   /   moncynnes Weard
24. firum foldan,   /   Frea ælmihtig
25. breostgehygdum;   /   forðon him brego sægde
26. sceaðum scyldfullum.   /   Ongyn þe scip wyrcan
27. innan and utan   /   eorðan lime
28. ofer stæðweallas.   /   Strang wæs and reðe
29. fyrdgesteallum.   /   Gewiton feorh heora
30. þe him ær tweowe sealdon   /   mid heora folcgetrume

ÆLFRIC:
The Devil and the Apostate

British Museum, MS Cotton Julius E. 7, folios 19ʳ–21ʳ. Previous edition: W. W. Skeat, ed., *Ælfric's Lives of Saints*, E.E.T.S., 76 (1881), pp. 72–78.

This excerpt, typically characteristic of Ælfric's narrative form and style, is one of the episodes, or miracles, recounted in the homily of the life of Saint Basil (*Depositio Sancti Basilii Episcopi*; number III in Skeat's *Lives*). Ælfric's style, generally referred to as metrical, or rhythmical, prose, shows parallels with vernacular poetic style, and his texts have sometimes been printed in poetic lines representing his usual structure of sentences composed of phrasal pairs, rhythmically balanced, with alliterative links; thus, in Skeat's text, the opening sentence of this episode appears as:

Sum arwurþe þegn hæfde ane dohter
þa he wolde gebringan   binnan sumum mynstre.

For discussion of Ælfric's style, see Angus McIntosh, "Wulfstan's Prose" [which contains comments on Ælfric], *Proceedings of the British Academy*, 34 (for 1948); and especially Peter Clemoes, "Ælfric," in *Continuations and Beginnings*, ed. E. G. Stanley (London, 1966), pp. 176–209, and John C. Pope, ed., *Homilies of Ælfric: A Supplementary Collection*, E.E.T.S., 259 (1967), pp. 105–136 ("Ælfric's Rhythmical Prose").

[*Glossary symbol:* AI]

Sum arwurþe þegn hæfde ane dohter þa he wolde gebringan
binnan sumum mynstre and Criste betæcan, to his clænan þeowdome. Þa wearð an his cnapena to cuð þam mædene,[1] and þurh
deofles tihtinge hi digollice lufode; ac he ne dorste ameldian his
5 ungemetegodan lufe. Eode þa to anum drymen þe deofles cræft
cuðe, and behet him sceattes gif he mid his scyncræfte him þæt
mæden mihte gemacian to wife. Þa gebrohte se dryman þone
cnapan to his deofle, and se deofol befran þone dweligendan cnapan
gif he wolde on hine gelyfan, and his Hælende wiðsacen wið þam
10 þe he[2] gefremode his fulan galnysse. Þa stod se earming ætforan
þam arleasan deofle þær he healice sæt mid his helcnihtum, and
cwæð he wolde wiðsacan his Criste, and gelyfan on hine gif he his
lust gefremode. Þa cwæð se sceocca eft: "Ge synd swiðe unge-
treowa. Þonne ge min behofiað þonne ic helpe eow, and ge wiþ-
15 sacað me eft and cyrrað to eowrum Criste, se þe is swiðe myldheort
and myldelice eow underfehþ. Ac wryt me nu sylfwylles[3] þæt
þu wiðsaca Criste and þinum fulluhte, and ic gefremme ðinne lust;
and þu beo on domes dæge fordemed mid me. Ða awrat se earming
mid his agenra hande swa swa se deofol him gedihte þone pistol.
20 And se deofol sona sænde to ðam mædene his fulan gastas, þe
galnysse styriað, and ontendan þæt mæden to þæs mannes lustum.
Heo wearð þa geangsumod mid þæra ormætan ontendnysse, and
feoll adune færlice hrymende: "Eala þu min fæder, gemyltsa
þinre dehter, and forgif me þam men þe min mod me to spenð,
25 elles ic mot sweltan sarlicum deaðe.

Þa weop se fæder; wolde hi gefræfrian, and cwæð mid mycelre
sarnysse to þære seocan dehter: "Ic wolde mid clænnysse Criste
þe beweddian, to engla gefærredena, to frofre minre sawle, and
þu þus wodlice wilnast ceorles." Heo ne rohte his worda for þæra
30 wodlican ontendnysse, and cwæð þæt heo sceolde sweltan forraðe
gif se fæder nolde gefremman hyre wyllan. Se fæder þa æt nextan,
be his freonda ræde, forgeaf þa earman dohter þam deofles

---

1. **wearð ... to cuð þam mædene**: *became acquainted with the girl.*
2. **wið þam þe he**:*providing that he* [*the devil*].
3. **sylfwylles**: an adverbial genitive, *of your own accord.*

cnihte mid mycclum æhtan[4], and his man nyste. Ða nolde se deofles
cniht cuman næfre to circan, ne Godes word gehyran ne þa halgan
35 messan. Wearð þa geopenad his earman wife his manfullan behat
þam hetolan deofle, and heo mid mycelre angsumnysse arn to
Basilie, and cydde him be endebyrdnysse[5] hyre cnihtes wiþersæc.
Þa het se halga wer hine to him gefeccan[6], and befran gif hit swa
wære swa his wif him sæde. And he sæde mid wope hu he beswican
40 wearð. Þa axode se bisceop: "Wylt þu bugan eft to Criste?" Se
wyþersaca cwæð: "Ic wylle georne, leof. Ac ic ne mæg, þeah ic
wylle, forþan þe ic wiðsoc Criste, and on gewryte afæstnode þæt
ic wære þæs deofles." Se halga wer him cwæð to: "Ne hoga þu
embe þæt. Ure Hælend is swiþe welwyllende, and wyle þe eft
45 underfon gif þu mid soðre dædbote gecyrst eft to him."

Hwæt, þa Basilius gebletsode þone cniht, and beleac hine onsundron on sumere digelre stowe, and tæhte[7] him bota and gebæd
for hine. Com eft ymbe ðry dagas and[8] axode hu he mihte.[9] Ða
cwæð se dædbeta: "Þa deoflu cumað to me and me swiðe geegsiað,
50 and eac swylce torfiað, and habbað him on hande min agen
handgewryt. Cweðað þæt ic come to him and na hi to me." Basilius
him cwæð to: "Ne beo ðu afyrht. Gelyf soðlice on God." And
senode hine eft, beleac eft þa duru, and lede him his mete. He com
eft ymbe feawa daga and cunnode þæs mannes. Se cniht cwæð to
55 ðam halgan were: "Ic gehyre[10] þa deoflu feorran and hyra egslican
þiwracan, ac ic hi ne geseo." He beleac hine eft on þa ylcan wysan
oð þone feowerteoðogan dæg, and fandode his siððan. Þa sæde se
cnapa þæt he swiðe wel mihte: "Nu todæg ic seah hu ðu oferswið-
dest þone deofol." Basilius þa on mergen gebrohte þone cnapan
60 into Godes huse, and het gegaderian þæt folc, and bæd hi ealle
wacian þær on niht mid him, and ðingian þam earman men to
þam ælmihtigan Gode. Mid þam þe hi swiðost bædon binnan þæra

4. MS æhtam.
5. be endebyrdnysse: *in the order of events; in proper order.*
6. het . . . hine . . . gefeccan: *commanded him to be brought.*
7. MS tæhta.
8. and not in MS.
9. hu he mihte: *freely, how he was; if he were in good spirits;* Cp. BTD, magan (II).
10. MS gehyra.

cyrcan, þa com se wælreowa deofol. Wolde geniman þone cnapan
of Basilius handum, hetolice teonde; and cwæð to ðam halgan þæt
65 he hine berypte: "Ne sohte ic na hine, ac he sylf com to me. Her ic
habbe his handgewryt, þæt ic hit gehealde mid me to þam gemæne-
lican dome on þam mycclum dæge.¹¹" Ða cwæð se halga wer: "We
clypiað to ðam Hælende upahafenum handum oð þæt þu þæt
handgewryt agife." Ða clypodon hi ealle 'Kyrrieleyson' upahafe-
70 num handum wið heofonas weard¹² — and efne þa æfter fyrste
feol þæt ylce gewryt ufon of þære lyfte to ðam geleaffullan biscope.
He þancode þa Gode mid gastlicra blysse, and axode þone cnapan
gif he oncneowe þæt gewryt. He cwæð: "Ic oncnawe þas cartan
fulgeare; þis ic sylf awrat þam awyrgedan deofla." Hwæt, þa
75 Basilius hi¹³ sona totær, and gehuslode þone cnapan and þam
Hælende betæhte, and lærde hine georne hu he lybban sceolde on
Cristes geleafan oð his lifes ende.

11. **þam mycclum dæge**: *on the Day of Judgment.*
12. **wið . . . weard**: a phrasal, *toward.*
13. **hi** = **heo** = **cartan**.

Three Riddles

The Exeter Book, folios 107ᵛ–108ᵛ, 109ᵛ–110ᵛ, 112ᵛ–113ʳ. Previous editions: F. Tupper, ed., *The Riddles of the Exeter Book* (New York, 1910), riddles 30, 40, 48; G. P. Krapp and E. V. K. Dobbie, eds., *The Exeter Book* (New York, 1936), riddles 29, 39, 47.

Old English poetry includes some ninety-five riddles, all of which are contained in the Exeter Book. Although a few of these are derivative of or modeled on Latin riddles (e.g., by Aldhelm), and many contain subjects found universally in riddles, the largest proportion of Old English riddles was cultivated from the subjects of everyday life. The subjects (or problems) of the riddles are varied, and typically concrete, such as sword, shield, horn, lyre, plow, key, oyster, onion, badger, cuckoo, storm, and moon. The subjects of Latin riddles are often identified in a title ("*Nox*," "*Clypeus*," "*De Creatura*," etc.), but the Exeter Book riddles have no titles and hence the solutions proposed by editors and commentators are based on analogues in riddle literature and on ingenuity; for this reason, many of the Old English riddles have been "solved" in quite different ways: thus, the subject of riddle 32 (in the Krapp-Dobbie edition) has been interpreted by different readers as "wagon," "millstone," "ship," or "wheel." But it is perhaps just as well that the Old English riddles do not have titles which specify their literal subjects, because their fundamental appeal is not so much to "solve problems" as to stimulate our delight in the mysteries and wonders which their descriptions and narratives, personifications and paradoxes, symmetries of word and phrase evoke.

The three riddles selected here illustrate, when taken together, the habits of thought and of style which dominate the genre in Old English. Riddle 29 develops by narrative progress and the figures of treasure and exile the widespread riddle motif of the Moon. Riddle 39 ("Day," or "Moon"), while less detailed and realistically concrete than many riddles, is complex in stylistic variety, in emotional expression, and in the intertwining of subordinate paradoxes with the dominant paradox of a creature which is the lowliest of all creatures but a great blessing to men. Riddle 47 ("Bookworm") is one of the finest examples among the riddles of incisive, witty paradox.

[*Glossary symbols*: *R29, R39, R47*]

Riddle 29

Ic wiht geseah   wundorlice
hornum bitweonum[1]   huþe[2] lædan,
lyftfæt leohtlic,[3]   listum[4] gegierwed,
huþe to þam ham   of þam heresiþe.
5   Walde[5] hyre[6] on þære byrig   bur atimbran,[7]
searwum asettan,   gif hit swa meahte.[8]
Ða cwom wundorlicu wiht   ofer wealles hrof[9] —
seo is eallum cuð   eorðbuendum;

1. **hornum bitweonum**] MS **horna abitweonū**.
2. **huþe** here and in line 4 is the accusative object of **lædan**.
3. **leohtlic**: freely, *shining*, but the literal sense of **lēoht-līc**, *light-like*, is contextually apt.
4. **listum**: a dative (or instrumental) plural with adverbial function, *artfully*.
5. **walde**: a variant of **wolde**.
6. **hyre**: reflexive.
7. **atimbran**] MS **atimbram**.
8. **gif hit swa meahte**: ellipsis of **beon**; freely, *if she* [**wiht**] *might*.
9. **ofer wealles hrof**: may be taken to mean something like *over the horizon*, but within the (figurative) terms of the poem the roof's wall refers back to the **byrig** in line 5.

ahredde þa þa huþe,   ond to ham[10] bedraf[11]
10 wreccan ofer willan[12];   gewat hyre west þonan
fæhþum[13] feran,   forð onette.[14]
Dust stonc to heofonum,   deaw feol on eorþan,
niht forð gewat.   Nænig siþþan
wera gewiste   þære wihte sið.

Riddle 39

Gewritu secgað[1]   þæt seo wiht sy
mid moncynne   miclum tidum[2]
sweotol ond gesyne.   Sundorcræft hafað
maran[3] micle[4]   þonne[5] hit men witen.
5 Heo wile gesecan   sundor æghwylcne
feorhberendra;   gewiteð eft feran on weg.[6]
Ne bið hio næfre   niht þær oþre,[7]

10. **to ham**: apparently in some contrastive sense to **to þam ham** (= **hame**) in line 4; perhaps read *at (her) home, from home*.

11. **bedraf**] MS **bedræf**. Cp. the citation under **niht** in BTD, p. 720: **Swa swa se beorhta dæg todræfþ ða dimlican þeostru ðære sweartan nihte.**

12. **ofer willan**: a phrasal, *against her* [the **wiht** of line 1] *will*.

13. **fæhþum**: the only dative/instrumental plural form recorded, with uncertain meaning; literally (?) *by means of* (or, *because of*) *feuds, in feud*; freely (?) *hostilely.* Cp. **here-siþe**, line 4.

14. **onette**]MS **o netteð**.

1. **Gewritu secgað**: the only occurrence of this formula in the Riddles; as a formula it is related to the introductory **Ic wat, Ic gefrægn, Ic (ge)seah**, all of which occur often in the Riddles as an initial means of eliciting expectation, inviting the listener/reader to a mystery, and of evoking the indirection so essential to riddle-craft. In addition, **gewritu secgað** (repeated in line 13) suggests a didactic intent, which may also be implicit in line 4b. Cp. the recurrence of **(ge)secgan(ne)** in lines 22 ff.

2. **miclum tidum**: This appears to be the only instance in which **micel** modifies **tid**; the precise meaning is unclear. Translate (?) *for much time*, (?) *for many hours*, (?) *at many times*.

3. **maran**] MS **maram**.

4. **maran micle**: another unusual construction with **micel**; probably, *much (far) greater* [**sundorcræft**].

5. **þonne**: *when*.

6. **on weg**: a phrasal, *away*.

7. **Ne ... oþre**: literally, *She* [**wiht**] *is never there another (? the next) night*; that is, never stationary, never fixed in time or place, but also (in the paradox of service to men and exile from them) never allowed to remain.

ac hio sceal wideferh   wreccan laste[8]
hamleas hweorfan   — no þy heanre biþ.
10 Ne hafað hio fot ne folme,[9]   ne æfre foldan hran,
ne eagena[10]   ægþer twega,
ne muð hafaþ   ne wiþ monnum spræc,
ne gewit hafað,   ac gewritu secgað
þæt seo sy earmost[11]   ealra wihta
15 þara þe æfter gecyndum[12]   cenned wære.
Ne hafað hio sawle ne feorh,   ac hio siþas sceal
geond þas wundorworuld   wide dreogan.
Ne hafaþ hio blod ne ban,   hwæþre bearnum wearð
geond þisne middangeard   mongum to frofre.
20 Næfre hio heofonum hran   ne to helle mot,
ac hio sceal wideferh   wuldorcyninges[13]
larum lifgan.[14]   Long is[15] to secganne
hu hyre ealdorgesceaft   æfter gongeð,
woh wyrda gesceapu[16]   — þæt is[17] wrætlic þing
25 to gesecganne!   Soð is æghwylc[18]
þara þe ymb þas wiht   wordum becneð:
'Ne hafað heo ænig[19] lim,   leofaþ efne seþeah.'
Gif þu mæge reselan   recene gesecgan
soþum wordum,[20]   saga hwæt hio hatte.[21]

8. **wreccan laste**: *on the trace (path) of exile.*

9. **folme**] MS **folm**.

10. **eagena**] MS **eage ne**, no doubt induced by the frequency of **ne**. Perhaps the original reading was **ne eagena [hafað]**.

11. **sy earmost**: Cp. line 9b.

12. **æfter gecyndum**: freely, *in nature*; *after the nature of things.*

13. **(-) cyninges**] MS **cyninge**.

14. **sceal . . . larum lifgan**: *must live by the teachings (laws).*

15. **Long is**: *It is too long (difficult)*; cp. BTD, Supp., **lang**, II.4.

16. **woh wyrda gesceapu**: literally, *woven (twisted) destinies of fates.*

17. **þæt is**] **is** not in MS.

18. **Soð is æghwylc**: *Each one is true (just).*

19. **heo ænig**] MS **he hænig**; **he** is scribally introduced by a different hand. This line is the concluding summary of the preceding paradoxes.

20. **soþum wordum**: Cp. **soð** and **wordum** in lines 25 and 26 respectively; the two collocations of **soð** and **word** have different functions: one refers to the truth or rightness of the paradox itself, the other is part of the invitation to solve the riddle-paradox, *in true words.*

21. **saga hwæt hio hatte**: a variation on the frequentative end-formula in riddles, **Saga (Frige) hwæt ic hatte.**

Riddle 47

Moððe word fræt.   Me þæt þuhte
wrætlicu wyrd   þa ic þæt wundor gefrægn,
þæt se wyrm forswealg   wera gied[1] sumes,
þeof in þystro,   þrymfæstne cwide
5   ond þæs strangan staþol.[2]   Stælgiest ne wæs
wihte þy gleawra   þe he þam wordum swealg.

---

1. The accusative appositives are **gied**, **cwide**, and **staþol**.

2. **þæs strangan staþol**: literally, *the foundation of the strong* (or, *of a strong man*); that is, a book, probably a Bible. Cp. the citations in BTD: — **Biþ Drihten ure se trumesta staþol**; — **On ðissum cwydum is se staðol ealles geleafan.**

ÆLFRIC:
St. John and the Wayward Boy

Bodleian MS Laud Misc. 509, folios 137ᵛ–133ʳ [folio 133 was misbound and follows folio 139]. Previous edition: S. J. Crawford, ed., *The Heptateuch*, E.E.T.S., O. S. 160 (London, 1922), pp. 62–68 (lines 1046–1153).

This self-contained narrative of St. John the Apostle occurs in Ælfric's long Letter to Sigeweard on the Old and New Testaments. The story, which Ælfric attributes to Jerome, takes place after John had been banished by Domitian to Patmos and then, following Domitian's death, returned to Ephesus where he administered the faith and appointed bishops in nearby towns.

Ælfric tells the story straightforwardly and with great simplicity of diction and syntax. Sentences and clauses beginning with **þa**, **and**, **he**, and **ac** are recurrent, but such syntactic repetition never becomes obtrusive or labored because Ælfric constantly alternates and varies his structures. Simple and direct as the narration may seem, it is also sustained by a sensitive attention to various forms of rhetorical symmetry and balance, such as: alliteration (**micelre mærþe ... mennisc**; **fyrste ferde ... foresædan**; **marum morð- dædum ... manfullum**), parallel phrasals (**stranglic on wæstme and wenlic on nebbe**; **glæd on mode and on anginne caf**), and repetition of affixes and head-words (**alædde ... aweg**; **ætburste ... ætfleon**; **mildsunge ... mildheorton**; **dæghwamlice ... deorwurð- lice**; **befæste ... besorh**).

[*Glossary symbol*: AII]

He becom þa to anre birig, swa swa he gebeden wæs, gehende
Ephesan, and þær bisceop gehadode, and þa circlican þeawas
him sylf þær getæhte þam gehadodum preostum ðe he þær gelo-
gode, and mid micelre mærþe þæt mennisc þæt lærde to Godes
geleafan mid glædre heortan.

Ða geseah Iohannes sumne cniht on þam folce iunglicre ylde
and ænlices hiwes, stranglic on wæstme and wenlic on nebbe,
swiðe glæd on mode and on anginne caf, and begann to lufienne
on his liðum þeawum[1] þone iungan cniht þæt he hine Criste ge-
strynde. Ða beseah Iohannes swa upp to þam bisceope, þe ða niwan
wæs gehadod, and him þus to cwæð: "Wite þu la bisceop, þæt ic
wille þæt þu hæbbe þisne iungan man mid þe on þinre lare æt
ham, and ic hine þe befæste mid healicre gecneordnisse on Cristes
gewitnysse and þissere gelaðunge." Hwæt, þa se bisceop bliðelice
underfeng þone foresædan cniht, and sæde þæt he wolde his
gimene habban mid geornfulnysse, swa he him bebead, on his
wununge mid him. Iohannes þa eft geedleahte his word and
gelome bebead þam bisceope mid hæsum, þæt he þone iungan
cniht gewissian sceolde to ðam halgan geleafan, and he ham þa
gewende eft to Efesan birig to his bisceopstole. Se bisceop þa
underfeng, swa swa him beboden wæs, þone iungan cniht, and him
Cristes lare dæghwamlice tæhte and hine deorwurðlice heold oð
þæt he hine gefullode mid fullum truwan þæt he geleafful[2] wære,
and he wunode swa mid him on arwurðnysse, oð þæt se bisceop
hine let faran be his wille,[3] wende þæt he sceolde on Godes gife
þurhwunian on gastlicum þeawum. He geseah þa sona þæt he his
sylfes geweold, on ungeripedum freodome and unstaðððigum
þeawum, and begann þa to lufienne leahtras to swiðe and fela
unðeawas mid his efenealdum cnihtum, þe unrædlice ferdon on
heora idelum lustum on gewemmednyssum and wolicum[4] gebær-
um. He and his geferan þa begunnon to lufienne þa micclan drunc-

1. **on his liðum þeawum**: *in his* [*John's*] *gentle way.*
2. Notice the repetition: ge_fu_llode ... fu_l_lum ... gelea_ffu_l.
3. **be his wille**: *of his* [*the bishop's*] *own will.*
4. MS **woclicum**.

ennisse on nihtlicum gedwylde, and hig þa hine on gebrohton[5]
þæt he begann to stelenne on heora gewunan,[6] and he gewenede
swa hine sylfne simble to heora synlicum þeawum and to marum
35 morðdædum mid þam manfullum flocce. He genam þa heardlice
þurh heora lare on his orþance þa egeslican dæda, and swa swa
modig hors þe ungemidlod byð and nele gehirsumian þam ðe
him on uppan sitt, swa ferde se cniht on his fracedum dædum,
and on morðdædum micclum gestrangod on orwennysse his
40 agenre hæle, swa þæt he ortruwode on his Drihtnys mildheortnysse,[7] and his fulluhtes ne rohte þe he underfangen hæfde. Him
þuhte þa to waclic þæt he wolde gefremman þa læssan[8] leahtras,
ac he leornode æfre maran and maran on his manfulnysse and ne
let nanne his gelican on yfele.[9] He ne geþafode þa þæt he under-
45 þeod wære yfelum gegadum, þe hine ær forlærdon, ac wolde beon
yldest on þam yfelan flocce, and geworhte his geferan to weald-
gengum ealle on widgillum dunum on ealre hreownysse.

Eft þa æfter fyrste ferde se apostol to þære foresædan byrig, ðe
se bisceop onwunode, þe þone cniht hæfde on his gimene æror,
50 swa swa Iohannes het, and he hine befæste and he swiðe bliðe
wæs æt þam bisceopstole. Syððan he gedon hæfde his Drihtenes
þenunga and þa ðing gefyllede, þe he fore gelaþod wæs. He
cwæð þa anrædlice: "Eala þu la bisceop, gebring me nu ætforan
þæt, þæt[10] ic ðe befæste on mines Drihtnes truwan, and on þære
55 gewitnysse, þe ðu wissian scealt on þissere gelaðunge." He wearð
þa ablicged and wende þæt he bæde sumes oþres sceattes oððe
sumes feos, þæs þe he[11] ne underfeng fram þam apostole. Ac he
eft beðohte þæt se eadiga Iohannes him leogan nolde, ne hine
þæs biddan þæt he ær ne befæste, and he forhtmod wafode.

---

5. **hine on gebrohton**: literally, *they brought him on (along?)*; perhaps read a composition, **ongebrohton**, *they induced him.*

6. **on heora gewunan**: *in their habit*; freely, *as was customary for them.*

7. MS **and his mildheortnysse** follows here redundantly, no doubt an oversight
as the scribe went on to **and his fulluhtes.**

8. MS **leasan**, probably induced by **leahtras.**

9. **ne let nanne . . .**: *he allowed* (or, *considered*) *no one (to be) his equal in evil.*

10. **gebring . . .**: *bring that now into my presence, that which . . . .*

11. **þæs þe he**: *such as he.*

Iohannes þa geseah þæt he sæt ablicged, and cwæð him eft þus
to: "Ic bidde æt þe nu þæs iungan cnihtes, þe ic þe befæste, and
þæs broþor sawle þe me besorh ys." Ða begann se ealda incuðlice
siccettan and mid wope wearð witodlice ofergoten, and cwæð to
Iohanne: "He, leof, ys nu dead." Ða befran Iohannes færlice and
cwæð: "Hu ys he la dead oððe hwilcum deaðe[12]?" He cwæð him
eft þus to andsware: "He is Gode dead, forþan þe he leahterfull
and geleafleas ætbærst, and he ys geworden nu to wealdgengan
and þæra sceaðena ealdor, þe he him sylf gegaderode, and wunað
on anre dune mid manegum sceaþum, þam þe he nu ys ealdor and
heretoga." Hwæt, þa Iohannes mid ormætre geomerunge cwehte
his heafod, and cwæð to þam bisceope: "Godne hyrde let ic þe,[13]
þæt þu þæs broðor sawle heolde. Ac beo me nu gegearcod an
gerædod hors and latteow þæs weges þe lið to þam sceaðum."
And man him sona funde, þæs þe he frimdig wæs, and he fram
þære ciricean sona swiðe efste, oð þæt he geseah þæra sceaþena
fær, and to þam weardmannum witodlice becom. Ða gelæhton þa
weardmen his wealdleðer fæste þæt he mid fleame huru ne ætburste. Ac he nolde him ætfleon ne nanes fleames cepan, ac he
clypode ofer eall: "Ic com me sylf to eow. Alædað me nu to butan
laðe[14] eowerne ealdor." Hig clipodon þa mid þam[15] þone cniht
him raðe to, þe hira heafodman wæs, and he com þa gewæmnod.
And he mid sceame wearð sona ofergoten, þa þa he oncneow þone
Cristes apostol, and began to fleonne fram his andweardnysse.
Iohannes ða heow þæt hors mid þam spuran and wearð him æfterweard—and his ylde ne gimde. Clypode þa hlude and cwæð to
þam fleondum: "Eala þu min sunu, hwi flihst þu þinne fæder?
Hwi flihst ðu þisne ealdan and ungewæpnodan[16]? Ne ondræd þe

12. **oððe hwilcum deaðe**: *and in which manner of death.*

13. The construction of this clause is unclear. Freely, *I considered you a good*
guardian; *I left you (to be) a good guardian.*

14. **butan laðe**: *without harm.* Crawford (following Grein) emends to **late**, apparently taking a construction **butan late** to mean *quickly*, but there is no evidence
to support such an idiom, and the phrase **butan laðe** occurs at least once elsewhere
in Old English.

15. **Hig . . . þam**: *Thereupon then they called.*

16. MS **ungewæpnode**.

la earming; git þu hæfst lifes hiht. Ic wille agildan gescead for
þinre sawle Criste, and ic lustlice wille min lif for þe syllan, swa
90   swa se Hælend sealde hine sylfne for us, and mine sawle ic sille
for þinre. Ætstand huru nu, and gehyr þas word, and gelyf þæt
se Hælend me asende to þe." Þa ætstod se wealdgenga syþþan
he þas word gehirde, and aleat to eorðan mid eallum lichaman,[17]
and awearp his wæmna and weop swiðe biterlice. And he bifiende
95   feoll to Iohannes fotum mid geomerunge and þoterunge mid tear-
um ofergoten, biddende miltsunge be þam ðe[18] he mihte. And
behydde his swiðran hand ofsceamod forðearle for þære morðdæde
þe he gedon hæfde, and for þam manslihte þe he sloh mid þære
handa. Þa swor se apostol þæt he soðlice wolde him mildsunge
100   begitan æt þam mildheortan Hælende. And eac he sylf aleat to
him and gelæhte his swiþran, for ðære þe he[19] ofdrædd wæs for
his morðdædum, and alædde hine[20] aweg wepende to circean,
and for hine gebæd mid broðorlicre lufe, swa swa he him behet,
to þam Hælende gelome, and eac mid fæste fela daga on an,[21] oð
105   þæt he him mildsunge beget æt þam mildheortan Criste. He hine
frefrode eac mid his fægeran[22] lare and his afyrhte mod swiþe fægerlice mid his frofre geliðewæhte, þæt he ne wurde ormod, and he
nateshwon ne geswac ær þan þe[23] his sawul wæs wiðinnan gegladod
þurh þone Halgan Gast and he mildsunge hæfde ealra his mis-
110   dæda. He hine hadode eac to þæs Hælendes þeowdome. Ac us
ne segð na seo racu to hwam he hine sette, buton þæt he sealde
soðe gebysnunge eallum dædbetendum þe to Drihtene gecyrrað,
þæt hig magon arisan, gif hig rædfæste beoð, fram heora sawle
deaþe and fram heora synna[24] bendum, and heora Scippend
115   gladian[25] mid soðre dædbote, and habban[25] þæt ece lif mid þam
leofan Hælende se þe a rixað on ecnysse. Amen.

17. MS **lichama**.
18. **be þam ðe**: *even as*.
19. **for ðære þe he**: freely, *because he* [the **cniht**].
20. **hine** not in MS.
21. **on an**: an adverbial phrase, *continuously*.
22. MS **fægera**.
23. **ær þan þe**: a phrasal, *before, until*.
24. MS **synnū** = **synnum**.
25. The subject (and auxiliary verb) of **gladian** and **habban** is **hig magon** in line 113.

The Wife's Lament

The Exeter Book, folio 115ʳ–115ᵛ. Previous editions: G. P. Krapp and E. V. K. Dobbie, eds., *The Exeter Book* (New York, 1936), pp. 210–211; R. F. Leslie, ed., *Three Old English Elegies* (Manchester, 1961), pp. 47–48.

In form, this poem is a monologue, spoken by a woman. Its content can perhaps best be described as an utterance of human deprivation and longing which expresses resignation close to despair. The speaker elliptically refers to the source of her grief: separation from her lord and husband because of his kin's hostility towards their being together, and the change of spirit which that hostility has caused within him. She exists in enforced exile, and the desolation of her heart is mirrored in the desolation of her habitat. The overgrown gloom of her dwelling and the realization of her privation are increased in each dawn, as she awakes alone, conscious of the contented bliss of lovers elsewhere and of the endless day of unending loneliness which awaits her. She reflects on the character and fate of any person yet untried by great sorrow, but soon returns to her own fate by imagining the condition of her lord as one identical with hers.

The style of *The Wife's Lament* is deliberate, restrained, and rhetorically unadorned. For example, there is little immediate (or focal) variation (**leofra . . . holda freonda**), schematic patterning (**þær ic sittan mot . . . þær ic wepan mæg**), or use of poetic epithets, adjectives, or compounds (**uhtceare, eorðsele, dreorsele**).

The pronoun **ic** occurs frequently but almost never in combination with the same word (such as a verb or adverb) more than once: **Ic þis**, **Ic þæt**, **hwæt ic**, **siþþan ic**, **A ic**, etc. This restraint and economy of phrasing is not unlike the plain style of some Elizabethan lyrics. But the style is also suggestive of metaphysical poetry in the intricacy of its interlacing vocabulary. The poet employs a relatively small, and in its simplex form (**mod, lond**, etc.) a simple, vocabulary, but he generates and redistributes a part of the vocabulary throughout the poem in different lexical combinations and syntactic patterns. For example, notice the recombinations (lexically, syntactically, and referentially) of the following: **lond, eorð(an)**; **geomor, ceare**; **leof(an), freond (frynd), wine**; **hyge(nd), mod**; **sið, wræc(ca)**; **(a)(ge)bidan, (be)dreogan, begietan**.

In the Exeter Book arrangement of poems *The Wife's Lament* immediately follows the first of two gatherings of riddles (nos. 1–59). Given the position of the poem in the codex it may not be too far-fetched to suppose that for the Anglo-Saxon compiler the poem represented a riddle, perhaps because it begins with **Ic**, as do many of the riddles (**Ic wæs . . .**, **Ic sceal . . .**, **Ic eom . . .**, **Ic wat . . .**, **Ic seah . . .**, etc.). For us *The Wife's Lament* remains something of a riddle, at least in the limited sense of puzzle. The brief summary given in the first paragraph reflects the traditional view of the poem. There is, however, great diversity in the scholarship concerning a unified interpretation, the meaning of particular words and allusive references, the syntax and punctuation of certain lines, and so on. Cited below (with the title of the poem abbreviated *WL*) are several essays illustrative of this diversity: S. B. Greenfield, "*The WL* Reconsidered," *PMLA*, LXVIII (1953); J. A. Ward, "*The WL*: An Interpretation," *JEGP*, LIX (1960); R. D. Stevick, "Formal Aspects of *The WL*," *JEGP*, LIX (1960); R. C. Bambas, "Another View of the Old English *WL*," *JEGP*, LXII (1963); J. L. Curry, "Approaches to a Translation of the Anglo-Saxon *The WL*," *Medium Aevum*, XXXV (1966); M. Stevens, "The Narrator of *The WL*," *Neuphilologische Mitteillungen*, LXIX (1968).   [*Glossary symbol*: WL]

Ic þis giedd wrece   bi me ful geomorre,
minre sylfre sið.[1]   Ic þæt secgan mæg
hwæt ic yrmþa gebad   siþþan ic up weox[2]
niwes oþþe ealdes,[3]   no ma þonne nu —
5 a ic wite wonn   minra wræcsiþa.
    Ærest min hlaford gewat   heonan of leodum
ofer yþa gelac;   hæfde ic uhtceare[4]
hwær min leodfruma   londes wære.
Ða ic me feran gewat   folgað secan,[5]
10 wineleas wræcca,   for minre weaþearfe;

1. Syntactically both **giedd** and **sið** are objects of **wrece**; thus, literally: *I utter this song, my own situation, concerning myself full sorrowful*; but freely: *I sing this song concerning myself full sorrowful, (concerning) my own plight.*

2. **weox**: Most previous editors, following Sievers, emend to **aweox** because of a presumed metrical deficiency in the half-line. Syntactically, a phrasal, **up aweoxe**, does occur at least once, in *Elene*, line 1225, and **up** combines with other verbs with **a**-prefix, such as **aræran**, **astigan**, **astandan**, **arisan**, and **ahon**, as well as with the unprefixed forms. Among the kinds of scribal omission in the Exeter Book both whole words (e.g., **hine** in *Guthlac A*, line 156) and initial **h** (as **his** in *Christ*, line 615) are omitted with relative frequency, but the omission otherwise of an *initial* letter or syllable is relatively infrequent (e.g., **g** omitted before **rene**, in *Phoenix*, line 154, **ge** before **siþa** in *Widsith*, line 110, **mon** before **dryhtne** in Riddle 58, line 6). The emendation to **aweox** may well be right, but given the inconclusiveness of metrical evidence alone it seems best not to emend.

3. **niwes oþþe ealdes**: adverbial genitives, modifying **yrmþa**: *of miseries new or old.*

4. **uhtceare**: **uht**- refers to early morning, the twilight period before dawn, often signifying in the poetry a time of extreme anxiety. Cp. *The Wanderer*, lines 8–9: 'Oft ic sceolde ana uhtna gehwylce/mine ceare cwiþan,' together with the analysis of this state of mind in the same poem (lines 34–50a), and *Resignation* (also in the Exeter Book), lines 95–96: **ond him bið a sefa geomor,/mod morgenseoc**. Cp. also the passage (and its context) in *Beowulf*, lines 3021–3023: **Forðon sceall gar wesan/monig morgenceald mundum bewunden,/hæfen on handa**.

5. **folgað secan**: a compressed and elliptical expression in this poem, the full semantic structure of which is 'to seek out my lord, my husband, to render my duty to him.' The surface expression and the reference contained in it seems somewhat impersonal, but this mood is consistent with much of the poem; moreover, the wife's loss of and quest for her lover-husband is blended, in compressed form, with the figure of the thane who has lost his lord (e.g., **leodfruma**, line 8) and travels about in exile (cp. the context of the **wineleas guma** in *The Wanderer*, line 45, and see **wineleas** in BTD).

ongunnon þæt þæs monnes   magas hycgan[6]
þurh dyrne geþoht,   þæt hy todælden unc
þæt wit gewidost   in woruldrice
lifdon laðlicost   —ond mec longade.
15   Het mec hlaford min   her eard niman.[7]
Ahte ic leofra lyt[8]   on þissum londstede,[9]
holdra freonda   —forþon is min hyge geomor.
    Ða ic me ful gemæcne   monnan funde,
heardsæligne,   hygegeomorne,
20   modmiþendne,   morþorhycgendne,[10]
bliþe gebæro.[11]   Ful oft wit beotedan
þæt unc ne gedælde   nemne deað ana
owiht[12] elles.   Eft is þæt onhworfen;
is nu fornumen[13]   swa hit no wære,

6. **ongunnon . . . hycgan**: literally, *meditated*; freely, *intended*.

7. **her eard**] MS **her heard**; **eard niman**: a phrasal, *to take up* (my) *dwelling*.

8. **leofra lyt**: litotes; that is, 'no one,' or 'not any.'

9. The place referred to by **her** (line 15) . . . on **þissum londstede** is the place of exile described in lines 27f.

10. **-hycgendne**] MS **hycgende**; **morþorhycgendne**: taken either as two words or as a compound, the meaning of the construction is unclear; (?) *mindful of great injury*, (?) *(having a) murderous* (? *hostile*) *mind*. For adjective compounds formed with a present participle, cp. in the dictionaries such words as **gleawhycgende, leoht-berende, sædberende, teargeotende**.

11. **bliþe gebæro**: The syntax of this phrasal is extremely difficult to determine. The main questions are: (1) Does the phrasal begin a new sentence at line 21, as an instrumental modifying **wit**? Or (2) does it conclude the sequence of adjectives describing the **monnan** (line 18)? Leslie (p. 55) argues that **bliþe gebæro** is unlikely to begin a sentence because of **ful oft**, which he claims "usually begins a sentence" (but see **fulloft, fuloft** in BTD). What may be more to the point is that a sentence or main clause beginning with an instrumental phrase would be unusual in Old English; cp. the very rare dative absolute, based on ablative absolute constructions in Latin (examples, R. Quirk and C. L. Wrenn, *An Old English Grammar*, art. 111). In line 44 **bliþe gebæro** occurs, in a noun series descriptive of **geong mon**, as the accusative object of **habban sceal**. It therefore seems likely that **bliþe gebæro** here is to be construed as part of the adjective series descriptive of **monnan**, not of course as an adjective, but as an instrumental phrase modifying the preceding adjectives.

12. **ne** modifies **owiht**, for the phrasal, **ne owiht elles**, *not anything else*. Cp. the form **nawiht** in BTD.

13. **fornumen**] not in MS. A word has been scribally lost in this line and the insertion follows Leslie.

25 freondscipe uncer.   Sceal¹⁴ ic feor ge neah
    mines felaleofan   fæhðu dreogan.¹⁵
    Heht mec mon¹⁶ wunian   on wuda bearwe
    under actreo   in þam eorðscræfe.
    Eald is þes eorðsele;   eal ic eom oflongad.
30 Sindon dena dimme,   duna uphea,
    bitre burgtunas,   brerum beweaxne,
    wic wynna leas.¹⁷   Ful oft mec her wraþe begeat
    fromsiþ frean.   Frynd sind on eorþan;¹⁸
    leofe lifgende   leger weardiað
35 þonne ic on uhtan   ana gonge
    under actreo   geond þas eorðscrafu,
    þær ic sittan¹⁹ mot   sumorlangne dæg,²⁰

14. **sceal**] MS **seal**.

15. **fæhðu dreogan**: *suffer (endure) the feud*; the **fæhðu** must refer to the cause of separation vaguely stated in lines 11–14a, the source of the lord's (husband's) state of mind described in lines 19–20.

16. **Heht mec mon**: At line 15 the subject of **het** (= **heht**) is **hlaford min**. Here, however, **mon** is probably not to be construed as **mon(n)** (that is, the speaker's **hlaford**), but as the indefinite pronoun: *One commanded me*, or simply *I was commanded*. Such a shift from specific to indefinite subject may be part of the progressive impersonality and abstraction of the speaker's tone.

17. The terms of lines 27–32 indicate that the speaker's dwelling, her enforced exile hall (**eorðsele**), is a cave or series of caves. It is likely, however, that for the poet the physical details of "place" were intended not so much as a description as an expression, a suggestion, of utter privation and desolation; the woman in the state of separation is depicted as an exile, a **wineleas wræcca** (10), and her abode is the proper setting for an exile, a **wic wynna leas** (32).

These lines contain contrasts and inversions: her hall (**-sele**) is of earth and old; its protective fortifications (**burgtunas**: hills and dales, **dena ... duna**) are overgrown with briars. A very similar set of propositions and inversions (embedded in equally terse statement) appears in the magnificent antithesis in *The Wanderer*, lines 32–33: **Warað hine wræclast, nales wunden gold,/ferðloca freorig, nalæs foldan blæd**.

18. **Frynd sind on eorþan**: Cp. lines 16–17a; **on eorþan** seems to have idiomatic force, perhaps to be rendered "alive," and hence related to **lifgende** in line 34. By contrast to the **frynd** (? *lovers*), who **leger weardiað** (**on uhtan** understood), the condition of the speaker (**on uhtan ana**, with **uhtceare** [7]), residing in a desolate "hall" devoid of the companionship of men and women, is as though one of death.

19. **sittan**] MS **sittam**, the error probably induced by **mot**, which follows.

20. **sumorlangne dæg**: idiomatically, "a long day." The expression is reinforced

þær ic wepan mæg　　　mine wræcsiþas,
earfoþa fela.　　Forþon ic æfre ne mæg
40　þære modceare　　　minre gerestan,
　　ne ealles þæs longaþes　　　þe mec on þissum life begeat.[21]
　　A scyle geong mon　　　wesan geomormod,
　　heard heortan geþoht;　　　swylce habban sceal
　　bliþe gebæro,　　　eac þon breostceare,
45　sinsorgna gedreag.　　　Sy æt him sylfum gelong
　　eal his worulde wyn,　　　sy ful wide fah
　　feorres folclondes[22]　　　— þæs[23] min freond siteð
　　under stanhliþe,　　　storme behrimed,
　　wine werigmod　　　wætre beflowen
50　on dreorsele.[24]　　　Dreogeð se min wine

---

by **ic æfre ne mæg . . . gerestan** in lines 39–40. Cp. *Juliana*, lines 494–497: **Ic asecgan ne mæg,/þeah ic gesitte sumerlongne dæg,/eal þa earfeþu þe ic ær ond siþ/ gefremede to facne**. Cp. *The Meters of Boethius*, 4.18–21, where **sumurlange dagas** has a more literal sense.

21. This long line (41) is a kind of incremented restatement of lines 32b–33a.

22. The syntax and meaning of lines 42–47 have been interpreted in several different ways; for a brief review see Leslie's note in his edition (pp. 57–58). Syntactically, the constructions **A scyle . . . habban sceal** indicate a gnomic application or generalization, and the two **sy** constructions, as imperatives or subjunctives (third-person singular), are most likely part of the gnomic statement.

From her own experience of suffering, the speaker seems to conclude that it is the lot of any person (**geong mon**) to be sad-minded and oppressed with woes, but that he should also be resolute (**heard heortan geþoht**) and of cheerful mien (**bliþe gebæro**). The **sy** phrases, like the phrases preceding, appear to represent opposites: the joys of his world may belong to (or, be dependent upon) himself, or he may be cast as an exile (and hence deprived of joys) into a far land. By **geong mon** the speaker may mean simply one who has yet to be tested as she and her **freond** have been tested (see **geong** in BTD).

23. **þæs**] MS **þæt**. Most editors retain **þæt**, but with labored, often uncertain, explanations. If the subject of the preceding **sy** phrase (line 46) is, as suggested above, the generic **geong mon**, then the adverbial conjunction **þæs**, *in respect of which, so* (cp. *Elene*, line 210; *Phoenix*, lines 409, 472; *Christ*, lines 829, 1360), provides a clear transition from the gnomic reflection on the general situation of (**geong**) men to the particular illustration of the woman's **freond**, whose miseries complement and compound her own.

24. The details of description in lines 48–50a, as similarly suggested in note 17 to lines 27–32, are more figurative than literal in what they mean poetically. The situation of the woman's **freond**, separated from her, is a projection of her own: he sits

micle modceare — he gemon to oft
wynlicran wic. Wa bið þam þe sceal
of langoþe[25] leofes abidan.

---

under a **stanhliþe** as she sits under an **actreo** (36); his hall is a **dreorsele** as hers is an **eald eorðsele** (29); he sits **storme behrimed** as her **burgtunas** are **brerum be-weaxne** (31); in contrast to the **wic wynna leas** (32) he remembers, as she remembers, a **wynlicran wic**.

25. **langoþe**: Notice how this word and its related verb, **(of)longian**, recur, almost as a refrain, throughout the poem (lines 14, 29, 41, 53).

WULFSTAN: *De falsis Diis*[1]

Bodleian MS Hatton 113, folios 58ᵛ–61. Previous editions: Arthur Napier, ed., *Wulfstan* (Berlin, 1883), pp. 104–107 (no. 18); Dorothy Bethurum, ed., *The Homilies of Wulfstan* (Oxford, 1957), pp. 221–224 (no. 12).

This homily is based on an excerpt Wulfstan took from a longer homily of the same subject by Ælfric; he. rewrote the part he borrowed. For a description of the changes made by Wulfstan and of the medieval background of the topic and references within it, see Professor Bethurum's excellent notes to her edition, pages 333–339, and also the discussion of Wulfstan's style in her Introduction, pages 87–98. Ælfric's *De falsis Diis* has been edited, with full apparatus and explanatory notes, by John C. Pope in *Homilies of Ælfric: A Supplementary Collection*, vol. II, pp. 676 ff., and Notes, pp. 713 ff.

Although Germanic and Scandinavian heathen beliefs and practices continued to have an influence in England during and beyond Wulfstan's time, his treatment of the origin of classical deities and their Scandinavian counterparts is here explicative rather than exhortative. The homily altogether lacks the emotional energy and elaborate rhetoric of Wulfstan's best known but least typical work,

---

1. Napier: *De falsis deis*; Bethurum: *De falsis dies* (on p. 32 of her edition Professor Bethurum has *deis*).

214

Sermo ad Anglos, but it is nevertheless an interesting example of clear exposition, rational judgment, and sardonic tone.

[*Glossary symbol:* W]

Eala, gefyrn is[2] þæt ðurh deofol fela þinga misfor, and þæt mancynn to swyðe Gode mishyrde, and þæt hæðenscype ealles[3] to wide swyðe gederede and gyt dereð wide. Ne ræde we þeah ahwar on bocum þæt man aræde ænig hæðengyld[4] ahwar on worulde on eallum
5   þam fyrste þe wæs ær Noes flode. Ac syððan þæt gewearð þæt Nembroð[5] and ða entas worhton þone wundorlican stypel æfter Noes flode, and him ða swa fela gereorda gelamp, þæs þe[6] bec secgað, swa ðæra wyrhtena wæs. Þa syððan toferdon hy wide landes,[7] and mancyn þa sona swyðe weox; and ða æt nyhstan wur-
10   don hi bepæhte þurh ðone ealdan deofol, þe Adam iu ær beswac, swa þæt hi worhton wolice and gedwollice him hæþene godas, and ðone soðan God and heora agenne Scyppend forsawon, þe hy to mannum gescop and geworhte. Hi namon eac him ða þæt to wisdome þurh deofles lare,[8] þæt hy wurðedon him for godas[9] þa
15   sunnan and ðone monan for heora scinendan beorhtnesse and him lac[10] þa æt nyhstan þurh deofles lare offrodon and forleton heora Drihten, þe hy gescop and geworhte. Sume men eac sædan be ðam scinendum steorrum þæt hi godas wæron, and agunnan

2. This introductory formula is exceptional among Wulfstan's works; he usually begins a homily with the standard homiletic formula **Leofan men**.

3. **ealles**: an adverbial genitive, *in every respect, entirely*.

4. MS **h** superscript.

5. That is, Nimrod, who is referred to in *Genesis*, chapter 10. For the medieval connection of Nimrod with the Tower of Babel, see the references given by Professor Bethurum in her edition, p. 334, and cp. Milton's *Paradise Lost*, Book XII, lines 24 ff.

6. **þæs þe**: *as*.

7. **wide landes**: an idiom, *far and wide over the earth*.

8. The syntax of this clause is ambiguous; translate, *Then through the devil's teaching they also took unto themselves that as wisdom.*

9. MS **godes**.

10. **him lac**: **him** is the indirect object, *to them* [the gods]; **lac** is the direct object of **offrodon**.

hy weorðian georne; and sume hy gelyfdon eac on fyr for his
20   færlicum bryne, sume eac on wæter, and sume hy gelyfdon on
ða eorðan forðan þe heo ealle þing fedeð. Ac hy mihton georne
tocnawan, gif hi cuðon þæt gescead, þæt se is soð God þe ealle þas
ðing gescop us mannum to brice and to note for his miclan godnesse,
þe[11] he mancynne geuðe. Ðas gesceafta eac ealle doð swa swa him
25   gedihte heora agen Scyppend and ne magon nan þing don butan
ures Drihtnes þafunge, forðam þe nan oðer Scyppend nis buton se
ana soða God þe we on gelyfað, and we hine ænne ofer ealle oðre
þing lufiað and wurðiaþ mid gewissum geleafan, cweþende mid
muðe and mid modes incundnesse[12] þæt se an is soð God þe ealle
30   ðing gescop and geworhte.

Gyt ða hæþenan noldon beon gehealdene on swa feawum godum
swa hy ær hæfdan, ac fengon[13] to wurðienne æt nyhstan mistlice
entas and strece woruldmen, þe mihtige wurdan on woruldafelum
and egesfulle wæran þa hwyle þe hy leofedon, and heora agenum
35   lustum fullice fulleodan.[14] An man wæs on geardagum eardiende
on þam iglande þe Creata hatte se wæs Saturnus gehaten, and se
wæs swa wælhreow þæt he fordyde his agene bearn ealle butan
anum and unfæderlice macode heora lif to lyre sona on geogoðe.[15]
He læfde swaþeah uneaðe ænne to life, þeah ðe he fordyde þa
40   broðra elles, and se wæs Iouis gehaten and se wearð hetol feond.
He aflymde his agene fæder eft of ðam ylcan foresædan iglande
þe Creta hatte, and wolde hine forfaran georne gif he mihte. And
se Iouis wearð swa swyðe gal þæt he on his agenre swyster gewifode, seo wæs genamod Iuno, and heo wearð swyðe healic gyden
45   æfter hæðenscype geteald. Heora twa dohtra wæron Minerua and

11. **þe**, the relative particle, refers back to **ealle þas ðing**.
12. MS **incunnesse**.
13. MS **fenge**.
14. The explanation of the origin of the gods here, and throughout the homily,
is known as euhemerism (the belief that mythological gods are derived from the
deification of mortals). For the medieval background of euhemeristic interpretation see the note in Professor Bethurum's edition, p. 335.
15. **macode heora lif . . .**: a periphrastic way of saying 'he killed them in their
youth'; Professor Bethurum points out (p. 336) the corresponding, blunt statement
in Ælfric's homily: **macode heora flæsc him to mete**.

Uenus. Þas manfullan men þe we ymbe specað wæron getealde
for ða mærostan godas þa on ðam dagum, and þa hæðenan wurðodon hy swyðe þurh deofles lare; ac se sunu wæs swaþeah swyðor
on hæðenscype gewurðod þonne se fæder wære, and he is geteald
0 eac arwurðost ealra þæra goda þe þa hæðenan on ðam dagum for
godas hæfdon on heora gedwylde. And he hatte Þor oðrum naman
betwux sumum þeodum; ðone Denisca leoda lufiað swyðost and
on heora gedwylde weorðiaþ geornost. His sunu hatte Mars, se
macode æfre gewinn and wrohte, and saca and wraca he styrede
5 gelome. Ðysne yrming æfter his forðsiðe wurðodon þa hæðenan
eac for healicne god, and swa oft swa hy fyrdedon oððe to gefeohte
woldon þonne offrodon hy heora lac on ær[16] to weorðunge þissum
gedwolgode. And hy gelyfdon þæt he miclum mihte heom fultumian on gefeohte, forðan þe he gefeoht and gewinn lufude on
0 life. Sum man eac wæs gehaten Mercurius on life, se wæs swyðe
facenfull and ðeah full snotorwyrde swicol on dædum and on leas-
bregdum. Ðone macedon þa hæðenan be heora getæle eac heom
to mæran gode,[17] and æt wega gelætum[18] him lac offrodon oft and
gelome þurh deofles lare, and to heagum beorgum him brohton
5 oft mistlice loflac. Ðes gedwolgod wæs arwurðe eac betwux eallum
hæðenum on þam dagum, and he is Oðon gehaten oðrum naman
on Denisce wisan. Nu secgað sume þa Denisce men on heora
gedwylde þæt se Iouis wære þe hy Þor hatað, Mercuries sunu,
þe hi Oðon namiað, ac hi nabbað na riht, forðan þe we rædað
0 on bocum, ge on hæþenum ge on Cristenum, þæt se hetula Iouis
to soðan[19] is Saturnes sunu. And sum wif hatte Uenus, seo wæs
Ioues dohtor, and seo wæs swa ful and swa fracod on galnysse
þæt hyre agen broðor wið hy gehæmde, þæs se man sæde, þurh
deofles lare, and ða yfelan wurðiað þa hæðenan eac for healice
75 fæmnan.

Manege eac oðre hæþene godas wæron mistlice fundene and

---

16. **on ær**: an adverbial phrase, *before, formerly.*

17. Translate: *According to their reckoning the heathens made him* [**Ðone** = *Mercurius*] *also (as) a famous god for themselves.*

18. **æt wega gelætum**: *at the meetings of ways, at the crossroads.*

19. **to soðan**: *in truth.*

eac swylce hæþene gydena on swyðlicum wyrðmente geond
middaneard mancynne to forwyrde, ac þas synd þa fyrmestan ðeh
þurh hæðenscipe getealde, þeah ðe hy fulice leofodon on worulde.

80 And se syrwienda deofol þe a swicað embe mancyn gebrohte þa
hæðenan men on þam healicon gedwylde, þæt hi swa fule him to
godum gecuran, þe heora fulan lust heom to lage sylfum gesettan
and on unclænnesse heora lif eal lyfedan þa hwile ðe hi wæran.[20]
Ac se bið gesælig þe eal swylc oferhogað and ðone soðan Godd

85 lufað and weorðað, þe ealle þing gescop and geworhte. An is ælmihtig God on þrym hadum, þæt is Fæder and Suna and Halig Gast.
Ealle þa ðry naman befehð an godcund miht and is an ece God,
Waldend and Wyrhta ealra gesceafta. Him symle sy lof and weorð-
mynt in ealra worulda woruld[21] a butan ende. Amen.

---

20. Professor Bethurum (her edition, p. 339) translates this complex sentence as
follows; *And the scheming devil who is ever plotting against mankind brought the heathen
people into such egregious folly that they chose for gods men so corrupt that they established
their own foul lust as a law for themselves and lived in uncleanness their whole life.*

21. **in ealra worulda woruld**: that is, *in saeculum saeculi.*

VAINGLORY

The Exeter Book, folios 83ʳ–84ᵛ. Previous edition: G. P. Krapp and E. V. K. Dobbie, eds., *The Exeter Book* (New York, 1936), pp. 147–149.

Vainglory belongs to a group of Old English religious poems which are explicitly didactic, but it is structurally far more formally homiletic, and in its diction and imagery more poetic, than most of them. Probably the closest analogue to the poem in the literature, both prose and poetry, is Hrothgar's long homiletic speech in *Beowulf*, lines 1700–1784.

Just as later English writers made use of the tavern as a scene of temptation and vice, the *Vainglory* poet introduces the feast as the setting for his exemplum of the vainglorious man. The feast, with its boisterous boasts of prowess, is set forth in battle terms (**Breah-tem stigeð,/cirm on corþre**; cp. *Genesis A* lines 2408–2418), and the arrogant man is figuratively depicted as a warrior who lets fly missiles of malice (**hygegar leteð,/scurum sceoteþ**) at others and is himself the target of the devil's arrows (**læteð inwitflan/brecan þone burgweal**). Because of its reverberations of details and motifs from Old English heroic poetry and the ingenuity of its diction and imagery, this introductory scene (lines 13–44a) may be considered the high point of the poem.

The explication (**Nu þu cunnan meaht....**) which follows balances the individualized exemplum with the exemplum of the fallen angels, and provides a contrast to the vainglorious man

219

by means of a description of the humble man (**Ðonne biõ þam oþrum ungelice...**) which includes its own, brief explication (**Wite þe be þissum...**). The concluding exhortation is in the form of a long, Ciceronian-like sentence, suspending to the very end its most important word, **Waldend**. Whereas the structure of *Vainglory* is defined and controlled by its homiletic pattern, the artistry of the poem as a whole is sustained by verbal and phrasal associations and symmetries (e.g., the recurrence of **bearn**, **wil(-)**, **(un)gelic(e)**, **sella(n)**, **lætan**, and **(a)stigan**). For a recent discussion of *Vainglory*, see B. F. Huppé, *The Web of Words* (Albany, 1970), pp. 8–26.

[*Glossary symbol: V*]

    Hwæt, me frod wita   on fyrndagum
    sægde, snottor ar,   sundorwundra fela.
    Wordhord onwreah[1]   witgan larum
    beorn boca gleaw,   bodan ærcwide,[2]
5 þæt ic soðlice   siþþan meahte
    ongitan bi þam gealdre   Godes agen bearn,
    wilgest[3] on wicum,   ond þone wacran swa some,[4]
    scyldum bescyredne,   on gescead witan.[5]
    Þæt mæg æghwylc mon   eaþe geþencan,
10 se þe hine ne læteð[6]   on þas lænan tid

1. **onwreah**] MS **onwearh**: the error probably by distant metathesis.

2. **bodan ærcwide**: Although it is possible to read **ærcwide** as instrumental or dative, the construction seems more likely to be an accusative object of **onwreah** in apposition with **wordhord**; translate: *ancient saying* (or *words*) *of the prophet*.

3. **wilgest**: For the meaning of **will**, especially in compounds (e.g. **wilboda**, **wilcuma**, **wilgedryht**), see BTD. The sense here seems to be *willing* (or *lovely*) *guest*; cp. **willum** (line 72) and **wilsum** (line 81). Notice the contrast in lines 45–46a.

4. **swa some**: a phrasal, *similarly.*

5. **on gescead witan**] MS **witon**: the phrase, *to know in distinction, to know by discrimination*, parallels **ongitan** (line 6).

6. **ne læteð**] **ne** is not in the MS, but it seems necessary; without **ne** the meaning of lines 9–12 in context would be obscure. To clarify the syntax and sense of lines 10–11, examine the slight rephrasing: **se þe hine ne læteð, modes gælsan, amyrran his gemyndum on þæs lænan tid.**

amyrran[7] his gemyndum   modes gælsan
ond on his dægrime[8]   druncen[9] to rice,
þonne monige beoð   mæþelhergendra,[10]
wlonce wigsmiþas   winburgum[11] in.

15   Sittaþ æt symble,[12] soðgied[13] wrecað,
wordum wrixlað,   witan fundiaþ
hwylc æscstede[14]   inne in ræcede
mid werum wunige,   þonne win hweteð
beornes breostsefan.   Breahtem stigeð,

20   cirm on corþre,   cwide scralletaþ[15]
missenlice.   Swa beoþ modsefan
dalum gedæled,   sindon dryhtguman
ungelice![16]   Sum on oferhygdo
þrymme þringeð[17]   — þrinteð him in innan

25   ungemedemad mod;   sindan to monige þæt!

---

7. **hine ne læteð . . . amyrran**: *does not let himself be hindered.*

8. Notice the parallel phrasing: **on þas lænan tid . . . on his dægrime**.

9. **druncen**] MS **drucen**: a noun, *drunkenness*, the object of **ne læteð**, *does not allow drunkenness into (for) rule*, or, with **weorðan** understood, *does not allow drunkenness to become too powerful.*

10. **mæþelhergendra**: sometimes emended to **-hegendra**, *council-holders*, but the MS reading, *speech-praisers* (boast-lovers) is apt here. Cp. **herigend** in BTD, Supp.

11. **winburgum**: The head-word may be **win** = *joyous* or **wīn** = *wine*; in this context the latter seems more likely. Cp. lines 18b and 41a, and in BTD the cmpds.: **winærn**, **winhus**, **winland**.

12. **wlonce wigsmiþas . . . Sittaþ æt symble**: Cp. the recomposition in lines 39–40.

13. **soðgied**: This word occurs once elsewhere, in *The Seafarer* line 1, apparently (but not certainly) with the literal sense, *true tales* (not legendary). Such a sense seems inexact in the context here, since the implication is really 'tall tales'; perhaps read 'well-known tales.'

14. **æscstede**: **stede**, m., often as a simplex and most usually as a head-word in compounds (such as **stedefæst**) means *firmness*, *steadiness*. But also as a simplex and always as a base-word in compounds, **stede** means *place*, *position*. The literal sense of **æscstede**, therefore, is probably *spear-place*, *place-of-spears*, *battlefield*. (See the **æsc**-cmpds. in BTD.) The sense in this context, however, seems to have ironic intent, since the battlefield on which these particular warriors fight is **inne in ræcede**.

15. **cwide scralletaþ**: In *The Fates (Fortunes) of Men*, line 83, it is the harper's plectrum which sounds loudly (**scralletan**).

16. **ungelice**: Cp. line 67b.

17. **þrymme þringeð**] MS **þrȳme þringe**. For the word **þrinteð**, cp. the Exeter Book, Riddle 37, line 2: **womb wæs on hindan þriþum aþrunten**.

Bið þæt æfþonca   eal gefylled
feondes fligepilum,[18]   facensearwum;
breodað he ond bælceð,   boð his sylfes
swiþor micle   þonne se sella mon.
30 Þenceð þæt his wise   welhwam þince
eal unforcuþ.   Biþ þæs oþer swice
þonne he þæs facnes   fintan sceawað.
Wrenceþ he ond blenceþ,   worn geþenceþ
hinderhoca[19];   hygegar leteð,
35 scurum sceoteþ.   He þa scylde ne wat
fæhþe gefremede;   feoþ[20] his betran
eorl fore æfstum;   læteð inwitflan
brecan þone burgweal   þe him bebead Meotud
þæt he þæt wigsteal[21]   wergan sceolde.[22]

---

18. **feondes fligepilum**: Cp. *Beowulf*, lines 1740–1746, and F. Klaeber's relevant remarks in "Die christlichen Elemente im *Beowulf*," *Anglia*, 35 (1912), 128–129. A similar reference to the devil's arrows appears in *Juliana*, lines 382–384. The *Vainglory* poet reapplies the arrow motif to the proud man in lines 34–35, then returns to the devil's arrows in lines 37–38.

19. **hinderhoca**: literally *hinder (behind)-hooks*, but the word most likely has an idiomatic sense, perhaps similar to '*backbite*'; cp. the following word, **hyge-gar**. Moreover, the word **hinder**, like the image of arrows (**fligepilum, hygegar, inwitflan**), in Old English is associated with the devil. An interesting passage occurs in Ælfric's homilies:

> He [Jesus] cwæð to þam deofle, 'Ga þu underbæc.' Deofles nama is gereht, 'Nyþer-hreosende.' Nyþer he ahreas, and underbæc he eode fram frimðe his anginnes, þa þa he wæs ascyred fram þære heofonlican blisse; on hinder he eode eft þurh Cristes to-cyme; on hinder he sceal gan on domes dæge, þonne he bið belocen on helle-witte on ecum fyre, he and ealle his gefaren; and hi næfre siþþan ut-brecan ne mæg. [*The Homilies of the Anglo-Saxon Church*: *First Part*: *Homilies of Ælfric*, ed. and trans. B. Thorpe (London, 1844), vol. I, pp. 172 and 174.]

Cp. **hinderscipe** in BTD; **niþer gebiged** in line 55 of this poem; *Guthlac A*, lines 676–677a; and *Solomon and Saturn*, lines 125b–126.

20. **feoþ**] MS **feoh**.

21. Literally, lines 37–39 mean *he allows the arrow of malice* (?or *malicious arrow*) *break the fortress wall which God entrusted to him so that he should defend that war-place*. The **burgweal**, with its appositive **wigsteal**, probably represents the proud man's own soul (or will) which has become, as he shoots barbs of hate at others, the target of the devil's barbs (**inwitflan**); a parallel to the figurative use of **burgweal** occurs

40   Siteþ symbelwlonc,   searwum læteð
     wine gewæged   word ut faran,
     þræfte þringan   þrymme gebyrmed,[23]
     æfæstum onæled,   oferhygda ful,
     niþum nearowrencum.[24]   Nu þu cunnan meaht,
45   gif þu þyslicne   þegn gemittest
     wunian in wicum.   Wite þe be þissum
     feawum forðspellum   þæt þæt biþ feondes bearn
     flæsce bifongen;   hafað fræte lif,
     grundfusne gæst   Gode orfeormne,
50   wuldorcyninge.   Þæt se witga song,
     gearowyrdig guma,   ond þæt gyd awræc:
     "Se þe[25] hine sylfne   in þa sliþnan tid[26]
     þurh oferhygda   up ahlæneð,
     ahefeð heahmodne,   se sceal hean wesan,
55   æfter neosiþum[27]   niþer gebiged
     wunian witum fæst,   wyrmum beþrungen.
     Þæt wæs geara iu   in Godes rice
     þætte mid englum   oferhygd astag,
     widmære gewin.[28]   Wroht ahofan,

in *Juliana*, lines 647–652a. Cp. again *Beowulf*, lines 1740–1746, and especially the devil's description of his device in attacking men in *Juliana*, lines 397b–409a. Notice the internal rime, **-weal**, **-steal**.

22. **sceolde**] MS **scealde**.

23. **þræfte þringan þrymme gebyrmed**: Cp. line 24. The word **gebyrmed**, similar to **þrinteð** in line 24, means *swollen*, but more specifically, *puffed up (in the process of fermentation)*. Cp. the poetic word **bolgenmod**, and **abylgnesse** in line 71. For a Biblical parallel of the vainglorious speaker of evil, cp. the Paris Psalter prose (ed. Bright and Ramsey [Boston, 1907]), Pss. XI, 2–4, XIII; for the structure of the poem as a whole Huppé (see Headnote) has noticed parallels with the Vulgate Ps. 35 and its medieval commentaries.

24. **niþum nearowrencum**: Since **niþ** elsewhere in Old English is always a noun, this construction is probably an instance of asyndetic parataxis (following the solution by Kock), *with evil, with deceitful tricks*.

25. **se þe**] MS **seþe**, with initial **e** scribally corrected from **i**.

26. Notice the interesting cluster of prepositions and prepositional affixes in lines 52–55.

27. **neosiþum**: See other **neo-** words in BTD and the cmpd. **orcnēas** at *Beowulf*, line 112; cp. **neorxenewang** in the Glossary.

28. Reference to the fall of the angels from heaven occurs frequently in Old

60　heardne heresiþ,　　heofon widledan[29];
　　forsawan hyra sellan　　þa hi to swice þohton
　　ond þrymcyning　　þeodenstoles
　　ricne beryfan,[30]　　swa hit ryht ne wæs,
　　ond þonne gesettan　　on hyra sylfra dom
65　wuldres wynlond.　　Þæt him wige forstod
　　fæder frumsceafta;　　wearð him seo feohte to grim.
　　Ðonne bið þam oþrum　　ungelice
　　se þe her on eorþan　　eaðmod leofað,
　　ond wiþ gesibbra gehwone　　simle healdeð
70　freode on folce,　　ond his feond[31] lufað
　　þeah þe he[32] him abylgnesse　　oft gefremede
　　willum in þisse worulde.　　Se mot in wuldres dream,[33]
　　in haligra hyht　　heonan astigan
　　on engla eard.　　Ne bið þam oþrum swa,
75　se þe on ofermedum　　eargum dædum
　　leofaþ in leahtrum,　　ne beoð þa lean gelic
　　mid wuldorcyning."　　Wite þe be þissum,
　　gif þu eaðmodne　　eorl gemete,
　　þegn on þeode,　　þam bið simle
80　gæst gegæderad,　　Godes agen bearn,[34]
　　wilsum in worlde,　　gif me se witega ne leag.
　　Forþon we sculon a hycgende　　hælo rædes
　　gemunan in mode　　mæla gehwylcum
　　þone selestan　　sigora Waldend. Amen.

English poetry; especially relevant here are the passages in *Genesis B*, lines 261–264, and *Juliana*, lines 422–424. The poet uses this commonplace integrally and climactically as part of his delineation of an arrogant man's course and fall.

29. **widledan**] MS **wid lædan**.

30. **þa . . . beryfan**, lines 61b–63a: *when they thought about (considered) treachery and (thought) to deprive the powerful (**ricne**) glory-King of His princely throne.*

31. **feond**] MS **freond**, perhaps induced by **fre-ode** in the same line.

32. **he**: refers to **feond**.

33. **in wuldres dream**] **in** is not in the MS, but it seems required both syntactically and semantically.

34. **Wite . . . bearn**, lines 77b–80: Cp. lines 44b–47.

Of the Phoenix

British Museum MS Cotton Vespasian D. XIV (MS V), folios 166ʳ–168ʳ, with readings from Corpus Christi College, Cambridge MS 198 (MS C), folios 374ᵛ–377ʳ. Previous editions: (MSS C and V) F. Kluge, ed., "Zum Phönix," *Englische Studien*, VIII (1885), 474–79; (MS V) R. D.-N. Warner, ed., *Early English Homilies*, E.E.T.S., O.S., 152 (London, 1917), pp. 146–48; (MS C) A. S. Cook, ed., *The Old English Elene, Phoenix, and Physiologus* (New Haven, 1919), pp. 128–131; (MS V) N. F. Blake, ed., *The Phoenix* (Manchester, 1964), pp. 94–96.

The ancient myth of the Phoenix, early allegorized in Christian tradition (as in the *Physiologus*) and widespread among medieval writers (such as Ambrose), had two extended forms in Old English: (1) The Exeter Book poem *The Phoenix*, the first part (lines 1–380) of which is a free paraphrase of the *Carmen de ave phoenice* attributed to Lactantius and the second part (lines 381–end) a poetic commentary on the Christian allegory; and (2) the rhythmical prose homily edited here.

Compared with the text of the Phoenix homily in MS V, the text in MS C is slightly longer because of the inclusion of more didactic matter, its syntax is occasionally clearer, and its orthography is more consistent; in content, and for the most part in style, the two texts are approximately identical. Given the similarity of the two texts, a choice on substantive grounds of a preferred text would be difficult apart from the fact that MS C is the earliest of the two. The version in MS V is given here because the scribal form of its language illustrates some of the symptoms of transition between late Old English and early Middle English (the approximate date of MS V is the middle of the twelfth century): e.g., inflectional reduction and generalization to zero /-**e**/**en**, -**eð**/-**et**; syllabic contraction (as in **wurlde**); **æi/ei** before palatal **g** (as in **reign**, **dæig**); **æ** for **e** (**ængel**); **e** for **ea** (as **heh**, **geseh**); **y** for **i** (**synden**) and **i** for **y** (**-cinn**); **þone** sporadically for **þonne**, etc. For discussion of the onset of Middle English, see K. Malone, "When Did Middle English Begin?" *Curme Volume, Language Monographs* No. 7 (1930), pp. 110–17; R. Derolez, "Periodisering en Continuïteit of: 'When Did Middle English Begin?'" *Album Edgard Blancquaert* (Tongeren, 1958), pp. 77–84; and A. H. Marckwardt, "Verb Inflections in Late Old English," *Philologica* (Baltimore, 1949), pp. 79–88. For another, poetic, text showing similar transitional features, see "Instructions for Christians," ed. J. L. Rosier, in *Anglia*, 82 (1964), 4–22; 84 (1966), 74.

The dominance of alliteration and the frequency of rhythmical (or metrical) phrases and patterns of phrases suggest a close affinity between the style of this homily and Ælfric's style. Both Kluge and Cook printed the text partially in prose, partially in metrical lines; an illustration from Kluge's print of MS C (lines 18–22) follows:

Sunne þær scineð seofanfealdlucor and beorhtlicor ðone her deð. Ðær wuniaþ on Godes ænglas unrim mid þam halgum saulum oþ Domæsdæg. Ðær wunað on

an fæger fugol,   Fenix haten;
he is mycel and mære,   swa se Ælmihtiga hine sceop.

(Abbreviations in notes: MS C and MS V, explained in the head-note above; *Ph.* = The Exeter Book poem *The Phoenix*; *Carmen* = *Carmen de ave phoenice*, the text of which follows the homily.)

[*Glossary symbol:* P]

Sanctus Johannes geseh ofer garseg swylc hit an land wære.[1]
Þa genam hine se ængel and gebrohte hine to neorxenewange.[2]
Neorxenewange nis naðer ne on heofene ne on eorðe. Seo boc
sægð þæt Noes flod wæs feowrtig fedmen heh ofer þa hegesta
dunen þe on middenearde synden, and neorxenewang is feowrtig
fedme herre þone Noes flod wæs. And hit hangeð betwonen
heofonen and eorðen wunderlice, swa hit se Eallwealdend gescop.
And hit is eall efenlang and efenbrad. Nis þære naðer ne dene ne
dune. Ne þære ne byð ne forst, ne snaw, ne hagel, ne reign. Ac
þær is Fons Uite, þæt is lifes welle. Þonne Kalendas Januarii inn
gað þonne flowð seo welle swa fægere and swa smoltlice, and na
deoppere þone mann mæig gewæten his finger on forewarde[3]
ofer eall þæt land. And swa gelice[4] ælce monðe, ane siðe þonne[5] se
monð inn cumð, seo welle onginð flowen. And þær is se fægere
wudeholt, þe is genemmed Radionsaltus. Þær is ælc treow swa
riht swa bolt[6] and swa heh þæt nan eorðlic mann ne geseh swa heh,[7]
ne seggen ne cann hwilces cynnes heo synden. Ne fealleð þær
næfre leaf of, ac heo byð singrene, wlitig and wynsum, welena
unrim. Neorxenewange is upprihte on eastewearde[8] þisse wurlde.
Nis þær ne hete ne hunger, ne þær niht nefre ne byð, ac simble
dæig. Sunne þær scineð seofen siðe brihtlycor þone on þissen earde.
Þær wuneð on[9] Godes ængles unrim mid þan halgen sawlen oðð
domes dæig.

1. **hit an land wære**: so MS C, **hit land wære**; by **land** is probably meant *island*,
as *Ph.*, line 9: **Ænlic is þæt iglond**.

2. **neorxenewange**: The Old English term for Paradise; in connection with
Latin texts the word glosses both *paradisus* and *eliseum*. The word is recorded in
more than fifteen different forms, and these in turn have given rise to about as
many explanations of its etymology, the most recent of which is H. D. Meritt, *Some
of the Hardest Glosses in Old English* (Stanford, 1968), pp. 78–80.

3. **on forewarde**: *on the tip* (of the finger).

4. **swa gelice**: a phrasal, *similarly*.

5. **ane siðe þonne**: a phrasal idiom, *as soon as*, *once*.

6. **saw riht swa bolt**: literally, *as straight as a bolt*; freely, 'bolt upright,' 'as straight
as an arrow.' Cp. Chaucer's 'upright as a bolt,' in *The Canterbury Tales*, A3264.

7. **geseh swa heh**: *has seen so high* (?or, *as high* [a tree]); MS C **geseon meahte**.

8. **upprihte on eastewearde**: *straight up* (directly overhead) *in the East*.

9. **wuneð on**: The construction **wunian on** is normally followed by an object in
the dative, but here it is apparently a phrasal, *dwells*; cp. **onwunian** in BTD.

Þær wuneð on[9] an fugel fæger, Fenix gehaten: he is mycel and
25 mære swa se Mihtige hine gescop. He is hlaford ofer eall fugel-
cynn. Ælcere wuca ane siðe[10] se fægere fugel hine baðeð on þære
lifes welle; and þonne flihð se fugel, and gesett uppe þæt hegeste
trow ongean þære haten sunne. Þonne scinð he swa sunneleome,
and he gliteneð swilc he gyldene seo. His feðeren synden ængles
30 feðeren gelice. His breost and bile brihte scineð fægere and fage —
feawe synden swylce. Hwat! his eagene twa æðele synden swa
clæne swa cristal and swa scire swa suneleome. His fet synden
blodreade begen and se bile hwit. Hwæt! se fægre fugel flihð of
his earde, se þe is fægere Fenix gehaten. Þonne wuneð he witod-
35 lice on Egiptelande fiftene wucan feste togædere.[11] Þonne cumeð
him to, swaswa to[12] heora kinge, fageninde swyðe eall þæt fugelcinn; and fægere gegreteð ealle Fenix, writigeð and singeð ealle
abuten him. Ælc on his wisen, ealle hine herigeð. Þonne ferð
þæt folc feorrene, swyðe wafigeð and wundrigeð, wylcumigeð
40 Fenix: "Hal beo þu, Fenix, fugele fægerest. Feorren þu come.
Þu glitenest swa read gold, ealra fugela king, Fenix gehaten."
Þonne wyreceð heo of wexe and writeð Fenix, and meteð hine
fægere þær se madme stant.[13] Þonne fagenegeð þære fugeles
ealle fægere and fage; feale togædere fealleð to foten, Fenix
45 greteð. His stemne is swa briht swa beme, and his sweora swylce

---

10. **Ælcere wuca ane siðe**: *once each week.*
11. **feste togædere**: MS C **fæste ætgædere**; freely, *continuously.*
12. **swaswa to**] MS V **swaswa to to**; MS C **swylce hi cyning wære.**
13. Cp. *Ph.*, lines 331–335:

> Ðonne wundriað   weras ofer eorþan
> wlite ond wæstma,   ond gewritum cyþað,
> mundum mearciað   on marmstane,
> hwonne se dæg ond seo tid   dryhtum geeawe
> frætwe flyhthwates,

and *Carmen*, lines 153–54:

> protinus exsculpunt sacrato in marmore formam
> et titulo signant remque diemque nouo.

MS C omits any reference to **madme: metað Fenix and hine mærlice þær wordum
heriað, fugela fægerest Fenix haten.**

smete gold; and his forebreost fægere geheowed swylce marmelstan mæres cinnes.[14] And him on read heow rudeð on þan hrycge.[15]
Goldfelle gelic gliteneð Fenix.

Þonne færð eft se fugel fægere to his earde emb fiftene wucan,
and fugeles manige ealle him abuten efne ferden ufene and nyðene,
and on ælce healfe oððet heo nehiget neorxenewange. Þær inn
gefærð Fenix fugele fægerest, and eall oðer fugelcinn to heora
earden gewændeð. Nu sæigð her Sanctus Johannes soðen worden,
swa se wyrhte cann, þæt æfre binnen an þusend wintren[16] þynceð
Fenix þæt he forealdod seo, gegadered togædere ofer eall Paradis
þa deorwurðe boges and heapeð tosamne. And þurh Godes mihte
and þære sunneleome se heap byð onæled.[17] And þonne fealleð
Fenix on middan þæt micele fyr and wurð forbærned eall to duste.
Þonne on þan þriddan dæge ariseð se fægere fugel Fenix of deaðe
and byð eft edgung and færð to þære lifes welle and baðað hine
þærinne. And him wexeð on feðeren swa fægere swa heo æfre
fægerest wæren. Þuss he deð æfre binne þusend wintren—he
hine forbærnð and eft edgung uppariseð. And næfð he nænne
gemaca, and nan mann ne wat hweðer hit is þe karlfugel þe
cwenefugel bute God ane.[18] Þes halge fugel is Fenix gehaten,
wlitig and wynsum, swa hine God gescop. And þuss he sceal drigen
Drihtenes wille, se þe is on heofone heh and halig, ealra kinge

---

14. **marmelstan mæres cinnes**: *marble of an excellent kind*; MS C **mærost cynnes**.

15. **hrycge**] MS V **hrynge**; MS C **ricge**.

16. MS C: **Nu sagað her Sanctus Johannes soðum wordum, wislice and wærlice, swa se wertacen, þæt six þusend her on worolde Crist forestihte, ðone æfre embe an þusend geara farað Fenix, se fægra fugel, wlitig and wundorlic.**

17. MS C: **and þurh Godes mihte se hate sunne scineþ, and þurh þara sunnan hatnesse and hire lioman se heap wyrðeþ onæled.**

18. Cp. *Ph.*, lines 355–360:

> God ana wat,
> Cyning ælmihtig,   hu his gecynde bið,
> wifhades þe weres;   þæt ne wat ænig
> monna cynnes,   butan Meotod ana,
> hu þa wisan sind   wundorlice,
> fæger fyrngesceap,   ymb þæs fugles gebyrd.

King. Crist us generige þæt we on wynne wunigen mote mid þan
þe leofeð and rixeð a bute ænde.[19] Amen.

Annex:
Lactantius: Carmen de ave phoenice[1]

Est locus in primo felix oriente remotus,
  qua patet aeterni maxima porta poli.
nec tamen aestiuos hiemisue propinquus ad ortus
  sed qua sol uerno fundit ab axe diem.
illic planities tractus diffundit apertos,   5
  nec tumulus crescit nec caua uallis hiat,
sed nostros montis, quorum iuga celsa putantur,
  per bis sex ulnas imminet ille locus.
hic Solis nemus est et consitus arbore multa
  lucus perpetuae frondis honore uirens.   1
cum Phaethonteis flagrasset ab ignibus axis,
  ille locus flammis inuiolatus erat;
et cum diluuium mersisset fluctibus orbem
  Deucalioneas exsuperauit aquas.
non huc exsangues Morbi, non aegra Senectus   1
  nec Mors crudelis nec Metus asper adest,
nec Scelus infandum nec opum uesana Cupido
  aut Sitis aut ardens caedis amore Furor;

---

19. The conclusion in MS C is expanded:
    Nu is us andgyt forgyfen, mancenne: Fugelas heriaþ Crist. Nu gedafenað us
    þæt we herian urne Drihten mid ælmæssan and mid halgunge bedum and mid
    eallum þingum; þæt [we] witon þæt Gode leof is and gescildan us wiþ ða eahta
    heahsynna þæt we þa ne fremman: þæt is morþor and stala, mane aþas and
    unrihtgitsunge and unrihthæmedu and gifernesse, leasunga and attorcræftas
    dyrneligera, and twispæce and ofermodignæss. Beorgan we us wiþ ealle þas
    heahsynna and lufian urne Drihten mid eallum mægene and mid eallum mode.
    Se God þe leofað and rixaþ, se ðe on heofonum is heah and halig, ealra cyn-
    inga Cyning. Crist us generie þæt we on wynne wunian moton, se ðe leofað
    and rixað soðlice mid Fæder and Sunu and mid þam Halgan Gaste a buton
    ænde. Amen.
    1. From H. W. Garrod, ed., *The Oxford Book of Latin Verse* (Oxford: 1912), pp.
362, 367.

Luctus acerbus abest et Egestas obsita pannis
    et Curae insomnes et uiolenta Fames.   20
non ibi tempestas nec uis furit horrida uenti
    nec gelido terram rore pruina tegit;
nulla super campos tendit sua uellera nubes
    nec cadit ex alto turbidus umor aquae.
est fons in medio, quem uiuum nomine dicunt,   25
    perspicuus, lenis, dulcibus uber aquis;
qui semel erumpens per singula tempora mensum
    duodecies undis inrigat omne nemus.
hic genus arboreum procero stipite surgens
    non lapsura solo mitia poma gerit.   30
hoc nemus, hos lucos auis incolit unica Phoenix,
    unica si uiuit morte refecta sua.
paret et obsequitur Phoebo ueneranda satelles:
    hoc Natura parens munus habere dedit.
lutea cum primum surgens Aurora rubescit,   35
    cum primum rosea sidera luce fugat,
ter quater illa pias inmergit corpus in undas,
    ter quater e uiuo gurgite libat aquam.
tollitur ac summo considit in arboris altae
    uertice, quae totum despicit una nemus,   40
et conuersa nouos Phoebi nascentis ad ortus
    exspectat radios et iubar exoriens.
atque ubi Sol pepulit fulgentis limina portae
    et primi emicuit luminis aura leuis,
incipit illa sacri modulamina fundere cantus   45
    et mira lucem uoce ciere nouam;
quam nec aedoniae uoces nec tibia possit
    musica Cirrhaeis adsimulare modis,
et neque olor moriens imitari posse putetur
    nec Cylleneae fila canora lyrae.   50
postquam Phoebus equos in aperta effudit Olympi
    atque orbem totum protulit usque means,
illa ter alarum repetito uerbere plaudit
    igniferumque caput ter uenerata silet.

atque eadem celeris etiam discriminat horas   55
    innarrabilibus nocte dieque sonis,
antistes luci nemorumque uerenda sacerdos
    et sola arcanis conscia, Phoebe, tuis.
quae postquam uitae iam mille peregerit annos
    ac si reddiderint tempora longa grauem,   60
ut reparet lapsum spatiis uergentibus aeuum,
    adsuetum nemoris dulce cubile fugit;
cumque renascendi studio loca sancta reliquit,
    tunc petit hunc orbem, mors ubi regna tenet.
derigit in Syriam celeris longaeua uolatus,   65
    Phoenicen nomen cui dedit ipsa uetus,
secretosque petit deserta per auia lucos,
    sicubi per saltus silua remota latet.
tum legit aerio sublimem uertice palmam,
    quae Graium Phoenix ex aue nomen habet,   70
in quam nulla nocens animans prorepere possit,
    lubricus aut serpens aut auis ulla rapax.
tum uentos claudit pendentibus Aeolus antris,
    ne uiolent flabris aera purpureum,
neu concreta noto nubes per inania caeli   75
    submoueat radios solis et obsit aui.
construit inde sibi seu nidum siue sepulcrum:
    nam perit ut uiuat, se tamen ipsa creat.
colligit hinc sucos et odores diuite silua,
    quos legit Assyrius, quos opulentus Araps,   80
quos aut Pygmaeae gentes aut India carpit
    aut molli generat terra Sabaea sinu.
cinnamon hic auramque procul spirantis amomi
    congerit et mixto balsama cum polio.
non casiae mitis nec olens suffimen acanthi   85
    nec turis lacrimae guttaque pinguis abest.
his addit teneras nardi pubentis aristas
    et sociat myrrae uim, Nabathaea, tuae.
protinus instructo corpus mutabile nido
    uitalique toro membra uieta locat.   90

ore dehinc sucos membris circumque supraque
    inicit exsequiis inmoritura suis.
tunc inter uarios animam commendat odores,
    depositi tanti nec timet illa fidem.
interea corpus genitali morte peremptum   95
    aestuat, et flammam parturit ipse calor,
aetherioque procul de lumine concipit ignem,
    flagrat et ambustum soluitur in cineres.
quos uelut in massam generans in morte coactos
    conflat; et effectum seminis instar habet.   100
complerit mensum si fetus tempora certa,
    sese oui teretis colligit in speciem;
hinc animal primum sine membris fertur oriri,
    sed fertur uermi lacteus esse color:
ac uelut agrestes, cum filo ad saxa tenentur,   105
    mutari tineae papilione solent:
inde reformatur quali fuit ante figura
    et Phoenix ruptis pullulat exuuiis.
non illi cibus est nostro concessus in orbe
    nec cuiquam inplumem pascere cura subest;   110
ambrosios libat caelesti nectare rores,
    stellifero tenues qui cecidere polo.
hos legit, his alitur mediis in odoribus ales,
    donec maturam proferat effigiem.
ast ubi primaeua coepit florere iuuenta,   115
    euolat ad patrias iam reditura domus.
ante tamen, proprio quicquid de corpore restat,
    ossaque uel cineres exuuiasque suas
unguine balsameo myrraque et ture soluto
    condit et in formam conglobat ore pio.   120
quam pedibus gestans contendit Solis ad urbem
    inque ara residens ponit in aede sacra.
mirandam sese praestat praebetque uerendam:
    tantus aui decor est, tantus abundat honor.
praecipuus color est, quali sunt sidera caeli,   125
    praecoqua uel qualis Punica grana tegit:

qualis inest foliis, quae fert agreste papauer,
    cum pandit uestes Flora rubente solo.
hoc humeri pectusque decens uelamine fulgent,
    hoc caput, hoc ceruix summaque terga nitent;   130
caudaque porrigitur fuluo distincta metallo,
    in cuius maculis purpura mixta rubet;
aura auri pennas insignit, desuper Iris
    pingere ceu nubis splendida rore solet;
albicat insignis mixto uiridante smaragdo   135
    et puro cornu gemmea cuspis hiat;
ingentis oculos credas geminos hyacinthos
    quorum de medio lucida flamma micat;
arquata est rutilo capiti radiata corona
    Phoebei referens uerticis alta decus;   140
crura tegunt squamae Tyrio depicta ueneno,
    ast unguis roseo tinguit honore color.
effigies inter pauonis mixta figuram
    cernitur et pictam Phasidis inter auem.
magnitiem, terris Arabum quae gignitur, ales   145
    uix aequare potest, seu fera seu sit auis.
non tamen est tarda, ut uolucres quae corpore magno
    incessus pigros per graue pondus habent,
sed leuis ac uelox, regali plena decore;
    talis in aspectu se tenet usque hominum.   150
huc uenit Aegyptus tanti ad miracula uisus
    et raram uolucrem turba salutat ouans.
protinus exsculpunt sacrato in marmore formam
    et titulo signant remque diemque nouo.
contrahit in coetum sese genus omne uolantum,   155
    nec praedae memor est ulla nec ulla metus.
alituum stipata choro uolat illa per altum
    turbaque prosequitur munere laeta pio.
sed postquam puri peruenit ad aetheris auras,
    mox redit; illa suis conditur inde locis.   160
o fortunatae sortis finisque uolucrem,
    cui de se nasci praestitit ipse deus!

o felix, seu mas seu femina siue necutrum,
    felix quae Veneris foedera nulla coit!
mors illi Venus est, sola est in morte uoluptas: 165
    ut possit nasci, appetit ante mori.
ipsa sibi proles, suus est pater et suus heres,
    nutrix ipsa sui, semper alumna sibi.
ipsa quidem, sed non eadem est; eademque nec ipsa est,
    aeternam uitam mortis adepta bono.   170

The Whale

The Exeter Book, folios 96ᵛ–97ᵛ. Previous editions: A. S. Cook, ed., *The Old English Elene, Phoenix, and Physiologus* (New Haven, 1919), pp. 77–80; G. P. Krapp and E. V. K. Dobbie, eds., *The Exeter Book* (New York, 1936), pp. 171–174.

The medieval Latin versions of the Greek *Physiologus* (or *Bestiary*, as it was sometimes later called) contained between twenty-six and forty-nine chapters, each devoted to a real or legendary creature together with its interpreted moral or theological significance; in Old English only three of these chapters (*The Panther*, *The Whale*, and *The Partridge*) are extant, and it is possible that these were the only parts of the *Physiologus* ever rendered into Old English.

In *The Whale*, the larger rhetorical structure of comparison (of aspects of the whale and their equations in religious terms) and the sequence of details closely follow the Latin, as may be seen by comparing the text with the two Latin versions appended to it. The poet naturalizes his model by using poetic compounds (such as **ferðgrim**, **deaðsele**, **feorgbona**, **heoloþhelm**, **mistglom**, **sæ(yð)-mear**, **mereweard**, and **herehuþ**); by focal (or immediate) and cross (or distant) variation (e.g., **fareðlacendum**, **niþþa gehwylcum** [lines 5–6], **scinna þeaw**, **deofla wise** [lines 31–32]; **wægliþende** [line 11]—**faroðlacende** [line 20]—**sæliþende** [line 48]); by lexical juxtapositions (**ealond/unlond/eglond**); and by figurative uses (e.g., **grund/fæstenne** = **deaðsele** = *hell*). In addition, both halves (the whale, the devil) of each part (the illusion of safety and the

236

descent; the tempting lure: **þurh wynsum [swetne] stenc**), and both halves of the poem as a whole, are coalesced and balanced by lexical and phrasal recomposition and repetition; for example, notice the incidence and permutations of: **(bi)fæste(-)**, **fer(h)þ(e)/ ferht-**, **(un)will(-)**, **facn(-)/fæcn(-)**, **beswican** (and **bi**-derivatives), **cræftig**, **on(-)/ on** (phrasals).

[*Glossary symbol:* Wh]

Nu ic fitte gen[1]   ymb fisca cynn
wille woðcræfte   wordum cyþan
þurh modgemynd   bi þam miclan hwale.
Se bið unwillum[2]   oft gemeted,
5 frecne ond ferðgrim   fareðlacendum,
niþþa gehwylcum;   þam[3] is noma cenned,
fyrnstreama geflotan,   Fastitocalon.[4]
Is þæs hiw gelic   hreofum stane,
swylce worie   bi wædes ofre,
10 sondbeorgum ymbseald,   særyrica mæst,[5]
swa þæt wenaþ   wægliþende
þæt hy on ealond sum   eagum wliten,[6]
ond þonne gehydað[7]   heahstefn scipu

1. **gen**: *next* (in the sequence of chapters in, or examples of, the Physiologus).
2. **unwillum**: an adverbial dative, *unwillingly*.
3. **þam**] MS þæm, with hoop of **e** in **æ** uncompleted.
4. **Fastitocalon**: This word, through several stages of transformation, represents Greek 'ασπιδοχελ'ωνη, Latin *aspidoceleon* (*-chelone*), *asp*, or *shield, turtle*. The Old English form of the word was probably influenced by an Irish form (*fascitocalon*) of the Latin.
5. It is likely that this clause (lines 9–10), introduced by **swylce**, is an explanation or clarification of **gelic hreofum stane**; translate, *as if a great bed of seaweed* (? *-rushes*), *encompassed by sand banks, were moving about (rising and falling) by the water's edge.* The etymology, and hence the precise meaning, of **særyrica** is unclear; cp. **earisc**, **earixe** in BTD.
6. The verb **wlitan** frequently occurs with **on**.
7. **gehydað**: Contextually, this verb must mean 'they guide' or 'they secure (fasten),' but etymologically it is unclear (? = **gehēdan**, *to guard*; **gehȳdan**, *to hide*; **hȳð**, *a harbor*, in a verb form, **gehȳðan**, *to put in harbor*). Kemp Malone (*Jespersen*

    to þam unlonde,[8]   oncyrrapum
15 sælaþ[9] sæmearas   sundes æt ende,[10]
    ond þonne in þæt eglond   up gewitað
    collenferþe.   Ceolas stondað
    bi staþe fæste,   streame[11] biwunden.
    Ðonne gewiciað   werigferðe;
20 faroðlacende   frecnes ne wenað.
    On þam ealonde   æled weccað,
    heahfyr ælað.   Hæleþ beoþ on wynnum,
    reonigmode,   ræste geliste.
    Þonne gefeleð   facnes cræftig
25 þæt him þa ferend on   fæste wuniaþ,[12]
    wic weardiað   wedres on luste,[13]
    ðonne[14] semninga   on sealtne wæg
    mid þa nowe[15]   niþer gewiteþ

heed; but this verb never occurs elsewhere in a context of ships and the contexts in which it does occur seem far removed from *to heed* (a ship). As supporting evidence, he refers to Psalm 55, line 7, of the Paris Psalter—**þæt heo gehyden hælun mine**—but this evidence is inconclusive.

8. **unlonde** reinforces the illusory aspect of **hy on ealond sum eagum wliten** (line 12). Literally the word means *non-land*, or, contextually, 'seeming land,' but notice also in BTD the sense of **un-** in such words as: **undæd, ungetimu, ungeðanc, ungifu, unlār, unlust, unlyft, unsæd, unswefn, unwidere.**

9. **sælaþ**] MS **setlaþ**. The emendation follows A. S. Cook (*The Old English Elene, Phoenix, and Physiologus* [New Haven, 1919], p. 137). Apart from the MS form in this poem there is no evidence for a verb, **setlan**; but **sælan**, *to moor* (a ship), occurs several times in the poetry, in markedly similar contexts and syntax, such as *Beowulf*, line 1917: **sælde to sande sidfæþme scip oncerbendum fæst.**

10. **sundes æt ende**: *at the end of* (their = **sæmearas**) *swimming* (or, freely, *sea-journey*).

11. **streame**] MS final **e** scribally altered from **a**.

12. The syntax is: **þa ferend wuniaþ fæste on him.**

13. **wedres on luste**: *in the pleasure of fine weather.*

14. **Ðonne** (line 24)...**ðonne** (line 27): *When . . . then*; similarly in lines 51 and 53, 71 and 76.

15. **nowe**] MS **noþe**. Most editors retain the MS reading (see Krapp and Dobbie's edition for a summary and BTD at **noþ**, p. 726.) but without substantial evidence. Syntactically we expect a noun and contextually the noun that seems apt would be a word meaning *ship, men,* or *load*. The emendation (**now** = *ship*) follows H. D. Meritt's suggestion (in *Fact and Lore* [Stanford, 1954], 2A, 47) as the most satisfying, although in Old English **now** is attested solely in a derivative form, **nowend**, and **nowend** exists only as a gloss to Latin *nauclerus*.

garsecges gæst,   grund geseceð —
30 ond þonne in deaðsele   drence[16] bifæsteð
scipu mid scealcum.   Swa bið scinna þeaw,
deofla wise,   þæt hi drohtende
þurh dyrne meaht   duguðe beswicað
ond on teosu tyhtaþ   tilra dæda;[17]
35 wemað on willan[18]   þæt hy wraþe secen
frofre to feondum,   oþþæt hy fæste ðær
æt þam wærlogan   wic[19] geceosað.
Þonne þæt gecnaweð   of cwicsusle
flah feond gemah,[20]   þætte fira gehwylc
40 hæleþa cynnes   on his hringe[21] biþ
fæste gefeged,   he him feorgbona
þurh sliþen searo   siþþan weorþeð,
wloncum ond heanum,   þe his willan her
firenum fremmað,   mid þam[22] he færinga,
45 heoloþhelme biþeaht,   helle seceð,

16. **drence**: *in* (or, *by means of*) *drowning*. **drenc** occurs once elsewhere in the poetry, in *Elene*, lines 136–137: **sume drenc fornam on lagostreame lifes æt ende.**

17. **duguðe . . . tilra dæda**: (?) *from the virtue (excellence) of good deeds.*

18. **wemað on willan**: Probably elliptic for *they* [*devils*] *persuade (tempt) them in their wills*; **on willan**: because of **geceosað** in line 37, the sense of **willa** is most likely the faculty of the will, which here is seduced by false (or apparent) goods (as the sailors are led astray by the *appearance* of an island) to make wrong choices. The function of the will is explained in the following citation from BTD (**willa**): **Ðæs mannes sawl hæfð on hire . . . gemynd and andgit and willa . . . Of ðam willan cumaþ geþohtas and word and weorc, ægðer ge yfele ge gode . . . þurh ðone willan heo wile swa hwæt swa hire licaþ.**

19. **wic**: Cp. **gewiciað** in line 19.

20. **flah feond gemah**: *the cruel (and) wicked fiend.* Cp. the similar construction in the Exeter Book *Riming Poem*, line 62: **flah mah** (or **flahmah**) **fliteþ**. In the Exeter Book poem *The Phoenix*, line 595, occurs a variant construction: **fah feond gemah.**

21. **hringe**: If this is the correct reading of the poem, the precise meaning of **hring** in context is unclear (? *fetters*, ? *orb of dominion*). Cosijn suggested **hricge**, *on his back*, which gives good sense, in cross reference to the whale and in direct reference to the devil who is often referred to in legend, and graphically depicted, as carrying off sinners on his back. However, the basic meaning of the verb **(ge)-fēgan**, *to join together, to join one thing to another*, would seem to support the MS **hringe**. For the sense of *ring* as a means of constraint, cp. the citations under **hring** (III) in BTD, Supp.

22. **mid þam**: *when.*

goda geasne,[23]   grundleasne wylm
under mistglome,   swa se micla hwæl,
se þe bisenceð   sæliþende
eorlas ond yðmearas.

                He hafað oþre gecynd,
50 wæterþisa[24] wlonc,   wrætlicran gien.
Þonne hine on holme   hungor bysgað
ond þone aglæcan   ætes lysteþ,
ðonne se mereweard   muð ontyneð,
wide weleras.   Cymeð wynsum stenc
55 of his innoþe   þætte oþre þurh þone,
sæfisca cynn,   beswicen weorðaþ;
swimmað sundhwate   þær se sweta stenc
ut gewiteð.[25]   Hi þær in farað
unware weorude[26]   oþþæt se wida ceafl
60 gefylled bið   — þonne færinga
ymbe þa herehuþe   hlemmeð togædre
grimme goman.   Swa biþ gumena gehwam,
se þe oftost his   unwærlice
on þas lænan tid   lif bisceawað;
65 læteð hine beswican[27]   þurh swetne stenc,[28]
leasne willan,[29]   þæt he biþ leahtrum fah
wið wuldorcyning.   Him se awyrgda ongean
æfter hinsiþe   helle ontyneð,
þam þe leaslice   lices wynne

---

23. **goda geasne**: *deprived of good*, modifying **he** (line 44) (= **feond**), who is in a state of privation, deprived of God.

24. **wæterþisa**: freely, *water-charger*. The same word occurs in *Guthlac B*, line 1329, in apposition with **bat** and **wæghengest** (literally, *wave-stallion*).

25. **gewiteð**] MS -að, probably induced by contiguous verbs in -að.

26. **unware weorude**: *as an unwary throng*. With **unware**, notice **beswicen** in line 56 and the following citations (under **unwær**) from BTD: **Deofol wile beswican ðone unwaran.** — **Deofol deð swyðe lytelice, ðær he ongyt unwære menn.**

27. **beswican**: With **læteð hine** the infinitive forms a passive construction, *lets himself be deceived.*

28. **þurh swetne stenc**: a parallel occurs in *The Blickling Homilies* (ed. R. Morris, E.E.T.S., O.S. 58, 63, 73 [1880], p. 55: **deofles wise bið þæt he wile symle þone unwaran man beswican þurh þa swetnesse þara synna.**

29. **leasne willan**: *deprived of will*, modifying **hine** in line 65. Cp. notes 18 and 23.

70 ofer ferhtgereaht[30]   fremedon on unræd.[31]
Þonne se fæcna   in þam fæstenne
gebroht hafað,   bealwes cræftig,
æt þam edwylme,   þa þe him on cleofiað,
gyltum gehrodene,[32]   ond ær georne his
75 in hira lifdagum   larum hyrdon,
þonne he þa grimman   goman bihlemmeð
æfter feorhcwale   fæste togædre,
helle hlinduru[33]   — nagon hwyrft ne swice,
utsiþ æfre,   þa þær in cumað,
80 þon ma[34] þe þa fiscas   faraðlacende
of þæs hwæles fenge   hweorfan motan.
Forþon is eallinga[35] . . .
dryhtna dryhtne,[36]   ond a deoflum wiðsace
wordum ond weorcum,   þæt we wuldorcyning
85 geseon moton.   Uton a sibbe[37] to him
on þas hwilnan tid   hælu secan,
þæt we mid swa leofne   in lofe motan
to widan feore   wuldres neotan.

30. **ofer ferhtgereaht**: For a summary of the interpretations of this construction, see the Krapp-Dobbie edition, p. 316. The element **ferht(-)** probably is a form of **ferhð**, *mind, spirit,* as all editors agree; cp. the attested form **ferhtlice** (*rational*). The form **(-)gereaht** can only, on the evidence of attested forms, be a preterite singular or past participle of **gereccan**. Although no cmpds are recorded with **gereccan** as a final element, the by-form **reccan** does occur in cmpds, as in **oferreccan**. Cook (in his edition, p. 138) assumes a conversion-noun, **-gereaht** (*guidance*), and among the solutions this seems to be the most tenable; following Cook, **ofer ferhtgereaht** (Cook emends to **ferhð-**) means *contrary to the guidance of mind* (or, *reason*). Cp. the similar **ofer** phrases in BTD, **ofer** II.9 (p. 730). Moreover, such a rendering is conceptually consistent with **wemað on willan** (line 35) and **leasne willan** (line 66).

31. **on unræd**: *in folly*; perhaps adverbial, *irrationally*.

32. **gyltum gehrodene** modifies **þa þe** in line 73; cp. **leahtrum fah** in line 66.

33. **hlinduru** occurs also in *Andreas*, line 993, where it refers literally to a prison door or gate. Two related cmpds, **hlinræced** (*prison*) and **hlinscua** (*shadows of prison* [or, *of hell*]), occur in *Juliana*, lines 243 and 544 respectively.

34. **þon ma**: *any more than.*

35. The MS continues with no gap, but it is clear that the scribe has left out a half line and probably at least another whole line.

36. **dryhtne**] MS **dryhtene**: medial **e** scribally underdotted, signifying deletion.

37. **sibbe** in form may be dative or the accusative object (together with **hælu**) of **secan**; the syntax suggests dative, *Let us always in peace* (or, *friendship*) *to Him.* A clearer instance occurs in *Andreas*, line 809: **secan mid sybbe swegles dreamas**.

Annex: Two Versions of the The Whale in the Latin Physiologus

B Version[1]

Est belua in mare quae dicitur graece aspidochelone, latine autem aspido testudo; cetus ergo est magnus, habens super corium suum tamquam sabulones, sicut iuxta littora maris. Haec in medio pelago eleuat dorsum suum super undas maris sursum; ita ut nauigantibus nautis non aliud credatur esse quam insula, praecipue cum uiderint totum locum illum sicut in omnibus littoribus maris sabulonibus esse repletum. Putantes autem insulam esse, applicant nauem suam iuxta eam, et descendentes figunt palos et alligant naues; deinde ut coquant sibi cibos post laborem, faciunt ibi focos super arenam quasi super terram; illa uero belua, cum senserit ardorem ignis, subito mergit se in aquam, et nauem secum trahit in profundum maris.

Sic patiuntur omnes qui increduli sunt et quicumque ignorant diaboli astutias, spem suam ponentes in eum; et operibus eius se obligantes, simul merguntur cum illo in gehennam ignis ardentis: ita astutia eius.

Secunda eius beluae natura haec est: quando esurit, aperit os suum, et quasi quemdam odorem bene olentem exhalat de ore suo; cuius oderem, mox ut senserint minores pisces, congregant se intra os ipsius; cum autem repletum fuerit os eius diuersis piscibus pusillis, subito claudit os suum et transglutit eos.

Sic patiuntur omnes qui sunt modicae fidei, voluptatibus ac lenociniis quasi quibusdam odoribus diabolicis adescati subito absorbentur ab eo sicut pisciculi minuti; maiores enim se continent ab illo et neque appropiant ei. Sic ergo qui Christum semper in sua mente habent, magni sunt apud eum; et si sunt perfecti, agnoscunt multiformes astutias diaboli, et custodiunt se ab eo et magis resistunt: ille uero fugit ab eis. Dubii autem et modicae fidei homines, dum uadunt post uoluptates et luxurias diaboli, decipiuntur;

---

1. From Francis Carmody, ed., *Physiologus Latinus* (Paris, 1939), pp. 44–45.

dicente scriptura: Unguentis et uariis odoribus delectantur, et sic confringitur a ruinis anima [Proverbs 27:9].

Y Version[2]

Phisiologus autem dixit de ceto quoddam, quod est in mari, nomine aspidoceleon uocatur, magnum nimis, simile insule, et plus quam harena grauis, figuram habens diabuli. Ignorantes autem naute, alligant ad eum naues sicut ad insulam, et anchoras et palos nauis configunt in eo; et accendunt super eum ignem ad coquendum sibi aliquid; si autem excaluerit cetus, urinat, descendens in profundum, et demergit omnes naues. —Sic et tu, o homo, si suspendas te et aligas teipsum in spe diabuli, demergit te secum simul in gehennam ignis.

Aliut naturale habet cetus: si autem esurierit, multum adaperit os suum, et omnis odor bonus per os eius procedit; odorantes autem pusilli pisciculi, secuntur eius odorem, et conponant se in ore magni ceti illius; cum autem impletum fuerit os eius, concludit os suum, et gluttit pusillos omnes illos pisciculos, hoc est modicos in fide. —Maiores autem et perfectos pisces non inuenimus adpropiare ad cetum: consummati enim sunt perfecti; etenim Paulus apostolus dixit: Non enim eius *uersutias* ignoramus [II Corinthians 2:11]. Iob perfectissimus piscis est, Moises et reliqui alii prophete; Ioseph effugiit cetum magnum, principis cocorum mulierem, sicut in Genesis scripturum est [cp. Genesis 39]; sicut et Thecla Thamyridum, sicut Susanna duos senes Babylonicos iniquos; Hester et Iudit effugerunt Artaxersen et Olofernem; tres pueri Nabuchodonosor regem, magnum cetum; et Sarra filia Raguelis Nasmodeum (sicut in Tobia). Bene ergo Phisiologus dixit de aspidoceleon ceto magno.

---

2. From Francis Carmody, ed., "Physiologus Latinus Versio Y," *University of California Publications in Classical Philology*, XII (Berkeley, 1944), 125.

Bede: CÆDMON

Bodleian MS Tanner 10, pages 596–599 (MS), with readings from Corpus Christi College, Cambridge MS 41 (MS B), Cambridge Univ. Lib. MS Kk. 3.18 (MS Ca), Corpus Christi College, Oxford MS 279 (MS O). Previous editions: T. Miller, ed., *Bede's Ecclesiastical History*, E.E.T.S., 95 (London, 1890), pp. 343–349; J. Schipper, ed., in *Bibliothek der angelsächsischen Prosa*, IV (Leipzig, 1899), pp. 480–492.

The story of Cædmon was first recorded in Latin by Bede in his *Historia Ecclesiastica Gentis Anglorum* (book IV, chapter xxiv; ed. C. Plummer, 2 vols. [Oxford, 1896]), which was later translated into Old English. The only dates we have for the period during which Cædmon flourished are 657–680, the period when Hild served as Abbess at Strenæshalc (Streaneshalh). Bede's account refers to Cædmon's considerable repertoire of poetic composition based on Biblical narrative, but the only recorded text that can be attributed to him is the Hymn, translated by Bede into Latin from a vernacular version, which is extant in seventeen manuscripts, the earliest of which is the Moore Manuscript (ca. 737), Cambridge Univ. Lib. MS Kk. 5. 16; the text of the Hymn, in Northumbrian dialect, from this manuscript is printed in the annex to "Cædmon." For a brief survey of the manuscripts containing the Hymn, see E. V. K. Dobbie, ed., *The Anglo-Saxon Minor Poems* (New York, 1942), pp. xciv–c.

The sudden transformation of Cædmon the tongue-tied keeper of cattle to Cædmon the inspired composer of religious songs has

been read, or interpreted, as a biographical example of the training of an Old English **scop** (*poet*, derived from **scieppan**, *to create*),
who learns to sing and compose orally by listening to and absorbing
the rhythms and formulas of other singers; we may be sure,
however, that for Bede and the Anglo-Saxons Cædmon's gift was
the result of a divine miracle rather than of an acquired (and for a
time, latent) talent.

[*Glossary symbol:* C]

In ðeosse abbudissan mynstre[1] wæs sum broðor syndriglice mid
godcundre gife gemæred ond geweorðad, forþon he gewunade
gerisenlice leoð wyrcan, þa ðe to æfestnisse ond to arfæstnisse
belumpon,[2] swa ðætte swa hwæt swa he of godcundum stafum þurh
5   boceras geleornode, þæt he æfter medmiclum fæce in scopgere-
orde mid þa mæstan swetnisse ond inbryrdnisse geglængde ond in
Engliscgereorde wel geworht forþ brohte. Ond for his leoþsongum
monigra monna mod oft to worulde forhogdnisse ond to geþeod-
nisse þæs heofonlican lifes onbærnde wæron. Ond eac swelce[3]
10 monige oðre æfter him in Ongelþeode ongunnon æfeste leoð
wyrcan, ac nænig hwæðre him þæt gelice[4] don ne[5] meahte forþon
he nalæs from monnum ne þurh mon gelæred wæs þæt he þone
leoðcræft leornade, ac he wæs godcundlice gefultumod[6] ond þurh
Godes gife þone songcræft onfeng. Ond he forðon næfre noht
15 leasunge ne idles leoþes wyrcan ne[7] meahte, ac efne þa an þa ðe[8]
to æfæstnisse belumpon, ond his þa æfæstan tungan gedeofanade
singan.[9]

---

1. The monastery for monks and nuns at Strenæshalc (Whitby), founded and
presided over by Abbess Hild (or Hilda).
2. From MS O **-on**; MS **-en**.
3. **eac swelce**: *likewise.*
4. **him . . . gelice**: literally, *in like manner to him.*
5. **ne**] from MS Ca.
6. From MS O **-mod**; MS **-med**.
7. **ne**] from MS Ca.
8. **ac efne þa an þa ðe**: *but just those (songs) alone which.*
9. The clause beginning **ond**: *and which it was suitable for his pious tongue to sing;*

Wæs he se mon in weoruldhade geseted oð þa tide þe he wæs
gelyfdre ylde, ond næfre nænig leoð geleornade. Ond he forþon
20 oft in gebeorscipe, þonne þær wæs blisse intinga[10] gedemed, þæt
heo ealle sceoldon[11] þurh endebyrdnesse[12] be hearpan singan,
þonne he geseah þa hearpan him nealecan þonne aras he for
scome[13] from þæm symble ond ham eode to his huse. Þa he þæt
þa sumre tide dyde, þæt he forlet þæt hus þæs gebeorscipes ond ut
25 wæs gongende to neata scipene, þara heord him wæs þære neahte
beboden. Þa he ða þær in gelimplice tide his leomu on reste gesette
ond onslepte, þa stod him sum mon æt þurh swefn ond hine halette
ond grette ond hine be his noman nemnde: "Cedmon, sing me
hwæthwugu." Þa ondswarede he ond cwæð: "Ne con ic noht
30 singan ond ic forþon of þeossum gebeorscipe uteode ond hider
gewat, forþon ic naht singan ne cuðe." Eft he cwæð, se ðe wið
hine sprecende wæs: "Hwæðre þu meaht singan." Þa cwæð he:
"Hwæt sceal ic singan?" Cwæð he: "Sing me frumsceaft." Þa he
ða þas andsware onfeng, þa ongon he sona singan in herenesse
35 Godes Scyppendes þa fers ond þa word þe he næfre gehyrde, þara[14]
endebyrdnesse þis is:

> Nu we[15] sculon herigean heofonrices Weard,
> Meotodes meahte ond his modgeþanc,
> weorc Wuldorfæder, swa he wundra gehwæs,
40 > ece Drihten, or onstealde.
> He ærest sceop eorðan bearnum
> heofon to hrofe,[16] halig Scyppend;

the accusative **þa** (rather than the dative **þære** after **gedeofanade**) probably represents the Latin construction: *religiosam ejus linguam decebant.*

10. **blisse intinga**: *an occasion of joy*; **intinga**, rather than the expected accusative
(**-an**), renders Latin *causa* as nominative rather than as ablative: *cum esset laetitiae
causa decretum.*

11. From MS B; MS **sealde**.

12. **þurh endebyrdnesse**: *in order*; freely, *each one in turn.*

13. MS **for forscome**.

14. From MS O; MS **þære**.

15. **we**] from MSS Ca and O (superscript).

16. **to hrofe**: *as (for) a roof.*

þa middangeard   moncynnes Weard,
ece Drihten,   æfter teode
5   firum foldan,   Frea ælmihtig.

Þa aras he from þæm slæpe, ond eal þa þe he slæpende song,[17] fæste in gemynde hæfde, ond þæm wordum sona monig word in þæt ilce gemet Gode wyrðes songes togeþeodde.[18] Þa com he on morgenne to þæm tungerefan, þe his ealdormon wæs. Sægde him hwylc gife he onfeng, ond he hine[19] sona to þære abbudissan gelædde ond hire þæt[20] cyðde ond sægde. Þa heht heo gesomnian ealle þa gelæredestan men ond þa leorneras, ond him ondweardum[21] het secgan þæt swefn ond þæt leoð singan, þæt ealra heora dome gecoren wære,[22] hwæt oððe hwonon þæt cumen wære. Þa wæs him eallum gesegen swa swa hit wæs, þæt him wære from Drihtne sylfum heofonlic gifu forgifen. Þa rehton heo him ond sægdon sum halig spell ond godcundre lare word; bebudon him þa, gif he meahte, þæt he in swinsunge leoþsonges þæt gehwyrfde. Þa he ða hæfde þa wisan onfongne, þa eode he ham to his huse, ond cwom eft on morgenne, ond þy betstan leoðe geglenged him asong ond ageaf þæt him beboden wæs[23].

Ða ongan seo abbudisse clyppan ond lufigean þa Godes gife in þæm men, ond heo hine þa monade ond lærde þæt he woruldhad anforlete ond munuchad onfenge, ond he þæt wel þafode. Ond heo hine in þæt mynster onfeng mid his godum, ond hine geþeodde to gesomnunge þara Godes þeowa, ond heht hine læran þæt getæl

---

17. The clause beginning **ond**: *and all those (songs) which he sang while sleeping*, i.e., in his dream.

18. The clause beginning **ond** is a closely literal rendering of Bede's Latin: *et eis [cuncta quae cantaverat] mox plura in eundem modum verba Deo digni carminis adiunxit.* **in þæt ilce gemet = on þæm ilcan gemete. Gode wyrðes]** from MSS B, Ca, O; MS **godes wordes.**

19. **he = ealdormon; hine** = Cædmon.

20. From the other MSS; MS **þa.**

21. **him ondweardum:** *to them (who were) present.*

22. The clause beginning **þæt**: *so that it* [the **hwæt** clause which follows] *might be determined by the judgment of them all.*

23. The clause beginning **ond þy** may be clarified by the rephrasing: **ond asong ond ageaf him** [*to them*] **þæt him** [*to him*] **beboden wæs geglenged þy betstan leoðe.**

þæs halgan stæres ond spelles. Ond he eal þa he in gehyrnesse
geleornian meahte, mid hine gemyndgade ond, swa swa clæne
neten eodorcende, in þæt sweteste leoð gehwyrfde[24]. Ond his song
70   ond his leoð wæron swa wynsumu to gehyranne, þætte seolfan þa
his lareowas æt his muðe wreoton ond leornodon. Song he ærest
be middangeardes gesceape ond bi fruman moncynnes ond eal
þæt stær Genesis, þæt is seo æreste Moyses booc, ond eft bi utgonge
Israhela folces of Ægypta londe ond bi ingonge þæs gehatlondes;
75   ond bi oðrum monegum spellum þæs halgan gewrites canones
boca; ond bi Cristes menniscnesse, ond bi his þrowunge ond bi his
upastignesse in heofonas; ond bi þæs Halgan Gastes cyme, ond þara
apostola lare; ond eft bi þæm dæge þæs toweardan domes, ond bi
fyrhtu þæs tintreglican wiites, ond bi swetnesse þæs heofonlecan
80   rices, he monig leoð geworhte. Ond swelce eac oðer monig be
þæm godcundan fremsumnessum ond domum he geworhte. In
eallum þæm he geornlice gemde þæt he men atuge from synna
lufan ond mandæda, ond to lufan ond to geornfulnesse awehte
godra dæda. Forþon he wæs se mon swiþe æfæst ond regollecum
85   þeodscipum eaðmodlice underþeoded. One wið þæm þa ðe in oðre
wisan don woldon, he wæs mid welme micelre ellenwodnisse
onbærned. Ond he forðon fægre ende his lif betynde ond
geendade.

Forþon þa ðære tide nealæcte his gewitenesse ond forðfore,[25]
90   þa wæs he feowertynum dagum ær, þæt he wæs lichomlicre untrym-
nesse þrycced ond hefgad, hwæðre to þon[26] gemetlice þæt he ealle þa
tid meahte ge sprecan ge gongan. Wæs þær in neaweste untrumra
monna hus, in þæm heora þeaw wæs þæt heo þa untruman[27] ond
þa ðe æt forðfore wæron in lædan[28] sceoldon[29], ond him þær

---

24. From MSS Ca, O; MS **gehwerfde**.

25. The clause beginning **Forþon**: *Whereupon when it drew near to the time of his
death and departure.*

26. **to þon**: a phrasal, *to that extent, to such an extent.*

27. From MS O; MS **untrumran**.

28. From MS O; MS **-on**.

29. The clause beginning **in þæm** may be rephrased thus for clarity: **in þæm
wæs heora þeaw þæt heo [= hie] sceoldon lædan in þa untruman ond þa ðe
wæron æt forðfore.**

95 ætsomne þegnian. Þa bæd he his þegn on æfenne þære neahte þe
he of worulde gongende wæs þæt he in þæm huse him stowe
gegearwode, þæt he gerestan meahte. Þa wundrode se þegn for
hwon[30] he ðæs bæde, forþon him þuhte þæt his forðfor swa neah ne
wære; dyde hwæðre swa swa he cwæð ond bibead. Ond mid þy[31] he

100 ða þær on reste eode, ond he gefeonde mode sumu þing mid him
sprecende ætgædere ond gleowiende wæs þe þær ær inne wæron[32],
þa wæs ofer middeneaht þæt he frægn, hwæðer heo ænig husl inne
hæfdon. Þa ondswarodon heo ond cwædon: "Hwylc þearf is ðe
husles? Ne þinre forþfore swa neah is, nu þu þus rotlice ond þus

105 glædlice to us sprecende eart." Cwæð he eft: "Berað me husl to." Þa
he hit þa on honda hæfde, þa frægn he hwæþer heo ealle smolt
mod ond buton eallum[33] incan bliðe to him hæfdon. Þa ondswaredon hy ealle, ond cwædon þæt heo nænigne incan to him wiston, ac
heo ealle him swiðe bliðemode wæron. Ond heo wrixendlice hine

110 bædon þæt[34] he him eallum bliðe wære. Þa ondswarade he ond
cwæð: "Mine broðor, mine þa leofan, ic eom swiðe bliðemod to eow
ond to eallum Godes monnum." Ond he[35] swa wæs hine getrym-
mende mid þy heofonlecan wegneste ond him oðres lifes ingong
gegearwode. Þa gyt he frægn hu neah þære tide wære þætte þa

115 broðor arisan sceolden,[36] ond Godes lof ræran ond heora uhtsong
singan. Þa ondswaredon heo: "Nis hit feor to þon." Cwæð he:
"Teala, wuton we wel þære tide bidan." Ond þa him[37] gebæd ond
hine gesegnode mid Cristes rodetacne, ond his heafod onhylde[38]
to þam bolstre, ond medmicel fæc onslepte—ond swa mid stilnesse

120 his lif geendade.

30. **for hwon**: *why*.
31. **mid þy**: *when*.
32. The order of the clause beginning **ond he** may be recomposed thus: **ond he,
gefeonde mode, wæs gleowiende ond sprecende sumu þing ætgædere mid him,
[mid þæm] þe wæron inne ær**.
33. **eallum**: an adverbial dative, *entirely*.
34. **þæt**: freely, *if*.
35. **he**] from the other MSS.
36. MS **scolden**.
37. **him**: reflexive.
38. **on-**] from the other MSS; MS **oh-**.

Ond swa wæs geworden þætte swa swa he[39] hluttre mode ond
bilwitre ond smyltre wilsumnesse Drihtne þeode, þæt he eac
swylce swa smylte deaðe middangeard wæs forlætende, ond to his
gesihðe becwom. Ond seo tunge þe swa monig halwende word in
þæs Scyppendes lof gesette, he ða swelce eac þa ytmæstan word in
his herenisse, hine seolfne segniende ond his gast in his honda
bebeodende, betynde[40]. Eac swelce þæt is gesegen þæt he wære
gewis his seolfes forðfore of þæm þe[41] we nu secgan hyrdon.[42]

125

Annex: Cædmon's Hymn, the earliest version

Cambridge Univ. Lib., MS Kk. 5. 16, folio 128ᵛ.

Nu scylun hergan	hefaenricaes Uard,
Metudæs maecti	end his modgidanc,
uerc Uuldurfadur,	sue he uundra gihuaes,
eci Dryctin,	or astelidæ.
He aerist scop	aelda barnum
heben til hrofe,	haleg Scepen.
Tha middungeard	moncynnæs Uard,
eci Dryctin,	æfter tiadæ
firum foldu,	Frea allmectig.

5

Primo cantauit Caedmon istud carmen.

10

---

39. **he**] from the other MSS.

40. Syntactically the subject of **betynde** seems to be **seo tunge**; Sweet (*Anglo-Saxon Reader* [Oxford, 1950], p. 208) observed that the translator in error took *illa lingua* as nominative rather than as ablative. The proper construction would be: **(he) betynde (his lif)**.

41. **þe**] from the other MSS.

42. Additional note, to line 32, **þu meaht singan**: It has several times been disputed whether the text should read **þū meaht singan** or **þū mē āht singan**; for discussion of the problems, see B. Mitchell, "Postscript on Bede's *mihi cantare habes*," *NM* 70 (1969), 369–80.

Genesis A

Bodleian MS Junius 11, pages 64–73, 92–96. Previous editions: F. Holthausen, ed., *Die Ältere Genesis* (Heidelberg, 1914), lines 668–879, 1344–1479; G. P. Krapp, ed., *The Junius Manuscript* (New York, 1931), lines 1285–1496, 1960–2095.

Genesis A begins with a prologue of the revolt of the angels in Heaven, their fall and the creation of Hell, and the moving of God's will to create the World. The rest of the poetic narrative is a partial translation, sometimes quite literal and sometimes in free paraphrase, of chapters 1–22:13 of the Vulgate Genesis. It is unknown whether the translation-paraphrase originally was more extensive than the text which remains in manuscript.

The two sections edited here, *The Flood* and *The Capture and Rescue of Lot*, are representative of the paraphrast's talent as a narrative poet well nurtured in his own heroic poetry, the style, idiom, and spirit of which are in many ways (e.g., the use of patronymics and formulas; the heroic relationships) sympathetic to those of Old Testament narrative. Each of the three parts of the Flood — God's command and the preparation of the ark, the deluge, the subsiding of the waters — is recounted at a measured and suspended pace as the poet reshapes the familiar story in his native style, with its variations, exclamatory formulas, collocations and compounds. Aside from the fact that it is a Biblical event, the feud and battle between Abraham and the Elamites might as well be an event out of the history or heroic legend of the Anglo

Saxons themselves, so thoroughly does the poet naturalize the details and narrative sequence. The continuity of traditional diction, motifs and themes in Old English heroic poetry can be seen by comparing Abraham's rescue of Lot with the magnificent Hrefnawudu drama in *Beowulf* (lines 2922–2998) and with the eleventh-century *Maldon*.

(Note: The line numbers refer to the line enumeration of the complete text [as edited by Krapp] of *Genesis A*.)

[*Glossary symbol:* G]

The Flood

1285　Noe wæs god,　　Nergende leof,
　　　　swiðe gesælig,　　sunu Lameches,
　　　　domfæst and gedefe.　　Drihten wiste
　　　　þæt þæs æðelinges　　ellen dohte
　　　　breostgehygdum;　　forðon him Brego sægde,
1290　halig æt hleoðre,　　Helm allwihta,
　　　　hwæt he fah werum[1]　　fremman wolde.
　　　　Geseah unrihte　　eorðan fulle,
　　　　side sælwongas　　synnum gehladene,
　　　　widlum gewemde.　　Þa Waldend spræc,
1295　Nergend usser,　　and to Noe cwæð:
　　　　"Ic wille mid flode　　folc acwellan,
　　　　and cynna gehwilc　　cucra wuhta
　　　　þara þe lyft and flod　　lædað and fedað,[2]
　　　　feoh and fuglas.　　Þu scealt frið habban
1300　mid sunum þinum　　ðonne sweart wæter,
　　　　wonne wælstreamas　　werodum swelgað,
　　　　sceaðum scyldfullum.　　Ongyn þe scip wyrcan,
　　　　merehus micel,　　on þam þu monegum scealt
　　　　reste geryman,　　and rihte setl

1. **he fah werum**: Syntactically **fah** modifies **he**, *he* [God] *hostile*, but the syntax of the whole line is unclear: (?) *what He, hostile to men, would do*; (?) *what He, (being) hostile, would do to men.*

2. **lædað and fedað**: *bring forth and nourish*; cp. the similar collocations in the Exeter Book *Fates of Men*: [the mother and father] **temiaþ** [MS **tennaþ**] **ond tæcaþ** [MS **tætaþ**] (4). **fergað swa ond feþað** [their child] (7).

1305 ælcum æfter agenum[3]   eorðan tudre;
gescype[4] scylfan   on scipes bosme.
Þu þæt[5] fær gewyrc   fiftiges wid,
ðrittiges heah   and[6] þreohund lang
elngemeta,   and wið yða gewyrc[7]
1310 gefeg fæste.   Þær sceal fæsl wesan
cwiclifigendra   cynna gehwilces
on þæt wudufæsten,   wocor gelæded[8]
eorðan tudres.   Earc sceal[9] þy mare."
Noe fremede[10]   swa hine Nergend heht,
1315 hyrde þam halgan   Heofoncyninge,
ongan ofostlice   þæt hof wyrcan,
micle merecieste.   Magum sægde
þæt wæs þrealic þing   þeodum toweard,
reðe wite.   Hie ne[11] rohton þæs.
1320   Geseah þa ymb wintra worn   wærfæst Metod
geofonhusa mæst   gearo hlifigean,
innan and utan   eorðan lime
gefæstnod wið flode,   fær Noes,
þy selestan[12];   þæt is syndrig cynn —
1325 symle bið þy heardra   þe[13] hit hreoh wæter,

3. **æfter agenum**: (?) *for his own*; or *after (according to the needs of) his own kind.*
4. **gescype**] y corrected in MS from an original i or u.
5. **þæt**] MS **þær**, perhaps because of **fær** which follows.
6. **and**] not in MS.
7. **wið yða gewyrc**: **gewyrc** is usually construed here as a verb (as in line 1307) in apposition with **gefeg** with *hit* (= **fær**) understood, and **yða** accordingly is taken as an accusative plural. Such an appositional construction, however, would be unusual in this poem, and **gewyrc** in 1309 may be open to question. It seems possible that the word is a scribal error for **gewealc**, which occurs with some frequency elsewhere in a construction, **yða gewealc**, *rolling of waves* (see BTD at **gewealc**). The scribe's eye may have wandered to the **gewyrc** of line 1307 which in the manuscript (p. 65) stands in the line above to the left.
8. The verbal construction is **sceal wesan gelæded**, with **fæsl** and **wocor** the subject.
9. **sceal**: **beon** understood; this is a common ellipsis in the poetry.
10. **fremede**] MS **freme**.
11. **ne**] Before **n** there is an erasure of one letter, perhaps **g**.
12. **þy selestan** modifies **lime** in line 1322.
13. **þe**: The instrumental **þē** forms a correlative construction with **þy**.

swearte sæstreamas,   swiðor beatað.

    Ða to Noe cwæð   Nergend usser:
"Ic þe þæs[14] mine,[15]   monna leofost,
wære gesylle,   þæt þu weg nimest,[16]
1330   and feora fæsl   þe þu ferian scealt
geond deop wæter   dægrimes worn
on lides bosme.   Læd, swa ic þe hate,
under earce bord   eaforan þine,
frumgaran þry,   and eower feower wif[17];
1335   ond[18] þu seofone genim   on þæt sundreced
tudra gehwilces   geteled rimes,[19]
þara þe to mete   mannum lifige,[20]
and þara oðerra[21]   ælces twa.
Swilce þu of eallum   eorðan wæstmum
1340   wiste under wægbord   werodum gelæde,
þam þe mid sceolon   mereflod nesan.
Fed freolice   feora wocre
oð ic þære lafe   lagosiða eft,
reorde under roderum,   ryman wille.
1345   Gewit þu nu mid hiwum   on þæt hof gangan,
gasta werode.   Ic þe godne wat,
fæsthydigne;   þu eart freoðo[22] wyrðe,
ara mid eaforum.   Ic on andwlitan
nu ofor seofon niht   sigan læte
1350   wællregn ufan   widre eorðan.[23]

14. þæs: semi-adverbial, *therefor*.

15. **mine** modifies **wære**, a noun, in the next line.

16. **weg nimest**: an idiom, here apparently in the sense *lead forth, take the way*; the subject of the verb is both **þu** and **fæsl** (1330).

17. That is, Noah's three sons (Shem, Ham, Japheth), their wives, and Noah's.

18. **ond**] The initial letter, a capital **O**, appears over a pen-stroke, probably the abbreviation 7 = **and**.

19. **seofone . . . geteled rimes**: *seven . . . counted of (in) number*.

20. **lifige** is singular because of **gehwilces** (1336).

21. **oðerra**] MS **oðe ra**; one letter erased after **e**.

22. **freoðo**: genitive singular; the genitive of this word in *Genesis A* always has this form.

23. **on andwlitan** (line 1348b) makes a construction with **widre eorðan. ofor**

Feowertig daga   fæhðe ic wille
on weras stælan,[24]   and mid wægþreate
æhta and agend   eall acwellan
þa beutan beoð   earce bordum
1355 þonne sweartracu   stigan[25] onginneð.''
        Him þa Noe gewat,   swa hine Nergend het,
under earce bord   eaforan lædan,[26]
weras on wægþel[27]   and heora wif somed;
and eall þæt to fæsle   Frea ælmihtig
1360 habban wolde   under hrof gefor
to heora ætgifan,   swa him ælmihtig
weroda Drihten   þurh his word abead.[28]
Him on hoh[29] beleac   heofonrices Weard
merehuses muð[30]   mundum sinum,
1365 sigora Waldend,   and segnade
earce innan   agenum spedum
Nergend usser.   Noe hæfde,
sunu Lameches,   syxhund wintra[31]
þa he mid bearnum   under bord gestah,

seofon niht: *seven nights (days) from now*; perhaps emend **ofor** to **ofer**, the usual spelling in *Genesis A*.

24. Translate: *For forty days I intend to make a charge of enmity against men*; **ic wille** forms a construction with both **stælan** and **acwellan** (1353). For the use of **stælan** (**on**), see BTD, and cp. the poem *Christ and Satan* (in the Junius MS), lines 638b–39a: **stæleð feondas fæhðe and firne**.

25. **stigan**: Cp. line 1375, **Sæs up stigon**.

26. **Him þa Noe gewat … lædan**: *Then Noah went to lead . . . .* **Him** is reflexive and unnecessary to translate.

27. **wægþel**] In -**þel**, **e** is a scribal change from an original **æ**; **þel** or **þell** is, however, the usual spelling in the poem.

28. Lines 1359–1362 seem compressed and elliptical; perhaps translate, *and all that as offspring* [*i.e., the living creatures*], (*which*) *the almighty God wished to have under the roof, came to their provider* [*Noah*], *as the almighty Lord of hosts had commanded to him* [*Noah*] *by His word.*

29. **Him on hoh**: An idiom, otherwise unattested in Old English, *behind Him*.

30. **muð**: *mouth* used to refer to a door occurs elsewhere in Old English; see BTD, and particularly *Beowulf*, lines 723–724: [Grendel] **onbræd þa bealohydig, ða he gebolgen wæs,/recedes muþan**. (The word **duru** occurs in line 721.)

31. **Noe hæfde … syxhund wintra**: *Noah was six hundred years old.*

1370 gleaw mid geogoðe,[32]   be Godes hæse,
      dugeðum dyrum.   Drihten sende
      regn from roderum   and eac rume let
      willeburnan   on woruld þringan
      of ædra[33] gehwære,   egorstreamas
1375 swearte swogan.   Sæs up stigon
      ofer stæðweallas.   Strang wæs and reðe
      se ðe wætrum weold: wreah and þeahte
      manfæhðu bearn   middangeardes
      wonnan wæge,[34]   wera eðelland;
1380 hof hergode,   hygeteonan wræc
      Metod on monnum.   Mere swiðe grap
      on fæge folc   feowertig daga,
      nihta oðer swilc.[35]   Nið wæs reðe,
      wællgrim werum.   Wuldorcyninges
1385 yða wræcon   arleasra feorh
      of flæschoman.   Flod ealle wreah
      hreoh under heofonum   hea beorgas[36]
      geond sidne[37] grund   and on sund ahof
      earce from eorðan,   and þa æðelo mid
1390 þa segnade   selfa Drihten,
      Scyppend usser,   þa he þæt scip beleac.
          Siððan wide rad   wolcnum under
      ofer holmes hricg[38]   hof seleste,

32. **mid bearnum ... mid geogoðe ... dugeðum dyrum** are appositives.

33. **ædra**: A parallel use of **æder** occurs in a passage attributed to Wulfstan: **Ealle eorðan æddre onsprungon ongean ðam heofonlican flode** (cited in BTD, Supp., p. 10).

34. **manfæhðu** (line 1378) is genitive singular following **bearn**. **wonnan wæge** forms a phrase with **middangeardes**.

35. **oðer swilc**: literally, *another (of) such* (**feowertig**); freely, *forty days and forty nights*.

36. **Flod** is modified by **hreoh**; **ealle** modifies **hea beorgas**, perhaps in an adverbial function, *entirely*.

37. **sidne**] d, over n, erased.

38. **hricg**] MS **hrincg**: A form **hrincg** also occurs once elsewhere in *Genesis A* in the phrase **hrincg þæs hean landes** (line 2855). Both there and here in line 1393 the form has been taken as **hring**, *ring*, in a special sense, *circuit, sea or land enclosed by*

       for mid fearme.   Fære ne moston
1395 wægliðendum   wætres brogan
       hæste hrinon,   ac hie halig God[39]
       ferede and nerede.   Fiftena stod
       deop ofer dunum   se[40] drenceflod
       monnes elna[41];   þæt is mæro wyrd!
1400 Þam æt niehstan   wæs nan to gedale
       nymþe heo wæs ahafen   on þa hean lyft.[42]

the horizon, although in no other instance is OE **hring/hrincg** (note in BTD that the cluster **-cg** occurs infrequently among forms of **hring**) associated with sea or land as an aspect of height or expanse. It is altogether probable that in these two places in *Genesis A* **hrincg** is a scribal error for **hricg**, *ridge, back*, which occurs elsewhere in the poetry in such phrases as: **on sæs hricg, ofer sæs hrygc, ofer wæteres hrycg, on wæteres hricg, ofer hreone hrycg, yða hrycgum; sundhrycg.**

39. Lines 1394b–1396b contain the following problems involving ambiguous forms: Is **fære** a dative singular form of **fær** (*ship*) in a kind of apposition with **wægliðendum**, or of **fær** (*danger, terror*), both of which occur unambiguously elsewhere in *Genesis A*? Is **hæste** (1) an adjective (*violent*) modifying **brogan**, (2) a ds. of **hæst** (*violence*) in apposition with **fære** (*terror*), or (3) an adverb (*violently*)? A choice among these possibilities is difficult, but perhaps translate, *The terrors of the water might not violently* (**hæste** = adverb) *touch the ship* (**fære**), *the wave-farers*; with this rendering the **hie** of line 1396 most likely refers to the immediate antecedent, **wægliðendum**, rather than collectively to this word and its presumed near-appositive, **fære**.

40. **se**] MS **sæ**, corrected scribally to **se**.

41. **Fiftena** (line 1397b) forms a construction with **monnes elna** (line 1399a).

42. A possible reading of lines 1400–1401, the meaning of which is uncertain, is: *To them* [that is, **wægliðendum** of line 1395] *finally there was no other alotment* (**nan to gedale**) *except that the ark* (**heo**) *was lifted high into the air* (literally, *into the high air*). That is, as the flood rose and destroyed the **eorðan tuddor** (line 1402), the apportionment to Noah and his companions in God's covenant was that they should be lifted above the flood's destruction and thereby be saved. The poet's intent in **nan to gedale nymþe . . .** may be slightly ironic.

For the phrase **to gedale**, in legal contexts, see BTD, Supp., p. 311. Other editors emend **heo** to **heof**, *lamentation*, but such a reading is inconsistent with the movement of this passage, and nothing is said elsewhere in the Flood narrative about Noah and his companions lamenting. Moreover, the spelling **heof** would be unusual in *Genesis A* since the one instance of the word's appearance in the poem is in the usual form, **heaf**, in line 923: **þurh wop and heaf**. Another possible reading is K. Sisam's (in *Studies in the History* of *Old English Literature* [Oxford, 1962], p. 42); he translates *Fifteen of our* (**monnes**) *ells above the mountains stood the whelming flood (that was a great marvel!); and at last there was none to divide the flood* (**þam . . . to gedale**) *unless it* (sc. **seo dun** [= **dunum**, line 1398]) *rose up to the high firmament.*

Þa se egorhere   eorðan tuddor
eall acwealde,   buton þæt earce bord
heold heofona Frea   þa hine[43] halig God
1405   ece upp forlet   ed monne[44]
streamum stigan,   stiðferhð Cyning.
    Þa gemunde God   mereliðende,
sigora Waldend   sunu Lameches
and ealle þa wocre   þe he wið wætre beleac,
1410   lifes Leohtfruma,   on lides bosme.
Gelædde þa wigend   weroda Drihten
worde ofer widland.   Willflod ongan
lytligan eft;   lago ebbade,
sweart under swegle.   Hæfde soð Metod
1415   eaforum egstream   eft gecyrred,
torhtne[45] ryne,   regn gestilled.
For famig scip   L and C[46]
nihta under roderum,   siððan nægledbord,
fær seleste,   flod up ahof,
1420   oðþæt rimgetæl   reðre þrage
daga forð gewat.   Ða on dunum gesæt
heah mid hlæste   holmærna mæst,
earc Noes,   þe Armenia
hatene syndon.   Þær se halga bad,
1425   sunu Lameches,   soðra gehata
lange þrage,   hwonne him lifes Weard,
Frea ælmihtig,   frecenra siða

---

43. **hine**: Presumably this pronoun refers back to **egorhere** in line 1402.

44. **ed monne**] This is the MS reading, which probably represents both scribal error and omission. Previous editors emend in different ways: **edniowne flod** (*ever-renewing flood*, Holthausen); **e[acne an]d wonne** (*swollen and dark* [*flood*], Holthausen); **edmodne flod** (*obedient flood*, Wülker, and Krapp). None of these solutions holds up well to scrutiny, and since no other (more acceptable) emendation has suggested itself, it has been thought best to leave the half-line as it stands in the MS. Freely, the meaning of the lines seems to be: *when holy, eternal God, the stern-minded King, released* (**upp forlet**) *the deluge* (**hine**) *to mount in floods*.

45. **torhtne**] MS **torht**.

46. **L and C**: that is, **fiftig and hundteontig**.

reste ageafe,   þæra[47] he rume dreah
þa hine on sunde   geond sidne grund
1430 wonne yða   wide bæron.
        Holm wæs heononweard.   Hæleð langode,
wægliðende,   swilce wif heora,
hwonne hie of nearwe   ofer nægledbord
ofer streamstaðe   stæppan mosten
1435 and of enge ut   æhta lædan.
        Þa fandode   forðweard scipes
hwæðer sincende   sæflod þa gyt
wære under wolcnum.   Let þa ymb worn daga —
þæs þe[48] heah hlioðo   horde onfengon
1440 and æðelum eac   eorðan tudres —
sunu Lameches   sweartne fleogan
hrefn ofer heahflod   of huse ut.
        Noe tealde   þæt he[49] on neod hine,
gif he on þære lade   land ne funde,
1445 ofer sid wæter   secan wolde
on wægþele.   Eft[50] him seo wen geleah,
ac se feond[51] gespearn   fleotende hreaw;
salwigfeðera   secan nolde.

---

47. **þæra**] MS **þære**, which may represent a scribal conflation of an original **þæra þe**.

48. **þæs þe**: *after*.

49. **he**: the raven, the subject of **secan wolde** in line 1445; **hine** refers to Noah.

50. **Eft**: The basic meanings of **eft** are *again, afterwards*; at the head of a sentence or clause, in a sequence of time or of events, however, **eft** often has a function similar to that of the adverb **þa**, with the meaning *then* or *thereupon*.

51. **se feond**: *the evil creature* = the raven; other editors emend, perhaps rightly, to **feonde**, *he rejoicing*; the verb **fēon** occurs twice elsewhere in the poem (lines 1468 and 1523) in the form **gefēon**.

The Vulgate Genesis reports simply that the raven 'went out and did not return,' but the poet adds that it 'perched upon floating corpses' and then, rhetorically (noticing **secan wolde** of line 1445) that **salwigfeðera secan nolde (hine)**. The detail of the raven perching, or treading upon, corpses is often found in medieval commentaries on *Genesis*, such as Isidore's (. . . *emissus corvus non est reversus, aut aquis utique interceptus, aut aliquo supernante cadavera illectus* [*P. L.* 83, 233]), and in medieval Latin poetry, such as Claudius Marius Victor's *Alethias*, Book II, lines 498–500 (ed. C. Schenkl) and Avitus's *De Diluvio*, Book IV, verse 566 (ed. Peiper). For the

He þa ymb seofon niht[52]   sweartum hrefne
1450   of earce forlet   æfter fleogan
ofer heah wæter   haswe culufran[53]
on fandunga   hwæðer famig sæ,
deop þa gyta,   dæl ænigne
grenre eorðan   ofgifen hæfde.
1455   Heo wide hire   willan sohte
and rume fleah.   Nohweðere reste fand,
þæt heo for flode   fotum ne meahte
land gespornan   ne on leaf treowes
steppan for streamum,   ac wæron steap hleoðo
1460   bewrigen mid wætrum.   Gewat se wilda fugel
on æfenne   earce secan
ofer wonne wæg,   werig sigan,
hungri to handa   halgum rince.
Ða wæs culufre eft   of cofan sended
1465   ymb wucan wilde.   Seo wide fleah
oðþæt heo rumgal   reste stowe
fægere funde   and þa fotum stop
on beam hyre;   gefeah bliðemod
þæs þe[54] heo gesittan[55]   swiðe werig

Genesis A poet, however, the detail may have derived from the native poetic motif of the raven as one of the Beasts of Battle which devour corpses left after a battle (here, after the Deluge).

An argument against the emendation, **se feonde**, is that such a construction would be unusual in *Genesis A*. The poet may have referred to the raven as **se feond** simply because the bird, with its predatory instincts, **secan nolde**; but it may also be considered that medieval exegesis saw in the Genesis account of the raven a figure of the devil, and **feond** in Old English often means *the devil*. Bede, for example, explains: "Corvus dimissus, et non reversus, *figuram peccatoris vel diaboli tenet, ad regnum Dei non revertentis*" (*P. L.* 91, 226); cp. also Rabanus Maurus, *P. L.* 107, 522. For another objection to **feonde**, from a different point of view, see K. Sisam, *Studies* (cited above in note 42), pp. 40–42.

52. **ymb seofon niht**: that is, a week later; cp. **ymb wucan** in line 1465.

53. The syntax of lines 1449–1451 may be clarified by juxtaposing word-order: **of earce forlet haswe culufran fleogan ofer heah wæter æfter sweartum hrefne. heah**] Final **h** appears added above the line.

54. **þæs þe**: *when*.

55. **gesittan**] MS **gesette**, which the scribe may have thought was the needed verb before noticing **moste**.

1470 on treowes telgum   torhtum moste.
      Heo feðera onsceoc,   gewat fleogan eft
      mid lacum hire;   liðend[56] brohte
      elebeames twig   an[57] to handa,
      grene blædæ.   Þa ongeat hraðe
1475 flotmonna frea   þæt wæs frofor cumen,
      earfoðsiða bot.   Þa gyt se eadega wer,
      ymb wucan þriddan,   wilde culufran
      ane sende.   Seo eft ne com
      to lide fleogan,   ac heo land begeat,
1480 grene bearwas.   Nolde gladu æfre
      under salwed bord[58]   syððan ætywan
      on þellfæstenne,   þa hire þearf ne wæs.
      Þa to Noe spræc   Nergend usser,
      heofonrices Weard,   halgan reorde:
1485 "Þe is eðelstol   eft gerymed,
      lisse on lande,   lagosiða rest
      fæger on foldan.   Gewit on freðo gangan
      ut of earce,   and on eorðan bearm
      of þam hean hofe   hiwan læd þu,
1490 and ealle þa wocre   þe ic wægþrea on
      liðe[59] nerede   þenden lago hæfde
      þrymme geþeahtne[60]   þriddan[61] eðyl."

56. **liðend**: freely, *the sea-going one* (= **culufre**).

57. **an** modifies **twig**, as an indefinite article; cp. **ane** in line 1478.

58. **salwed bord**: BTD suggests that the ship is described as **salwed** because of the pitch which holds it together, and to this point cp. lines 1322–1324a, and **þellfæstenne** in line 1482.

59. **liðe**] MS **hliðe**.

60. ~~geþeahtne~~] MS ~~geþeahte~~.

61. **þriddan**] MS **þridda**. The phrase **þriddan eðyl** in context seems to refer to **eorðan** and has been explained (after Kock) as a condensed reference to a scheme such as heaven, ocean, and earth. BTD, under **þridda**, cites two quotations which might, as examples of similar enumeration, support this suggestion: **Heofonwaru and eorðwaru, helwaru þridde**; **On nanum heolstrum heofenan, oþþe eorþan, oþþe sæ þriddan**. It is possible, however, that the line has been scribally garbled and that **þriddan eðyl** is a ghost-phrase. Cp. the similarity of diction in lines 1377–1379: **þeahte . . . wera eðelland**.

He fremede swa   and frean hyrde,
stah ofer streamweall,   swa him seo stefn bebead,
1495   lustum miclum,   and alædde þa
of wægþele   wraðra lafe.

The Capture and Rescue of Lot

1960   Ða ic aldor gefrægn[1]   Elamitarna,
fromne folctogan,   fyrd gebeodan,
Orlahomar;   him Ambrafel
of Sennar   side werode[2]
for on fultum.   Gewiton hie feower þa
1965   þeodcyningas   þrymme micle
secan suð ðanon   Sodoman and Gomorran.
Þa wæs guðhergum   be Iordane
wera eðelland   wide geondsended,
folde feondum.[3]   Sceolde forht monig
1970   blachleor ides   bifiende gan
on fremdes fæðm[4];   feollon wergend
bryda and beaga,   bennum seoce.
Him þa togeanes   mid guðþræce
fife foron[5]   folccyningas
1975   sweotum suðon;   woldon Sodome burh
wraðum[6] werian.   Þa wintra XII

1. **ic ... gefrægn**: Although the formula *I* [the poet, the narrator] *have heard* [literally, *learned by asking*], and formulas of the same function (such as **we nu gehyrað**) appear infrequently in *Genesis A* as a whole, they occur with a relatively high frequency in this particular section, probably because it is a sustained battle narrative, which the poet-paraphrast develops and controls in the idiom of his native heroic poetry. See lines 2013b–2014a and 2060.

2. **werode**] MS **worulde**. The phrase **side worulde** in itself is straightforward (*in the wide world*; *widely in the world*), but in this context it seems awkward. The emendation (*with a large troop*) follows Bouterwek, who emended to **worude**; the word is, however, consistently spelled **werod** (or **wered**) in *Genesis A*, hence the reading adopted here. Cp. **þrymme micle** in line 1965.

3. The appositives in lines 1967–1969 are: **guðhergum - feondum, eðelland - folde**.

4. **on fremdes fæðm**: *into a stranger's embrace*.

5. **foron**] MS **foran**; cp. line 1982.

6. **wraðum**: freely, *against the enemy*.

norðmonnum ær   niede sceoldon
gombon gieldan   and gafol sellan,
oðþæt þa leode   leng ne woldon
1980 Elamitarna   aldor swiðan
folcgestreonum,   ac him from swicon.[7]
   Foron þa tosomne   — francan wæron hlude —
wraðe wælherigas.   Sang se wanna fugel[8]
under deoreðsceaftum,   deawigfeðera,
1985 hræs on wenan.   Hæleð onetton
on mægencorðrum,   modum þryðge,[9]
oðþæt folcgetrume   gefaren hæfdon
sid tosomne   suðan and norðan,[10]
helmum þeahte.   Þær wæs heard plega,
1990 wælgara wrixl,   wigcyrm micel,
hlud hildesweg.   Handum brugdon
hæleð of scæðum   hringmæled sweord,
ecgum dihtig.   Þær wæs eaðfynde
eorle orlegceap,[11]   se ðe ær ne wæs
1995 niðes genihtsum.   Norðmen wæron
suðfolcum swice[12];   wurdon Sodomware
and Gomorre   goldes bryttan

7. **him from swicon**: literally, *they turned from him*; that is, they turned away from their former allegiance, rendering *recesserunt ab eo* (*Genesis* 14:4).

8. **se wanna fugel**: the raven, one of the Beasts of Battle, the mention of which here, at the outset of battle, signifies impending carnage. Notice the association of **francan wæron hlude** and **sang se wanna fugel**, and cp. the similar poetic preparation for combat in **Maldon**, lines 106–107: **Þær wearð hream ahafen, hremmas wundon, / earn æses georn. Wæs on eorþan cyrm**. At the defeat of the Elamites the **fuglas** reappear (lines 2088–2089) to fulfill their expectation of corpses (**hræs on wenan**).

9. **þryðge**] MS **þrydge**.

10. The syntax of lines 1987–1988 is awkward; translate: *until they* [the **Hæleð** of line 1985] *had come from the south and north, extensive together, in* (or *into*) *a host.*

11. **orlegceap** appropriately describes **hringmæled sweord** (that is, splendid war-gear), although the heroic irony of the sentence suggests a figurative meaning of **orlegceap**, something like '*a wealth of violence*.'

12. **swice**: literally the meaning seems to be *deceptive*, but the precise meaning in the context is unclear. The poet's use of the word here may have something to do with the references to tribute and booty (lines 1978, 1981, and 1994), and by association, **goldes bryttan** in line 1997.

æt þæm lindcrodan   leofum[13] bedrorene,
fyrdgesteallum.   Gewiton feorh heora
2000 fram þam folcstyde   fleame nergan,
secgum ofslegene[14];   him on swaðe[15] feollon
æðelinga bearn,   ecgum ofþegde,
willgesiððas.   Hæfde wigsigor
Elamitarna   ordes wisa;
2005 weold wælstowe.   Gewat seo wæpna laf
fæsten secan.   Fynd gold strudon,
ahyðdan[16] þa mid herge   hordburh wera,
Sodoman and Gomorran,   þa sæl ageald,[17]
mære ceastra.   Mægð siðedon,
2010 fæmnan and wuduwan,   freondum beslægene,
from hleowstole.   Hettend læddon
ut mid æhtum   Abrahames mæg
of Sodoma byrig.   We þæt soð magon
secgan furður,   hwelc siððan wearð
2015 æfter þæm gehnæste   herewulfa sið,[18]
þara þe læddon Loth   and leoda god,
suðmonna sinc   — sigore gulpon!
    Him[19] þa secg hraðe   gewat siðian,
an gara laf,   se ða guðe genæs,
2020 Abraham secan.   Se þæt orlegweorc
þam Ebriscan   eorle gecyðde,
forslegen swiðe   Sodoma folc,
leoda duguðe,   and Lothes sið.
Þa þæt inwitspell   Abraham sægde

---

13. **leofum** modifies (**goldes**) **bryttan**.

14. **feorh heora** (line 1999) is the object of **nergan** and is modified by **secgum ofslegene**.

15. **him on swaðe**: *behind them* (*on the track*).

16. **ahyðdan**] MS **ahudan**.

17. **þa sæl ageald**: probably, *as opportunity* (or *time*) *permitted*; cp. *Beowulf*, lines 1665–1666: **Ofsloh ða æt þære sæcce, þa me sæl ageald, / huses hyrdas**.

18. Lines 2014–2015: Literally, *what course of the battle-wolves happened since, after the battle*; *what happened later to the battle-wolves after that battle*.

19. **Him**: reflexive; similarly in line 2045.

2025 freondum sinum;   bæd him[20] fultumes
      wærfæst hæleð   willgeðoftan,
      Aner and Manre,   Escol þriddan;
      cwæð þæt him wære   weorce on mode,
      sorga sarost,   þæt his suhtriga
2030 þeownyd þolode;   bæd him þræcrofe
      þa rincas þæs   ræd ahicgan,
      þæt his hyldemæg   ahreded[21] wurde,
      beorn mid bryde.   Him þa broðor þry
      æt spræce þære   spedum miclum
2035 hældon hygesorge,   heardum wordum
      ellenrofe,[22]   and Abrahame
      treowa sealdon,   þæt hie his torn mid him
      gewræcon[23] on wraðum,   oððe on wæl feollon.[24]
      Þa se halga heht   his heorðwerod
2040 wæpna onfon.[25]   He þær wigena fand,
      æscberendra,   XVIII
      and CCC eac,[26]   þeodenholdra,[27]
      þara þe he wiste   þæt meahte wel æghwylc
      on fyrd wegan   fealwe linde.
2045 Him þa Abraham gewat,   and þa eorlas þry
      þe him ær treowe sealdon   mid heora folcgetrume[28];
      wolde his mæg huru,

---

20. **him**, here and in line 2030: *for himself*; for this construction see BTD, Supp., **biddan** (IV).

21. **ahreded**] MS **ahred**.

22. **heardum wordum ellenrofe**: *the brave ones by means of brave words*.

23. **his torn** is the object of **gewræcon**.

24. **feollon**] MS **feallan**.

25. **onfon**] MS **ofon**, the **n** of **on-** superscribed in front of **f**.

26. **XVIII and CCC eac**: a frequent way of expressing large numbers; cp. BTD, **eac**.

27. **þeodenholdra**] MS **þeonden holdra**.

28. **folcgetrume**] MS **folce getrume**. This line, with non-distinctive alliteration, and line 2047, which is incomplete, indicate some kind of scribal error. Since there is no apparent break in the meaning, no attempt has been made to improve upon the MS reading; for various editorial improvements, see Krapp's notes to his edition, p. 186.

Loth alynnan   of laðscipe.

Rincas wæron²⁹ rofe³⁰;   randas wægon³¹

2050 forð fromlice   on foldwege.

Hildewulfas   herewicum neh

gefaren hæfdon.   Þa he his frumgaran,

wishydig wer,   wordum sægde,

Þares afera,   him wæs þearf micel

2055 þæt hie on twa healfe³²

grimme guðgemot   gystum eowdon

heardne handplegan;   cwæð þæt him se halga,

ece Drihten,   eaðe³³ mihte

æt þam spereniðe   spede lænan.

2060   Þa ic neðan gefrægn   under nihtscuwan

hæleð to hilde.   Hlyn wearð on wicum

scylda and sceafta,   sceotendra fyll,

guðflana gegrind;   gripon unfægre

under sceat³⁴ werum   scearpe garas,

2065 and feonda feorh   feollon ðicce.

Þær hlihende   huðe feredon

secgas and gesiððas.   Sigor eft ahwearf

of norðmonna   niðgeteone,

æsctir wera.   Abraham sealde

2070 wig to wedde,   nalles wunden gold,

for his suhtrigen³⁵;   sloh and fylde

feond on fitte   —him on fultum grap

heofonrices Weard!   Hergas wurdon

---

29. **wæron**] MS **waron**.

30. **rofe**] **f** scribally corrected from **r**.

31. **wægon**] **g** scribally corrected from **r**.

32. Line 2055: A half-line is all that the MS provides, as for line 2047; **hie**] MS **he**; **on twa healfe**: *on both sides.*

33. **eaðe**] MS **eað**.

34. **under sceat**: literally, *beneath* (or *through*) *their clothes*: figuratively, 'under their breasts,' into their hearts.

35. With characteristic Old English (poetic) irony, in this antithesis (lines 2069–2071) the poet states that Abraham gave not ransom (**wunden gold**) for Lot's return, but war. For a more detailed and dramatic use of the same antithesis, cp. *Maldon,* lines 45–61.

feower on fleame, folccyningas,
2075 leode ræswan; him on laste stod[36]
hihtlic heorðwerod, and hæleð lagon;
on swaðe sæton,[37] þa þe Sodoma
and Gomorra golde berofan,
bestrudon stigwitum. Him þæt stiðe geald[38]
2080 fædera Lothes. Fleonde wæron[39]
Elamitarna aldorduguðe,
dome bedrorene, oðþæt hie Domasco
unfeor wæron. Gewat him Abraham ða
on þa wigrode wiðertrod seon
2085 laðra monna. Loth wæs ahreded,
eorl mid æhtum; idesa hwurfon,
wif on willan.[40] Wide gesawon
freora feorhbanan fuglas slitan
on ecgwale. Abraham ferede
2090 suðmonna eft sinc and bryda,
aðelinga bearn, eðle[41] nior,
mægeð heora magum. Næfre mon ealra
lifigendra her lytle werede
þon wurðlicor wigsið ateah,
2095 þara þe wið swa miclum mægne geræsde.[42]

---

36. **him on laste stod**: *followed (pursued) them*; literally, *stood behind* (**on laste**) *them*. Cp. line 2001, **him on swaðe**, and *The Battle of Brunanburh*, line 22: **on last legdun laþum þeodum**.

37. **on swaðe sæton**: freely, *they* [**hæleð** = **norþmenn**] *remained* (dead) *behind* (*on the track*).

38. **geald**: Notice the use of this word together with **nalles wunden gold** (2070) and lines 1976b–1978.

39. **wæron**] not in MS.

40. **hwurfon . . . on willan**: *returned in joy*.

41. **eðle**] MS oðle.

42. The relationships of this long sentence (lines 2092b–2095) may be seen by rephrasing it: **Næfre mon ealra lifigendra, þara þe wið swa miclum mægne geræsde, þon wurðlicor wigsið ateah her lytle werede.**

Annex:/ Genesis VI:9–VIII:19; XIV:1–16[†]

Noe vir iustus atque perfectus fuit in generationibus suis
cum Deo ambulavit
et genuit tres filios Sem Ham et Iafeth
corrupta est autem terra coram Deo et repleta est iniquitate
cumque vidisset Deus terram esse corruptam
omnis quippe caro corruperat viam suam super terram
dixit ad Noe finis universae carnis venit coram me
repleta est terra iniquitate a facie eorum
et ego disperdam eos cum terra
fac tibi arcam de lignis levigatis
mansiunculas in arca facies
et bitumine linies intrinsecus et extrinsecus et sic facies eam
trecentorum cubitorum erit longitudo arcae
quinquaginta cubitorum latitudo
et triginta cubitorum altitudo illius
fenestram in arca facies et in cubito consummabis summitatem
ostium autem arcae pones ex latere deorsum
cenacula et tristega facies in ea
ecce ego adducam diluvii aquas super terram
ut interficiam omnem carnem
in qua spiritus vitae est subter caelum
universa quae in terra sunt consumentur
ponamque foedus meum tecum
et ingredieris arcam tu et filii tui
uxor tua et uxores filiorum tuorum tecum
et ex cunctis animantibus universae carnis
bina induces in arcam ut vivant tecum
masculini sexus et feminini
de volucribus iuxta genus suum

---

†From A. Henricus Quentin, ed., *Genesis* (vol. 1 of *Biblia Sacra*) (Rome 1926), pp. 163–171, 193–196. The full text is given here to illustrate what the poet chose to omit from his paraphrase as well as what he chose to include.

et de iumentis in genere suo

et ex omni reptili terrae secundum genus suum

bina de omnibus ingredientur tecum ut possint vivere

tolles igitur tecum ex omnibus escis quae mandi possunt et comportabis apud te

et erunt tam tibi quam illis in cibum.

Fecit ergo Noe omnia quae praeceperat illi Deus [*VII*] dixitque Dominus ad eum

ingredere tu et omnis domus tua arcam

te enim vidi iustum coram me in generatione hac

ex omnibus animantibus mundis tolles septena septena masculum et feminam

de animantibus vero non mundis duo duo masculum et feminam

sed et de volatilibus caeli septena septena masculum et feminam

ut salvetur semen super faciem universae terrae

adhuc enim et post dies septem ego pluam super terram

quadraginta diebus et quadraginta noctibus

et delebo omnem substantiam quam feci de superficie terrae.

Fecit ergo Noe omnia quae mandaverat ei Dominus

eratque sescentorum annorum quando diluvii aquae inundaverunt super terram

et ingressus est Noe et filii eius

uxor eius et uxores filiorum eius cum eo in arcam propter aquas diluvii

de animantibus quoque mundis et inmundis

et de volucribus et ex omni quod movetur super terram

duo et duo ingressa sunt ad Noe in arcam masculus et femina

sicut praeceperat Deus Noe

cumque transissent septem dies aquae diluvii inundaverunt super terram.

Anno sescentesimo vitae Noe mense secundo septimodecimo die mensis

rupti sunt omnes fontes abyssi magnae

et cataractae caeli apertae sunt

et facta est pluvia super terram quadraginta diebus et quadraginta noctibus

in articulo diei illius ingressus est Noe et Sem et Ham et Iafeth filii
eius

uxor illius et tres uxores filiorum eius cum eis in arcam

ipsi et omne animal secundum genus suum

universaque iumenta in genus suum

et omne quod movetur super terram in genere suo

cunctumque volatile secundum genus suum

universae aves omnesque volucres

ingressa sunt ad Noe in arcam bina et bina

ex omni carne in qua erat spiritus vitae

et quae ingressa sunt masculus et femina ex omni carne introierunt

sicut praeceperat ei Deus

et inclusit eum Dominus deforis

factumque est diluvium quadraginta diebus super terram

et multiplicatae sunt aquae et elevaverunt arcam in sublime a terra

vehementer inundaverunt et omnia repleverunt in superficie
terrae

porro arca ferebatur super aquas

et aquae praevaluerunt nimis super terram

opertique sunt omnes montes excelsi sub universo caelo

quindecim cubitis altior fuit aqua super montes quos operuerat

consumptaque est omnis caro quae movebatur super terram

volucrum animantium bestiarum omniumque reptilium quae
reptant super terram

universi homines et cuncta in quibus spiraculum vitae est in terra
mortua sunt

et delevit omnem substantiam quae erat super terram ab homine
usque ad pecus

tam reptile quam volucres caeli

et deleta sunt de terra

remansit autem solus Noe et qui cum eo erant in arca

obtinueruntque aquae terras centum quinquaginta diebus.

[VIII] Recordatus est autem Deus Noe cunctorumque animantium

et omnium iumentorum quae erant cum eo in arca

adduxit spiritum super terram et inminutae sunt aquae

et clausi sunt fontes abyssi et cataractae caeli

et prohibitae sunt pluviae de caelo

reversaeque aquae de terra euntes et redeuntes

et coeperunt minui post centum quinquaginta dies

requievitque arca mense septimo vicesima septima die mensis super montes Armeniae

at vero aquae ibant et decrescebant usque ad decimum mensem

decimo enim mense prima die mensis apparuerunt cacumina montium

cumque transissent quadraginta dies

aperiens Noe fenestram arcae quam fecerat dimisit corvum

qui egrediebatur et revertebatur donec siccarentur aquae super terram

emisit quoque columbam post eum ut videret si iam ccssassent aquae super faciem terrae

quae cum non invenisset ubi requiesceret pes eius reversa est ad eum in arcam

aquae enim erant super universam terram

extenditque manum et adpraehensam intulit in arcam

expectatis autem ultra septem diebus aliis rursum dimisit columbam ex arca

at illa venit ad eum ad vesperam

portans ramum olivae virentibus foliis in ore suo

intellexit ergo Noe quod cessassent aquae super terram

expectavitque nihilominus septem alios dies et emisit columbam

quae non est reversa ultra ad eum.

Igitur sescentesimo primo anno primo mense prima die mensis inminutae sunt aquae super terram

et aperiens Noe tectum arcae aspexit viditque quod exsiccata esset superficies terrae

mense secundo septima et vicesima die mensis arefacta est terra

locutus est autem Deus ad Noe dicens

egredere de arca tu et uxor tua

filii tui et uxores filiorum tuorum tecum

cuncta animantia quae sunt apud te ex omni carne

tam in volatilibus quam in bestiis

et in universis reptilibus quae reptant super terram

educ tecum et ingredimini super terram

crescite et multiplicamini super terram.

Egressus est ergo Noe et filii eius

uxor illius et uxores filiorum eius cum eo

sed et omnia animantia iumenta et reptilia quae repunt super terram

secundum genus suum arcam egressa sunt.

XIV: 1–16

Factum est autem in illo tempore ut Amrafel rex Sennaar

et Arioch rex Ponti

et Chodorlahomor rex Elamitarum

et Thadal rex Gentium

inirent bellum contra Bara regem Sodomorum

et contra Bersa regem Gomorrae

et contra Sennaab regem Adamae

et contra Semeber regem Seboim

contraque regem Balae ipsa est Segor

omnes hii convenerunt in vallem Silvestrem quae nunc est mare salis

duodecim enim annis servierant Chodorlahomor

et tertiodecimo anno recesserunt ab eo

igitur anno quartodecimo venit Chodorlahomor et reges qui erant cum eo

percusseruntque Rafaim in Astaroth Carnaim

et Zuzim cum eis

et Emim in Save Cariathaim

et Chorreos in montibus Seir

usque ad campestria Pharan quae est in solitudine

reversique sunt et venerunt ad fontem Mesfat ipsa est Cades

et percusserunt omnem regionem Amalechitarum

et Amorreum qui habitabat in Asasonthamar

et egressi sunt rex Sodomorum et rex Gomorrae

rexque Adamae et rex Seboim

necnon et rex Balae quae est Segor

et direxerunt contra eos aciem in valle Silvestri

scilicet adversum Chodorlahomor regem Elamitarum
et Thadal regem Gentium
et Amrafel regem Sennaar
et Arioch regem Ponti
quattuor reges adversus quinque
vallis autem Silvestris habebat puteos multos bituminis
itaque rex Sodomorum et Gomorrae terga verterunt ceciderunt-
    que ibi
et qui remanserant fugerunt ad montem
tulerunt autem omnem substantiam Sodomorum et Gomorrae
et universa quae ad cibum pertinent et abierunt
necnon et Loth et substantiam eius
filium fratris Abram qui habitabat in Sodomis
et ecce unus qui evaserat nuntiavit Abram Hebreo
qui habitabat in convalle Mambre Amorrei
fratris Eschol et fratris Aner
hii enim pepigerant foedus cum Abram
quod cum audisset Abram captum videlicet Loth fratrem suum
numeravit expeditos vernaculos suos trecentos decem et octo
et persecutus est eos usque Dan
et divisis sociis inruit super eos nocte
percussitque eos et persecutus est usque Hoba quae est ad laevam
    Damasci
reduxitque omnem substantiam et Loth fratrem suum cum sub-
    stantia illius
mulieres quoque et populum.

Two Texts

The following texts, from *Christ* (lines 1007–1038) and *Beowulf* (lines 1623–1676), are unedited here in different degrees. The word-division and metrical distribution have been normalized for the *Christ* passage, but the text is unpunctuated. The *Beowulf* passage is an approximate, literal transcription of the text as it appears in the manuscript; the pointing is retained, but the occasional accent marks and point over **y** are omitted; the scribal contractions are **7 = ond**, **ū = um**, **n̄ = ne**, **Þ = þæt**; the insular 3 and runic ρ are printed as **g** and **w**. These particular texts have been selected, for practice in textual study, because they require no emendation.

From CHRIST
The Exeter Book, folios 22ᵛ–23ʳ.

[*Glossary symbol:* X]

Ðonne mihtig god   on þone mæran beorg
mid þy mæstan   mægenþrymme cymeð
heofonengla cyning   halig scineð
wuldorlic ofer weredum   waldende god   1c
ond hine ymbutan   æþelduguð betast
halge herefeðan   hlutre blicað
eadig engla gedryht   ingeþoncum
forhte beofiað   fore fæder egsan

forþon nis ænig wundor   hu him woruldmonna   1015
seo unclæne gecynd   cearum sorgende
hearde ondrede   ðonne sio halge gecynd
hwit ond heofonbeorht   heagengla mægen
for ðære onsyne beoð   egsan afyrhte
bidað beofiende   beorhte gesceafte   1020
dryhtnes domes   daga egeslicast
weorþeð in worulde   þonne wuldorcyning
þurh þrym þreað   þeoda gehwylce
hateð arisan   reordberende
of foldgrafum   folc anra gehwylc   1025
cuman to gemote   moncynnes gehwone
þonne eall hraðe   adames cynn
onfehð flæsce   weorþeð foldræste
eardes æt ende   sceal þonne anra gehwylc
fore cristes cyme   cwic arisan   1030
leoðum onfon   ond lichoman
edgeong wesan   hafað eall on him
þæs þe he on foldan   in fyrndagum
godes oþþe gales   on his gæste gehlod
geara gongum   hafað ætgædre bu   1035
lic ond sawle   sceal on leoht cuman
sinra weorca wlite   ond worda gemynd
ond heortan gehygd   fore heofona cyning.

From *BEOWULF*

British Museum, MS Cotton Vitellius A XV, folios 165ᵛ–166ᵛ,
and the Thorkelin transcripts.

[*Glossary symbol*: Y]

Com þato lande lid manna helm swið
mod swymman sæ lace gefeah mægen
byrþenne þara þe he him mid hæfde.   [1625]
Eodon him þato geanes gode þancodon
ðryð lic þegna heap þeodnes ge fegon
þæs þe hi hyne ge sund ne geseon moston.

ða wæs of þæm hroran helm 7 byrne
lungre alysed lagu drusade wæter   [163
under wolcnum wæl dreore fag. ferdon
forð þonon feþe lastum ferhþum
fægne fold weg mæton cuþe stræte
cyning balde men from þæm holm
clife hafelan bæron earfoðlice heora   [163
æg hwæþrū fela modigra feower scoldon
on þæm wælstenge weorcum geferian to
þæm gold sele grendles heafod opðæt
semninga tosele comon frome fyrd
hwate feowertyne geata gongan gum   [16
dryhten mid modig onge monge meodo
wongas træd. ðacom ingan ealdor
ðegna dæd cene mon dome ge wurþad
hæle hilde deor hroðgar gretan. þa
wæs befeaxe on flet boren grend les   [16
heafod þær guman druncon egeslic for
eorlum 7þære idese mid wlite seon wræt
lic weras onsawon.

XXIIII

Beowulf maþelode bearn ecg þeowes
hwæt we þe þas sælac sunu healfdenes   [16
leod scyldinga lustū brohton tires
to tacne þe þu her tolocast. ic þ un
softe ealdre ge digde wigge under
wætere weorc geneþde earfoðlice   [1
æt rihte wæs guð ge twæfed nymðe
mec god scylde. Ne meahte ic æthil
de mid hruntinge wiht ge wyrcan
þeah þ wæpen duge. ac me ge uðe
ylda waldend þ ic onwage geseah wlitig
hangian eald sweord eacen oftost wisode   [1
winigea leasum þic ðy wæpne gebræd.
ofsloh ða æt þære sæcce þame sæl

ageald huses hyrdas þa þ hilde bil for
barn brogden mæl. swa þ blod gesprang
hatost he[a] þo swata ic þ hilt þanan feon   [166₅
dum æt ferede fyren dæda wræc deað
cwealm denigea swa hit gedefe wæs. ic
hit þe þoñ ge hate þþu on heorote most
sorh leas swefan mid þinra secga gedryht
7 þegna ge hwylc þinra leoda duguðe 7io   [167₀
goþe þ þu him on drædan neþearft þeo
den scyldinga on þa healfe aldor bealu
eorlum swa þu ær dydest.

The manuscript illustrations of four of the preceding edited texts represent scribal hands in the period c970–c1150. By comparing the plates with the edited texts, notice the special forms for **g**, **r**, **s**, **w**, and the abbreviation signs for **and/ond**, **þæt**, **-m**, and **-ne**. By comparing the plates with one another, observe the variations in letter forms, especially for **a**, **c**, **d**, **e**, **f**, **g**, **h**, **t**, **y**, and ligatures (such as **st**). Some letters in the same plate have more than one distinctive form; notice the position and distribution of variant forms, including capitals, in each plate. What kind of distinction does there seem to be in the use of **g**-forms in Plate 5? Punctuation in these plates is marked by a mid-line point (not to be confused with an occasional dotted-curve tail of final letters). Plate 5 shows the point on the line and a few instances of the inverted semicolon and hyphen. Does there seem to be any consistent function to the pointing, corresponding to modern punctuation practice? Notice especially the use of pointing in Plate 3 (of *Genesis A*): in what way and to what degree does the manuscript pointing in this plate agree with the punctuation of the edited text?

It may be useful, as a means of gaining preciseness in detail, to write out a description of the physical appearance (size and shape) of letter forms (alone and in combination) in one or more plates. Listed below are some of the terms commonly used in paleographical description; each term is followed by an *example* of a letter to which it may be applied. In using these terms, or others of your own devising, the aim should be a *concise* and *clear* description of graphic form.

> pointed [**a**], square(d) [**a**], round(ed) [**a**],
> straight-back(ed)/round-back(ed) [**d**],
> open-topped [**e**], descender [**r**, **s**], ascender [**f**, **s**],
> bow(ed) [**p**], low/long/round [**s**], straight-limbed [**y**],
> cross-bar [**ð**], tail [**g**], head [**s**], limb [**h**, **y**],
> split/tagged [**ð**, **þ**], down stroke/up stroke [**p**, **ð**],
> ligature [**e** + another letter].

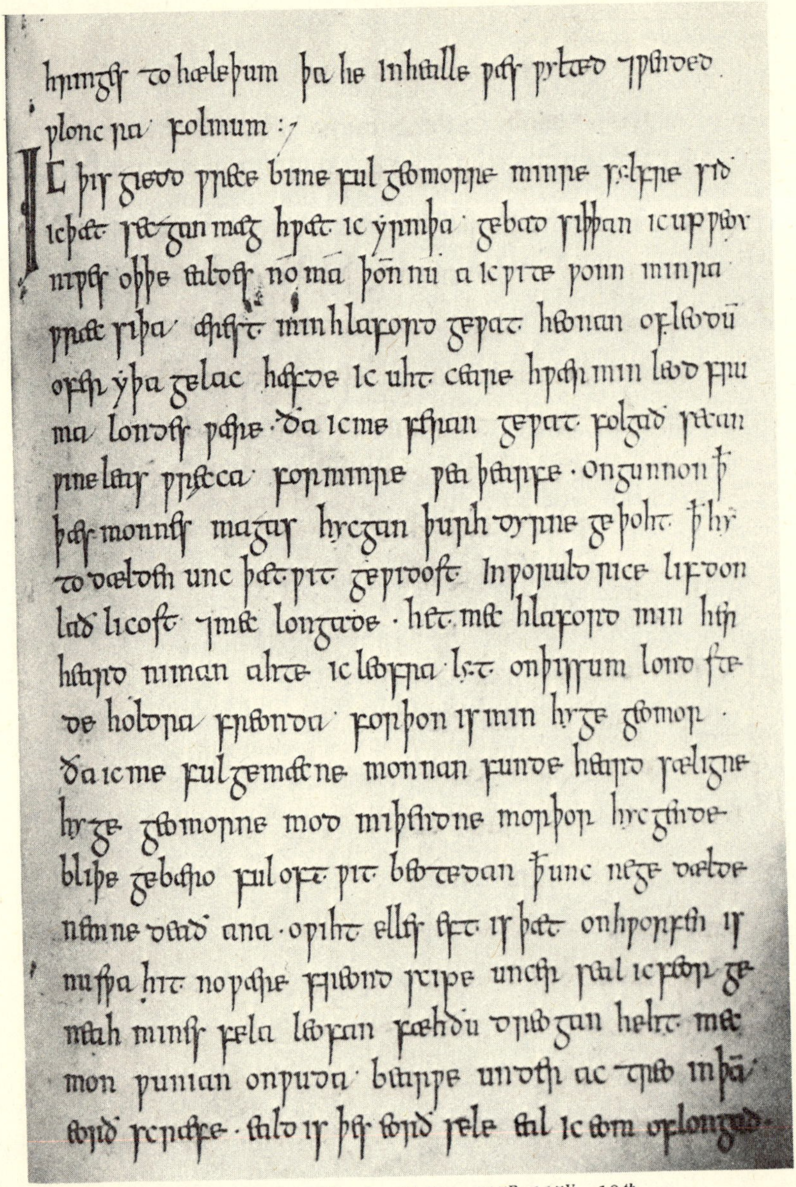

Plate 1 MS: The Exeter Book, Folios 115ᴿ–115ⱽ; 10th century, second half. Text: "The Wife's Lament."

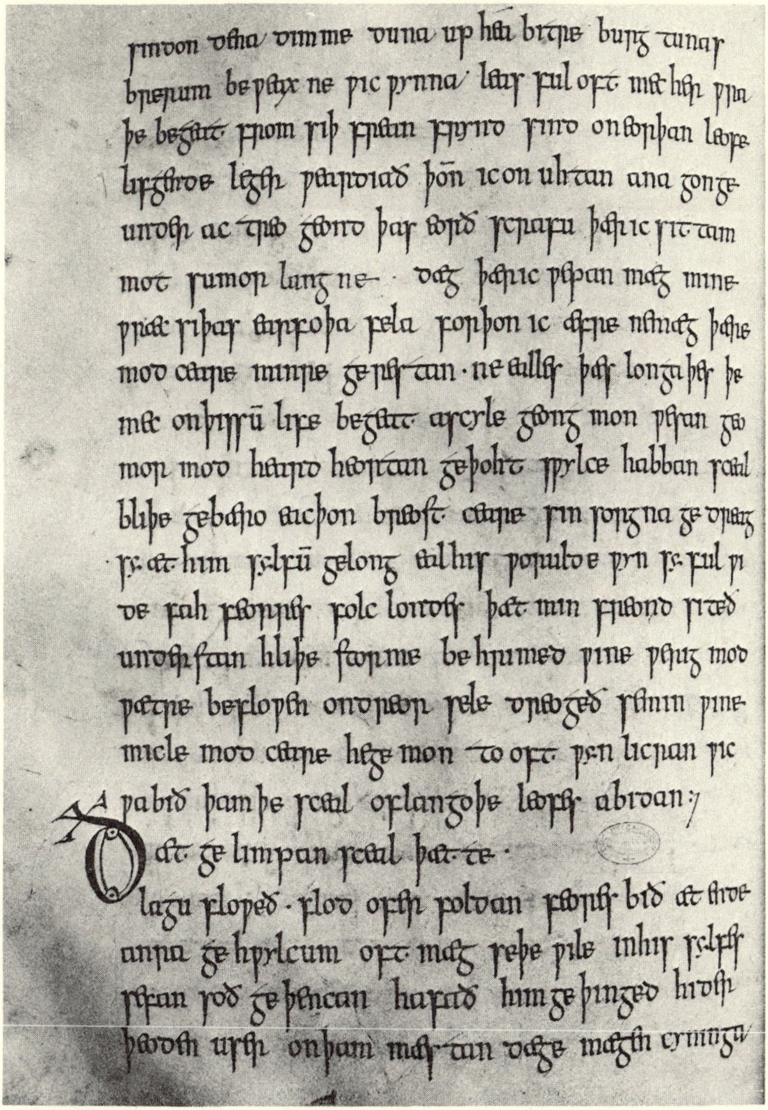

Plate 2

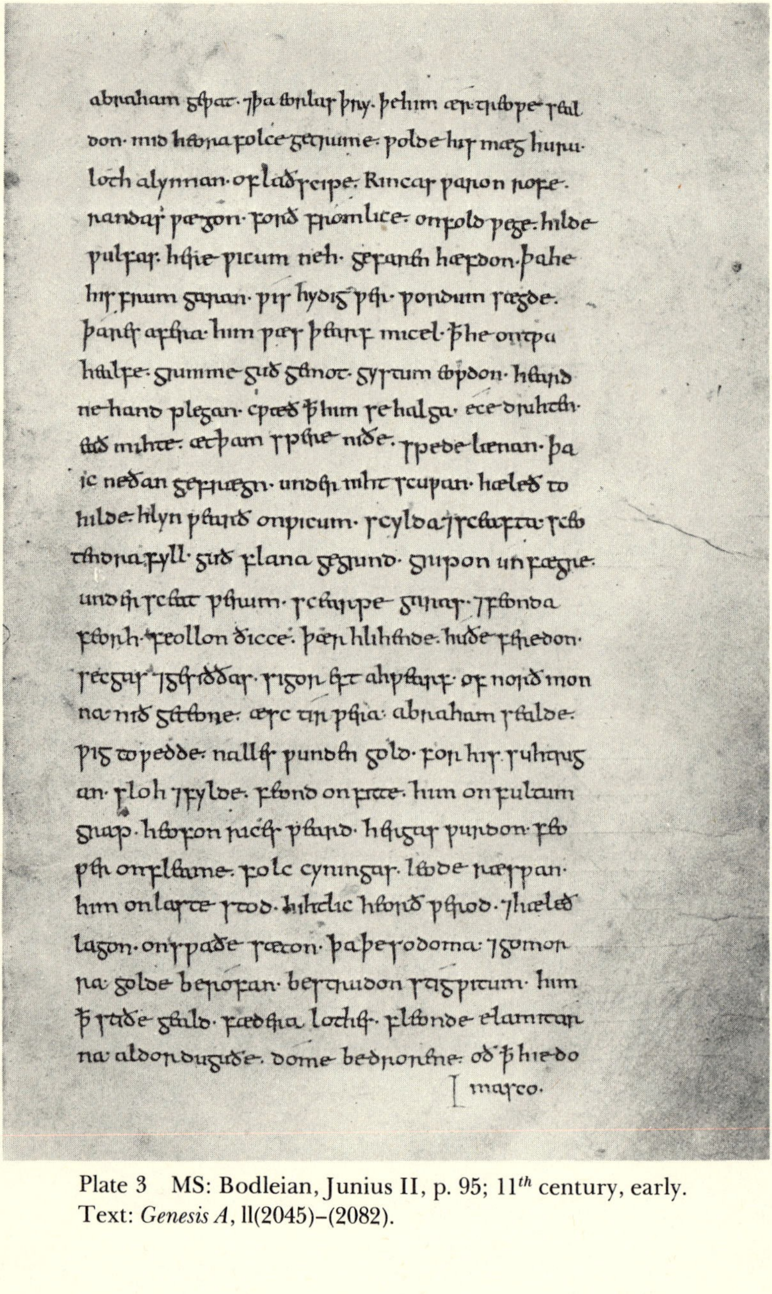

Plate 3   MS: Bodleian, Junius II, p. 95; 11th century, early.
Text: *Genesis A*, ll(2045)–(2082).

20.

ƿæt nextan · be hiſ ſƿeonda ræde · ſoþ geaf þa tan
man dohteſ þam deofleſ cnihte · mid mycclū
æhtam · ⁊hiſ man nyſte · Ða nolde ſe deofleſ
cniht · cuman næſſe to cirican · ne goeſ ſoþo
ge hyþan · ne þa halgan meſſan · Þeaþid þa
ge opnad hiſ raſman ſiſe · hiſ man ſullan
be hat · þam hetolan deofle · ⁊heo mid miſ
celſe angſum nyſſe · aſin to baſilie · ⁊cyode
him be enoſ byþonyſſe hyþe cnihteſ ſiſſen
ſæc · þa hec ſe halga þeſ · hine to him geſæc
can · ⁊be ſſian giſ hiſ ſſa þeſie · þa hiſ ſiſ
him ſæde · ⁊hſ ſæde mid þoþe hu he beſſican
þeaþid · Þa aſode ſe biſceop ·ſylc þu bugan
æſt to xþe · Se þyſſeſ ſaca ic ſylle goþne
leoſ · ac ic ne mæg · þeah ic ſylle · ſoſ þan þe ic
ſid ſoc cuſte · ⁊on ſe þſyce aſæſtnode þic þæſie
þaſ deofleſ · Se halga þeſ him cæd to · Ne ho
ga þu embe þ · uſe haleno lſ ſſſe ſel ſyllen
de · ⁊ſyſle þe æſt undeſ ſon · giſ þu mid ſoſue
dæd bote ſe cyſſe æſt to him · Hſæt þa baſi
luſ ſe blæc ſode þone cniht · ⁊be leac hine
on ſunoþon · on ſumeſe diſelſe ſtoþe · ⁊tæhta
him bota · ⁊ſe bæd ſoſ hine · Com æſt ymbe
dſy daſuſ · aſode hu he mihte · Ða cæd ſe
dæd beta · þa deoflu cumað to me · ⁊me ſſide
ge eſſiað · ⁊eac ſſylce toſſiad · ⁊habbað hı
on haſnod · min aſen hand ſe þſyc · cþædad þ
ic comeᵗ hı · ⁊na hı tome · Baſiluſ him cæd
to · ne beo ðu aſyſht · ſe lyſ ſod licr ongod·
⁊ſenode hine æſt · be leac æſt þa duſuſ·
⁊ lede him hiſ mete · He comſ æſt ym be
ſeaþa daſa · ⁊cunnode þæſ manneſ · Se cniht

Plate 4 MS: British Museum, Cotton Julius E. VII, Folio
20ᴿ; 11th century, early. Text: Ælfric, "The Devil and the
Apostate."

mes dæg. Þær wuneð on an fugel wrætlic
fenix ge haten. he is micel ⁊ mære swa se
mihtige hine gescop. he is hlaford ofer
eall fugel cynn. ælc cepe þuca ane side
se wrætlic fugel hine baðeð. on þære liþes
pelle. ⁊ þon whild se fugel ⁊ ge sett up
pe þ begeste þrop on gean þære hatan
sunne þon scind he swa sunne leome the
glitened swile he gyldene seo. his feðeren
synden ængles feðeren gelice. his breost
⁊ bile bryhte scined wrætlic ⁊ wrage. fea
þe synden swylce. hwæt his eagene swa
aðele synden swa clæne swa cristal ⁊ swa
sciene swa suneleome. his fet synden blod
reade begen. ⁊ se bile hwit. hwæt se wræt
þe fugel whild of his eande. se þe is wræt
þe fenix ge haten. þone wuneð he prud
lice on egipte lande. fiftene þusan reste
to gadere. þone cumeð him to swa swa to
to heora kinge wægeninde spyde. eall þ fu
gel cynn. ⁊ wrætlic gegrieted ealle fenix.
wriciged ⁊ singed. ealle abuten hun. ælc

Plate 5 MS: British Museum, Cotton Vespasian D. XIV,
Folio 167^{R}; 12th century, middle. Text: "Of the Phoenix."

GLOSSARY

Arrangement and Contents of the Glossary

The order of the Glossary is alphabetical: æ initially and internally follows **ad**; all words beginning with the prefix **ge-** are grouped under **G**; words beginning with **þ** are grouped together in a section which follows words beginning with **t**. Proper names appear, alphabetically, at the end of the Glossary proper. Cross-references are made throughout to variant forms of head-words (**fram**, see **from**), some forms of nouns, pronouns, and adjectives (**fēos**, see **feoh**; **hīe**, see **hē**; **cucra**, see **cwic**), and many tense-forms of verbs (**cūðe**, see **cunnan**; **dyde**, see **dōn**).

The style and sequence of syntactic description is:

1. *For nouns*: singular forms, nominative-genitive-dative-dative/instrumental-accusative; plural forms, nominative through accusative.

2. *For adjectives and pronouns*: declensional case + number + gender (e.g., nsm. = nominative singular masculine, aplm.wk. = accusative plural masculine weak); comparative and superlative forms (of adjectives).

3. *For verbs*: (a) infinitive; (b) present-tense forms, first to third persons (e.g., pres. 1s. = present first-person singular); present subjunctive and negative present forms; (c) past-tense forms (e.g., pret. 3pl. = preterite third-person plural); preterite subjunctive and negative preterite forms; (d) imperative, present participle, past participle, and gerund forms. Verbs are classified by the traditional grammatical category to which they belong: strong (or vocalic) verbs, classes 1–7 (Arabic numbers); weak (or consonantal) verbs, classes I–III (Roman numbers); preterite-present, anomalous, and contract verbs.

Syntactic description and citation of occurring forms are intended to be exhaustive for nouns, adjectives, verbs, and some pronouns. A few non-ambiguous forms of relative high frequency are given but not listed by text, and these are capitalized and followed by the citation of first appearance plus *etc.*; such forms are **CWÆÐ** (pret. 3s. of **cweðan**), **DĒOFLES** (gs. of **dēofol**), **GODES** (gs. of **god**), **HÆFDE** (pret. 3s. of **habban**), **SINGAN** (inf.), and

WEARÐ (pret. 3s. of **weorðan**). Fully recorded but in most cases not cited by text are adverbs (and their phrasals), prepositions (and their phrasals), conjunctions, interjections, personal pronouns, the forms of **eom-wesan**, and the forms of **sē** (**sēo**, **þæt**). A form which is identical with the head-word, usually a nominative singular or infinitive, is not repeated but cited by text-reference alone; a form which differs from the head-word by inflection, internal change, or orthographical variation is cited in full (e.g., **axode**, **ǣdra**), or by the inflection added to the stem (e.g., **-e**, **-an**, **-um**, **-ne**), or by part of the head-word internally changed and/or inflected (e.g., **-wrigen**, **-burste**); the distinction between **þ** and **ð** is normally made in citations, but in some headwords and multiple citations of a given form **þ** may appear for **ð** and vice versa. Following any given syntactic category (such as ns., or pret. 3s.), the relevant text-references are given in alphabetical order, AI to Y (see Abbreviations, below).

The meanings given for words, based on present lexicographical knowledge, are those which are appropriate to the texts; for the full record of meanings and usage of a word throughout its history in Anglo-Saxon the reader should consult the Bosworth-Toller Dictionary and Supplement, and occasionally the Middle English Dictionary. In cases in which more than one meaning is given the meanings are not prescriptively classified by text or context; here the reader must make a choice among the possibilities. In many instances, particularly for compounds, an attempt has been made to give both literal and transferred (often figurative) meanings, since one *kind* of meaning may throw light upon another. Extended meanings, of words chiefly in the poems, considered apt to a particular context are suggested but usually prefixed by a question mark.

Abbreviations

absol. = absolute (as of adjectives used as nouns)
a./acc. = accusative
adj. = adjective
adv. = adverb, adverbial
anom.v. = anomalous verb

art. = article
comp. = comparative (forms of adjectives and adverbs)
conj. = conjunction
contr.v. = contract verb
cp. = compare
d./dat. = dative
dem. = demonstrative
d-i = dative-instrumental
Eng. = Modern English
f. = feminine (gender)
g./gen. = genitive
ger. = gerund
Ger. = Modern German
Gk. = Greek
imper. = imperative (forms of verbs)
impers. = impersonal
indef. = indefinite
inf. = infinitive
inst. = instrumental
interj. = interjection
Lat. = Latin
lit. = literally
m. = masculine (gender)
MS = manuscript
n. = neuter (gender)
n./nom. = nominative
neg. = negative
num. = number, numeral
O.Ic. = Old Icelandic
pers. = personal
pl. = plural
poss. = possessive
pp. = past participle
prep. = preposition
pres. = present (tense)
pres.p. = present participle
pret. = preterite (tense)
pret.-pres.v. = preterite-present verb
pron. = pronoun
rd. = reduplicating (verb)
rel. = relative (pronoun); related to (etymologically)
s. = singular
st. = strong (of verb classes)

subj. = subjunctive
superl. = superlative (forms of adjectives and adverbs)
v./vb. = verb
voc. = vocative
w. = with
wk. = weak (of verb classes and declensional forms)

AI = Ælfric: *The Devil and the Apostate*
AII = Ælfric: *St. John and the Wayward Boy*
C = Bede: *Cædmon*
G = *Genesis A*
P = *Of the Phoenix*
R29 = *Riddle 29* (followed by line number)
R39 = *Riddle 39* (followed by line number)
R47 = *Riddle 47* (followed by line number)
V = *Vainglory*
W = Wulfstan: *De falsis Diis*
Wh = *The Whale*
WL = *The Wife's Lament*
X = *Christ*
Y = *Beowulf*

(n) signifies that a form is contained in a note to one of the texts: For Prose texts, the number given is the *Footnote number*, as P(n18) = *Of the Phoenix*, Footnote 18; for Poetic texts, the number refers to the *line* for which there is a note, as G(n1298) = *Genesis A*, note to line 1298.

A number of words throughout the Glossary have variant spellings for the same case- or tense-form in the same text, or in different texts, or in both (e.g., see **cōm/cwōm**, pret. 3s. of **cuman**). The principal spelling variations which occur involve the following graphic (and often phonological) contrasts: **e/i/y** (as **-ness**, **-niss**, **-nyss**), **a/o** (as **and**, **ond**), **æ/e** (as **fæste**, **feste**), intervocalic or final single/doubled consonant (as **-l-/-ll-**, **-s/-ss**).

Head-Words: A List of the Chief Variant Forms and Spellings

æfest/æfst
and/ond

be/bī
bebēodan/bibēodan
bitwēonum/betwonen
bliss/blyss
bōc/booc

cwic/cucu
cwide/cwyde
cynn/cinn

drihten/dryhten

engel/ængel

fæste/feste
fela/feale
forðām/forðon
from/fram

gangan/gongan
gehwilc/gehwylc
gēn/gīen
gewrit/gewryt
gīeman/gēman
gīet/gīt

hand/hond
hēah/hēh
hiht/hyht
hīw/hēow

hring/hryng
hwæt/hwat
hwæðer/hweðer
hwanan/hwonan
hwīl/hwȳl
hwilc/hwylc/hwelc

igland/iglond
ilca/ylca

lago/lagu
land/lond
lang/long
langian/longian
langoþ/longaþ
libban/lifgan/lifian

manig/monig
man(n)/mon(n)
mergen/morgen
micel/mycel
mildheort/myldheort

nā/nō
nalæs/nal(l)es/nealles
nama/noma
nān/nǣn
nēah/nēh
nerian/nergan
-ness/-niss/-nyss
niht/neaht
niðer/nyðer
nōht/nāht

ræced/reced
regn/reign
rest/ræst
riht/ryht

samod/somed
sawol/saw(u)l
sceamu/scomu
sellan/syllan
sibb/sybb
siððan/syððan
standan/stondan
stefn/stemne
swilc/swylc
swilce/swelce/swylc(e)
swiðe/swyðe

sylf/self/seolf

tōsamne/tōsomne

ufan/ufene/ufon

wann/wonn
welm/wylm
weorðment/wyrðment
werian/wergan
werod/weorud
wiht/wuht
woruld/wurld
wræcca/wrecca

ymb(e)/emb(e)

A

ā, adv., *always, ever, continually*; **ā butan ende/ā bute ænde**, *world without end, for ever.*

abbudisse, f., *abbess*; ns. C62; gs. **-dissan** C1; ds. **-dissan** C50. [Lat. *abbātissa*]

ābēodan, st. v. 2, *order, command*; pret. 3s. **ābēad** G1362. [Ger. *bieten*]

ābīdan, st.v.1, w. gen., *await*; inf. WL53. [Eng. *abide*]

āblicgan, wk.v.I, *be astonished, grow pale*; pp. nsm. **āblicged** AII 56, 60.

ābūtan/-en, prep., *about, around.*

ābylgness, f., *anger, hostility*; as. **-e** V71. [**-bylg-**, rel. **belg**, m., *bag, bellows*; **belgan**, st.v.3, *become angry*]

ac, conj., *but.*

acsian, wk.v.II, *ask, demand*; pret. 3s. **axode** AI 40, 48, 72.

āctrēo, n., *oak tree*; ds. WL28, 36.

ācwellan, wk.v.I, *kill, destroy*; inf. G1296, 1353; pret. 3s. **ācwealde** G1403. [rel. Eng. *quell*]

adūne, adv., *down, downward.*

ǣdre, f., *fountain, spring, vein of water*; npl. G(n1374); gpl. **ǣdra** G1374. [Ger. *Ader*]

ǣfen(n), n. (and m.), *evening*; ds. **-e** C95, G1461.

æfest/æfst, f., *envy*; dipl. **-um** V37, **æfæstum** V43.

ǣfest/ǣfæst, adj., *devout, pious*; nsm. C84; asf. **-an** C16; apln. **-e** C10. [ǣ- = ǣ/ǣw, f., *law, covenant*]

ǣfeste, adv., *devotedly, piously.*

ǣfestniss/ǣfæstniss, f., *devotion, religion*; ds. **-e** C3, 16.

ǣfre, adv., *ever, always.*

æfter, prep. w. dat., *after* (in time or space); *according to*; *in the course of.*

æfter, adv., *after(wards), then.*

æfterweard, adj., *after, following*; nsm. AII 84.

æfþonca, wk.m., *insult, anger*; ?*egregious person*; ns. V26. [æf- = prep., *of, from*; þanc(a), *thought*]

ǣghwæðer, pron., *each*; dsm. **-þrum** Y.

ǣghwylc, adj. and pron., *each (one), every (one)*; nsm. G2043, V9; nsn. R39: 25; asm. **-ne** R39: 5.

ǣgðer (= **ǣghwæðer**), pron., *each (of two), either*; as. R39:11.

ǣht, f., *possessions, goods; wealth*; dpl. **-um** G2012, 2086; **-an** AI 33 [MS **-am**]; apl. **-a** G1353, 1435. [rel. **āgan**]

ǣlan, wk.v.I, *kindle*; pres. 3pl. **ǣlað** Wh22.

ǣlc, adj. pron., *each, any*; nsm. absol. P38; nsn. P15; gsn. **-es** G1338; dsm. **-e** P13; dsf. **-e** P51, **-ere** P26; dsn. **-um** G1305.

ǣled, m., *fire*; as. Wh21.

ælmesse, f., *alms (giving)*; dpl. **-mæssan** P(n19). [Lat., Gk. *eleēmosyna*]

ælmihtig, adj., *almighty*; nsm. C45, G1359, 1361, 1427, P(n18), W85; dsm.wk. **-an** AI 62. [cp. Lat. *omnipotens*]

ænd, see **end**.

ængel, see **engel**.

ǣnig, adj. (and pron.), *any, anyone*; nsm. absol. P(n18); nsn. X1015; asn. C102, R39: 27 [MS **hænig**], W4; asm. **-ne** G1453.

ǣnlic, adj., *excellent, singular*; nsn. P(n1); gsn. **-es** AII 7. [ǣn-, rel. **ān**, adj., *one, unique*]

ænre, see **an**.

ǣr, adv., *before, formerly, already*; prep., *before*; **ǣr þan þe**, *before, until*; **ǣr ond sīþ**, *before and since*.

ǣrcwide, m., *former (ancient) saying, pronouncement*; *?old prophecy*; *?as*. V4.

ǣrest(e), superl. adv. (of **ǣr**), *earliest, first*.

ǣror, comp. adv. (of **ǣr**), *earlier, beforehand*.

ǣs, n., *food, carrion*; gs. **-es** G(n1983). [Ger. Aas]

æscberend, m., *(ash) spear-* or *lance-bearer*; gpl. **-ra** G2041. [Ger. Esche]

æscstede, f., *spear-place*; *?battlefield*; ns. V17.

æsctīr, m., *spear-glory, glory in war*; ns. G2069.

æt, prep. w. dat., *at, in, by, to*; **æt nextan/niehstan/nyhstan**, *at last, finally*.

ǣt, f., *food*; gs. **-es** Wh52. [rel. Eng. *eat*]

ætberstan, st.v.3, *break out, break away*; pres. 3s. **-bærst** AII 67; pret. subj. 3s. **-burste** AII 77.

ætferian, wk.v.I, *carry away*; pret. 1s. **-ferede** Y.

ætflēon, st.v.2, w. dat., *flee, escape*; inf. AII 78.

ætforan, prep. w. dat., *before, in front of*.

ætgædere, adv., *together*.

ǣtgifa, wk.m., *food-giver, provider*; ds. **-n** G1361.

ætrihte, adv., *immediately*.

ætsomne, adv., *together*.

ætstandan, st.v.6, *stand still, stop, stay*; imper. s. **-stand** AII 91; pret. 3s. **-stōd** AII 92.

ætȳwan, wk.v.I, *show, reveal (oneself)*; inf. G1481.

æðelduguð, f., *noble retinue*; ns. X1011.

æðele, adj., *noble*; npln. P32. [Ger. *edel*]

æðeling, m., *nobleman, prince*; gs. **-es** G1288; gpl. **-a** G2002, 2091.

æðelu, n., *descent, noble origin*; dpl. **-m** G1440; apl. **æðelo** G1389.

āfæstnian, wk.v.II, *fasten, confirm*; pret. 1s. **-node** AI 42.

afera (= **eafora**), wk.m., *son*; ns. G2054.

āflȳman, wk.v.I, *cause to flee, put to flight, drive away*; pret. 3s. **āflȳmde** W41.

āfyrht, pp. adj. (of **āfyrhtan**, I), *frightened, terrified*; nsm. AI 52; asn. **-e** AII 106.

āfyrhtan, wk.v.I, *frighten, terrify*; pp. nplm. **āfyrhte** X1019.

āgan, pret.-pres.v., *have, possess*; pret. 1s. **āhte** WL16; pres. neg. 3pl. **nāgon** Wh78. [Eng. *owe, ought*; cp. **æht**, f.]

āgen, adj., *own, proper*; nsm. W25, 73; nsn. V80; gsf. **-re** AII 40; dsf. **-re** W43, **-ra** AI 19; dsn. G1305; asm. **-e** W41, **-ne** W12; asn. AI 50, V6; dplm. **-um** W34; dplf. **-um** G1366; apln. **-e** W37.

āgend, m., *owner, lord*; apl. G1353.

āgifan, st.v.5, *give (back), render, return*; pres. 2s. **āgife** AI 69; pret. 3s. **āgēaf** C61, **āgēafe** G1428.

āgildan, st.v.3, *pay, render, repay; provide; permit*; inf. AII 88; pret. 3s. **āgeald** G2008, (n2008), Y. [Eng. *yield*; rel. Eng. *guild*, Ger. *Geld*]

āginnan, st.v.3, *begin, undertake*; pret. 3pl. **āgunnan** W18.

āglǣca, wk.m., *monster, fiend*; as. **-n** Wh52.

āhebban, st.v.6, *lift, heave up; exalt*; pres. 3s. **āhefeð** V54; pret. 3s. **āhof** G1388, 1419; pret. 3pl. **āhofan** V59; pp. **āhafen** nsm. G(n1983), nsf. G1401. [Eng. *heave*]

āhicgan, wk.v.III, *devise, invent, find*; inf. G2031.

āhlǣnan, wk.v.I, *set (oneself) up, incline (oneself)*; pres. 3s. **-eð** V53. [Ger. *lehnen*]

āhreddan, wk.v.I, *snatch away (by force); rescue*; pret. 3s. **āhredde** R29:9; pp. nsm. **āhreded** G2032 [MS **ahred**], 2085.

āhrēosan, st.v.2, *rush down, fall*; pret. 3s. **āhrēas** V(n34).

āhte, see **āgan**.

āhwār, adv., *anywhere*.

āhweorfan, st.v.3, *turn away, avert*; pret. 3s. **āhwearf** G2067.

āhȳðan, wk.v.I, *destroy, lay waste*; pret. 3pl. **āhȳðdan** G2007 [MS **ahudan**].

ālǣdan, wk.v.I, *lead (out)*; pret. 3s. **ālǣdde** AII 102, G1495; imper. pl. **ālǣdað** AII 79.

aldor, m. (= **ealdor**), *elder, chief, prince*; as. G1960, 1980.

aldorbealu, n., *injury to life, death*; as. Y. [**-bealu**, Eng. *bale*]

aldorduguð, m., *chief nobility*; npl. **-e** G2081.

ālēat, see **ālūtan**.

allwihte, f.pl., *all creatures*; gpl. **-wihta** G1290.

ālūtan, st.v.2, *incline, bow down*; pret. 3s. **āleat** AII 93, 100. [rel. Eng. *lout*]

ālynnan, st.v.3, *deliver, release*; inf. G2048.

ālȳsan, wk.v.I, *loosen, take off*; pp. nsm. **ālȳsed** Y.

āmeldian, wk.v.II, *betray, make known*; inf. AI 4. [Ger. *melden*]

Amen, Latin end-formula, *may it be so!*

āmyrran, wk.v.I, *disturb, damage, corrupt*; inf. V11. [Eng. *mar*]

ān, adj., *one, sole, only*; indef. pron. function, *a, an*; nsm. AI 3, G2019, P24, W29, 35, 85, 87; nsm. wk. **-a** W27, WL22, (n7); nsf. W85; nsf.wk. **-a** WL35; nsn. AII 72, P1; dsm. **-um** AI 5, W38, **-e** P13, 26; dsf. **-re** AII 1, 69; asm. **ænne** W27, 39; asf. **-e** AI 1, G1478; asn. G1473, P54; gpl. **-ra** X1025, 1029; see next word.

ān/āna/āne, adv., *alone*; C15, P65, (n18), WL 22, 35.

and/ond, conj., *and*.

andgit/-gyt, n., *understanding*; ns. P(n19); as. Wh(n35). [**git**, rel. (be)**gietan**, st.v.5, *get*]

andswaru, f., *answer*; ds. **-sware** AII 66; as. **-sware** C34.

andweardnyss, f., *presence*; ds. **-e** AII 83.

andwlita, wk.m., *face, surface*; as. **-n** G1348.

ānforlǣtan, st.v.7, *relinquish, forsake*; pret. subj. 3s. **-lēte** C64.

angin, n., *conduct, resolve; beginning, purpose*; gs. **-nes** V(n34); ds. **-ne** AII 8.

angsumnyss, f., *anguish, anxiety, sorrow*; ds. **-e** AI 36. [Ger. *eng*]

ānrǣdlīce , adv., *resolutely*. [**ān** (*one*) + **rǣd**, m., *counsel*; cp. Lat. *unanimiter*]

apostol, m., *apostle*; ns. AII 48, 99; ds. **-e** AII 57; as. AII 83; gpl. **-a** C78. [Lat. *apostolus*]

ār, m., *messenger, bearer of wisdom*; ns. V2.

ār, f., *honor, favor*; gpl. **-a** G1348. [Ger. *Ehre*]

ārǣran, wk.v.I, *raise up*; pret. 3s. **ārǣrde** W4.

ārfæstniss, f., *honor-firmness, piety, virtue*; ds. **-e** C3.

ārīsan, st.v.1, *arise*; inf. AII 113, C115, X1024, 1030; pres. 3s. **ārīseð** P59; pret. 3s. **ārās** C22, 46.

ārlēas, adj., *void of honor, infamous, cruel*; dsm. wk. **-an** AI 11; gplm. **-ra** G1385.

arn, see **irnan**.

ārwurð, adj., *honorable, venerable*; nsm. **-e** AI 1, W65; superl. nsm.
    -ost W50.

ārwurðnyss, f., *honor, dignity*; ds. **-e** AII 24.

āscyran, wk.v.I, *cut off*; pp. nsm. **āscyred** V(n34). [Eng. *shear*]

āsecgan, wk.v.III, *relate, assert*; WL (n37).

āsendan, wk.v.I, *send forth*; pret. 3s. **āsende** AII 92.

āsettan, wk.v.I, *place, set (up)*; inf. R29:6.

āsingan, st.v.3, *sing*; pret. 3s. **āsong** C61.

āstīgan, st.v.1, *climb, mount (up), ascend*; inf. V73; pret. 3s. **āstāg**
    V58. [Ger. *steigen*]

ātēon, st.v.2, *draw out, lead out*; pret. 3s. **ātēah** G2094; pret. subj.
    3s. **ātuge** C82. [rel. Ger. *ziehen*]

ātimbran, wk.v.I, *build*; inf. R29:5.

attorcræft, m., *poisonous, evil art*; apl. **-as** P(n19).

āð, m., *oath*; apl. **-as** P(n19). [Ger. *Eid*]

āðrintan, st.v.3, *swell (up)*; pp. nsf. **āþrunten** V(n24).

āweccan, wk.v.I, *awake, arouse*; pret. subj. 3s. **āwehte** C83.

āweg, adv., *away*.

āweorpan, st.v.3, *throw down, cast away*; pret. 3s. **āwearp** AII 94.
    [Ger. *werfen*]

āwrecan, st.v.5, *sing, recite*; pret. 3s. **āwræc** V51.

āwrītan, st.v.1, *write out*, or *down*; pret. 1s. **āwrāt** AI 74; pret. 3s.
    āwrāt AI 18.

awyrged, pp. adj. (of **awyrgan**), *accursed*; nsm.wk. absol. **awyrgda**
    Wh67; dsm.wk. **awyrgedan** AI 74.

axode, see **acsian**.

B

bād, see **bīdan**.

bæd(e), **bædon**, see **biddan**.

bælcan, wk.v.I, *roar*; ?*belch*; pres. 3s. **-ceð** V28.

bæron, see **beran**.

bān, n., *bone*; as. R39:18. [Ger. *Bein*]

baðian, wk.v.II w. reflex. pron., *bathe*; pres. 3s. **baðeð** P26, **baðað** P60.

be/stressed **bī**, prep. w. dat., *by, beside*; *about, concerning*; *according to*; **be þām þe**, *just as, even as*.

bēag, m., *ring, bracelet*; gpl. **-a** G1972.

bealohȳdig, adj., *murderous-minded, angry*; nsm. G(n1364). [**hȳdig** = **hygdig, hygd**, fn., *mind*]

bealu, n., *evil, malice*; gs. **bealwes** Wh72. [Eng. *bale*]

bēam, m., *tree*; as G1468. [Ger. *Baum*]

bearm, m., *bosom, lap*; as. G1488.

bearn, n., *child, son*; ns. V47, 80, Y; as. V6 (Christ); npl. G2002; dpl. **-um** C41, G1369, R39:18; apl. G1378, 2091, W37. [Scottish *bairn*]

bearu, m., *grove, wood*; *barrow*; ds. **bearwe** WL27; apl. **bearwas** G1480.

bēatan, st.v.7, *beat, hit, thrust*; pres. 3pl. **bēatað** G1326.

bebēodan/bi-, st.v.2, *command, order*; *offer*; pret. 3s. **-bēad** AII 16, 18, C98, G1494, V38; pret. 3pl. **-budon** C57; pres. p. nsm. **-bēodende** C127; pp. **-boden** nsm. AII 21, nsf. C26, nsn. C61.

bēc, see **bōc**.

bēcnan, wk.v.I, *indicate, explain*; pres. 3s. **bēcneð** R39:26. [Eng. *beckon*; rel. Eng. *beacon*]

becuman, st.v.4, *come, arrive*; *happen*; pret. 3s. **-com** AII 1, 76, **-cwom** C124.

bed, n., 'bead,' *prayer*; dpl. **-um** P(n19).

bedrīfan, st.v.1, *drive, go*; pret. 3s. **-drāf** [MS **-dræf**] R29:9.

bedroren, pp. adj. (of **bedrēosan**, st.v.2), w. dat./inst., *deprived* (*of*); nplm. **-e** G1998, 2082.

befæstan, wk.v.I, *commend, commit, entrust*; *receive*; pres. 1s. **-fæste** AII 13; pret. 1s. **-fæste** AII 54, 61; pret. 3s. **-fæste** AII 50, 59.

beflōwan, st.v.7, *flow around, encompass*; pp. nsm. **-flowen** WL49.

befōn, st.v.7, *comprehend, encompass, contain*; pres. 3s. **-fēhð** W87. [rel. Ger. *fangen*]

befrīnan, st.v.3, *ask*; pret. 3s. **-frān** AI 8, 38, AII 64. [**frīnan** = **frignan**]

bēgen, adj., *both*; nplm. P33; npln. **bū** X1035.

begietan, st.v.5, *get, find, seize*; inf. **-gitan** AII 99; pret. 3s. **-geat** G1479, WL32, 41, **-get** AII 105.

beginnan, st.v.3, *begin*; pret. 3s. **-gan(n)** AII 7, 28, 33, 62, 81; pret. 3pl. **-gunnon** AII 31.

behāt, n., *promise, vow*; ns. AI 35.

behātan, st.v.7, (freq. with dat. of person and gen. of thing), *promise*; pret. 3s. **-hēt** AI 6, AII 103.

behōfian, wk.v.II, w. gen., *need, have need of*; pres. 2pl. **-hōfiað** AI 14. [Eng. *behove*]

behrīman, wk.v.I, *cover with rime, ice over*; pp. nsm. **-hrīmed** WL48.

behȳdan, wk.v.I, *hide, conceal*; pret. 3s. **-hydde** AII 97.

belimpan, st.v.3, *concern, regard, pertain*; pret. 3pl. **-lumpon** C4, 16.

belūcan, st.v.2, *lock up, enclose, shut up*; pret. 3s. **-lēac** AI 46, 53, 56, G1363, 1391, 1409; pp. **-locen** V(n34).

bēme, ?m., *trumpet*; ns. P45.

ben(n), f., *wound*; dpl. **-um** G1972. [rel. **bana**, wk.m., *murderer*]

bend, f., *bond*; dpl. **-um** AII 114. [Ger. *Band*; rel. **bindan**, st.v.3, *bind*]

bēon — wesan, anom. v., *be*; pres. 1s. **eom**, **bēo**; 2s. **bist**, **eart**; 3s. **is/ys**, **bið/byð**; pres. 1–3 pl. **sindon/syndon**, **sindan**, **synden**, **sind/synd**, **bēoð**; pres. subj. 1–3s. **sēo**, **sȳ**, **bēo**; pres. subj. 1–3pl. **sīen**; imper. 2s. **bēo**, pl. **bēoð**; neg. pres. 1 and 3s. **nis**. Pret. 1s. **wæs**, 2s. **wære**, 3s. **wæs**; pret. pl. 1–3 **wæron/wæran**; pret. subj. 1–3s. **wære**, 1–3pl. **wæren**; neg. pret. 3s. **næs**.

beorg, m., *mountain, hill*; as. X1007; dpl. **-um** W64; apl. **-as** G1387. [Eng. *barrow*; Ger. *Berg*]

beorgan, st.v.3, *protect, defend*; inf. with **witon** understood P(n19).

beorht, adj., *bright*; nsm.wk. **-a** R29(n9); nplf. **-e** X1020.

beorhtness, f., *brightness*; ds. **-e** W15.

beorn, m., *man; warrior*; ns. G2033, V4; gs. **-es** V19. (not to be confused with **bearn**).

bēotian, wk.v.2, *vow; boast*; pret. 1pl. **bēotedan** WL21.

bēoð, see **bēon**.

bepǣcan, wk.v.I, *deceive, seduce*; pp. nplm. **-pæhte** W10.

beran, st.v.4, *bear, carry*; imper. pl. **berað** C105; pret. 3pl. **bæron** G1430, Y; pp. nsn. **boren** Y.

berēofan , st.v.2 (or **berebban**, st.v.6), *deprive of*; pret. 3pl. **-rōfan** G2078.

berȳfan, wk.v.I, *rob*; inf. V63.

berȳpan, wk.v.I, *deprive, rob*; pret. 3s. **-rȳpte** AI 65.

bescierian, wk.v.II, *deprive (of)*, *separate (from)*; pp. asm. **-scyredne** V8. [Eng. *shear*]

besēon, st.v.5, *look*; pret. 3s. **-sēah** AII 10.

beslēan, st.v.6, *deprive of (by violence)*; pp. nplf. **-slægene** G2010.

besorh, adj., *dear, beloved*; nsf. AII 62.

bestrūdan, st.v.2, *despoil, deprive (of)*, *rob*; pret. 3pl. **-strūdon** G2079.

beswīcan, st.v.1, *deceive, entice, seduce*; inf. Wh65, (n59, 65); pres. 3pl. **-swīcað** Wh33; pret. 3s. **-swāc** W10; pp. **-swican** AI 39, **-swicen** Wh56.

betǣcan, wk.v.I, *commit, deliver*; inf. AI 2; pret. 3s. **-tǣhte** AI 76.

betera, comp. adj. (of **gōd**), *better*; asm. **betran** V36.

betsta, superl. adj. (of **gōd**), *best*; nsf. **betast** X1011; disn. **-n** C60.

betwonen, prep., *between*.

betwux, prep., *between, among*.

betȳnan, wk.v.I, *close, shut*; pret. 3s. **-tȳnde** C87, 127.

beþencan, wk.v.I, *consider, bear in mind*; pret. 3s. **-ðōhte** AII 58.

beþringan, st.v.3, *beset (upon)*, *oppress*; pp. nsm. **-þrungen** V 56. [rel. Ger. *dringen*]

beūtan, prep. w. dat., *outside of*.

beweaxan, st.v. 7, *grow over*; pp. nplm **-weaxne** WL31.

beweddian, wk.v.II, *espouse, wed*; inf. AI 28.

bewindan, st.v.3, *grasp, wind about*; pp. **bewunden** WL (n7).

bewrēon, contr.v.1, *cover, put a covering on*; pp. npln. **-wrigen** G1460.

bi, see **be**.

bīdan, st.v.1, *abide, wait*; *endure*; inf. C117; pres. 3pl. **bīdað** X1020; pret. 3s. **bād** G1424.

biddan, st.v.5, *bid, ask, entreat, exhort*; *pray*; inf. AII 59; pres. 1s. **bidde** AII 61; pret. 3s. **bæd** AI 60, C95, G2025, 2030; pret. subj. 3s. **bæde** AII 56, C98; pret. 3pl. **bædon** AI 62, C110; pres. p. nsm. **biddende** AII 96. [Ger. *bitten*]

bifæstan, wk.v.I, *fasten, make secure*; pres. 3s. **-fæsteð** Wh30.

bifian, wk.v.II, *tremble, shake*; pres. 3pl. **beofiað** X1014; pres. p. **beofiende** X1020, **bifiende** AII 94, G1970. [Ger. *beben*]

bifōn, contr.v.7, *encase*; pp. nsn. **-fongen** V48.

bihlemman, wk.v.I, *snap, clash together*; pres. 3s. **-hlemmeð** Wh76.

bile, m., *bill, beak*; ns. P30, 33.

bilwit, adj., *mild*; disf. **-re** C122.

binnan/binne(n), prep. w. dat., *within, in, inside of, into*.

birig, see **burg**.

biscēawian, wk.v.II, *look on, regard*; pres. 3s. **-scēawað** Wh64.

bisceop, m., *bishop*; voc.s AII 11, 53; ns. AI 40, AII 14, 20, 24, 49; ds. **-e** AII 10, 18, 71, **biscope** AI 71, AII 10; as. AII 2. [rel. Lat. *episcopus*]

bisceopstōl, m., *bishop's seat, episcopal see*; ds. **-e** AII 20, 51. [-stōl, Eng. *stool*]

bisencan, wk.v.I, *sink*; pres. 3s. **-senceð** Wh48.

bist, see **bēon**.

biter, adj., *bitter*; *painful*; *grim*; nplm. **bitre** WL31.

biterlīce, adv., *sharply, bitterly*.

bitwēonum/betwonen, prep. w. dat., *between*; R29:2 [MS **abit-weonū**].

bið, see **bēon**.

biþeccan, wk.v.I, *cover*; pp. nsm. **-þeaht** Wh45. [rel. Eng. *thatch*]

biwindan, st.v.3, *wind about, encompass*; pp. nplm. **-wunden** Wh 18.

blāchlēor, adj., *having a pale face, fair*; nsf. G1970. [**blāc-** < **blīcan**, st.v.1]

blæd, f., *blade, leaf*; *twig*; as. **-æ** G1474.

blencan, wk.v.I, *deceive, delude*; pres. 3s. **blenceþ** V33. [rel. Eng. *blench*]

blīcan, st.v.1, *shine, gleam, sparkle*; pres. 3pl. **blīcað** X1012.

bliss/blyss, f., *bliss, joy, exultation*; gs. **-e** C19; ds. **-e** AI 72, V(n34).

blīðe, adj., *blitheful, happy*; nsm. AII 50, C110; disn. WL 21; asn. WL44; nplm. C107.

blīðe, adv., *joyfully, gladly*.

blīðelīce, adv., *gladly, joyfully*.

blīðemōd, adj., *blithe of mind, cheerful*; nsm. C111; nsf. G1468; nplm. **-e** C109.

blōd, n., *blood*; ns. Y; as. R39:18.

blōdrēad, adj., *blood-red, deep red*; nplm. **-e** P33.

bōc/booc, f., *book*; ns. C73, P3; npl. **bēc** W7; gpl. **bōca** C76, V4; dpl. **bōcum** W3, 70.

bōcere, m., *writer, scribe, author*; apl. **boceras** C5.

boda, wk.m., *messenger, prophet*; gs. **-n** V4. [rel. **bēodan**, st.v.2, *command*; Ger. *Bote*]

bōg, m., *bough, branch, twig*; apl. **-es** P56.

boian (or **bogian**), wk.v.II, *cast, throw*; *?boast*; pres. 3s. **bōð** V28.

bolster, m., *pillow (for the head)*; ds. **bolstre** C119. [Ger. *Polster*]

bolt, m., *bolt, crossbow for shooting arrows*; (idiom.) *something straight and taut*; ns. P16.

bord, n., *board, gangplank, side of a ship*; as. G1333, 1357, 1369, 1403, 1481; dpl. **-um** G1354. [as Eng., *to go on board (a ship, train, plane)*]

boren, see **beran**.

bōsm, m., *bosom, breast*; *ship's hold*; ds. **bōsme** G1306, 1332, 1410. [Ger. *Busen*]

bōt, f., *help, relief*; *penance*; ns. G1476; apl. (?gpl.) **-a** AI 47.

bōð, see **boian**.

breaht(e)m, m., *noise, clamor*; ns. V19.

brecan, st.v.4, *break (into, through)*; inf. V38.

bregdan, st.v.3, *swing, draw (forth)*; pret. 3pl. **brugdon** G1991. [Eng. *braid*]

brego, m., *ruler, lord*; *God*; ns. G1289.

breodian, wk.v.II, *cry out, shriek*; pres. 3s. **breodað** V28.

brēost, n., *breast*; ns. P30.

brēostcearu, f., *breast-care, innermost anxiety*; as. **-ceare** WL44.

brēostgehygd, f. and n., *inmost thought*; dipl. **-um** G1289.

brēostsefa, wk.m., *mind, spirit*; as. **-n** V19.

brēr, m., *briar*; dipl. **-um** WL 31.

brice, n., *use, service*; ds. W23. [rel. **brūcan**, st.v.2, *use*]

briht (= **beorht**), adj., *bright, clear*; nsm. **-e** P30; nsf. P45.

brihtlȳcor, comp. adv. (of **beorhtlīce**), *more brightly*.

bringan, wk.v.I (pres., st.v.3), *bring, carry*; pret. 3s. **brōhte** C7, G1472; pret. 3pl. **brōhton** W67, Y.

brōga, wk.m., *terror*; npl. **-n** G1395.

brogdenmǣl, n., *damascened sword*; ns. Y. [literally, *woven* (**bregdan**, st.v.3, *weave*) *ornament* (**mǣl**)]

brōðor, m., *brother*; ns. Cl, W73; gs. AII 62, 72; npl. C111, 115, G2033; apl. **brōðra** W40.

brōðorlic, adj., *brotherly*; dsf. **-re** AII 103.

brugdon, see **bregdan**.

brȳd, f., *woman about to be married*; *wife*; ds. **-e** G2033; gpl. **-a** G1972; apl. **-a** G2090.

bryne, m., *flame, heat*; ds. W20. [rel. **biernan**, st.v.3, *burn*]

brytta, wk.m., *breaker* (*of rings*), *dispenser*; *prince*; npl. **-n** G1997. [rel. **brēotan**, st.v.2, *break in pieces*]

bū, see **begen**.

būgan, st.v.2, *bow, submit, yield*; inf. AI 40.

būr, n., *bower, bedchamber* or *living-chamber*; as. R29 : 5.

burg/burh, f., *fortified place* or *dwelling*; ds. **birig** AII 1, 20, **byrig**, AII 48, G2013, R29 : 5; as. G1975.

burgtūn, m., *protective covering* (*residence*); *fortified habitation*; npl. **-as** WL31. [**-tūn**, Eng. *town*]

burgweal, m., *fortress wall*; ?Figuratively, *the heart* or *mind, container of the soul*; as. V38.

būton/būtan/būte, conj., *unless, except* (*that*); prep. w. dat., *out of, without*.

byrig, see **burg**.

byrne, f., *corselet, coat of mail*; ns. Y.

bysgian, wk.v.II, *make busy, trouble, torment*; pres. 3s. **bysgað** Wh51.

C

cāf, adj., *quick, sharp*; nsm. AII 8.

cann, see **cunnan**.

canon, m., *sacred canon*; gs. **-es** C75. [Lat. Gk.]

carte, f., (*piece of*) *paper*; as. **cartan** AI 73. [Lat. *charta*]

ceafl, m., *mouth, jaw(s)*; ns. Wh59.

cearu, f., *care, sorrow*; as. **ceare** WL(n7); dpl. **-m** X1016.

ceaster, f., *city*; apl. **ceastra** G2009. [Lat. *castra*]

cennan, wk.v.I, *bring forth, beget, create*; *devise*; pp. **cenned** R39:15, Wh6.

cēol, m., *keel of a ship*; *ship*; npl. **-as** Wh17.

ceorl, m., *freeman of the lowest class*; *husband*; gs. **-es** AI 29. [Eng. *churl*]

cēpan, wk.v.I, with gen., *desire, take*; inf. AII 78. [rel. **cēap**, m., *gain, property*; Eng. *cheap*]

cinn, see **cynn**.

circe, f., *church*; ds. **circan** AI 34, **ciricean** AII 75, **circean** 102, **cyrcan** AI 63. [late Lat. *cyrīca*]

ci(e)rm, m., *shout, uproar*; ns. **cyrm** G(n1983), V20.

circlic, adj., *like a church, ecclesiastical*; aplm. **-an** AII 2.

clǣne, adj., *clear, pure*; nsn. C68; dsm.wk. **clǣnan** AI 2; npln. P32.

clǣne, adv., *entirely, completely*.

clǣnnyss, f., *cleanness, chastity, purity*; ds. **-e** AI 27.

cleofian, wk.v.III, *cleave, adhere*; pres. 3pl. **-iað** Wh73.

clypian/clipian, wk.v.II, *call, speak, cry out*; pres. 1pl. **-iað** AI 68; pret. 3s. **clypode** AII 79, 85; pret. 3pl. **clypodon** AI 69, **clipodon** AII 80.

clyppan, wk.v.I, *embrace, clasp*; inf. C62.

cnapa, wk.m., *boy, young man*; ns. AI 58; as. **-n** AI 8, 8, 59, 63, 72, 75; gpl. **cnapena** AI 3. [Ger. *Knabe*]

cniht, m., *boy, youth*; ns. AI 34, 54, AII 38; gs. **-es** AI 37, AII 61; ds. **-e** AI 33; as. AI 46, AII 6, 9, 15, 19, 21, 49, 80; dpl. **-um** AII 29. [Eng. *knight*]

cofa, wk.m., *coffer, chamber*; *ark*; ds. **-n** G1464.

collenferhð, adj., *bold (of spirit)*; nplm. **-e** Wh17.

cōm(e), **cōmon**, see **cuman**.

con, see **cunnan**.

corðor, f. n., *troop, throng*; ds. **-þre** V20.

cræft, m., *craft, skill*; *power*; as. AI 5.

cræftig, adj., *skilled, skillful*; nsm. Wh24, 72.

cristal, m. (? or n.), *crystal*; ns. P32. [Lat. *crystallus*]

Cristen, adj., *Christian*; dplf. **-um** W70. [Lat. *Chrīstīnus*]

cucra, see **cwic**.

culufre, f., *dove*; ns. G1464; as. **-fran** G1451, 1477. [Eng. *culver*]

cuman, st.v.4, *come, proceed*; *happen*; inf. AI 34, X1026, 1036; pres. 1s. **come** AI 51; pres. 3s. **cumð** P14, **cumeð** P35, **cymeð** Wh54, X1008; pres. 3pl. **cumað** AI 49, Wh 79, (n35); pret. 1s. **com** AII 79; pret. 2s. **cōme** P40; pret. 3s. **cōm** AI 48, 53, 63, 65. AII 81, C48, G1478, Y, **cwōm** C60, R29:7; pret. 3pl. **cōmon** Y; pp. **cumen** nsf. G1475, nsn. C54.

cunnan, pret.-pres.v., *know (how)*; inf. V44; pres. 1s. **con** C29; pres. 3s. **cann** P17, 54; pret. 1s. **cūðe** C31; pret. 3s. **cūðe** AI 6; pret. 3pl. **cūðon** W22.

cunnian, wk.v.II, w. gen., *try, inquire, examine*; pret. 3s. **cunnode** AI 54.

cūð, adj., *known, familiar*; *intimate*; nsm. AI 3; nsf. R29:8; asf. **-e** Y . [as Eng. *uncouth*]

cūðe, cūðon, see **cunnan**.

cweccan, wk.v.I, *move, shake*; pret. 3s. **cwehte** AII 70.

cwēnfugel, m., *hen-bird*; ns. P65. [**cwēn**, f., *woman*; Eng. *queen*]

cweðan, st.v.5, *say, speak, declare*; pres. 3pl. **cweðað** AI 51; pret. 3s. **CWÆð** AI 12 etc., AII 11 etc., C29 etc., G1295 etc.; pret. 3pl. **cwædon** C103, 108; pres.p. nplm. **cweþende** W28. [rel. Eng. *quoth, bequeath*]

cwic/cucu, adj., *living, alive*; nsm. X1030; gpln. **cucra** G1297. [Eng. *quick,* 'living']

cwiclifigende, adj., *living*; gpln. **-dra** G1311.

cwicsūsl, n., *living-punishment, hell-torment*; ds. **-e** Wh38.

cwide/cwyde, m., *speech, discourse, saying*; ?dis., ?as. V20; as. R47:4; dpl. **cwydum** R47 (n5). [rel. **cweðan**]

cwiþan, wk.v.I, *lament*; inf. WL(n7).

cwōm, see **cuman**.

cȳdde, see **cȳðan**.

cyme, m., *coming*; *advent*; ds. C77, X1030.

cymeð, see **cuman**.

cyning, m., *king, ruler*; *God*; ns. G1406, P(n18, 19), X1009; as. X1038; gpl. **-a** P(n19); see also **king**.

cyningbald, adj., *royally brave, very brave*; nplm. **-e** Y. [**bald**, Eng. *bold*]

cynn (also **cinn**), n., *kind, race, family*; *kindred*; *nature (of something)*; ns. G1324, X1027; gs. **-es** P17(n18), 48, Wh40; as. Wh1; npl. Wh56; gpl. **-a** G1297, 1311.

cyrm, see **ci(e)rm**.

cyrcan, see **circe**.

cyrran, wk.v.I, *turn, go, return*; pres. 2pl. **cyrra∂** AI 15.

cy∂an, wk.v.I, *make known, proclaim, reveal*; inf. Wh2; pres. 3pl. **cy∮a∂** P(n13); pret. 3s. **cydde** AI 37, **cy∂de** C51. [rel. **cū∂**]

D

dǣd, f., *deed, action*; gp. **-a** C84, Wh34; dpl. **-um** AII 38, W61; dipl. **-um** V75; apl. **-a** AII 36.

dǣdbēta, wk.m., *deed-amender, penitent*; ns. AI 49. [rel. **bētan**, wk.v.I, *amend*; cp. **dǣdbōt**]

dǣdbētend, m., *penitent, deed-amender*; dpl. **-um** AII 112.

dǣdbōt, f., *amends-deed, repentance*; ds. **-e** AI 45, AII 115.

dǣdcēne, adj., *daring in deeds*; nsm. Y. [Eng. *keen*]

dæg, m., *day*; **dōmes dæg**, *the Judgment Day*; ns. P(n13), R29 (n9), **dæig** P21; ds. **-e** AI 18, 67, C78, P59, V(n34); as. AI 57, WL37, (n37), **dæig** P23; gpl. **daga** AI 54, AII 104, G1351, 1382, 1421, 1438, X1021; dpl. **dagum** C90, W47, 50, 66; apl. **dagas** AI 48.

dæghwāmlice, adv., *daily*. [**(ge)hwǣmlīc**, *each, every*; cp. **gehwā**]

dægrīm, n., *number of days*; gs. **-es** G1331; ds. **-e** V12.

dǣl, m., *share, part, portion, division*; as. G1453; dipl. **dālum** V22. [Eng. *deal*].

dēad, adj., *dead*; nsm. AII 64, 65, 66.

dēa∂, m., *death, dying*; ns. WL22, dis. **-e** AI 25, AII 65, 114, C123, P59.

dēa∂cwealm, m., *slaughter*; as. Y.

dēa∂sele, m., *death-hall*; *?hell*; ds. Wh30.

dēaw, m., *dew*; ns. R29 : 12.

dēawigfe∂era, adj., *dewy-feathered*; nsm. (absol.) G1984.

dehter, see **dohtor**.

Denisc, adj., *Danish, Scandinavian*; dsf. **-e** W67; nplm. **-e** W67; nplf. **-a** W52.

denu, f., *valley, vale*; ns. **dene** P8; npl. **dena** WL30.

dēofol, m. and n., *devil, the Devil*; ns. AI 8, 19, 20, 63, W80, Wh(n59); gs. **DĒOFLES** AI 4 etc., W14 etc., V(n34); ds. **dēofle** AI 8, 11, 36, V(n34), **dēofla** AI 74; as. AI 59, W1, 10; npl. **dēoflu** AI 49; gpl. **dēofla** Wh32; dpl. **dēoflum** Wh83; apl. **dēoflu** AI 55. [Lat. *diabolus*]

dēop, adj., *deep*; nsm. G1398, 1453; asn. G1331; comp. nsf. **-pere** P12.

deoreðsceaft, m., *dart-shaft, spear*; dpl. **-um** G1984. [**deoreð** = **daroð**; Eng. *dart*]

dēorwurðe, adj., *precious*; aplm. P56.

dēorwurðlīce, adv., *dearly*.

derian, wk.v.II, *injure, harm*; pres. 3s. **dereð** W3.

dēð, see **dōn**.

digel, adj., *secret*; dsf. **-re** AI 47.

dīgollīce, adv., *secretly*.

dihtig, adj., *doughty*; apln. G1993.

dim, adj., *dim, gloomy*; nplf. **-me** WL30.

dimlic, adj., *dim, dark*; aplf. **-an** R29(n9).

dohte, see **dugan**.

dohtor, f., *daughter*; ns. W72; ds. **dehter** AI 24, 27; as. **dohter** AI 1, 32; npl. **dohtra** W45.

dōm, m., *doom, judgment; praise, glory; power, will*; **dōmes dæg**, *the Day of Judgment*; gs. **-es** AI 18, C78, P23, V(n34), X1021; ds. **-e** AI 67, G2082, Y; dis. **-e** C54; as. V64; dpl. **-um** C81. [rel. **(ge)dēman**]

dōmfæst, adj., *just, renowned*; nsm. G1287.

dōn, anom. v., *do, make*; inf. C11, 86, W25; pres. 3s. **dēð** P62, Wh(n59); pres. 3pl. **dōð** W24; pret. 2s. **dydest** Y; pret. 3s. **dyde** C24, 99.

dorste, see **durran**.

drēam, m., *music; joy, pleasure*; ?as. V72; apl. **-as** Wh(n85). [Eng. *dream*, semantically influenced by Old Icelandic *draumr*]

drenc, m., *drowning*; ns. Wh(n30); dis. **-e** Wh30. [Eng. *drench*]

drenceflōd, m., *flood, deluge*; ns. G1398.

drēogan, st.v.2, *suffer, endure, undergoe*; inf. R39:17, WL26; pres.
3s. **drēogeð** WL50; pret. 3s. **drēah** G1428.

drēorsele, m., *desolate habitation*; *joyless hall*; ds. WL50. [**drēor-**, rel.
Eng. *dreary*]

drigian, (? = **drēogan**, st.v.2), *enjoy*; inf. **drigen** P66.

drihten/dryhten, m., *lord*; *God, Christ*; ns. C40, 44, G1287, 1362,
1371, 1390, 1411, 2058, R47 (n5); gs. **-es** AII 51, P67, **drihtnes**
AII 54, W26, X1021, **drihtnys**, AII 40; ds. **-e** AII 112, **drihtne**
C56, 122, Wh83 [MS **dryhtene**]; as. P(n19), W16; gpl. **dryhtna**
Wh83.

drincan, st.v.3, *drink*; pret. 3pl. **druncon** Y.

drohtian, wk.v.II, *dwell, live*; pres.p.nplm. **drohtende** Wh32.

druncen, n., *drunkenness*; as. V12 [MS **drucen**].

druncenniss, f., *drunkenness*; as. **-e** AII 31.

drūsian, wk.v.II, *stagnate*; pret. 3s. **drūsade** Y. [Eng. *drowse*]

dryht, f., *multitude*; ds. **-um** P(n13).

Dryhten, see **Drihten**.

dryhtguma, wk.m., *noble man, warrior*; npl. **-n** V22.

drȳman, m., *magician, sorcerer*; ns. AI 7; ds. **-men** AI 5. [**drȳ-**, Old
Irish *drúi*; rel. via Lat. to Eng. *druid*]

dugan, pret.-pres.v., *avail, thrive*; pres. subj. 3s. **duge** Y; pret. 3s.
dohte G1288.

duguð, f., *body of noble retainers, host, throng*; *men*; gs. **-e** Y; as. **-e**
G2023; dpl. **dugeðum** G1371; ?apl. **-e** Wh33.

dūn, f., *hill, mountain*; ns. **-e** P9; ds. **-e** AII 69; as. **-e** G(n1393); npl.
-a WL30; dpl. **-um** AII 47, G1398, 1421; apl. **-en** P5. [Eng.
down]

durran, pret. pres.v.5, *dare*; pret. 3s. **dorste** AI 4.

duru, f., *door*, as. AI 53.

dust, n., *dust, ash(es)*; ?*mist*; ns. R29: 12, ds. **-e** P58.

dwelian, wk.v.II, *err*; pres.p.asm.wk. **dweligendan** AI 8.

dyde, dydest, see **dōn**.

dȳre, adj., *dear*; dplf. G1371.

dyrne, adj., *hidden, secret, concealed*; asm. WL12; asf. Wh33.

dyrneligere, n., *adultery*; *fornication*; as. **-era** P(n19). [**-ligere** = **geligere**, n., *fornication*]

E

ēac, adv., *also*, *likewise*; **ēac swelce/swilce**, *likewise*; **ēac þon**, *besides*, *moreover*.

ēacen, pp. adj. (of **ēacan**, *increase*), *large*, *mighty*; asn. Y.

ēadig, adj., *happy*, *blessed*; *fortunate*; nsm.wk. **-a** AII 58, **ēadega** G1476; nsf. X1013.

eafora, wk.m., *son*, *child*; ns. **afera** G2054; dpl. **-rum** G1348, 1415; apl. **-n** G1333, 1357.

ēage, n., *eye*; npl. **-ne** P31; gpl. **-na** R39:11 [MS **eage ne**, ʔfor **ne eagena**]; dipl. **ēagum** Wh12.

eahta, num. adj., *eight*; aplf. P(n19).

eal, see **eal(l)**.

ēala, interj., *o*, *alas*.

eald, adj., *ancient*, *old*; nsm. WL29; nsm.wk. (absol.) **-a** AII 62; gs. (adverbial) **-es** WL4; asm.wk. **-an** AII 87 (absol.), W10.

ealdor, m., *chief*; ns. AII 68, 69, Y; as. AII 80.

ealdor, n., *life*; ds. **ealdre** Y. [Ger. *Alter*]

ealdorgesceaft, f., *condition (fate) of life*; ns. R39:23.

ealdormon, m., *alderman*; *chief*; ns. C49.

ealdsweord, n., *ancient sword*; as. Y.

eal(l), adj., *all*, *every*; absol., *everything*; nsm. P58, V26; nsf. WL46; nsn. P36, X1027, 1032; gsm. **-es** R47(n5), W2, WL41; dsm. **-um** AII 93, W4; dsf. **-re** AII 47; dsn. **-um** P(n19); asm. P55; asf. **-e** C91, G1409, 1490; asn. C72, (absol.) G1359, 1403, P13, 25, W83, 84; nplm. **-e** AI 69, C21, 106, 108, 109, P37, 38, 44, 50; nplf. **-e** G(n1374); npln. P52, **-e** W24; gplm. **-ra** C53, G2092, P41, 67, (n19), W50; gplf. **-ra** AII 109, R39:14, W89; gpln. **-ra** W88; dplm. **-um** AII 112, C55, 107, 110, G1339, R29: 8, W65; dpln. **-um** C82, P(n19); aplm. AII 79; **-e** AI 60, AII 47, C52, W87; aplf. **-e** P(n19); apln. C46, 67, (absol.) G1353, (?) **-e** G1386, W21, 22, 27, 29, 37, 85, WL(n37).

eal(l), adv., *entirely.*

ealles, adv., *entirely, in every respect.*

eallinga, adv., *altogether, entirely.*

eallwealdend, adj. (as noun), *all-ruling (one), God*; ns. P7.

ēalond, n., *sea-land, island*; ds. **-e** Wh21; as. Wh12. [**ēa**, f., *water*]

earc, f., *chest; ark*; ns. G1313, 1423; gs. **-e** G1333, 1354, 1357, 1403; ds. **-e** G1450, 1488; as. G1366, 1389, 1461. [Lat. *arca*]

eard, m., *(home)land, country, native dwelling*; gs. **-es** X1029; ds. **-e** P21, 34, 49; as. V74, WL15 [MS **heard**]; dpl. **-en** P53.

eardian, wk.v.II, *dwell, live*; pres.p. nsm. **eardiende** W35.

earfoð, n., *hardship, privation*; gpl. **-a** WL39; apl. **earfeþu** WL (n37).

earfoðlice, adv., *with difficulty.*

earfoðsīð, m., *troublesome, difficult journey*; gpl. **-a** G1476.

earg, adj., *cowardly, vile*; diplf. **-um** V75.

earm, adj., *poor, miserable, wretched*; dsm.wk. **-an** AI 61; dsf.wk. **-an** AI 35; asf.wk. **-an** AI 32; superl. nsf. **-ost** R39:14. [Ger. *arm*]

earming/yrming, m., *poor, miserable creature, wretch*; ns. AI 10, 18, AII 88; as. W55.

earn, m., *eagle*; ns. G(n1983). [rel. Ger. *Aar*]

eart, see **bēon**.

ēastweard, adv., *East, eastern part*; **on -e** P19.

ēaðe, adv., *easily, readily*; G2058 [MS **eað**].

ēaðfynde, adj., *easy to be found, easily found*; nsm. G1993.

ēaðmōd, adj., *humble, meek*; nsm. V68; asm. **-ne** V78.

ēaðmōdlice, adv., *humbly.*

ebbian, wk.v.II, *ebb*; pret. 3s. **ebbade** G1413.

ēce, adj., *eternal, everlasting*; nsm. C40, 44, G1405, 2058, W86; dsn. **ecum** V(n34); asn. AII 115.

ēce, adv., *eternally, evermore.*

ecg, f., *edge (of sword), blade; sword*; dpl. **-um** G1993, 2002.

ecgwæl, n., *sword-slaughter*; ds. **-wale** G2089.

ēcnyss, f., *eternity*; ds. **-e** AII 116.

edgung, adj. (= **-geong**), *young again*; nsm. P60, 63, X1032. [**ed-**, prefix, *again, back*]

edwylm, m., *heat of fire, burning heat*; ds. **-e** Wh73. [**ed-**, ?form of **ād**, m., *funeral pyre; fire*]

efenbrād, adj., *equally broad* (as long); nsm. P8. [**efen**, Eng. *even*]

efeneald, adj., *coeval, of the same age*; dp. **-um** AII 29.

efenlang, adj., *equally long* (as broad); nsm. P8.

efne, adv., *even, just (as)*; *precisely, exactly.*

efne, interj., *lo, behold; truly.*

efstan, wk.v.I, *hasten, make haste*; pret. 3s. **efste** AII 75.

eft, adv., *again, afterwards; back(wards).*

egesa, wk.m., *fear, awe*; dis. **egsan** X1014, 1019.

egesful, adj., *terrible, awe-inspiring*; nplm. **-le** W34.

egeslic, adj., *fearful, terrible, awful*; nsn. Y; aplf. **egslican** AI 55, **-an** AII 36; superl. nsm. **-ast** X1021.

ēglond, n., *island*; as. Wh16.

ēgorhere, m., *water-war* (or *force*), *flood*; ns. G1402.

ēgorstrēam, m., *water-stream, sea*; apl. **-as** G1374.

ēgstrēam, m., *water-stream, flood*; as. G1415.

elebēam, m., *olive tree*; gs. **-es** G1473. [**ele**, m., *oil*]

ellen, n., *courage, bravery*; ns. G1288.

ellenrōf, adj., *remarkably strong, brave*; nplm. **-e** G2036.

ellenwōdniss, f., *zeal, ardor*; gs. **-e** C86.

elles, adv., *else, otherwise.*

eln, f., *ell* (for Lat. *cubitum*: a unit of measure: $1\frac{1}{2}$ to 2 feet); gpl. **-a** G1399.

elngemet, n., *ell-measure, measurement by ells*; gpl. **-a** G1309.

emb(e), see **ymb(e)**.

ende, m., *end*; ds. W89, Wh15, (n30), X1029, **ænde** P69, (n19); dis. C86; as. AI 78.

endebyrdness, f., *order; turn*; ns. **-e** C36; ds. **-nysse** AI 37; as. **-e** C21.

engel/ængel, m., *angel, messenger*; ns. P2; gpl. **engla** AI 28, V74, X1013; **ængles** P22, 29; dpl. **englum** V58. [Lat. *angelus*]

engliscgereord, n., *English language*; ds. **-e** C7.

engu, f., *narrowness, confinement*; ds. **enge** G1435. [Ger. *eng*]

ent, m., *giant*; npl. **-as** W6; apl. **-as** W33.

ēode, ēodon, see **gān**.

eodorcan, wk.v.I, *chew, masticate, ruminate*; pres.p. nsn. **eordorcende** C69.

eom, see **bēon**.

eorl, m., *lord, nobleman, brave man*; ns. G2086; ds. **-e** G1994, 2021; as.
V37, 78; npl. **-as** G2045; dpl. **-um** Y; apl. **-as** Wh49. [Eng.
earl]

eorðbūend, m., *earth-dweller*; dpl. **-um** R29:8. [**būan**, anom. v.,
dwell, inhabit]

eorðe, f., *earth, ground, the earth*; gs. **eorðan** C41, G1305, 1313, 1322,
1339, 1350, 1402, 1440, 1454, 1488; ds. **eorðan** AII 93, G1389,
G(n1983), **eorðe** P3, **eorðen** P7, **on eorðan**, ?alive WL33; as.
eorðan G1292, P(n13), R29:12, V68, W21.

eorðlic, adj., *earthly, terrestrial*; nsm. P16.

eorðscræf, n., *earth-cave, barrow-tunnel*; ds. **-e** WL28; apl. **-scrafu**
WL36.

eorðsele, m., *earth-hall, habitation made of earth, cave*; ?*barrow (burial-
mound)*; ns. WL29.

ēow, see **gē**.

ēowan, wk.v.I, *show, manifest*; pret. 3pl. **ēowdon** G2056.

ēower, poss. pron., *your(s)*; nsm. G1334; dsm. **ēowrum** AI 15; asm.
-ne AII 80; see **gē**.

ēðel, m., *home, native land*; ds. **ēðle** G2091 [MS **oðle**]; as. **ēðyl**
G1492.

ēðelland, n., *fatherland, country*; ns. G1968; as. G1379.

ēðelstōl, m., *native (paternal) seat ('stool'), home*; ns. G1485.

F

fācen, n., *deceit, treachery, wickedness*; gs. **fācnes** V32, Wh24; ds.
fācne WL(n37).

fācenfull, adj., *deceitful, crafty*; nsm. W61.

fācensearu, n., *deceitful cunning, treachery*; dipl. **-m** V27.

fæc, n., *space, interval (of time)*; ds. **-e** C5; as. C119. [Ger. *Fach*]

fǣcne, adj., *deceitful, wicked*; nsm.wk. (absol.) **fǣcna** Wh71.

fæder, m., *father*; *God the Father*; ns. AI 23, 26, 31, 31, V66, W48,
86; gs. X1014; ds. P(n19); as. AII 86, W41.

fædera, wk.m., *father's brother, uncle,* ns. G2080.

fǣge, adj., *doomed, fated*; asn. G1382. [Scottish *fey*]

fægen, adj., *glad, rejoicing*; aplm. **fægne** Y. [Eng. *fain*]

fæger/fǣger, adj., *fair, beautiful, lovely*; nsm. P24, **-e** P26, 34, 49, 59, **fægre** P33, **fægra** P(n16); nsf. G1487; nsn. **-e** P14, 46, **fæger** P(n18); dism. **fægre** C87; dsf. **-an** AII 106 [MS **-a**]; asm. **-e** P43; asf. **-e** G1467; nplm. **-e** P30, 44; nplf. **-e** P61; superl. **-est**, nsm. P40, 52, (n13); nplf. P62.

fægere, adv., *beautifully, pleasantly*.

fægerlice, adv., *gently*.

fægnian, wk.v.II, *rejoice*; pres. 3pl. **fagenegeð** P43; pres.p. nsn. **fageninde** P36.

fæhð(u), f., *feud, violence, hostility*; ?dis. ?as. **-e** V36; as. WL26, **fæhðe** G1351, (n1351); dipl. **-um** (?adverbial, *hostilely*) R29:11.

fæmne, f., *virgin, maiden, woman*; as. **fæmnan** W73; npl. **fæmnan** G2010.

fær, n., *ship, ark*; *way, passage*; ds. **-e** G1394; as. AII 76, G1307, 1323, 1419. [rel. **faran**]

færinga, adv., *suddenly*.

færlic, adj., *sudden, quick*; dsm. **-um** W20.

færlice, adv., *immediately*.

færð, see **fēran**.

fæsl, m. and n., *seed, offspring, progeny*; ns. G1310, 1330; ds. **-e** G1359.

?fæst, n., *fasting (abstinence from food)*; ds. **-e** AII 104 (? for **fæstene**).

fæst, adj., *fast, fixed, firm*; nsm. V56; asn. Wh(n15); nplm. **-e** Wh18.

fæste/feste, adv., *fast, firmly*; *permanently*; **feste togædere/-ætgædere**, *continuously, ?altogether*.

fæsten, n., *fastness, fortress*; ds. **-ne** Wh71; as. or pl. G2006.

fæsthȳdig, adj., *constant, steadfast*; asm. **-ne** G1347. [**-hȳdig**, *mindful, heedful*]

fæðm, m., *embrace*; *fathom, cubit*; as. G1971; npl. **fedmen** P4, **fedme** P6. [Eng. *fathom*]

fāg, adj., *many-colored, variegated in color*; *bloodstained*; nsm. or n. Y; nplm. **-e** P30, 44.

fagenegeð, see **fægnian**.

fāh, adj., *outcast, outlawed, exiled*; *hostile*; *guilty*; nsm. G1291, Wh66, (n39), WL46.

fāmig, adj., *foamy*; nsm. G1452; nsn. G1417.

fand, see **findan**.

fandian, wk.v.II, often w. gen., *try, test, search out*; pret. 3s. **fandode** AI 57, G1436.

fandung, f., *test, probe, trial*; as. **-a** G1452.

faran, st.v.6, *go, proceed, advance*; inf. AII 25, V41; pres. 3pl. **faraðð** P(n16), Wh58; pret. 3s. **fōr** G1394, 1417, 1964; pret. 3pl. **fōron** G1974 [MS **foran**], 1982. [Eng. *fare*, Ger. *fahren*]

faroðlācende, part. adj., *seafaring*; *swimming*; nplm. Wh20, **faroð-** Wh80; dplm. absol. **fareðlācendum** Wh5. [**faroð**, m., *stream*; **lācan**, st.v.7, *move (upon)*]

Fastitocalon, Gk.-Lat., *asp-turtle, whale*; ns. Wh7.

feale, see **fela**.

feallan, st.v.7, *fall*; *fail, decay, die*; pres. 3s. **fealleð** P17, 57; pres. 3pl. **fealleð** P44; pret. 3s. **fēol(l)** AI 23, 71, AII 94, R29:12; pret. 3pl. **fēollon** G1971, 2001, 2038 [MS **-an**], 2065.

fealu, adj., *yellow, dusky*; asf. **fealwe** G2044. [Eng. *fallow*]

fearm, m., *provision, food*; ds. **-e** G1394.

feax, n., *hair (of the head)*; ds. **-e** Y.

fēawe, adj., *few*; nplm. P31; dplm. **fēawum** W31; dpln. **fēawum** V47; aplm. **fēawa** AI 54.

fēdan, wk.v.I, *feed, nourish*; *produce*; pres. 3s. **fēdeð** W21; pres. 3pl. **fēdað** G1298; imper. s. **fēd** G1342.

fedme, fedmen, see **fæðm**.

fela/feale, adj., indecl. w. gen. pl., *many*; as noun, **feale** P44.

felalēof, adj., *very dear*; *dearly beloved*; gsm.wk. (absol.) **-an** WL26.

felamōdig, adj., *very brave*; gpl. **-ra** Y.

feng, m., *grasp, embrace*; ds. **-e** Wh81. [cp. **fōn**]

fēngon, see **fōn**.

feoh, n., *cattle*; *money, property*; gs. **fēos** AII 57; as. G1299. [Ger. *Vieh*, Eng. *fee*]

feohte, wk.f., *battle, fight*; ns. V66.

fēol(l), fēollon, see **feallan**.

fēon, st.v.5, *exult (over)*; pres. 3s. **fēoþ** V36 [MS **feoh**].

fēond, m., *fiend, enemy*; *the Devil*; ns. ?G1447, W40, Wh39, (n39); gs. **-es** V27, 47; as. G2072, V70 [MS **freond**]; npl. **fȳnd** G2006; gpl. **-a** G2065; dpl. **-um** G1969, Wh36, Y.

feor(r), adv., *far*; **feor ge nēah**, *far and near*; see **feorr**, adj.

feorh, n., *life*; *soul*; ds. **feore** Wh88: **tō wīdan feore**, *forever*; as. G1385, R39:16; npl. G2065; gpl. **feora** G1330, 1342; apl. G1999.

feorhbana, wk.m., *life-destroyer*, *murderer*; ns. **feorg-** Wh41; apl. **-n** G2088.

feorhberend, m., *life-bearer*, *man*; gpl. **-ra** R39:6.

feorhcwalu, f., *life-slaughter*, *death*; ds. **-cwale** Wh77. [**-cwalu**, rel. **cwelan**, st.v.4, *die*]

feorr, adj., *far*, *distant*; gsn. **-es** WL47.

feorran/feorren(e), adv., *from afar*.

fēos, see **feoh**.

fēoþ, see **fēon**.

fēower, num. adj., *four*; nm. G1964, 2074, Y; an. G1334.

fēow(e)rtig, num. adj., *forty*; nm. P4, 5; as noun G1351, 1382.

fēowertēoða, num. adj., *fourteenth*; asm.wk. **-tēoðogan** AI 57.

fēowertȳne, num. adj., *fourteen*; nom. Y; dm. **-tynum** C90.

fēran, wk.v.I, *go, journey*; inf. R29: 11, R39: 6, WL9; pres. 3s. **fērð** P38, **færð** P49, 60; pret. 3s. **fērde** AII 38, 48; pret. 3pl. **fērdon** AII 29, Y, **fērden** P50.

fērend, m., *traveler, sailor*; npl. Wh25.

?ferhtgereaht, n., *guidance of mind, ?reason*; as. Wh70.

ferhð, m., *mind, heart, spirit*; dpl. **-um** Y.

ferian, wk.v.I, *carry, convey, bring*; inf. G1330; pres. 3pl. **fergað** G(n1298); pret. 3s. **ferede** G1397, 2089; pret. 3pl. **feredon** G2066. [Eng. *ferry*]

fers, n., *verse, sentence*; apl. C35. [Lat. *versus*]

ferðgrim, adj., *fierce of spirit*; nsm. Wh5. [**ferð-** = **ferhð**]

feste, see **fæste**.

fēt, see **fōt**.

fēðan, wk.v.I, *lead (in walking)*; pres. 3pl. **fēðað** G(n1298).

fēðelāst, m., *walking-track, step*; dpl. **-um** Y.

feðer, f., *feather*; pl. *wings*; npl. **-en** P29, 61; dpl. **-en** P30; apl. **-a** G1471.

fīf, num. adj., *five*; nm. **-e** G1974.

fīftēne, num. adj., *fifteen*; acc. absol. **-tēna** G1397; af. P35, 49.

fīftig, num. adj., *fifty*; gen. **-es** G1307.

findan, st. v.3, *find*; pret. 1s. **funde** WL18; pret. 3s. **funde** AII 74, G1467; pret. 3s. **fand** G1456, 2040; pret. subj. 3s. **funde** G1444; pp. nplm. (*to be found*) **fundene** W76.

finger, m., *finger*; as. P12.

finta, wk.m., *tail*; *consequence*; as. **-n** V32.

fīras, mpl., *living beings*, *men*; *mankind*; gen. **fīra** Wh39; dat. **fīrenum** Wh44, **fīrum** C44.

firen, f., *sin*; as. **firne** G(n1351); dipl. **-um** Wh45.

fisc, m., *fish*; npl. **-as** Wh80; gpl. **-a** Wh1.

fit, f., *song, poem*; as. **-te** Wh 1.

fitt, n., *strife, fight*; ds. **-e** G2072. [Eng. *fit*]

flǣsc, n., *flesh*; dis. **-e** V48, X1028; as. W(n15).

flǣschoma, wk.m., *the flesh-covering, body*; *carcass*; ds. **-n** G1386. [**-homa** = **hama**, m., *covering*]

flāh, adj., *insidiously artful, craftily deceitful*; nsm. Wh39.

flēam, m., *flight*; gs. **-es** AII 78; ds. **-e** AII 77, G2000, 2074.

flēogan, st.v.2, *fly*; inf. G1441, 1450, 1471, 1479; pres. 3s. **flīhð** P27, 33; pret. 3s. **flēah** G1456, 1465.

flēon, contr.v.2, *fly from, flee*; pres. 2s. **flīhst** AII 86, 87; pres.p. nplm. **flēonde** G2080, dsm. (absol.) **flēondum** AII 86; ger. **tō flēonne** AII 83.

flēotende, part. adj. (of **flēotan**, st.v.2), *floating*; asn. G1447.

flet, n., *floor (of a hall)*; as. Y.

fligepīl, m., *flying dart, arrow*; dipl. **-um** V27. [Lat. *pīlum*]

flīhð, see **flēogan**.

flocc, m., *flock, band*; ds. **-e** AII 35, 46.

flōd, m., *flood, deluge*; ns. G1298, 1386, 1419, P4, 6; ds. **-e** G1296, 1323, 1457, (n1374), W5, 7.

flotmonn, m., *seafarer*; gpl. **-a** G1475.

flōwan, st.v.7, *flow*; inf. **flōwen** P14; pres. 3s. **flōwð** P11.

flyhthwæt, adj., *eager, strong-flying*; gsm. (absol.) **-hwates** P(n13). [**hwæt**, adj., *quick, active*]

folc n., *folk, people*; ns. P39; gs. **-es** C74; ds. **-e** AII 6, V70; as. AI60, G1296, 1382, 2022, X1025.

folccyning, m., *king (of the people)*; npl. **-as** G1974, 2074.

folcgestrēon, n., *public treasure*; dpl. **-um** G1981.

folcgetrum, n., *host of people*; ds. **-e** G1987, 2046 [MS **folce-**].

folclond, n., *folk-land, inhabited country*; gs. **-es** WL47.

folcstyde, m., *folk-place, dwelling place*; ds. G2000.

folctoga, wk.m., *leader of the people*; as. **-n** G1961.

folde, wk.f., *earth, (dry) land*; ns. G1969; ds. **foldan** G1487, R39:10, X1033; as. **foldan** C45.

foldgræf, n., *earth grave*; dpl. **-grafum** X1025.

foldræst, f., *rest in the earth*; gs. **-e** X1028.

foldweg, m., *earth-way, earth, land*; ds. **-e** G2050; as. Y.

folgað, m., *service, duty; office of duty*; as. WL9.

folm, f., *hand, palm (of hand)*; as. **-e** R39:10 [MS **folm**].

fōn, st.v.7, *seize, take*; pret. 3pl. **fēngon** W32 [MS **fenge**].

Fons Vitae, Lat., *the Fountain of (eternal) Life*; ns. **Uite** P10.

for, prep. w. dat. or acc., *for, because of*; **for hwon**, *for what reason, why*; **for þære þe**, *because, for the reason that*.

fōr, fōron, see **faran**.

forbærnan, wk.v.I, *be consumed (by burning)*; pres. 3s. **-bærnð** P63; pp. nsm.**-bærned** P58.

forbyrnan, st.v.3, *burn up*; pret. 3s. **-barn** Y.

fordēman, wk.v.I, *condemn, damn*; pp. nsm. **-dēmed** AI 18.

fordōn, anom.v., *kill*; pret. 3s. **-dyde** W37, 39.

fore, prep. w. dat., *for, by.*

forealdian, wk.v.II, *become old, grow old*; pp. **forealdod** P55.

forebrēost, n., *breast, chest*; ns. P46.

foresæd, adj., *aforesaid, previously mentioned*; dsf.wk. **-an** AII 48; dsn.wk. **-an** W41; asm.wk. **-an** AII 15.

forestihtian, wk.v.II, *fore-ordain*; pret. 3s. **-stihte** P(n16).

forewarde, adv., **on forewarde**, *at the beginning, on the tip*; P12.

forfaran, st.v.6, *destroy, kill*; inf. W42.

forgifan, st.v.5, *grant, give*; pret. 3s. **-gēaf** AI 32; imper. 2s. **-gif** AI 24; pp. nsf. **-gifen** C56, nsn. **-gyfen** P(n19).

forhogdniss, f., *contempt, disdain*; ds. **-e** C8. [?rel. **forhycgan**, wk.v.III, *despise*]

forht, adj., *fearful, timid, afraid*; nsf. G1969; nplm. **-e** X1014.

forhtmōd, adj., *afraid, timid*; nsm. AII 59.

forlæran, wk.v.I, *mis-teach, seduce, corrupt*; pret. 3pl. **-lærdon** AII 45.

forlǣtan, st.v.7, *let go, leave*; *abandon*; pret. 3s. **-lēt** C24, G1405, 1450; pret. 3pl. **-lēton** W16; pres. p. nsm. **-lǣtende** C123.

forniman, st.v.4, *take away*; pret. 3s. **-nam** Wh(n30); pp. **-numen** WL24 [not in MS].

forraðe, adv., *very quickly*.

forsēon, st.v.5, *scorn, reject*; pret. 3pl. **-sāwan** V61, **-sāwon** W12.

forslēan, st.v.6, *strike down, kill*; pp. asn. **-slegen** G2022.

forst, m., *frost*; ns. P9.

forstandan, st.v.6, w. dat., *withstand, oppose*; pret. 3s. **-stōd** V65.

forswelgan, st.v.3, *swallow up, consume*; pret. 3s. **-swealg** R47:3.

forð, adv., *forth, away*; *forwards*; *henceforth*.

forðām/forðan/forðon (þe), adv., *therefore*; conj. *for, because*.

forðearle, adv., *very much, greatly*.

forðfōr f., *going forth, departure*; *death*; ns. C98; gs. **-e** C89, 128; ds. **-e** C94, 104. [**fōr**, f., *going*; rel. **faran**]

forðsīð, m., *departure*; *death*; ds. **-e** W55. [**sīð**, m., *going, journey*]

forðspell, n., *declaration*; dipl. **-um** V47. [**spell**, n., *discourse, message*]

forðweard, m., *leader, guide*; ns. G1436.

forwyrd, f., *fall, death*; *damnation*; ds. **-e** W78. [rel. **forweorðan**, st.v.3, *perish*]

fōt, m., *foot*; as. R39:10; npl. **fēt** P32; dpl. **-um** AII 95, G1457, 1467, **fōten** P44.

fraced, adj., *abominable*; nsf. **fracod** W72; dplf. **-um** AII 38.

frǣgn, see **frignan**.

frǣt, see **fretan**.

frǣt, adj., *proud, perverse*; asn. **-e** V48; see **fretan**.

frǣtwe, fpl., *adornments*; *perfection*; acc. P(n13).

fram/from, prep.w. dat., *from*.

franca, wk.m., *javelin, lance*; npl. **-n** G1982.

frēa, wk.m., *lord*; *God*; ns. C45, G1359, 1404, 1427, 1475; gs. **-n** WL33; ds. **-n** G1493.

frēcen, n., *peril, danger*; gs. **frēcnes** Wh20.

frēcne, adj., *terrible, perilous*; nsm. Wh5; gplm. **frēcenra** G1427.

frēfrian, wk.v.II, *comfort, console*; pret. 3s. **-frode** AII 106.

fremde, adj., *strange, foreign (one)*; gs. **fremdes** G1971. [Ger. *fremd*]

fremman, wk.v.I, *perform, do, bring about*; inf. G1291, P(n19);

pres. 3pl. **fremmaรฐ** Wh44; pret. 3s. **fremede** G1314 [MS **freme**], 1493; pret. 3pl. **fremedon** Wh70.

fremsumness, f., *kindness, mercy*; dpl. **-um** C81. [**frem-**, rel. **fremu**, f., *kindness, benefit*]

frēo, adj., *free(-born), having liberty*; *noble*; gplm. **frēora** G2088.

frēod, f., *peace*; as. **-e** V70.

frēodōm, m., *freedom, liberty*; ds. **-e** AII 27.

frēolīce, adv., *freely, readily*.

frēond, m., *friend*; *lover*; ns. WL47; npl. **frȳnd** WL33; gpl. **-a** AI 32, WL17; dpl. **-um** G2010, 2025.

frēondscipe, m., *love*; ns. WL25.

fre(o)รฐo, wk.f., indecl., *peace, security*; gs. G1347; ds. **freรฐo** G1487; see **friรฐ**.

fretan, st.v.5, *devour*; pret. 3s. **frรฆt** R47:1. [Ger. *fressen*]

frignan, st.v.3, *ask, inquire*; pret. 3s. **frรฆgn** C102, 106, 114.

frimdig, adj., *desirous*; nsm. AII 74.

frimรฐ, f., *origin*; ds. **-e** V(n34); cp. **fruma**.

friรฐ, m. and n., *peace, security*; as. G1299. [Ger. *Friede*]

frōd, adj., *old, wise*; nsm. VI.

frōfor, f., *help, consolation, support*; ns. G1475; ds. **frōfre** AI 28, AII 107, R39:19; ?ds./as. **frōfre** Wh36.

from/fram, prep. w. dat., *from*; see next word.

from, adj., *firm, strong*; *bold, brave*; asm. **-ne** G1961; nplm. **-e** Y.

fromlīce, adv., *stoutly, boldly*. [see preceding word]

fromsīรฐ, m., *departure, separation*; ns. WL33.

fruma, wk.m., *beginning, origin*; ds. **-n** C72.

frumgāra, wk.m., *leader*; *patriarch*; ds. **-n** G2052; apl. **-n** G 1334. [**frum**, adj., *first, original* + **gār**, m., *spear*; cp. Lat. *primipilus*]

frumsceaft, f., *first Creation, beginning*; as. C33; gpl. **-a** V66.

frȳnd, see **frēond**.

fugel, m., *fowl, bird*; ns. G1460, 1983, P24, 26, 27, 33, 49, 59, 65, (n16); gs. **fugles** P(n18); npl. **-es** P43, 50, **-as** P(n19); gpl. **-a** P41, P(n13), ?**-e** P40, 52; apl. **fuglas** G1299, 2088.

fugelcinn/-cynn, n., *bird-flock*; ns. P36; as. P25; npl. P52.

fūl, adj., *foul, dirty, impure*; nsf. W72; asm.wk. **-an** W82; asf.wk. **-an**

AI 10; aplm.wk. **-an** AI 20, absol. **-e** W81. [not to be confused with **ful(l)**]

fulgeare, adv., *full well, fully, thoroughly.*

fūlice/fūllice, adv., *foully, shamefully.*

ful(l), adj., *full (of), complete, entire*; nsm. V43; dsm. **-um** AII 23; asf. **-e** G1292.

ful(l), adv., *most, completely, full*; *very*; **ful oft**, *very often.*

fullgān, anom.v., w.dat., *perform, fulfill*; pret. 3pl. **-ēodan** W35.

fulluht, n., *baptism*; gs. **-es** AII 41; ds. **-e** AI 17.

fultum, m., *help, assistance*; gs. **-es** G2025; as. G1964, 2072.

fultumian, wk.v.II, *help, support*; inf. W58 (?w. **wolde** or **scolde** understood).

funde, **fundene**, see **findan**.

fundian, wk.v.II, *seek, attempt* (w. inf.); pres. 3pl. **fundiaþ** V16.

furður, adv., *further, more.*

fyll, m., *fall*; *destruction, death*; ns. G2062.

fyllan, wk.v.I, *fell, cut down*; *kill*; pret. 3s. **fylde** G2071.

fȳr, n., *fire*; ds. **-e** V(n34); as. P58, W19.

fyrd, f., *army, expeditionary force*; as. G1961, 2044.

fyrdgestealla, wk.m., *comrade in arms*; dpl. **-steallum** G1999.

fyrdhwæt, adj., *active, eager in war*; nplm. **-hwate** Y.

fyrdian, wk.v.II, *go with an army, march forth, be at war*; pret. 3pl. **fyrdedon** W56. [rel. **fyrd**]

fyrendǣd, f., *wicked deed, crime*; apl. **-a** Y.

fyrhto, f., *fright, terror*; ds. **fyrhtu** C79.

fyrmest, adj., *foremost, first*; nplm.wk. **-an** W78.

fyrndagas, mpl., *days of yore*; dpl. **-dagum** V1 (**on –dagum**, *long ago*), X1033. [**fyrn-**, adj., *ancient, former*]

fyrngesceap, n., *ancient decree*; ns. P(n18).

fyrnstrēam, m., *ancient-stream, the ocean*; gpl. **-a** Wh7.

fyrst, m., *space of time, time*; ds. **-e** AI 70, AII 48, W5.

G

gǣlsa, wk.m., *wantonness, evil*; as. V11.

gæst, m., *guest*; *enemy*; ns. Wh29 (?or **gāst/gǣst**, *spirit*); gpl. **gasta** G1346; dpl. **gystum** G2056; see **gāst**.

gafol, n., *tax, tribute*; as. G1978.

gāl, n., *wantonness, evil*; gs. **-es** X1034.

gāl, adj., *licentious, wanton* ; nsm. W43.

gālnyss, f., *lustfulness, lust*; ds. **-e** W72; as. **-e** AI 10, 21.

gān, anom.v., *go*; *advance*; *come*; inf. G1970, Y; pres. 3s. **gāð** P11; pret. 3s. **ēode** AI 5, C23, 59, 100, V(n34); pret. 3pl. **ēodon** Y; imper. 2s. **Gā** V(n34).

gangan/gongan, st.v.7, *go, proceed, move (about, along)*; *happen*; inf. C92, G1345, 1487, Y; pres. 1s. **gonge** WL 35; pres. 3s. **gongeð** R39:23; pres.p. nsm. **gongende** C25, 96.

gār, m., *spear*; *weapon*; ns. WL(n7); npl. **-as** G2064; gpl. **-a** G2019. [Eng. *gar (fish)*, *gar*lic]

gārsecg, m., *ocean, sea*; gs. **-es** Wh29; as. **-seg** P1. [no known cognates or etymology]

gāst, m., *breath*; *soul, spirit, life*; **Hālig Gāst**, *the Holy Ghost* (third person of the Trinity); ns. V80, W87; gs. **-es** C77; ds. **-e** P(n19), X1034; as. AII 109, C126, **gǣst** V49; apl. **-as** AI 20; see **gǣst**.

gāstlic, adj., *ghostly, spiritual*; dsf. **-ra** AI 72; dplm. **-um** AII 26.

ge, conj., *and*; **ge ... ge**, *both ... and*.

gē, pers. pron., 2pl. *ye*; npl. **gē**, gpl. **ēower**, dpl. **ēow**, apl. **ēow**; see **þū** and the poss. pron. **ēower**.

geald, see **gieldan**.

gealdor, n., *sound, (mysterious) song*; ds. **gealdre** V6.

geangsumian, wk.v.II, *make anxious, vex*; pp. **-sumod** AI 22.

gēar, m., *year*; gpl. **-a** P(n16), X1035.

gēara/geāra, adv., *of yore, formerly*; **gēara iū**, *in former times*, V57.

gēardagas, m.pl., *days of old, former times*; dpl. **-dagum** W35.

gearo, adj., *ready*; asn. G1321.

gearowyrdig, adj., *ready-of-speech, eloquent*; nsm. V51. [**wyrdig**, rel. **word**, n.]

gēasne, adj., *deprived of, void of*; nsm. Wh46.

gebād, see **gebīdan**.

gebæd, see **gebiddan**.

gebǣro, ?n. or f. (indecl.), *demeanor, disposition*; dis. WL21; as. WL44; dpl. **-bǣrum** AII 30.

gebeden, see **gebiddan**.

gebelgan, st.v.3, *swell up*; *enrage*; pp. nsm. **gebolgen** G(n1364). [rel. **belg**, m., *sack*; Eng. *belly*]

gebēodan, st.v.2, *command, order, summon*; inf. G1961.

gebēorscip, m., *feast, convivial gathering*; gs. **-es** C24; ds. **-e** C20, 30. [**bēor**, n., *beer, mead* + suffix *-ship*]

gebīdan, st.v.1, *experience, endure*; pret. 1s. **gebād** WL3. [Eng *bide*]

gebiddan, st.v.5, *bid, urge, intreat*; *pray*; pret. 3s. **gebæd** AI 47, AII 103, C117; pp. nsm. **gebeden** AII 1. [Ger. *bitten*]

gebīegan, wk.v.I, *bend, turn; debase*; pp. **gebīged** V55.

gebletsian, wk.v.II, *bless*; pret. 3s. **gebletsode** AI 46.

gebolgen, see **gebelgan**.

gebregdan, st.v.3, *draw*; pret. 1s. **gebrǣd** Y.

gebringan, wk.v.I (pres., st.v.3), *bring, lead, bear*; inf. AI 1; pret. 3s. **gebrōhte** AI 7, 59, P2, W80; pret. 3pl. **gebrōhton** AII 32, (?on **gebrōhton**, *caused, induced*); imper. 2s. **gebring** AII 53; pp. nsm. **gebroht** Wh72.

gebyrd, f., *nature*; as. P(n18). [Ger. *Geburt*]

gebyrman, wk.v.I, *swell, puff up* (in fermentation); pp. nsm. **gebyrmed** V42. [rel. **beorma**, wk.m., *yeast*]

gebysnung, f., *example*; ?dis./as. **-e** AII 112.

gecēosan, st.v.2, *choose, decide, elect*; pres. 3pl. **gecēosað** Wh37; pret. 3pl. **gecuran** W82; pp. nsn. **gecoren** C54.

gecnāwan, st.v.7, *know, perceive*; pres. 3s. **gecnāweð** Wh38.

gecneordniss, f., *diligence, care*; ds. **-e** AII 13.

gecoren, **gecuran**, see **gecēosan**.

gecynd, f., *nature, (natural) manner, kind*; *sex*; ns. **-e** P(n18), X1016, 1017; as. Wh49; dpl. **-um** R39:15.

gecyrran, wk.v.I, *turn; convert, change*; pres. 2s. **gecyrst** AI 45; pres. 3pl. **gecyrrað** AII 112; pp. **gecyrred** G1415.

gecȳðan, wk.v.I, *make known, tell, relate*; pret. 3s. **gecȳðde** G2021. [cp. **cūð, cȳðan**]

gedǣlan, wk.v.I, *divide, part*; pret. subj. 3s. **gedǣlde** WL22; pp. **gedǣled** V22. [cp. **dǣl, gedāl**]

gedafenian, wk.v.II, impers. (usually with dat.), *be becoming* or *fit, behoove*; pres. 3s. **-fenað** P(n19); pret. 3s. **gedeofanade** C16 (w.acc).

gedāl, n., *distinction, division, allotment*; ds. **-e** G1400.

gedēfe, adj., *honorable, good; fitting, proper*; nsm. G1287; nsn. Y.

gedēman, wk.v.I, *deem, judge, determine*; pp. nsm. **gedēmed** C20. [cp. **dōm**]

gederian, wk.v.II, *injure, afflict*; pret. 3s. **gederede** W3.

gedīgan, wk.v.I, *survive, endure*; pret. 1s. **gedīgde** Y.

gedihtan, wk.v.I, *put in order, compose, direct*; pret. 3s. **gedihte** AI 19, W25. [Eng. *dight*, rel. Lat. *dictāre*]

gedōn, anom.v., *do, make, perform*; pp. AII 51, 98.

gedreag, n., *multitude*; as. WL45.

gedryht, f., *troop, band of retainers*; ns. X1013; as. Y.

gedwolgod, m., *false god, idol*; ns. W65; ds. **-e** W58.

gedwollīce, adv., *heretically, erroneously*.

gedwyld, n., *wandering; error, heresy*; ds. **-e** AII 32, W51, 53, 68, 81. [rel. **(ge)dwellan**, wk.v.I, *lead astray*]

geēawan, wk.v.I, *reveal, make manifest*; pres. subj. 3s **geēawe** P(n13).

geedlǣcan, wk. v.I, *repeat*; pret. 3s. **-lēahte** AII 17.

geegsian, wk.v.II, *frighten*; pres. 3pl. **geegsiað** AI 49.

geendian, wk.v.II, *end, finish, complete*; pret. 3s. **geendade** C88, 120.

gefǣrrēden, f., *companionship, fellowship*; ds. **-a** (for **-e**) AI 28. [cp. **gefēra**]

gefæstnian, wk.v.II, *fasten, make firm*; pp. asn. **gefæstnod** G1323.

gefara, wk.m., *companion, fellow traveler*; npl. **gefaren** V(n34).

gefaran, st.v.6, *set forth, go*; pret. 3s. **gefōr** G1360; pp. **gefaren** G1987, 2052.

gefēah, see **gefēon**.

gefeccan, wk.v.I, *fetch, bring to*; inf. AI 38 (with **hēt**, *to be brought*).

gefēgan, wk.v.I, *join, fit together*; imper. s. **gefēg** G1310; pp. **gefēged** Wh41.

gefēlan, wk.v.I, *feel*; pres. 3s. **gefēleð** Wh24.

gefeoht, n., *fight, battle, war*; ds. **-e** W56, 59; as. W59.

gefēon, st.v.5, *be glad, rejoice, exult*; pret. 3s. **gefēah** G1468, Y; pret. 3pl. **gefēgon** Y; pres.p. disn. **gefēonde** C99.

gefēra, wk.m., *companion, associate*; npl. **-n** AII 31; apl. **-n** AII 46.

gefēran, wk.v.I, *go, proceed*; pres. 3s. **gefǣrð** P52.

geferian, wk.v.II, *carry*; inf. Y.

geflota, wk.m., *floater, swimmer*; ds. **-n** Wh7.

gefōr, see **gefaran**.

gefrǣfrian, wk.v.II, *comfort, console*; inf. AI 26.

gefrǣg(e)n, see **gefrignan**.

gefremman, wk.v.I, *perform, accomplish*; inf. AI 31, AII 42; pres. 1s. **gefremme** AI 17; pret. 1s. **gefremede** WL(n37); pret. 3s. **-fremede** V71; pret. subj. 3s. **-fremode** AI 10, 13; pp. asf. **-fremede** V36.

gefrignan, st.v.3, *ask, learn by asking, hear of*; pret. 1s. **gefrǣg(e)n** G1960, 2060, R47 : 2.

gefullian (= **-fullwian**), wk.v.II, *baptize*; pret. 3s. **-lode** AII 23. [cp. **fulluht**]

gefultumian, wk.v.II, *help, assist*; pp. nsm. **-tumod** C13.

gefyllan, wk.v.I, *fill, fulfill*; pp. nsm. **gefylled** V26, Wh60, **gefyllede** AII 52.

gefyrn, adv., *of old, formerly*.

gegada, wk.m., *fellow, companion*; dpl. **gegadum** AII 45.

gegad(e)rian, wk.v.II, *gather, assemble, unite*; *associate with*; inf. AI 60; pres. 3s. **gegadered** (?for **-deraðed** or **-dereð**) P55; pret. 3s. **gegaderode** AII 68; pp. **gegæderad** V80.

gegearcian, wk.v.II, *prepare*; pp. nsn. **gegearcod** AII 72.

gegearwian, wk.v.II, *prepare, make ready*; pret. subj. 3s. **gegearwode** C96, 114.

gegierwan, wk.v.I, *adorn*; pp. **-wed** R29 : 3.

gegladian, wk.v.II, *make glad, comfort*; pp. nsf. **gegladod** AII 108.

geglengan, wk.v.I, *adorn, embellish*; pret. 3s. **geglængde** C6; pp. asn. **geglenged** C60.

gegrētan, wk.v.I, *greet*; pres. 3pl. **gegrēteð** P37.

gegrind, n., *grinding together, clashing*; ns. G2063.

gehādian, wk.v.II, *ordain, consecrate*; pret. 3s. **gehādode** AII 2; pp. nsm. **gehādod** AII 11, dplm. **-um** AII 3.

gehǣman, wk.v.I, *lie with, commit fornication*; pret. 3s. **gehǣmde** W73.

gehāt, n., *promise, vow*; gpl. **-a** G1425.

gehātan, st.v.7, *call, name*; pres. 1s. **gehāte** Y; pp. **gehāten** P24, 35, 41, 65, W36, 40, 60, 66.

gehātlond, n., *promised land*; gs. **-es** C74.

gehealdan, st.v.7, *keep, hold*; pres. subj. 1s. **gehealde** AI 66; pp. nplm. **gehealdene** W31 (**gehealdan on**, *satisfied with*).

gehende, adv. and prep., *near, nigh*.

gehirde, see **gehȳran**.

gehirsumian, wk.v.II, *be obedient, obey*; inf. AII 37.

gehīwian, wk.v.II, *form, shape*; pp. nsn. **gehēowed** P46.

gehladan, st.v.6, *load, burden*; pret. 3s. **gehlod** X1034; pp. aplm. **gehladene** G1293.

gehnǣst, n., *conflict, slaughter*; ds. **-e** G2015. [rel. **hnītan**, st.v.1, *thrust, clash*]

gehrēodan, st.v.2, *adorn, cover (over)*; pp. nplm. **gehrodene** Wh74.

gehūslian, wk.v.II, *give the housel* (the eucharist), *consecrate*; pret. 3s. **gehūslode** AI 75.

gehwā, gehwæt, pron. w. part. gen., *each, every*; gsn. **gehwæs** C39; dsm. **gehwām** Wh62; dsf. **gehwǣre** G1374; asm. **gehwone** V69, X1026.

gehwǣr(e), adv., *everywhere, in all directions*; see also **gehwā**.

gehwilc/gehwylc, pron. w. part. gen., *each (one)*; nsm. X1029, Wh39; gsn. **-es** G1311, 1336; dsm. **-um** Wh6, **-e** WL(n7); asm. Y; asf. **-e** X1023; asn. G1297, X1025; ?dipln. **-um** V83.

gehwyrfan, wk.v.I, *change, turn, convert*; pret. 3s. **gehwyrfde** C69; pret. subj. 3s. **gehwyrfde** C58.

?gehȳdan, wk.v.I, *?fasten, secure*; *?put in harbor*; pres. 3pl. **gehȳdað** Wh13.

gehygd, f., *reflection, thought*; ns. X1038.

gehȳran, wk.v.I, *hear*; inf. AI 34; pres. 1s. **gehȳre** AI 55 [MS **gehyra**]; pret. 3s. **gehȳrde** C35, **gehirde** AII 91; imper. s. **gehȳr** AII 91; ger. **tō gehȳranne** C70.

gehȳrness, f., *hearing, report*; ds. **-e** C67.

gelāc, n., *play, tossing*; *tumult*; as. WL7.

gelæccan, wk.v.I, *take, catch, seize*; pret. 3s. **gelæhte** AII 101; pret. 3pl. **gelæhton** AII 76.

gelǣdan, wk.v.I, *guide, conduct, bring*; pres. subj. 2s. **gelǣde** G1340; pret. 3s. **gelǣdde** C51, G1411; pp. nsmnf. **gelǣded** G1312.

gelǣran, wk.v.I, *teach, educate, instruct*; pp. nsm. **gelǣred** C12; superl. aplm. **gelǣredestan** C52.

gelǣte, n., *meeting, juncture*; dpl. **gelǣtum** W63.

gelamp, see **gelimpan**.

gelaðian, wk.v.II, *invite, summon*; pp. nsm. **gelaþod** AII 52.

gelaðung, f., *congregation, church*; gs. (?or ds.) **-e** AII 14; ds. **-e** AII 55.

geléafa, wk.m., *belief, faith*; gs. **-n** R47(n5); ds. **-n** AI 77, AII 5, 19, W28.

geléafful, adj., *full of belief, faithful*; nsm. AII 23; dsm.wk. **-lan** AI 71.

geléafléas, adj., *belief-less, unbelieving*; nsm. AII 67.

geléogan, st.v.2, *belie, deceive, betray*; pret. 3s. **geléah** G1446.

geleornian, wk.v.II, *learn, inquire*; inf. C68; pret. 3s. **geleornode** C5, **-nade** C19.

gelīc, adj., *like*(w. dat.), *alike, similar, equal*; nsm. P48, Wh8; asm. **-an** AII 44; nplf. **-e** P30; npln. V76.

gelīce, adv., *in like manner, similarly, likewise*.

gelimpan, st.v.3, *occur, happen, befall*; pret. 3s. **gelamp** W7.

gelimplic, adj., *fit, suitable*; dsf. **-e** C26.

gelistan, wk.v.I, *desire, to be eager (for)*; pp. npln. **geliste** Wh23.

geliðewǣcan, wk.v.I, *calm*; pret. 3s. **-wǣhte** AII 107.

gelōgian, wk.v.II, *place; regulate*; pret. 3s. **gelōgode** AII 3.

gelōme, adv., *continually, repeatedly*.

gelong, adj., *belonging to, dependent on* (**æt**); nsf. WL45.

gelȳfan, wk.v.I, *believe, trust, confide*; inf. AI 9, 12; pres. 1pl. **gelȳfað** W27; pret. 3pl. **gelȳfdon** W19, 20, 58; imper. 2s. **gelȳf** AI 52, AII 91.

gelȳfed, adj., *weakened; advanced*; gsf. **gelȳfdre** C19.

gemaca, f., *mate, spouse*; as. P64.

gemacian, wk.v.II, *make, cause*; inf. AI 7.

gemǣc, adj., *suitable*; asm. **-ne** WL18.

gemǣnelic, adj., *common, general*; dsm. **-an** AI 66.

gemǣran, wk.v.I, *celebrate, glorify*; pp. nsm. **gemǣred** C2.

gemāh, adj., *malicious, impious, shameless*; nsm. Wh39, Wh(n39).

gēmde, see **gīeman**.

gemet, n., *measure, manner*; as. C48.

gemētan, wk.v.I, *find (out), encounter*; pres. subj. 2s. **gemēte** V78; pp. **gemēted** Wh4.

gemetlīce, adv., *moderately.*

gemittan, wk.v.I, *meet (with), find*; pres. 2s. **gemittest** V45.

gemon, see **gemunan**.

gemong, n., *mingling together, throng, troop*; ds. **-e** Y. [rel. Eng. *among*]

gemōt, n., *assembly, council*; ds. **-e** X1026. [Eng. *moot*]

gemunan, pret.-pres.v., *remember, be mindful of*; inf. V83; pres. 3s. **gemon** WL51; pret. 3s. **gemunde** G1407.

gemyltsian, wk.v.II, *show mercy, have compassion, pity*; imper. 2s. **gemyltsa** AI 23.

gemynd, f., i-stem, *mind, memory, remembrance*; *thought*; ns. X1037; ds. **-e** C46; as. Wh(n35); dipl. **-um** V11.

gemyndgian, wk.v.II, *remember, be mindful of*; pret. 3s. **gemynd-gade** C68.

gēn/gīen, adv., *next (in order), still.*

genæs, see **genesan**.

genam, see **geniman**.

genamian, wk.v.II, *name, call*; pp. nsf. **genamod** W44.

genemnan, wk.v.I, *name*; pp. nsn. **genemmed** P16.

generian, wk.v.II, *save, deliver*; pres. subj. 3s. **generige** P68, **generie** P(n19).

genesan, st.v.5, *be saved, escape from*; pret. 3s. **genæs** G2019.

geneðan, wk.v.I, *engage in, dare*; pret. 1s. **geneðde** Y.

genihtsum, adj., *abundant, copious, plentiful*; nsm. G1995. [**-niht-** = **nyht**, n., *abundance*]

geniman, st.v.4, *take, receive*; *undertake*; inf. AI 63; pret. 3s. **genam** AII 35, P2; imper. **genim** G1335.

geofonhūs, n., *sea-house, ship*; *ark*; gpl. **-a** G1321.

geoguð, f., *youth*; gs. **iogoþe** Y; ds. **geogoðe** G1370, W38.

gēomerung, f., *groaning, lamentation*; ds. **-e** AII 70, 95.

gēomor, adj., *sad*; nsm. WL17, (n7); dsf. **-re** WL1.

gēomormōd, adj., *sad-minded, sorrowful*; nsm. WL42.

geond, prep. w. acc., *through(out), over.*

geondsendan, wk.v.I, *overspread*; pp. nsn. **-sended** G1968.

geong, adj., *young*; nsm. WL42; see also **iung**.

geopenian, wk.v.II, *open, manifest, reveal*; pp. nsn. **geopenad** AI 35.

georn, adj., w. gen., *eager (for)*; nsm. G(n1983). [Eng. *yearn*]

georne, adv., *eagerly, earnestly; gladly*; superl. **geornost**.

geornfulness/-nyss, f., *eagerness, zeal, diligence*; ds. **-e** AII 16, C83.

geornlīce, adv., *earnestly, diligently, zealously*.

geornost, see **georne**.

gerǣdod, adj., *harnessed*; nsn. AII 73.

gerǣsan, wk.v.I, *rush, attack*; pret. 3s. **gerǣsde** G2095.

gereccan, wk.v.I, *explain, interpret*; pp. nsm. **gereht** V(n34).

gereord, n., *language*; gpl. **-a** W7.

gerestan, wk.v.I, *rest; take a rest from* (w.gen.); inf. C97, WL40.

gerisenlīce, adv., *fittingly, suitably*.

gerȳman, wk.v.I, *make room, expand, open*; inf. G1304; pp. nsm. **gerȳmed** G1485.

gesǣlig, adj., *happy, blessed, prosperous*; nsm. G1286, W84.

gesæt, see **gesittan**.

gesāwon, see **gesēon**.

gescēad, n., *distinction, discretion; argument, account*; as. AII 88, V8, W22.

gesceaft, n., *creation, created being*; npl. **-a** W24, **-e** X1020; gpl. **-a** W88.

gesceap, n., *fate, destiny; creation*; ds. **-e** C72; npl. **-u** R39:24. [Eng. *shape*]

gescildan, wk.v.I, *shield, guard against, protect*; inf. P(n19).

gescippan, st.v.6, *make, form, create*; pret. 3s. **gescōp** P7, 25, 66, W13, 17, 23, 30, 85; imper. s. **gescype** G1306.

gesēah, see **gesēon**.

gesēcan, wk.v.I, *seek (out), set out for, search for*; inf. R39:5; pres. 3s. **gesēceð** Wh29.

gesecgan, wk.v.II, *say, tell, declare*; inf. R39: 28; ger. **tō -ne** R39: 25.

gesēgen, see **gesēon**.

gesegnian, wk.v.II, w. reflex. (acc.) pron., *make the sign of the Cross, bless*; pret. 3s. **gesegnode** C118.

gesēon, contr.v.5, *see, behold*; inf. Wh85, Y; pres. 1s. **gesēo** AI 56; pret. 1s. **geseah** R29:1, Y; pret. 3s. **geseah** AII 6, 26, 60, 75, C22, G1292, 1320, **geseh** P1, 16; pret. 3pl. **gesāwon** G2087; pp. nsn. **gesēgen** C55, 127.

gesettan, wk.v.I, *set, place, occupy*; *establish*; inf. V64; pres. 3s. **gesette**
C26, **gesett** P27; pret. 3s. **gesette** C125; pret. 3pl. **gesettan**
W82, pp. nsm. **geseted** C18.

gesibb, f., *kinsman*, gpl. **-ra** V69.

gesihð, f., *sight*; ds. **-e** C124. [rel. **gesēon**]

gesittan, st.v.5, *sit (down), settle*; inf. G1469 [MS **gesette**]; pres. 1s.
gesitte WL(n37); pret. 3s. **gesæt** G1421.

gesið, m., *companion*; npl. **-ðas** G2067.

gesomnian, wk.v.II, *assemble, collect*; inf. C51.

gesomnung, f., *congregation, church*; ds. **-e** C66.

gespornan, st.v.3, *strike against*; *tread*; inf. G1458; pret. 3s. **gespearn**
G1447.

gespringan, st.v.3, *spring forth*; pret. 3s. **gesprang** Y.

gestīgan, st.v.1, *climb, ascend*; pres. 2s. **gestīgest** G(n1393); pret. 3s.
gestāh G1369. [Ger. *steigen*]

gestillan, wk.v.I, *still, calm, stop*; pp. **gestilled** G1416.

gestrangian, wk.v.II, *make strong, confirm*; *?harden*; pret. 3s.
gestrangod AII 39.

gestrȳnan, wk.v.I, *obtain, acquire, win over*; pret. subj. 3s. **gestrȳnde**
AII 9.

gesund, adj., *sound, safe, unharmed*; asm. **-ne** Y.

geswīcan, st.v.1, *leave off, stop*; pret. 3s. **geswāc** AII 108.

gesyllan, wk.v.I, *give*; pres. 1s. **gesylle** G1329.

gesȳne, adj., *seen, visible*; nsf. R39:3. [rel. **gesēon**]

getǣcan, wk.v.I, *teach, instruct, declare*; pret. 3s. **getǣhte** AII 3.

getæl, n., *reckoning, estimation*; *number, series*; ds. **-e** W62; as. C66.

getellan, wk.v.I, *reckon, count*; pp. **geteled** G1336; nsm. **geteald**
W49; nsf. **geteald** W45; nplm. **getealde** W46, 79.

getrymman, wk.v.I, *confirm, strengthen, encourage*; pres.p. nsm.
-mende C112. [rel. Eng. *trim*]

getwǣfan, wk.v.I, *separate, part*; *put an end to*; pp. **getwǣfed** Y.

geþafian, wk.v.II, *permit, allow, assent*; pret. 3s. **geþafode** AII 44.

geþeccan, wk.v.I, *cover (over)*; pp. asm. **geþeahtne** G1492 [MS
geþeahte]. [Eng. *thatch*]

geþencan, wk.v.I, *think, consider, determine*; inf. V9; pres. 3s. **geþen-
ceð** V33.

geþēodan wk.v.I, *join, unite*; pret. 3s. **geþēodde** C65.

geþēodniss, f., *joining, association*; ds. **-e** C8.

geþōht, m., *thought*; *intention, purpose*; ns. WL43; as. WL12; npl. **-as** Wh(n35).

geunnan, pret.-pres.v., *give, grant*; pret. 3s. **geūðe** W24, Y.

gewǣgan, wk.v.I, *afflict, overcome*; pp. nsm. **gewǣged** V41.

gewǣmnian (= **gewǣpnian**), wk.v.II, *arm*; pp. nsm. **gewǣmnod** AII 81.

gewǣn-, see **gewen-**.

gewǣtan, wk.v.I, *wet(ten)*; inf. **-en** P12.

gewāt, see **gewītan**.

gewealdan, st.v.7, w. gen., *wield, rule, have power over*; pret. 3s. **gewēold** AII 27.

gewemman, wk.v.I, *defile, besmirch*; pp. aplm. **gewemde** G1294. [rel. **wamm**, mn., *spot, stain*]

gewemmednyss, f., *corruption, defilement*; ds. **-um** AII 30.

gewendan, wk.v.I, *go, return*; pres. 3pl. **gewǣndeð** P53; pret. 3s. **gewende** AII 20. [Ger. *wenden*]

gewenian, wk.v.II, *accustom, habituate*; pret. 3s. **gewenede** AII 33.

gewēold, see **gewealdan**.

geweorðan, st.v.3, *happen, come to pass*; pret. 3s. **gewearð** W5; pp. **geworden** AII 67, C121.

geweorðian, wk.v.II, *honor, dignify*; pp. **geweorðad** C2, Y, **gewurðod** W49.

gewīcian, wk.v.II, *dwell, encamp*; pres. 3pl. **gewīciað** Wh19. [cp. **wīc**]

gewīdost, superl. adv. (of **wīde**), *farthest (apart)*.

gewīfian, wk.v.II, with **on** + dat., *take a wife, marry*; pret. 3s. **gewifode** W43.

gewin(n), n., *battle, war, contest*; ns. V59; as. W54, 59. [rel. **winnan**, st.v.3, *fight, struggle*]

gewis, adj., *certain, sure, knowing*; nsm. C128; dsm. **-sum** W28.

gewissian, wk.v.II, *instruct, inform*; inf. AII 19.

gewit(t), n., *mind, understanding*; as. R39:13.

gewitan, pret.-pres.v., *know*; pret. 3s. **gewiste** R29:14.

gewītan, st.v.1, *go; depart; come*; pres. 3s. **gewīteð** R39:6, Wh28, 58 [MS **-að**]; pres. 3pl. **gewitað** Wh16; pret. 1s. **gewāt** C31, WL9; pret. 3s. **gewāt** G1356, 1421, 1460, 1471, 2005, 2018, 2045, 2083, R29:10, 13, WL6; pret. 3pl. **gewiton** G1964, 1999; imper. 2s. **gewīt** G1345, 1487.

gewiteness, f., *departure*; gs. **-e** C89.

gewitnyss, f., *witness, charge*; ds. **-e** AII 14, 55.

gewitt, see **gewit**.

geworden, see **geweorðan**.

geworht(e), see **gewyrcan**.

gewrecan, st.v.5, *wreak, avenge, revenge*; pret. 3pl. **gewrǣcon** G2038.

gewrit/gewryt, n., *something written, writing; a book*; ns. AI 73; gs. **-es** C75; ds. **-e** AI 43; as. AI 73; npl. **-u** R39:1, 13; dipl. **-um** P(n13: MS **-u**).

gewuna, wk.m., *custom, wont, manner*; ds. **-n** AII 33.

gewunian, wk.v.II, *be accustomed*; pret. 3s. **gewunade** C2.

gewurðod, see **geweorðian**.

gewyrcan, wk.v.I, *form, make, construct, prepare*; inf. Y; pret. 3s. **geworhte** AII 46, C80, 81, W13, 17, 30, 85; imper. s. **gewyrc** G1307, ?1309; pp. asn. **geworht** C7.

gied(d), n., *word, speech; song*; as. R47:3, WL1, **gyd** V51.

gieldan, st.v.3, *pay, render*; inf. G1978; pret. 3s. **geald** G2079.

gieman/gēman, wk.v.I, w. gen., *care for, regard, seek*; pret. 3s. **gīmde** AII 85, **gēmde** C82.

gien, see **gēn**.

gīet/gīt, adv., *yet*.

gif, conj., *if*.

gīferness, f., *gluttony, greediness*; as. **-e** P(n19).

gifu, f., *gift, grace*; ns. C56; ds. **gife** AI 25, C2; as. **gife** C14, 50, 62.

gīmde, see **gīeman**.

gimen, f., *care; charge*; ds. **-e** AII 49; as. **-e** AII 16. [rel. **gīeman**]

gīt, see **gīet**.

gladian, wk.v.II, *make glad, gladden*; inf. AII 115.

glæd, adj., *glad, joyous*; nsm. AII 8; nsf. **-u** G1480; dsf. **-re** AII 5.

glædlīce, adv., *gladly, pleasantly*.

glēaw, adj., *prudent, wise, skillful; good*; nsm. G1370, V4; comp. nsm. **-ra** R47:6.

glēowian, wk.v.II, *jest*; pres.p. nsm. **glēowiende** C101.

glitenian, wk.v.II, *glitter, glisten, shine*; pres. 2s. **glitenest** P41; pres. 3s. **gliteneð** P29, 48.

god/God(d), m., *god, God*; ns. G1396, 1404, 1407, P65, 66, (n18, 19), W22, 27, 29, 84, 86, Y; gs. **GODES** AI 34 etc.; ds. **-e** AI 62, 72, AII 66, C48, P(n19), V49, W2, 63, Y; as. AI 52, W12, 56, 84; npl. **-as** W18, 76; gpl. **-a** W50; dpl. **-um** W31, 82; apl. **-as** W11, 14 [MS **-es**], 47, 51.

gōd, adj., *good*; nsm. G1285; asm. **-ne** AII 71, G1346; nplm. **-e** Wh(n35); gplf. **-ra** C84.

gōd, n., *bounty, good (thing); possession*; gs. **-es** X1034; as. G2016; gpl. **-a** Wh46; dpl. **-um** C65.

godcund, adj., *of the nature of God, divine*; nsf. W87; gsf. **-re** C57; dsf. **-re** C2; dplm. **-um** C4; dplf. **-an** C81.

godcundlīce, adv., *divinely, from heaven*.

gōdness, f., *goodness, worth*; ds. **-e** W23.

gold, n., *gold, as adornment or precious possession*; ns. P41, 46; gs. **-es** G1997; ds. **-e** G2078; as. G2006, 2070.

goldfyll, ?n., *gold-leaf (foil)*; ds. **-felle** P48.

goldsele, m., *gold-hall; wondrous, secure hall*; ds. Y.

gōma, wk.m., *palate*; pl. *jaws*; npl. **-n** Wh62; apl. **-n** Wh76. [Ger. *Gaumen*, Eng. *gum(s)*]

gombe, ?wk.f., *tribute*; as. **gombon** G1978.

gong, m., *coming, course; revolution*; dpl. **-um** X1035. [rel. **gangan**]

gonge, gongeð, gongende, see **gangan**.

grāp, see **grīpan**.

grēne, adj., *green; living*; gsf. **grēnre** G1454; aplm. G1480; aplf. G1474.

grētan, wk.v.I, *greet; address*; inf. Y; pres. 3pl. **grēteð** P45; pret. 3s. **grētte** C28.

grim, adj., *grim, savage*; nsf. V66; asn. G2056; nplm. **-me** Wh62; aplm. wk. **-man** Wh76.

grīpan, st.v.1, *assail, attack, seize*; pret. 3s. **grāp** G1381, 2072; pret. 3pl. **gripon** G2063.

grund, m., *ground, bottom*; *earth, land, country*; as. G1388, 1429, Wh29.

grundfūs, adj., *earth-eager, mortal-bound*; asm. **-ne** V49. [**fūs**, adj., *pressing forward, eager*]

grundlēas, adj., *bottomless, endless*; asm. **-ne** Wh46.

gulpon, see **gylpan**.

guma, wk.m., *man*; ns. V51; npl. **-n** Y; gpl. **gumena** Wh62.

gumdryhten, m., *lord, chief, of men*; ns. Y.

gūð, f., *war, battle, fight*; ns. Y; as. **-e** G2019.

gūðflān, m./f., *war-dart, arrow*; gpl. **-a** G2063.

gūðgemōt, n., *battle-meeting, battle*; apl. G2056.

gūðhere, m., *war band, army*; dpl. **-hergum** G1967.

gūðþracu, f., *war-force*; ds. **-þræce** G1973.

gyd, see **gied(d)**.

gyden, f., *goddess*; ns. W44; npl. **-a** W77.

gylden, adj., *golden*; nsm. **-e** P29.

gylpan, st.v.3, *boast, exult*; pret. 3pl. **gulpon** G2017. [Eng. *yelp*]

gylt, m., *crime*; *sin*; dipl. **-um** Wh74. [Eng. *guilt*]

gystum, see **gæst**.

gȳt/gȳta, adv., *yet. still*; *again*.

H

habban, wk.v.III, *have, possess*; inf. AII 16, 115, G1299, 1360, WL43; pres. 1s. **habbe** AI 66; pres. 2s. **hæfst** AII 88; pres. subj. 2s. **hæbbe** AII 12; pres. 3s. **hafað** R39: 3, 10, 12, 16, 18, 27, V48, X1032, 1035, Wh49, 72, **hæfð** Wh (n35); pres. 3s. neg. **næfð** P63; pres. 3pl. **habbað** AI 50; pres. 3pl. neg. **nabbað** W69; pret. 1s. **hæfde** WL7; pret. 3s. **HÆFDE** AI 1 etc.; pret. 3pl. **hæfdon** C103, 107, G1987, 2052, W51, **hæfdan** W33.

hād, m., *person*; dpl. **-um** W86.

hādian, wk.v.II, *ordain, consecrate*; pret. 3s. **hādode** AII 110.

hæf-, see **habban**.

hǣlan, wk.v.I, *heal, cure*; *assure*; pret. 3pl. **hǣldon** G2035.

hæle, m., *man, warrior*; *hero*; ns. Y; cp. **hæleð**.

hǣlend, m., *the healer, Jesus Christ*; ns. AI 44, AII 90, 92; gs. **-es** AII 110; ds. **-e** AI 9, 68, 76, AII 100, 104, 116.

hæleð, m., *man, warrior*; ns. G2026; npl. G1431, 1985, 1992, 2076, Wh22; gpl. **-a** Wh40; apl. G2061.

hǣl(u), f., *healing, salvation*; gs. **hǣlo** V82; ?gs. **hǣle** AII 40; as. Wh86.

hǣs, f., *(be)hest, command*; ds. **-e** G1370; dpl. **-um** AII 18. [rel. **hātan**]

hǣst, f., *violence, force*; ds. **-e** ?G1396.

hǣste, adv., *violently*; ?G1396.

hǣðen, adj., often absol. as noun, *pagan, heathen*; nplm. **-e** W76; nplm. wk. **-an** W31, 47, 50, 55, 62, 74; nplf. **-e** W77; dplm. **-um** W66; dplf. **-um** W70; aplm. **-e** W11; aplm. wk. **-an** W81.

hǣðengyld, n., *heathen (pagan) worship, idol*; as. W4.

hǣðenscipe/-scype, m., *paganism, heathendom*; ns. W2; ds. W45, 49, 79.

hafað, see **habban**.

hafela, wk.m., *head*; as. **-n** Y.

hagel, m., *hail*; ns. P9.

hāl, adj., *hale, whole; safe*; nsm. P40.

hālettan, wk.v.I, *salute, greet*; pret. 3s. **hālette** C27.

hālig, adj., *holy*; nsm. C42, G1290, 1396, 1404, P67, (n19), X1009, W85; nsm.wk. **hālga** AI 38, 43, 67, G1424, 2039, 2057, **hālge** P65; nsf.wk. **hālge** X1017; gsm. **hālgan** C75; gsn. **hālgan** C67, 75; dsm. **hālgum** G1463; dsm.wk. **hālgan** AI 55, 64, AII 19, G1315, P(n19); disf. **hālgan** G1484; asm.wk. **hālgan** AII 109; asf. **hālgan** AI 34; asn. C57; nplf. **hālge** X1012; gpl. (as noun) **-ra** V73; dplf. **hālgen** P22; dpln. **?hālgum** P(n19) [MS **-gunge**].

hālgung, f., ?as adj., *hallowing*; dpln. **-e** (? for **hālgum**; see **hālig**) P(n19). [cp. **(ge)hālgian**, wk.v.II, *hallow*]

hālwende, adj., *salutary, healing*; apln. C124.

hām, m., *home, house, abode*; ds. R29:4 (? for **hāme**), R29:9 (**tō hām**, ?*at [her] home, from home*); as. (adv.) AII 13, 19, C23, 59.

hāmlēas, adj., *homeless, destitute*; nsf. R39:9.

hand/hond, f., *hand*; ds. **-a** AII 97, C106, G1463, 1473, WL(n7), **-e** AI 19, 50; as. AII 97; dpl. **-um** AI 64, 68, 70, G1991; apl. **-a** C126.

handgewryt, n., *what is written by hand; contract*; as. AI 51, 66, 69.

handplega, wk.m., *hand-combat, fighting*; as. **-n** G2057.

hangian, wk.v.II, *hang, be suspended*; inf. Y; pres. 3s. **hangeð** P6.

hāt, adj., *hot*; nsf. **-e** P(n17); dsf. **-en** P28; superl. **-ost** Y.

hātan, st.v.7 (rd.), *command; name, call*; (passive) *be called*; pres. 1s. **hāte** G1332; pres. 3s. **hāteð** X1024; pres. 3pl. **hātað** W68; pret. 3s. **hēt** AI 38, 60, AII 50, C53, G1356, WL 15, **heht** C51, 66, G1314, 2039, WL 27; passive 3s. **hātte** R39:29, W36, 42, 51, 53, 71; pp. nsm. **hāten** P(n13); nplf. **hātene** G1424.

hātness, f., *hotness, heat*; as. **-e** P(n17).

hē, hēo, hit, pers. pron. 3s., *he, she, it*; nsm. **hē**, nsf. **hēo/hīo**, nsn. **hit**; gsm. **his**, gsf. **hire/hyre**; gsn. **his**; dsm. **him**, dsf. **hire/hyre**, dsn. **him**; asm. **hine**, asf. **hīe/hī/hȳ**, asn. **hit**; npl. (all genders) **hīe, hī/hȳ, hēo, hig**; gpl. (all genders) **heora, hyra**; dpl. (all genders) **him, hēom**; apl. (all genders) **hī/hȳ, hīe**.

hēa, see **hēah**.

hēafod, n., *head*; ns. Y; as. AII 71, C118, Y.

hēafodman, m., *headman, leader*; ns. AII 81.

hēagengel, m., *archangel*; gpl. **-engla** X1018. [**hēag** = **hēah**]

hēah/hēh, adj., *high, tall, lofty*; nsm. P4, 16, 67, (n19); nsf. G1422; gsn. **hēan** G(n1393); dsn. G1489; asf. **hēan** G1401; asn. G1308, 1451; ?nplf. G1439; dplm. **hēagum** W64, apln. **hēa** G1387; comp. nsm. **hērre** P6; superl. asn. **hēgeste** P27; aplf. **hēgesta** P4; see **hēh**, and **hēan**.

hēahflōd, m., *high flood (-waters)*; as. G1442.

hēahfȳr, n., *high, large fire*; as. Wh22.

hēahmōd, adj., *(too) high-minded, proud, vain*; asm. **-ne** V54.

hēahstefn, adj., *high-prowed*; apln. Wh13. [**stefn/stemn**, Eng. *stem*]

hēahsynn, f., *deadly sin*; apl. **-a** P(n19).

healdan, st.v.7, *hold, possess; keep, maintain, preserve*; pres. 3s. **healdeð** V69; pret. subj. 2s. **hēolde** AII 72; pret. 3s. **hēold** AII 22, G1404.

healf, f., *half, side; part*; ds. **-e** P51; as. **-e** Y; apl. **-e** G2055.

hēalic, adj., *high, lofty, very great; especial*; nsf. W44; dsf. **-re** AII 13; dsn. **-on** W81; asm. **-ne** W56; asf. **-e** W74.

hēalīce, adv., *highly, on high, exalted.*

hēan, adj., *low(ly), abject, poor, mean*; nsm. V54; dplm. **-um** Wh43; comp. nsf. **-re** R39:9; see also **hēah**.

hēap, m., *heap*; ns. P57, (n17), Y.

hēapian, wk.v.II, *heap (up), collect*; pres. 3s. **hēapeð** P56.

heard, adj., *hard; severe; fierce; strong, brave*; nsm. G1989, WL43; asm. **-ne** G2057, V60; dpln. **-um** G2035; comp. nsn. **þȳ heardra** G1325.

hearde, adv., *exceedingly, greatly; grievously.*

heardlīce, adv., *severely; boldly; excessively.*

heardsǣlig, adj., *unfortunate, misfortuned*; asm. **-ne** WL19.

hearpe, f., *harp*; ds. **hearpan** C21; as. **hearpan** C22.

heaðoswāt, m., *battle-sweat, blood shed in battle*; gpl. **-a** Y.

hēawan, st.v.7, *strike, kick*; pret. 3s. **hēow** AII 84.

hebban, st.v.6, *raise*; pp. **hæfen** WL(n7). [Eng. *heave*]

hefigian, wk.v.II, *make heavy, afflict*; pp. nsm. **hefgad** C91.

hēgeste, see **hēah**.

hēh, adv., *high*; P16; see **hēah**.

heht, see **hātan**.

helcniht, m., *hellish servant*; dpl. **-um** AI 11.

hell, f., *hell*; gs. **-e** Wh78; ds. **-e** R39:20; as. **-e** Wh45, 68.

hellewīte, n., *hell-torment*; ds. V(n34).

helm, m., *covering, helmet; protector, lord, God*; ns. G1290, Y; dpl. **-um** G1989.

helpan, st.v.3, *help, aid, assist*; pres. 1s. **helpe** AI 14.

hēo, see **hē**.

heofon/heofen, m., *heaven*; ds. **-e** P3, 67, **-en** P7; as. C42, V60; gpl. **-a** G1404, X1038; dpl. **-um** G1387, P(n19), R29:12, R39:20; apl. **-as** AI 70, C77.

heofonbeorht, adj., *heavenly bright*; nsn. X1018.

heofoncyning, m., *King of Heaven*; ds. **-e** G1315.

heofonengel, m., *heavenly angel*; gpl. **-engla** X1009.

heofonlic, adj., *from heaven, heavenly*; nsf. C56; gsn. **-an** C9, **-lecan** C79; dsm. **-an** G(n1374); dsf. **-an** V(n34); disn. **-lecan** C113.

heofonrīce, n., *the Kingdom of Heaven*; gs. **-s** C37, G1363, 1484, 2073.

hēold(e), see **healdan**.

heoloðhelm, m., *cover of invisibility*; dis. **-e** Wh45.

heonan, adv., *from here, hence*.

heononweard, adj., *hence-ward, falling-back*; nsm. G1431.

heora, see **hē**.

heord, f., *herd, flock*; ns. C25.

heorte, f., *heart*; gs. **heortan** X1038, WL43; ds. **heortan** AII 5.

heorðwerod, n., *hearth-troop, band of household retainers; loyal, endeared followers*; ns. G2076; as. G2039.

hēow, see **hēawan**; see also **hīw**.

hēr, adv., *here; in this place, at this time*.

here, m., *army, host*; ds. **herge** G2007; npl. **hergas** G2073. [Ger. *Heer*]

herefēða, wk.m., *war-infantry*; npl. **-n** X1012.

herehūð, f., *battle-prey, booty*; as. **-e** Wh61.

hereness/-niss, f., *praise*; ds. **-e** C34, 126. [cp. **heri(ge)an**]

heresīð, m., *battle-journey*; ds. **-e** R29: 4; as. V60.

heretoga, wk.m., *leader of a (war) band, chief*; ns. AII 70.

herewīc, n., *battle-camp*; dpl. **-um** G2051.

herewulf, m., *war-wolf, vicious warrior*; gpl. **-a** G2015.

hergian, wk.v.II, *harry; ravage, plunder*; pret. 3s. **hergode** G1380.

heri(ge)an, wk.v.II, *praise, glorify*; inf. C37, P(n19); pres. 3pl. **herigeð** P38, **-iað** P(n13, 19).

hērre, see **hēah**.

hēt, see **hātan**.

hēte (= **hǣtu**), f., *heat*; ns. P20.

hetol, adj., *full of hate, hostile; evil*; nsm. W40; nsm.wk. **hetula** W70; dsm.wk. **hetolan** AI 36.

hetolīce, adv., *fiercely, violently*.

hettend, m., *enemy*; npl. G2011.

hī, see **hē**.

hider, adv., *hither*.

hīe, see **hē**.

hig, see **hē**.

hiht/hyht, m., *hope, joy*; as. AII 88, V73.

hihtlic, adj., *joyous*; nsn. G2076.

hild, f., *war, battle*; ds. **-e** G2061, Y.

hildebil, n., *battle sword*; ns. Y.

hildedēor, adj., *brave in battle*; nsm. Y.

hildeswēg, m., *battle-clamor, sound of battle*; ns. G1991.

hildewulf, m., *battle-wolf, hostile warrior*; npl. **-as** G2051.

hilt, n., *sword-hilt*; as. Y.

him, see **hē**.

hindan, adv.: **on hindan**, *behind*.

hine, see **hē**.

hinderhōc, m., *hinder-hook, a hook from behind: cunning trick, sneaky malice*; gpl. **-a** V34.

hinsīð, m., *journey hence, departure, death*; ds. **-e** Wh68.

hīo, see **hē**.

hire/hyre, see **hē**.

his, see **hē**.

hit, neut. pronoun; see **hē**.

hīw/hēow, n., *hue, appearance, form*; ns. P47, Wh8; gs. **hīwes** AII 7.

hīwan, wk.m. pl., *(members of a) family or household*; dat. **hīwum** G1345; acc. G1489.

hlæst, n., *burden, load, freight*; ds. **-e** G1422. [rel. **hladan**, st.v.6, *lade, load*]

hlāford, m., *lord and master; lord and husband*; ns. P25, WL6, 15.

hlemman, wk.v.I, *snap (up)*; pres. 3pl. **hlemmeð** Wh61.

hleoðo, see **hlið**.

hlēoðor, m./n., *speech; prophecy*; dis. **hlēoðre** G1290.

hlēowstōl, m., *place of protection, native dwelling*; ds. **-e** G2011. [**hlēo(w)**, mn., *covering, shelter*; **stōl**, m., *seat*; Eng. *stool*]

hlīfigean, wk.v.II, *tower (up)*; inf. G1321.

hlihhan, st.v.6, *laugh, exult*; pres.p. nplm. **hlihhende** G2066.

hlinduru, f., *grated door* or *gate*; apl. Wh78. [rel. **hlinian**, wk.v.I, *lean*]

hlið, n., *slope, hill*; npl. **hlioðo** G1439, **hleoðo** 1459.

hlūd, adj., *loud, sonorous*; nsm. G1991; nplm. **-e** G1982.

hlūde, adv., *aloud, loudly*.

hlūtre, adv., *clearly, brightly*.

hlūttor, adj., *clear, pure*; disn. **hlūttre** C121.

hlyn, m., *sound, noise, clamor*; ns. G2061.

hof, n., *enclosure, dwelling*; *the ark*; ns. G1393; ds. **-e** G1489; as. G1345, 1380. [Ger. *Hof*]

hogian, wk.v.II, *think*; *be anxious*; imper. 2s. **hoga** AI 43.

hōh, m., *heel*; as. **on hōh**, *behind* G1363. [Eng. *hough*]

hold, adj., *devoted*; gplm. **-ra** WL17.

holm, m., *wave, (high) sea*; ns. G1431; gs. **-es** G1393; ds. **-e** Wh51.

holmærn, n., *sea-dwelling, ship*; *the ark*; gpl. **-a** G1422.

holmclif, n., *sea-cliff*; ds. **-e** Y.

hord, n., *(treasure-)hoard*; ds. **-e** G1439.

hordburh, f., *treasure-hoard city*; *prosperous, secure dwelling*; apl. G2007.

horn, m., *horn*; dpl. **-um** R29:2 [MS **-a**].

hors, n., *horse*; ns. AII 37, 73; as. AII 84.

hræfnas, see **hrefn**.

hrǣw, n., *corpse*; gs. **hrǣs** G1985; as. **hrēaw** G1447.

hrān, see **hrīnan**.

hraðe, adv., *hastily, quickly*. [comp. **hraðor**, Eng. *rather*]

hrēam, m., *outcry, clamor*; ns. G(n1983). [rel. **hrȳman**]

hrēaw, see **hrǣw**.

hrefn, m., *raven*; ds. **-e** G1449; as. G1442; npl. **hremmas** G(n1983).

hrēof, adj., *rough*; dsm. **-um** Wh8.

hrēoh, adj., *rough, tempestuous*; nsm. G1387; npln. G1325.

hrēownyss, f., *fierceness, savagery*; ds. **-e** AII 47 (? for **hrēoh-**).

hricg/hrycg, m., *back, ridge*; as. G1393 [MS **hrincg**]; ds. **-e** P47 [MSS **hrynge, ricge**]

hrīnan, st.v.1, w. dat., *lay hold of, reach (at, toward), touch*; inf. ?**hrīnon** G1396; pret. 3s. **hrān** R39:10, 20.

hring, m., *ring-fetter, bond of constraint*; ds. **-e** Wh40.

hringmǣled, adj., *ornamented with linked (or inlaid) rings*; apln. G1992. [lit., *ring-marked*]

hrōf, m., *roof*; *sky*; ds. **-e** C42; as. R29:7, ?as. **under hrōf** (*into the ark*) G1360.

hrōr, adj., *agile, vigorous*; dsm.wk. **-an** Y.

hrycg, see **hricg**.

hrȳman, wk.v.I, *cry out, exclaim*; *lament*; pres.p. nsf. **hrȳmende** AI 23. [rel. **hrēam**, m.]

hū, adv., *how; what.*

hungor/hunger, m., *hunger;* ns. P20, Wh51.

hungri, adj., *hungry;* nsm. G1463.

hūru, adv., *at least, indeed, certainly.*

hūs, n., *house, dwelling; the ark;* ns. C93; gs. **-es** G(n2008), Y; ds. **-e** AI 60, C23, 59, 96, G1442; as. C24.

hūs(e)l, n., *housel, consecrated bread and wine;* gs. **hūsles** C104; as. C102, 105.

hūð(e), f., *booty, plunder;* as. G2066, R29:2, 4, 9.

hwā, hwæt, pron., *who, what; which;* nsn. C54, R39:29; dsn. **hwām** AII 111, dism. **for hwon**, *why* C97; asn. **hwæt** C4, 33, G1291, WL3.

hwæl, m., *whale;* ns. Wh47; gs. **-es** Wh81; ds. **hwale** Wh3.

hwǣr, conj., *where.*

hwæt, n., pron., *what, which;* see **hwā.**

hwæt/hwat, interj., *lo!*

hwæthwugu, pron., *something, somewhat, a little;* asn. C29.

hwæðer/hweðer, conj., *whether, if.*

hwæð(e)re, adv., conj., *yet, however, nevertheless.*

hwām, see **hwā.**

hwanan/hwonan, adv., *whence.*

hweorfan, st.v.3, *turn, move about, go;* inf. R39:9, Wh81; pret. 3pl. **hwurfon** G2086.

hwettan, wk.v.I, *whet, incite;* pres. 3s. **hweteð** V18.

hwī, adv., *why, wherefore.*

hwīl/hwȳl, f., *while, time, period of time;* as. **-e** W34, 83.

hwilc/hwylc/hwelc, adj., pron., *which, what;* nsm. G2014; nsf. C102, V17; gsn. **-es** P17; dsm. **-um** AII 65; asf. C50.

hwīlen, adj., *for a while only, transitory;* asf.wk. **hwīlnan** Wh86.

hwīt, adj., *white; bright, radiant;* nsm. P33; nsn. X1018.

hwon, see **hwā.**

hwonan, see **hwanan.**

hwonne, adv., conj., *when, until.*

hwurfon, see **hweorfan.**

hwyrft, m., *course, return;* as. Wh78.

hȳ, see **hē.**

hycgan, wk.v.III, *think, consider*; inf. WL11; pres. p. npl. **hycgende** V82.

hyge, m., *mind, thought*; ns. WL17.

hygegār, m., *heart/mind-spear*; *weapon of deceit*; as. V34.

hygegēomor, adj., *sad at heart*; asm. **-ne** WL19.

hygesorg, f., *heart/mind-care, anxiety*; as. **-e** G2035.

hygetēona, wk.m., *injury in (to the) mind, insult, offense*; as. **-n** G1380.

hyht, see **hiht**.

hyldemǣg, m., *dear, close companion, kin*; ns. G2032.

hyra, see **hē**.

hȳran, wk.v.I, *hear*; *hearken to, obey* (w. dat.); pret. 3s. **hȳrde** G1315, 1493; pret. 3pl. **hȳrdon** C128, Wh75.

hyrde, m., *guardian, keeper*; as. AII 71; apl. **hyrdas** G(n2008), Y.

hyre, see **hē**; and next word.

hȳre, adj., *gentle*, (absol.) *good one*; nsf. G1468.

I

ic, pers. pron. 1s., *I*; ns. **ic**, gs. **mīn**, ds. **mē**, as. **mē, mec**; see **wē**, and the pers. pron. **mīn**.

īdel, adj., *idle, empty*; *vain*; gsn. **īdles** C15; dplm. **-um** AII 30.

ides, f., *woman*; ns. G1970; ds. **-e** Y; npl. **-a** G2086.

īgland/īglond, n., *island*; ns. P(n1); ds. **-e** W36, 41. [cp. **ēalond** and **ēglond**]

ilca/ylca, pron. adj., *same*; nsn. **ylce** AI 71; dsn.wk. **-n** W41; asf. **-n** AI 56; asn. **ilce** C48.

in, prep. w. dat., *in*; w. acc., *into, to*; see also **in(n)**.

inbryrdniss, f., *in-breathing, inspiration*; ds. **-e** C6.

inca, wk.m., *cause of complaint, ill-will*; ds. **-n** C107; as. **-n** C108.

incundness, f., *inwardness*; ds. **-e** W29 [MS **incunnesse**].

incūðlīce, adv., *grievously, sorely*.

ingeþonc, m., *inmost thought*; dpl. **-um** X1013.

ingong, m., *entrance, entry*; ds. **-e** C74; as. C113.

in(n), adv., *in, within, into*.

innan, adv., *within, inside*.

inne, adv., *inside, within*.

innoð, m., *inwards (of the body)*; ds. **-e** Wh55.

intinga, wk.m., *cause, occasion*; ns. C20.

into, prep. w. dat., *into*.

inwitflān, m., *malice-arrow, spiteful barb*; as. V37.

inwitspell, n., *tale of evil, unfortunate news*; as. G2024.

iogoþe, see **geoguð**.

irnan, st.v.3, *run*; pret. 3s. **arn** AI 36.

is, see **bēon**.

iū, adv. *formerly, once*.

iung, adj. (= **geong**), *young*; gsm. **-an** AII 61; asm. **-an** AII 9, 12, 18, 21.

iunglic, adj., *youthful*; gsf. **-re** AII 6.

K

Kalendas Januarii, Lat., *the month of January, the first of January*; nom. P10.

karlfugel, m., *male bird, cock*; ns. P64. [**carl**, m., *man*; O.Ic. **karl**]

king, m. (= **cyning**), *king*; ns. P41, 68; ds. **-e** P36; gpl. **-e** P67.

Kyrrieleyson, Gk. (*Kyrie eleison*), *Lord have mercy*.

L

lā, interj., *lo, ah*.

lāc, n., *gift, offering*; *booty*; as. W16, 57, 63; dpl. **-um** G1472. [as in Eng. *wedlock*]

lād, f., *way, journey*; ds. **-e** G1444. [rel. **lǣdan**]

lǣdan, wk.v.I, *lead, conduct, take*; *bring forth*; *carry*; inf. C94, G1357, 1435, R29:2; pres. 3pl. **lǣdað** G1298; pret. 3pl. **lǣddon** G2011, 2016; imper. s. **lǣd** G1332, 1489.

lǣfan, wk.v.I, *leave*; pret. 3s. **lǣfde** W39.

lǣnan, wk.v.I, *lend, grant*; inf. G2059.

lǣne, adj., *transitory*; asf. **lǣnan** V10; asn. **lǣnan** Wh64. [lit., *on loan*; rel. **lǣn**, f., *loan, gift*, **lǣnan**, wk.v.I]

lǣran, wk.v.I, *teach, advise*; *exhort*; inf. C66 (passive, *be taught*); pret. 3s. **lǣrde** AI 76, AII 4, C63.

lǣssa, comp. adj. (of **lȳtel**), *smaller*; aplm.wk. **lǣssan** AII 42 [MS **leasan**].

lǣtan, st.v.7, *let, allow, cause to (be, do)*; pres. 1s. **lǣte** G1349; pres. 3s. **lǣteð** V10, 37, 40, Wh65, **lēteð** V34; pret. 1s. **lēt** AII 71; pret. 3s. **lēt** AII 25, 44, G1372, 1438.

lāf, f., *(what is)left, remnant*; ns. G2005, 2019; ds. **-e** G1343; as. **-e** G1496. [rel. **lǣfan**, wk.v.I, *leave, bequeath*]

lago/lagu, m., *sea, water*; ns. G1413, 1491, Y; see also **lagu**, f.

lāgon, see **licgan**.

lagosīð, m., *sea-journey*; gpl. **-a** G1343, 1486.

lagostrēam, m., *water-stream, river*; ds. **-e** Wh(n30).

lagu, f., *law, rule*; ds. **lage** W82; see also **lago**, m.

land/lond, n., *land, country*; ns. P1; gs. **-es** G(n1393), W9 (**wīde landes**, *far and wide over the land*), (adv.) WL8; ds. **-e** C74, G1486; as. G1444, 1458, 1479, P14.

lang/long, adj., *long*; nsn. R39: 22 (*too long a time, too difficult*); asf. **-e** G1426; asn. G1308.

lange, adv., *long, a long time*.

langian/longian, wk.v.II, impers. w. acc. of person, *long, long (for)*; pret. 3s. **longade** WL14; pret. 3pl. **langode** G1431.

langoþ/longaþ, m., *longing*; gs. **-es** WL41; ds. **-e** WL53.

lār, f., *lore, learning*; *precept*; gs. **-e** C57; ds. **-e** AII 12, 106, C78; as. **-e** AII 22, 36, W14, 16, 48, 64, 74; dpl. **-um** Wh75; dipl. **-um** R39:22, V3. [rel. **lǣran**]

lārēow, m., *teacher, master*; npl. **-as** C71.

lāst, m., *step, footstep, track*; ds. **on lāste**, *behind, after* G2075; dis. **-e** R39:8; as. G(n2075).

lāttēow, m., *guide*; ns. AII 73.

lāð, n., *harm*; ds. **-e** AII 80 [MS **late**].

lāð, adj., *hateful, hated, loathed*; gplm. **-ra** G2085; dplf. **-um** G(n2075). [Eng. *loath*]

lāðlicost, superl. adv., *most hatefully, wretchedly*.

lāðscipe, m., *painful condition, calamity*; ds. G2048.

lēaf, n. or f., *leaf, shoot*; pl. *foliage*; ns. P18; apl. G1458.

lēag, see **lēogan**.

leahtor, m., *crime, sin*; dipl. **leahtrum** V76, Wh66; apl. **leahtras** AII 28, 42.

leahterfull, adj., *full of vice, vicious*; nsm. AII 66.

lēan, n., *recompense, reward*; npl. V76.

lēas, adj., *devoid of; false, deceptive*; nsm. WL32; dsm. **-um** Y; asm. **-ne** Wh66.

lēasbregd, m., *deceit, deceptive trick*; dpl. **-um** W61. [**-bregd**, rel. **bregdan**]

lēaslīce, adv., *falsely, deceptively.*

lēasung, f., *lying, vain speech, hypocrisy, false witness*; gs. **-e** C15; as. **-a** P(n19).

lecgan, wk.v.I, *lay, place, put (before)*; pret. 3s. **lēde** AI 53; pret. 3pl. **legdun** G(n2075).

leger, n., *bed*; apl. WL34. [rel. **licgan**, st.v.5]

leng, comp. adv. (of **lange**), *longer.*

lēod, f./**lēode**, f. pl., *people, nation*; ns.voc. Y; gs. **-e** G2075; npl. G1979, **lēoda** W52; gpl. **lēoda** G2016, 2023, Y; dpl. **lēodum** G(n2075), WL6.

lēodfruma, wk.m., *people-ruler, lord*; ns. WL8.

lēof, adj., often w. dat. of person, *dear, beloved*; (absol.) *dear one*; nsm. AI 41, AII 64, gsm. **-es** WL53; dsm. G1285, wk. **-an** AII 116; asm. **-ne** Wh87; asn. P(n19); nplm. **-e** WL34, wk. **-an** C111; gplm. **-ra** WL16; superl. nsm. voc. **-ost** G1328.

leofaþ, **leofeð**, **leofodon**, see **libban**.

lēogan, st.v.2, *lie, tell a lie*; inf. AII 58; pret. 3s. **lēag** V81.

lēoht, n., *light, brightness*; as. X1036.

lēohtfruma, wk.m., *source (creator) of light, God*; ns. G1410.

lēohtlic, adj., *light-like, with the appearance of light; bright*; asn. R29:3.

leomu, see **lim**.

leornere, m., *learner, scholar*; apl. **leorneras** C52.

leornian, wk.v.II, *learn, study*; pret. 3s. **leornade** C13, **leornode** AII 43; pret. 3pl. **leornodon** C71.

lēoð, n., *song, poem*; gs. **-es** C15; dis. **-e** C60; as. C19, 53, 69; npl. C70; apl. C3, 10, 80.

lēoðcræft, m., *song-craft, art of poetry*; as. C13.

lēoðsong, m., *poetic song, poem-song*; gs. **-es** C58; dpl. **-um** C7.

leoðum, see **lið**.

lēt, lēteð, see **lǣtan.**

libban/lifgan/lifian, wk.v.III, *live*; inf. **lifgan** R39:22, **lybban** AI 76; pres. 3s. **leofaþ** P(n19), R39: 27, V68, 76, **leofeð** P69; pres. subj. 3s. **lifige** G1337; pret. 1pl. **lifdon** WL14; pret. 3pl. **leofedon** W34, **leofodon** W79, **lyfedan** W83; pres.p. nplm. **lifgende** WL34; pres. p. gplm. **lifigendra** G2093.

līc, n., *body*; gs. **-es** Wh69; as. X1036.

licgan, st.v.5, *lie, lie dead*; pret. 3pl. **lāgon** G2076.

līchama, wk.m., *body*; ds. **-n** AII 93 [MS **-hama**], **-homan** X1031.

līchomlic, adj., *bodily*; dsf. **-re** C90.

līcian, wk.v.II, impers. w. dat., *please*; pres. 3s. **līcað** Wh(n35).

lid, n., *ship, vessel*; gs. **-es** G1332, 1410; ds. **-e** G1479. [rel. **līðan,** st.v.1, *go, sail*]

lidmann, m., *seafarer*; gpl. **-a** Y.

līf, n., *life*; gs. **-es** AI 77, AII 88, C9, 113, G1410, 1426, P10, 27, 60, Wh(n30); ds. **-e** W39, 60, 60, WL41; as. AII 89, 115, C87, 120, V48, W83, Wh64; apl. W38.

lifd, see **libban.**

līfdæg, m., *day of life, time of living*; dpl. **-dagum** Wh75.

lifg-, see **libban.**

līm, m., *lime, mortar*; ds. **-e** G1322.

lim, n., *limb*; as. R39:27; apl. **leomu** C26.

lind, f., *linden-wood* (*shield*); as. **-e** G2044.

lindcroda, wk.m., *press of* (*linden-wood*) *shields, battle*; ds. **-n** G1998.

līoma, wk.m., *ray* (*of sun*); apl. **-n** P(n17).

liss, f., *joy, delight*; npl. **-e** G1486. [rel. **līðe,** adj.]

list, f., *art, skill*; dipl. **-um** (adv., *artfully*) R29:3. [Ger. *List*; rel. **lǣran**]

lið, n., *limb, member*; dpl. **leoðum** X1031.

līðan, st.v.1, *go*; *fly*; pres. 3s. **līð** AII 73; pres.p. nsf. (absol.) **līðend** G1472.

līðe, adj., *gentle, gracious*; dpl. **līðum** AII 9. [Eng. *lithe*]

līðe, adv., *gently, well*; G1491 [MS **hlīðe**].

lōcian, wk.v.II, *look*; pres. 2s. **lōcast** Y.

lof, m. and n., *praise*; ns. W88; ds. **-e** Wh87; as. C115, 125. [Ger. *Lob*]

loflāc, n., *offering as praise*; apl. W65.

lond, see **land**.

londstede, m., *country, place*; ds. WL16.

long, see **lang**.

longade, see **langian**.

longaþ, see **langoþ**.

lufi(ge)an, wk.v.II, *love*; inf. C62, with **witon** understood P(n19); pres. 3s. **lufað** V70, W85; pres. 1pl. **lufiað** W28; pres. 3pl. **lufiað** W52; pret. 3s. **lufode** AI 4, **lufude** W59; ger. **tō lufienne** AII 8, 28, 31.

lufu, f., *love*; ds. **lufe** AII 103, wk. **lufan** C83; as. **lufe** AI 5.

lungre, adv., *quickly, forthwith*.

lust, m., *desire, pleasure*; ds. **-e** Wh26; as. AI 13, 17, W82; dipl. **-um** AI 21, AII 30, G1495, W35, Y.

lustlīce, adv., *happily, willingly*.

lybban, **lyfedan**, see **libban**.

lyft, m. and f., *air, sky; cloud(s)*; ns. G1298; ds. **-e** AI 71; as. G1401. [Ger. *Luft*]

lyftfæt, n., *air-vessel* (*container*), *sky-vat*; as. R29:3. [**-fæt**, Eng. *vat*]

lyre, m., *destruction, loss*; ds. W38. [rel. **lēosan**, st.v.2, *lose*]

lystan, wk.v.I, *cause desire*; pres. 3s. **lysteþ** Wh52.

lȳt, adj., and as neuter substantive, indecl. w. gen. pl., *few*; acc. WL 16.

lȳtel, adj., *little*; disn. **lȳtle** G2093.

lytelīce, adv., *deceitfully*.

lȳtligan, wk.v.II, *lessen, diminish*; inf. G1413.

M

mā, n., as adv., *more*; conj., **þon mā**, *any (the) more (than)*.

macian, wk.v.II, *make, form, arrange; cause*; pret. 3s. **macode** W(n15), 38, 54; pret. 3pl. **macedon** W62.

mādum (= **māðum**), m., *treasure, ornament*; *?monument*; ns. **mādme** P43.

mæg, m., *kinsman*; as. G2012, 2047; npl. **māgas** WL11; dpl. **māgum** G1317, 2092.

mæg(e), see **magan**.

mæ(g)den, n., *maiden, girl, virgin*; ds. **-e** AI 3, 20; as. AI 7, 21.

mægen, n., *might, force*; *host, troop*; ds. **mægne** G2095, **mægene** P(n19); npl. X1018.

mægenbyrþenn, f., *mighty burden*; ds. **-e** Y.

mægencorðor, n., *powerful band*; dpl. **-corðrum** G1986.

mægenðrymm, m., *power, majesty*; *angelic host*; dis. **-e** X1008.

mǣgð, f., *maiden, woman*; npl. G2009; apl. **mǣgeð** G2092.

mæig, see **magan**.

mǣl, n., *time, occasion*; gpl. **-a** V83. [Ger. *Mal*]

mǣre, adj., *glorious, splendid, excellent*; nsm. P25; nsf. **mǣro** G1399; gsn. **-s** P47; dsm.wk. **mǣran** W63; asm.wk. **mǣran** X1007; aplf. G2009; superl. aplm.wk. **mǣrostan** W47.

mǣrlīce, adv., *gloriously*.

mǣrðu, f., *honor, glory*; ds. **mǣrþe** AII 4. [rel. **mǣre**, adj.]

mǣst, superl. adj. (of **micel**), *most, greatest*; nsn. G1422, Wh10; dsf. **mǣstan** C6; dism.wk. **-an** X1008; asn. G1321.

mǣton, see **metan**.

mǣðelhergend, m., *speech-praiser*; *boast-lover*; gpl. **-ra** V13.

magan, pret.-pres.v., *be able, can, may*; pres. 1s. **mæg** AI 41, WL2, 38, 39, (n37); pres. 2s. **meaht** V44; pres. subj. 2s. **mæge** R39:28; pres. 3s. **mæg** V9, **mæig** P12; pres. 1pl. **magon** G2013; pres. 3pl. **magon** AII 113, W25; pret. 1s. **meahte** V5, Y; pret. 2s. **meaht** C32; pret. 3s. **meahte** C11, 15, 58, 68, 92, 97, G1457, 2043, R29:6, **mihte** AI 48, 58, AII 96, W42, 58; pret. subj. 3s. **mihte** AI 7, G2058; pret. 3pl. **mihton** W21.

māgas, **māgum**, see **mǣg**.

man/mann, m., indef. pron., nom.s. *one*; AII 74, P12, W4, WL27; see **man(n)/mon(n)**.

mān, n., *crime, guilt, sin*; as. AI 33.

mān, adj., *false*; aplm. **-e** P(n19).

māndǣd, f., *evil deed, crime*; gpl. **-a** C83.

mānfǣhðu, f., *evil strife, wickedness*; gs. G1378.

mānfull, adj., *evil, wicked*; nsn. wk. **-an** AI 35; dsm. **-um** AII 35; nplm. wk. **-an** W46.

mānfulnyss, f., *wickedness*; ds. **-e** AII 43.

manig/monig, adj., *many*; nsf. G1969; asn. C80; nplm. **-e** C10, P51,

V13, 25, **manege** W75, gplm. **-ra** C8; dplm. **managum** AII 69,
monegum, C75, G1303; **mongum** R39:19; apln. C47, 80, 124.

man(n)/mon(n), m., *man*; ns. C18, 27, 84, G2092, P16, 64, V9, 29,
W35, 60, 73, WL42, Y; gs. **-es** AI 21, 54, G1399, Wh(n35), WL11;
ds. **men** AI 24, 61, C63; as. AII 12, C12; npl. **men** R39:4, W17,
46, 67, Y; gpl. **-a** C8, 93, G1328, 2085, P(n18); dpl. **-um** C12, 112,
G1337, 1381, R39:12, W13, 23; apl. **men** C52, 82, W81, **menn**
Wh(n59); see **monna**.

man(n)cyn(n)/moncynn, n., *mankind, men, the human race*; ns. W1, 9;
gs. **-es** C43, 72, X1026; ds. **-e** R39:2, W24, 78, **mancenne** P(n19);
as. W80.

mansliht, m., *manslaughter, homicide*; ds. **-e** AII 98. [**sliht**, *slaughter*,
rel. **slēan**, st.v.6]

māra, comp. adj. (of **micel**), *more, greater*; nsf. þӯ **māre** G1313; asm.
māran [MS **-m**] **micle**, ?*much greater*, R39:4; asm. **māran** AII
43; dplf. **mārum** AII 34.

marm(el)stān, m., (*piece of*) *marble*; ns. P46; ds. **-e** P(n13). [Lat.
marmor]

maþelian, wk.v.II, *speak, make a speech*; pret. 3s. **maþelode** Y.

mē, see **ic**.

meaht, f., *might, power*; as. Wh33, **-e** C38.

meaht(e), see **magan**.

mearcian, wk.v.II, *mark, inscribe*; pres. 3pl. **mearciað** P(n13).

mec, see **ic**.

medmicel, adj., *not great, moderate, small*; dsn. **-miclum** C5; asn.
C118. [**med-** (also **met-**), prefix]

menn, see **mann**.

mennisc, n., *men, people*; as. AII 4.

menniscness, f., *human nature; incarnation*; ds. **-e** C76.

meodowong, m., *mead-field, field of nectar-giving flowers*; apl. **-as** Y.

me(o)tod/meotud, m., *the measurer, God*; ns. G1320, 1381, 1414,
P(n18), V38; gs. **-es** C38. [rel. **metan**]

mere, m., *sea, ocean*; ns. G1381. [Ger. *Meer*]

mereciest, f., *sea-chest, the ark*; as. **-e** G1317.

mereflōd, m., *sea-flood, deluge*; as. G1341.

merehūs, n., *sea(-going) house, the ark*; gs. **-es** G1364; as. G1303.

mereliðende, m., *seafaring (man)*, *sailor*; apl. G1407. [cp. **liðan**]

mereweard, m., *sea-warder*; *the whale*; ns. Wh53.

mergen/morgen, m., *morning*; ds. **-ne** C49, 60; as. AI 59.

messe, f., *mass, church service*; as. **messan** AI 35.

mētan, wk.v.I, *design, paint*; pres. 3pl. **mēteð** P42, **mētað** P(n13); see next word.

metan, st.v.5, *measure* (as to go by measured step), *traverse*; pret. 3pl. **mǣton** Y.

mete, m., *meat, food*; ds. G1337, W(n15); as. AI 53.

metod, see **meotod**.

micel/mycel, adj., *great*; *much, many*; nsm. G1990, P24; nsn.wk. **micla** Wh47; nsf. G2054; gsf. **-re** C86; dsm. **mycclum** AI 67; dsm.wk. **miclan** Wh3; dism. **micle** G1965; dsf. **-re** AI 26, 36, AII 4; dsf.wk. **miclan** W23; dsn. **miclum** G2095; asf. **micle** G1317, WL51; asf.wk. **micclan** AII 31; asn. G1303, **-e** P58; dplm. **miclum** G1495, W58 (adv., *much*); dplf. **micclum/ mycclum** AI 33, AII 39, **miclum** G2034; diplf. **miclum tidum**, *?for much time, ?at many times*, R39:2; see **mǣst** and **māra**.

micle, is. of **micel**, adv. in comp., *much*; **swiðor micle**, *much the more, far greater*; V29.

mid, prep. w. dat., *with, by*; *amid, among*; **mid þām**, conj. *when*; **mid þȳ**, conj. *when*.

mid, adv., *with, at the same time*; *likewise*.

middan(g)eard, m., *the (mortal) world, the earth*; gs. **-es** C72, G1378; ds. **middenearde** P5; as. C43, 123, R39:19, W78.

midde, wk.f., ds. **on middan**, *in the middle* P58.

middeneaht, f., *midnight*; as. C102.

miht, f., *might, power*; ns. W87; as. **-e** P56, (n17).

mihte, see **magan**.

mihtig, adj., *mighty, powerful*; nsm. (absol. = God) **-e** P25; nsm. X1007; nplm. **-e** W33.

mihton, see **magan**.

mildheort/myld-, adj., *mild-hearted, merciful*; nsm. AI 15; dsm.wk. **-an** AII 100, 105. [rel. Lat. *misericors*]

mildheortnyss, f., *mild-heartedness, mercy, compassion*; ds. **-e** AII 40. [rel. Lat. *misericordia*]

miltsung/mild-, f., *mercy, compassion*; gs. **-e** AII 96; as. **-e** AII 99, 105, 109.

mīn, poss. pron., *my*; nsm. AI 23, AII 86, WL6, 8, 15, 17, 47, 50; nsn. AI 24; gsm. **-es** AII 54, WL26; ?gsm./asm. AI 14; gsf. **-re** AI 28, WL2, 40; dsf. **-re** WL10; asf. **-e** AII 90, G1328, WL(n7); asn. AI 50, AII 89; nplm. **-e** C111; gplm. **-ra** WL5; aplm. **-e** WL38; see **ic**.

misdǣd, f., *misdeed, transgression*; gpl. **-a** AII 109.

misfaran, st.v.6, *go astray, err*; pret. 3s. **-fōr** W1.

mishȳran, wk.v.I, *disobey, pay no attention to* (w. dat.); pret. 3s. **-hȳrde** W2.

missenlīce, adv., *diversely, variously*.

mistglōm, ?m., *misty gloom, phantasmal darkness*; ds. **-e** Wh47.

mistlic, adj., *diverse, various*; aplm. **-e** W32; apln. **-e** W65.

mistlīce, adv., *diversely, variously*.

mōd, n., *mind, heart*; *will*; ns. AI 24, V25, WL(n7); gs. **-es** V11, W29; dis. **-e** AII 8, C100, 121, G2028, P(n19), V83; as. AII 106, C107; npl. C8; dpl. **-um** G1986. [Ger. *Mut*, Eng. *mood*]

mōdcearu, f., *grief of heart*; gs. **-ceare** WL40; as. **-ceare** WL51.

mōdgemynd, n., *mind*; *intelligence*; as. Wh3.

mōdgeþanc, m., *mind, purpose of mind, counsel*; as. C39.

mōdig, adj., *high-spirited, proud*; *courageous*; nsm. Y; nsn. AII 37.

mōdmiþend, adj., *mind-locked, ?secretive, thought-concealing*; asm. **-ne** WL20. [**mīðan**, st.v.1, *conceal*]

mōdsefa, wk.m., *mind, soul*; npl. **-n** V21.

mōna, wk.m., *moon*; as. **-n** W15.

mōn(a)ð, m., *month*; ns. P14; ds. **-e** P13.

monegum, mongum, monig, see **manig**.

monian, wk.v.II, *admonish, exhort*; pret. 3s. **monade** C63.

monna, wk.m., *man*; as. **-n** WL18; see **mann/monn**.

mōnð, see **mōnað**.

morgenceald, adj., *morning-cold*; WL(n7).

morgensēoc, adj., *morning-troubled, anxious*; nsn. WL (n7).

morðdǣd, f., *deadly sin, evil deed*; ds. **-e** AII 97; dpl. **-um** AII 35, 39, 102.

morðor, m., *murder, a deadly sin*; as. P(n19).

morþorhycgend, adj., *?murderous-minded*; *?greatly distressed* (because of harm done to one); asm. **-ne** WL20 [MS **-hycgende**].

mōtan, pret.-pres.v., *may, must*; pres. 1s. **mōt** AI 25, WL37; pres. 2s. **mōst** Y; pres. 3s. **mōt** R39:20, V72; pres. 1pl. **mōtan/mōton** P(n19), Wh85, 87; pres. 3pl. **mōtan** Wh81; pres. subj. 1pl. **mōte** P68; pret. 3s. **mōste** G1470; pret. 3pl. **mōston** G1394, Y; pret. subj. 3pl. **mōsten** G1434.

moððe, f., *moth* (a vellum-eating worm); ns. R47:1.

mund, f., *hand*; dpl. **-um** G1364, P(n13), WL(n7). [rel. Lat *manus*]

munuchād, m., *monastic state, monkhood*; as. C64. [Lat. *monachus*]

mūð, m., *mouth*; *door, gate*; ds. **-e** C71, W29; as. G1364, R39:12, Wh53.

mūða, wk.m., *mouth*; *opening, door*; as. **-n** G(n1364).

myc-, see **micel**.

myldelīce, adv., *graciously, mercifully*.

myldheort, see **mild-**.

mynster, n., *religious house, monastery*; ds. **mynstre** AI 2, C 1; as. C65. [Lat. *monastērium*]

N

nā/nō, adv., *never, not* (*at all*).

nabbað, see **habban**.

nǣfre/nēfre (ne ǣfre), adv., *never*.

nǣfð, see **habban**.

nægledbord, adj., *having nailed sides*; as a noun, *ship*; asn. G1418, 1433.

nǣnig (ne ǣnig), adj., *not any, none*; pron., *no one*; nsm. C11, R29:13; asm. **-ne** C108; asn. C19.

nāgon, see **āgan**.

nāht, see **nōht**.

nalæs/nal(l)es/nealles (ne ealles), adv., *not, not at all*.

nama/noma, wk.m., *name*; ns. V(n34), Wh6; ds. **-n** C28; dis. **-n** W51, 66; apl. **-n** W87.

namian, wk.v.II, *name*; *give a name to*; pres. 3pl. **namiað** W69.

nāmon, see **niman**.

nān/nǣn (ne ān), adj. pron., *none, no one, nothing, not any*; nsm.

P16, 64, W25; nsn. G1400; gsm. **-es** AII 78; asm. **-ne** AII 44; asf. **nǣnne** P63, asn. W25.

nāteshwōn, adv., *not at all, by no means.* [**nāwihtes-**; **āwiht**, adv., *at all*; **hwōn**, adj., *little*, adv. *somewhat*]

nāðer (= **nāhwæðer**), conj., *neither.*

ne/nē, adv., *not; nor* (in series); conj., *nor.*

nēah/nēh, adv. prep. w. dat., *near*; comp. **nīor**; superl. adj., *at last, finally*: ds. **æt nēxtan** AI 31, **æt nīehstan** G1400, **æt nȳhstan** W9, 16, 32.

neaht, see **niht**.

nēalǣcan, wk.v.I, w. dat., *approach, draw near*; inf. **nēalēcan** C22; pret. 3s. **nēalǣcte** C89.

nearo, f., *narrowness, confinement*; ds. **nearwe** G1433.

nearowrenc, m., *crafty device, perfidious trick*; dipl. **-um** V44. [Eng. *wrench*]

nēat, n., *neat, ox, cow*; pl. *cattle*; gpl. **-a** C25: cp. **nēten**.

nēawest, f., *nearness, neighborhood*; ds. **-e** C92. [**nēah**; **-west**, rel. **wesan**]

nebb, n., *nib = beak = nose = face; countenance*; ds. **-e** AII 7.

nēhian (= **nēahwian**), wk.v.II, *draw near (to)*; pret. 3s. **nēhiget** P51.

nele, see **willan**.

nemnan, wk.v.I, *call (upon the name of), address (by name)*; pret. 3s. **nemnde** C28.

nemne, conj., *except.*

nēod, f., *demand, desire*; as. G1443. [Eng. *need*, Ger. *Not*].

neorxenewang(e) (= **neorxnawang**), m., *paradise*; ns. P3, 5, 19; ds. **-e** P2, 51. [**-wang**, m., *plain, field*, **neorxna-** = ?**nē**, *death* + **orc**, *infernal region, death*]

nēosīþ, m., *corpse-journey, death*; dipl. **-um** V55.

nēotan, st.v.2, w.gen., *make use of, enjoy*; inf. Wh88. [cp. **notu**]

nergend, m., *savior, preserver*; ns. G1295, 1314, 1327, 1356, 1367, 1483; ds. **-e** G1285. [rel. to the following word]

nerian/nergan, wk.v.I, *save, rescue; protect*; inf. G2000; pret. 1s. **nerede** G1491; pret. 3s. **nerede** G1397.

nesan, st.v.5, *escape from, survive*; inf. G1341.

nēðan, wk.v.I, *have courage (to do), venture*; inf. G2060.

nēten, n. (= **nīeten**), *animal*; ns. C69; cp. **nēat**.

nēxtan, see **nēah**.

nīed, f., *need, necessity, duty*; dis. **-e** G1977.

nīehstan, see **nēah**.

niht/neaht, f., *night*; ns. P20, R29: 13; gs. **-e** C95, R29(n9); ds. **-e** C25; as. AI 61, R39: 7; gpl. **-a** G1383, 1418; apl. G1349, 1449.

nihtlic, adj., *nightly, nocturnal*; dsn. **-um** AII 32.

nihtscūa, wk.m., *shadow(s) of night, darkness*; ds. **-scūwan** G2060.

niman, st.v.4, *take; receive; undertake*; inf. **eard niman**, *take up a dwelling*, WL 15; pres. 2s. **nimest** G1329; pret. 3pl. **nāmon** W13.

nīor, comp. adv. (of **nēah**), *nearer, closer*.

nis, see **bēon**.

niððas, m. pl., *man*; gpl. **niþþa** Wh6.

nīð, m., *violence, affliction; malice, spite*; ns. G1383; gs. **-es** G1995; dipl. **-um** V44.

niðer/nyðer, adv., *below, down(wards)*.

nīðgetēon, n., *dire attack, violent combat*; ds. **-e** G2068. [cp. **tēona**, wk. m., *injury, anger*]

nīwan, adv., *newly, recently*.

nīwes, adv. (gs. of **nīwe**), *new, recently*.

nō, see **nā**.

nōht/nāht (= **nō-wīht**), n., *naught, not a whit, nothing*; as. C14, 29, 31.

nōhweðer(e), adv., *in no wise*.

nolde, noldon, see **willan**.

noma, see **nama**.

norðan, adv., *from the north*.

norðmann, m., *man from the north*; npl. **-menn** G1995, gpl. **-monna** G2068; dpl. **-monnum** G1977.

notu, f., *use, advantage*; ds. **note** W23. [cp. Eng. '*of note*']

?nōw, f., *ship*; as. **-e** Wh28.

nū, adv., *now, at this time, at present*.

nȳhstan, see **nēah**.

nymðe, conj., *unless, except*.

nyste, see **witan**.

nyðene, adv., *from below, beneath*.

nyðerhrēosende, pres.p. as noun, *down-falling*; ns. V(n34).

O

of, prep. w. dat., *from, of, out of.*

ofdrǣdan, st.v.7, with weak pp., *be afraid, terrify*; pp. nsm. **ofdrǣdd** AII 101.

ofer, prep. w. dat., *over, above, upon, after, across*; w. acc. *over, across*; *contrary to, against*; *past (in time).*

ōfer, m., *bank, shore*; ds. **ōfre** Wh9. [Ger. *Ufer*]

ofergēotan, st.v.2, *cover (by pouring), suffuse*; pp. nsm. **-goten** AII 63, 82, 96.

oferhogian, wk.v.II, *contemn, despise*; pres. 3s. **-hogað** W84.

oferhygd, f. and n., *overbearing mind, pride*; *vain thought*; ns. V58; ds. **-o** V23; gpl. **-a** V43; ?apl. **-a** V53.

ofermēde, n., *immoderate self-esteem, vanity, pride*; dipl. **-mēdum** V75. [**mēde**, rel. **mōd**, n.]

ofermōdignæss, f., *pride, vainglory*; as. P(n19).

oferswīðan, wk.v.I, *prove stronger than, overcome*; pret. 2s. **-swīðdest** AI 58.

offrian, wk.v.II, *offer, bring a sacrifice in honor of*; pret. 3pl. **offrodon** W16, 57, 63.

ofgiefan, st.v.5, *give up, give over, leave*; pp. **ofgifen** G1454.

oflongian, wk.v.II, *grip, seize with longing*; pp. **oflongad** WL29.

ofostlīce, adv., *hastily, speedily.*

ofsceamian, wk.v.II, *put to shame, make ashamed*; pp. nsm. **ofsceamod** AII 97.

ofslēan, st.v.6, *strike (down), kill*; pret. 1s. **ofslōh** G(n2008), Y; pp. nplm. **ofslegene** G2001.

oft, adv., *often*; superl. **oftost.**

ofþecgan, wk.v.I, *consume, destroy*; pp. nplm. **ofþegde** G2002.

on, prep. w. dat., *in, on, among, at*; w. acc., *in, into, on, onto, upon*; *against, towards*; **on ǣr**, adv., *before*; **on ān**, adv., *continuously, persistently*; **on weg**, adv., *away*; **on hōh**, adv., *behind.*

onǣlan, wk.v.I, *inflame, kindle, ignite*; pp. nsm. **onǣled** P57, (n17), V43.

onbærnan, wk.v.I, *(en)kindle, light*; *inspire*; pp. nsm. **onbærned** C87; npln. **onbærnde** C9.

onbregdan, st.v.3, *swing open*; pret. 3s. **onbrǣd** G(n1364).

oncerbend, f., *anchor-bond, rope*; dpl. **-um** Wh(n15).

oncnāwan, st.v.7, *know, acknowledge*; pres. 1s. **oncnāwe** AI 73; pret. 3s. **oncnēow** AII 82; pret. subj. 3s. **oncnēowe** AI 73.

oncyrrāp, m., *anchor-rope*; dipl. **-um** Wh14.

ond, see **and**.

ondrǣdan, rd.v.7, w. reflex. dat., *fear, dread*; inf. Y; imper. s. **ondrǣd** AII 87; pret. subj. 3s. **ondrēde** X1017.

ondswarian, wk.v.II, *(give an) answer, respond*; pret. 3s. **-swarede** C29, **-swarade** C110; pret. 3pl. **-swaredon** C107, 115, **-swarodon** C102.

ondweard, adj., *present, in attendance*; dplm. **-um** C52.

ōnettan, wk.v.I, *hasten, move rapidly*; pret. 3s. **ōnette** R29:11 [MS **o netteð**]; pret. 3pl. **ōnetton** G1985.

onfōn, st.v.7, *receive, take; undertake*; inf. (w. gen.) G2040 [MS **ofon**], X1031; pres. 3s. **onfēhð** X1028; pret. 3s. **onfēng** C14, 34, 50, 65; pret. subj. 3s. **onfēnge** C64; pret. 3pl. **onfēngon** G1439; pp. nsm. **onfongne** C59.

ongan, see **onginnan**.

ongēan, prep. w. dat., *against; towards, before*.

Ongelþēod, f., *Anglian, English people (nation)*; ds. **-e** C10.

ongi(e)tan, st.v.5, *understand, realize, perceive*; inf. V6; pres. 3s. **ongyt** Wh(n59); pret. 3s. **ongeat** G1474.

onginnan, st.v.3, *begin, attempt, endeavor*; pres. 3s. **onginneð** G1355, **onginð** P14; imper.s. **ongyn** G1302; pret. 3s. **ongan/ongon** C34, 62, G1316, 1412; pret. 3pl. **ongunnon** C10, WL11.

onhweorfan, st.v.2, *change, reverse*; pp. nsn. **onhworfen** WL23.

onhyldan, wk.v.I, *incline, recline*; pret. 3s. **onhylde** C118.

onscacan, st.v.6, *shake*; pret. 3s. **onscēoc** G1471.

onslǣpan, wk.v.I, *sleep, fall asleep*; pret. 3s. **onslēpte** C27, 119.

onspringan, st.v.3, *spring (up)*; pret. 3pl. **onsprungon** G(n1374).

onstellan, wk.v.I, *institute, be the author of, create*; pret. 3s. **onstealde** C40.

onsundron, adv., *separately, apart*. [Eng. *asunder*]

onsȳn, f., *countenance, presence*; ds. **-e** X1019.

ontendan, wk.v.I, *kindle*; pret. 3pl. AI 21. [rel. Ger. *entzünden*]

ontendnyss, f., *burning, that which enkindles passion*; ds. **-e** AI 22, 30.

ontȳnan, wk.v.I, *open*; pres. 3s. **ontȳneð** Wh53, 68.

onwrēon, contr.v.1, *uncover, unlock*; pret. 3s. **onwrēah** V3 [MS **onwearh**].

onwunian, wk.v.II, *dwell (in), inhabit*; pret. 3s. **onwunode** AII 49.

ōr, n., *beginning, origin*; as. C40.

ord, m., *battle-line, army*; gs. **-es** G2004.

orfeorme, adj., *empty (of), destitute, deprived (of)*; asm. **orfeormne** V49. [**or-**, prefix, *lacking, without*]

orlegcēap, m., *battle-bargain, booty*; ?*wealth of violence*; ns. G1994.

orlegweorc, n., *war-work, action*; as. G2020.

ormǣte, adj., *measureless, immense*; dsf. **ormǣtre** AII 70; dsf.wk. **ormǣtan** AI 22.

ormōd, adj., *without courage, despairing*; nsm. AII 107.

ortrūwian, wk.v.II, *be without trust of, despair of*; pret. 3s. **ortrūwode** AII 40.

orðanc, m., *want of thought, thoughtlessness*; ds. **-e** AII 36.

orwēnnyss, f., *without expectation* or *hope*; *despair*; ds. **-e** AII 39.

oð/oðð, prep. w. acc., *to, up to, until*; conj. *until*.

ōðer, adj., *other, another*; *something else*; *next*; nsm. V31, W26; gsm. **ōðres** AII 56; gsn. **ōðres** C113; dsm. **ōðrum** V67, 74, W51, 66; dsf. **ōðre** C85; asf. **ōðre** R39:7, Wh49; asn. C80, G1383 (**ōðer swilc**, *another of such*); nplm. **ōðre** C10, W76; npln. **ōðre** Wh55, **ōðer** P52; gpln. **ōðerra** G1338 [MS **oðe ra**]; dplm. **ōðrum** C75; apln. **ōðre** W27.

oððæt/oððet, conj., *until*.

oððe, conj., *or*.

ōwiht, n., *anything, aught*; nsn. WL23: **ne ōwiht elles**, *not anything else*.

P

Paradīs, m., *Paradise*; as. P55. [Lat. Gk. *paradīsus*]

pistol, m., *epistle, letter*; as. AI 19. [Lat. *epistola*]

plega, wk.m., *(sword) play*; ns. G1989.

prēost, m., *priest*; dpl. **-um** AII 3. [Lat. Gk. *presbyter*]

R

racu, f., *narrative, story*; ns. AII 111.

rād, see **ridan**.

ræced/reced, m., *hall*; gs. **-es** G(n1364); ds. **-e** V17.

ræd, m., *advice, counsel*; gs. **-es** V82; ds. **-e** AI 32; as. G2031. [Ger. *Rat*]

rædan, st.v.7 and wk.v.I, *read*; pres. 1 pl. **rædað** W69, **ræde** W3.

rædfæst, adj., *stable in counsel, prudent, wise*; nplm. **-e** AII 113.

ræran, wk.v.I, *raise*; inf. C115. [rel. **rīsan**, st.v.1, *rise*]

ræst, see **rest**.

ræswa, wk.m., *counselor, leader*; npl. **-n** G2075.

rand, m., *boss (round metal center) of a shield, shield*; apl. **-as** G2049.

raðe, adv., (= **hraðe**), *quickly, directly*.

rēad, adj., *red* (of gold: *precious*); nsn. P41, 47.

reccan, wk.v.I, w. gen., *tell, speak of, reckon*; *care about*; pret. 3s. **rōhte** AI 29, AII 41; pret. 3pl. **rehton** C56, **rōhton** G1319.

reced, see **ræced**.

recene, adv., *quickly*.

regn/reign, m., *rain*; ns. P9; as. G1372, 1416.

regollec, adj., *regular, in accordance with monastic rule*; dplm. **-um** C84. [rel. Lat. *regula*]

rēodan, st.v.2, *redden, cover with red*; pret. 3s. **rūdeð** P47.

rēonigmōd, adj., *sad at heart, weary*; nplm. **-e** Wh23.

reord, f., *food, sustenance*; as. **-e** G1344.

reord, f. (or n.), *voice*; dis. **-e** G1484.

reordberend, m., *speech-bearer, man*; apl. **-e** X1024.

rēsele, f., *solution of a riddle*; as. **rēselan** R39 : 28.

rest/ræst, f., *rest, quiet*; *resting-place*; ns. G1486; gs. **-e** G1466, Wh23; ds. **-e** C26, 100; as. **-e** G1304, 1428, 1456.

rēðe, adj., *fierce, violent, harsh*; *terrible*; nsm. G1376, 1383; nsn. G1319; gsf. **rēðre** G1420.

rice, adj., *powerful, strong*; asm. **rīcne** V63; asn. V12.

rice, m., *kingdom, realm, dominion*; gs. **-s** C80; ds. V57. [Ger. *Reich*]

ricsian, wk.v.II, *rule, reign, govern*; pres. 3s. **rixað** AII 116, P(n19), **rixeð** P69.

rīdan, st.v.1, *ride, go*; pret. 3s. **rād** G1392.

riht/ryht, adj., *right, proper, true*; *straight*; nsn. V63; **swā riht swā bolt**, *as straight as a bolt, perfectly straight*, P15.

riht, n., *(that which is) right*; as. W69.

rihtan, wk.v.I, *set up, assign*; imper.s. **rihte** G1304.

rīm, n., *number, counting*; gs. **-es** G1336.

rīmgetæl, n., *number*; ns. G1420.

rinc, m., *man, warrior*; *hero*; ds. **-e** G1463; npl. **-as** G2049; apl. **-as** G2031.

rixað, rīxeð, see **rīcsian**.

rōdetācen, n., *sign of the rood (the cross)*; ds. **-tācne** C119.

rodor, m., *the heavens*; *sky*; dpl. **roderum** G1344, 1372, 1418.

rōf, adj., *valiant, strong*; nplm. **-e** G2049.

rōhte, rōhton, see **reccan**.

rōtlīce, adv., *cheerfully*.

rūdeð, see **rēodan**.

rūme, adv., *roomily, widely, abundantly*.

rūmgāl, adj., *revelling freely, rejoicing in free space*; nsf. G1466.

ryht, see **riht/ryht**.

rȳman, wk.v.I, *enlarge, increase, yield*; inf. G1344. [rel. **rūm**, adj., *roomy, spacious*]

ryne, m. and n., *running course, flow (of rain)*; as. G1416.

S

sacu, f., *distress, strife*; apl. **saca** W54. [rel. **sacan**, st.v.6, *struggle, fight*]

sǣ, m. or f., *sea, ocean*; ns. G1452; npl. **-s** G1375.

sæc(c), f., *fighting, battle*; ds. **-e** G(n2008), Y. [rel. **sacan**, st.v.6, *fight*]

sǣdan, sǣde, see **secgan**.

sǣfisc, m., *sea-fish*; gpl. **-a** Wh56.

sǣflōd, m. and n., *sea-flood, deluge*; ns. G1437.

sægð, sæigð, see **secgan**.

sǣl, m. or f., *time, opportunity*; ns. G2008, (n2008), Y.

sǣlāc, n., *sea-booty*; ds. **-e** Y; apl. Y.

sǣlan, wk.v.I, *moor, make (tie) fast*; pres. 3pl. **sǣlaþ** Wh15 [MS **set-laþ**]; pret. 3s. **sǣlde** Wh(n15). [Ger. *seilan*]

sǣliðend, m., *seafarer*; apl. **-e** Wh48.

sǣlwong, m., *fecund, fertile plain*; apl. **-as** G1293.

sǣmearh, m., *ocean-steed, ship*; apl. **-mearas** Wh15. [Eng. *mare*]

sænde, see **sendan**.

?sǣrȳric, n., *?sea-weed, ?reed-bed*; gpl. **-a** Wh10.

sǣstrēam, m., *sea-waters, sea-currents*; npl. **-as** G1326.

sæt, sǣton, see **sittan**.

saga(ð), see **secgan**.

salwed, adj., *darkened, black (with pitch)*; asn. G1481.

salwigfeðera, adj., *dark-plumaged*; nsm. G1448.

samod/somed, adv., *together, jointly*.

sanctus, Lat. m., *Saint*; ns. P1, 53, (n16).

sand, n., *sand, shore*; ds. **-e** Wh(n15).

sang, see **singan**.

sārost, superl. adj. (of **sār**), *most painful; grievous*; ns. G2029. [Eng. *sore*]

sārlic, adj., *sad, lamentable, grievous*; dism. **-um** AI 25.

sārnyss, f., *sadness, anguish, grief*; ds. **-e** AI 27.

sāwol/sāw(u)l, f., *soul; life*; ns. AII 108, Wh(n35); gs. **sāwle** AI 28, AII 62, 113; ds. **sāwle** AII 89; as. **sāwle** AII 72, 90, R39:16, X1036; dpl. **sāwlen** P22.

sāwon, see **sēon**.

sceaft, m., *shaft (of a spear or lance)*; gpl. **-a** G2062.

sceal, scealt, see **sculan**.

scealc, m., *retainer; man*; dpl. **-um** Wh31.

sceamu/scomu, f., *shame, confusion*; ds. **sceame** AII 82, **scome** C23.

scearp, adj., *sharp*; nplm. **-e** G2064.

scēat, m., *clothing; bosom*; as. G2064.

sceatt, m., *money, treasure*; gs. **-es** AI 6, AII 56. [rel. Ger. *Schatz*]

scēað, f., *sheath*; dpl. **scǣðum** G1992.

sceaða, wk.m., *evil doer, criminal*; gpl. **sceaðena** AII 68, 75; dpl. **sceaðum** AII 69, 73, G1302.

scēawian, wk.v.II, *see, behold*; pres. 3s. **scēawað** V32. [rel. Eng. *show*]

sceocca, wk.m., *fiend*; ns. AI 13.

sceolden, -an, see **sculan**.

scēotan, st.v.2, *shoot*; pres. 3s. **scēoteþ** V35.

scēotend, m., *shooter, warrior*; gpl. **-ra** G2062.

scieppan, st.v.6, *shape, form, create*; pret. 3s. **sceop** C41. [rel. **scop**, m., *poet*]

scīnan, st.v.1, *shine*; pres. 3s. **scīneð** P21, (n17), X1009, **scīnð** P28; pres. 3pl. **scīneð** P30.

scīnend, pres.p.adj. (of **scīnan**, 1), *shining*; dsf. **-an** W15; dplm. **-um** W18.

scinna, wk.m., *specter, demon*; gpl. Wh31. [rel. **scīnan**, st.v.1, *shine*]

scip, n., *ship*; ns. G1417; gs. **-es** G1306, 1436; as. G1302, 1391, Wh(n15); apl. **scipu** Wh13, 31.

scipen, f., *cattle-stall*; ds. **-e** C25.

scippend, see **scyppend**.

scīr, adj., *bright*; npln. **-e** P32.

scome, see **sceamu**.

scopgereord, n., *language of poetry, poetic speech*; ds. **-e** C5.

scrallettan, wk.v.I, *sound (?off) loudly*; pres. 3pl. **-lettaþ** V20.

sculan, pret.-pres.v., *shall, must; be obliged to; be fated*; pres. 1s. **sceal** C33, WL25 [MS **seal**]; pres. 2s. **scealt** AII 55, G1299, 1303, 1330; pres. 3s. **sceal** G1310, 1313, P68, R39:8, 16, 21, X1029, 1036, WL43, 52, **sceall** (n7); pres. subj., 3s. **scyle** WL42; pres. 1 pl. **sculon** V82; pres. 3pl. **sceolon** G1341, **sculon** C37; pret. 1s. **sceolde** WL(n7); pret. 3s. **sceolde** AI 30, 76, AII 19, 25, G1969, V39 [MS **scealde**]; pret. 3pl. **sceoldon** C21, 94, G1977, **scoldon** Y; pret. subj. 3pl. **sceolden** C115.

scūr, m., *shower*; dipl. **-um** V35.

scyld, m., *shield*; gpl. **-a** G2062.

scyld, f., *crime, sin, guilt*; ?as./apl. **-e** V35; dipl. **-um** V8. [Ger. *Schuld*]

scyldan, wk.v.I, *shield against, protect*; pret. subj. 3s. **scylde** Y.

scyldfull, adj., *sinful, guilty*; dplm. **-um** G1302.

scyle, see **sculan**.

scylfe, wk.f., *shelf; ?partition*; apl. **scylfan** G1306.

scyncræft, m., *illusory art, magic*; ds. **-e** AI 6. [**scinn**, n.; *specter, illusion*]

scyppend, m., *God, the Creator*; ns. C42, G1391, W25, 26; gs. **-es** C35, 125; as. **scippend** AII 114, W12. [rel. **scieppan**]

sē, **sēo**, **þæt**, dem. adj., def. art., and pron., *that, the, that one*; dem. pron. *that (one), those, he, she, it, they*; as rel. pron. (often w. rel. particle **þe**), *who, which, that*; as indef. pron. *he who, whoever*; nsm. **sē**, nsf. **sēo**, nsn. **þæt**; gsm. **þæs**, gsf. **þǣre/þǣra**, gsn. **þæs**; dsm. **þǣm/þām**, dsf. **þǣre/þǣra**, dsn. **þǣm/þām**; ism. and n. **þȳ**, **þon**, **þē**; asm. **þone**, asf. **þā**, asn. **þæt**. npl. (all genders) **þā**; gpl. (all genders) **þāra/þǣra**; dipl. (all genders) **þǣm/þām**; apl. (all genders) **þā**. Compound forms and phrasals: **ǣr þan (þe)/ ǣr þon**, *before, until*; **bē þām þe**, *even as*; **for þām/þǣm/þān/ þon**, *because*; **for þǣre þe**, *for the reason that, because*; **mid þām**, *when*; **mid þȳ**, *when*; **oþ þæt/oþ þet**, *until*; **tō þæs**, *to that extent*; **tō þon**, *to that degree*; **þæs** (conj.), *in respect of which, so*; **þæs þe**, *as, according to what, because*; **þon mā**, *any more than*; **þȳ lǣs**, *lest*; **þȳ . . . þē**, *the . . . the*.

sēah, see **sēon**.

sealde, **sealdon**, see **sellan**.

sealt, adj., *salt*; asm. **-ne** Wh27.

searo, n., *art*; *(cunning) device*; as. Wh42; dipl. **searwum** (adv. *skillfully*) R29:6, (adv. *cunningly*) V40.

sēcan, wk.v.I, *seek, seek out, search*; *visit*; inf. G1445, 1448, 1461, 1966, 2006, 2020, Wh(n85), 86, WL9; pres. 3s. **sēceð** Wh45; pres. subj. 3pl. **sēcen** Wh35; pret. 1s. **sōhte** AI 65; pret. 3s. **sōhte** G1455.

secg, m., *man*; ns. G2018; npl. **-as** G2067; gpl. **-a** Y.

secg, f., *sword*; dpl. **-um** G2001.

secgan, wk.v.III, *say, tell*; *declare*; inf. C53, 128, G2014, WL2, **seggen** P17; pres. 3s. **segð** AII 111, **sægð** P4, **sæigð** P53, **sagað** P(n16); pres. 3pl. **secgað** R39:1, 13, W8, 67; imper. 2s. **saga** R39:29; pret. 3s. **sǣde** AI 39, 39, 58, AII 15, W71, **sægde** C49, 51, G1289, 1317, 2024, 2053, V2; pret. 3pl. **sǣdan** W17, **sægdon** C57; ger. **tō secganne** R39:22.

sefa, wk. m., *mind, spirit*; ns. WL(n7).

segnian, wk.v.II, *make the sign of the cross*; *bless*; pret. 3s. **segnade** G1365, 1390, **sēnode** AI 53; pres. p. nsm. **segniende** C126.

sēl, adj., *good, excellent*; comp. nsm.wk. **sēlla**, V29; comp. as. (? or pl.) m. absol. **sēllan**, V61; see **sēlest**.

sele, m., *hall*; ds. Y.

sēlest, superl. adj. (of **sēl**), *best*; nsn. **-e** G1393; dism.wk. **-an** G1324; asm.wk. **-an** V84; asn. **-e** G1419.

self, see **sylf**.

sellan/syllan, wk.v.I, *give, offer*; *produce*; inf. AII 89, G1978; pres. 1s. **sille** AII 90; pret. 3s. **sealde** AII 90, 111, G2069; pret. 3pl. **sealdon** G2037, 2046. (Not to be confused with **sēllan**.)

sēlla(n), see **sēl**.

semninga, adv., *suddenly*.

sendan, wk.v.I, *send*; pret. 3s. **sænde** AI 20, **sende** G1371, 1478; pp. nsf. **sended** G1464.

sēnode, see **segnian**.

sēo, see **bēon** and **sē**.

sēoc, adj., *sick*; *exhausted (from illness)*; dsf.wk. **-an** AI 27; nplm. G1972.

seofon, num. adj., *seven*; acc. G1349, 1449, **-e** G1335, **seofen** P21.

seolf, see **sylf**.

sēon, contr.v.5, *see*; inf. G2084; pret. 1s. **sēah** AI 58; pret. 3pl. **sāwon** Y.

setl, n., *seat, place*; apl. G1304.

settan, wk.v.I, *appoint, assign*; pret. 3s. **sette** AII 111.

seþēah, adv., *however, nevertheless*.

sibb/sybb, f., *peace*; ds. **-e** Wh(n85), ?ds./as. **sibbe** Wh85. [Ger. *Sippe*]

siccettan, wk.v.I, *sigh, groan*; inf. AII 63.

sīd, adj., *wide, broad*; *large, vast*; disn. **-e** G1963; asm. **-ne** G1388, 1429; asn. G1445; npln. G1988; aplm. **-e** G1293. [Eng. *side*]

sīdfæþme, adj., *wide-embracing, roomy*; asn. Wh(n15).

sīen, see **bēon**.

sīgan, st.v.1, *sink, descend*; inf. G1349, 1462.

sigor, m., *victory, triumph*; ns. G2067; ds. **-e** G2017; gpl. **-a** G1365, 1408, V84. [Ger. *Sieg*]

sille, see **sellan**.

simble, see **symble**.

sīn, poss. pron., *his*; gpln. **-ra** X1037; dplm. **-um** G2025; dplf. **-um** G1364.

sinc, n., *treasure*; as. G2017, 2090.

sincan, st.v.3, *sink*; *subside*; pres.p. nsm. **sincende** G1437.

sind/synd, see **bēon**.

sindan/sindon, see **bēon**.

singan, st.v.3, *sing, tell (in song)*; inf. C17 etc.; pres. 3pl. **singeð** P37; imper. s. C28, 33; pret. 3s. **sang** G1983, **song** C46, 71, V50.

singrēne, adj., *forever green*; nsn. (or f.) P18. [**sin-**, prefix, *extensive, perpetual*]

sinsorg, f., *constant sorrow*; gpl. **-na** WL45.

sittan st.v.5, *sit*; *encamp*; inf. WL37 [MS **sittam**]; pres. 3s. **siteð** V40, WL47, **sitt** AII 38; pres. 3pl. **sittaþ** V15; pret. 3s. **sæt** AI 11, AII 60; pret. 3pl. **sǣton** G2077.

sīð, m., *journey, voyage*; *fate*; (*a period of*) *time, time* (as a unit of measure); ns. G2015; ds. (adv.) **āne sīðe**, *at a time, once* P13, 26; as. G2023, R29:14, WL2; gpl. **-a** G1427; apl. **-as** R39:16, **-e** P21.

sīðian, wk.v.II, *go (on a journey), travel*; inf. G2018; pret. 3pl. **sīðedon** G2009.

sīððan/syððan, adv., *afterwards, then*; conj., *after, since*.

six, num. adj., *six*; acc. P(n16).

slǣp, m., *sleep*; ds. **-e** C46.

slǣpan, wk.v.I, *sleep*; pres.p. nsm. **slǣpende** C46.

slēan, contr.v.6, *strike, beat*; *slay*; pret. 3s. **slōh** AII 98, G2071.

slītan, st.v.1, *slit, tear, rend*; inf. G2088.

slīþen, adj., *cruel, dire, malign*; asn. Wh42; asf. **slīþnan** V52.

slōh, see **slēan**.

smēte, adj., *pure, refined*; nsn. P46.

smolt, adj., *kind, peaceful, serene*; asn. C106.

smoltlīce, adv., *gently*.

smylte, adj., *quiet, serene*; dism. C123; disf. **smyltre** C122.

snāw, m., *snow*; ns. P9.

snottor, adj., *wise*; nsm. V2.

snotorwyrde, adj., *wise in speech, plausible*; nsm. W61.

Sodomware, m.pl., *the people of Sodom*; npl. G1996. [**-ware**, pl. suffix].

sōhte, see **sēcan**.

some, see **swā**.

sōna, adv., *soon, immediately, directly.*

sondbeorg, m., *sandbank* (or *dune*); dipl. **-um** Wh10.

song, m., *song, poetry*; gs. **-es** C48; npl. C69; see **singan**.

songcræft, m., *song-craft, art of composing poetry*; as. C14.

sorg, f., *sorrow, care*; gpl. **-a** G2029.

sorgian, wk.v.II, *grieve, sorrow*; pres.p. nsf. **sorgende** X1016.

sorhlēas, adj., *sorrow-less, free from care*; nsm. Y.

sōð, adj., *true, genuine; just, righteous*; nsm. G1414, W22, 29; nsm.wk.
  sōða W27; nsn. R39:25; dsm. **-an** W71; dsf. **-re** AI 45; AII 115;
  ?disf./asf. **-e** AII 112; asm. wk. **-an** W12, 84; gpln. **-ra** G1425;
  dipln. **-um** P(n16), R39:29, **-en** P53. [Eng. *sooth*]

sōð, n., *truth*; as. G2013.

sōðgied, n., *true tale*; *?presumptuous (boasting) tale*; as. (? or pl.) V15.

sōðlīce, adv., *truly, really.*

spanan, st.v.7, *entice*; pres. 3s. **spenð** AI 24.

specað, see **sprecan**.

spēd, f., *speed, quickness; success; power, might*; ds. **-e** G2059; dpl. **-um**
  G1366, 2034.

spel(l), n., *story, narrative, discourse*; gs. **-es** C67; as. C57; dpl. **-um**
  C75. [as Eng. *gospel*, from **gōdspel**]

sperenīð, m., *spear-strife, battle*; ds. **-e** G2059.

sprǣc, f., *speech; report*; ds. **-e** G2034; see **sprecan**.

sprecan, st.v.5, *speak, say*; inf. C92; pres. 1pl. **specað** W46; pret. 3s.
  sprǣc G1294, 1483, R39:12; pres.p. nsm. **sprecende** C32, 101,
  105.

spura, wk.m., *spur*; dpl. **-n** AII 84.

stæf, m., *staff, written character, letter*; dpl. **stafum** C4. [Ger. *Stab*]

stǣlan, wk.v.I, *lay to one's charge, accuse*; inf. G1352; pres. 3pl. **stǣ-
  leð** G(n1351).

stælgiest, m., *guest intent upon stealing*; ns. R47:5. [cp. **stala**, **stelan**]

stæppan/steppan, st.v.6, *step, go, advance*; inf. G1434, 1459; pret. 3s.
  stōp G1467.

stǣr, n., *history*; gs. **-es** C67; as. C73. [rel. Lat. *historia*]

stæð, n., *bank, shore*; ds. **staþe** Wh18. [Ger. *Gestade*]

stæðweall, m., *shore-wall, barrier of the shore*; apl. **-as** G1376.

stāh, see **stīgan**.

stala, f., *stealing*; as. P(n19).

stān, m., *stone*; ds. **-e** Wh8.

standan/stondan, st.v.6, *stand*; *remain*; pres. 3s. **stant** P43; pres. 3pl. **stondað** Wh17; pret. 3s. **stōd** AI 10, C27, G1397, 2075.

stānhlið, n., *stone cliff*, ?*barren cliff*; ds. **-e** WL48.

staþe, see **stæð**.

staðol, m., *station, foundation, support*; ns. R47(n5); as. R47:5.

stēap, adj., *high, prominent*; asf. **-e** G(n1393); npln. G1459.

stefn/stemne, f., *voice*; ns. G1494, P45.

stelan, st.v.4, *steal*; ger. **tō stelenne** AII 33.

stenc, m., *odor, fragrance*; ns. Wh54, 57; as. Wh65. [Eng. *stench*]

steorra, wk.m., *star*; dpl. **steorrum** W18.

stīgan, st.v.1, *climb, arise, mount up*; inf. G1355, 1406; pres. 3s. **stīgeð** V19; pret. 3s. **stāh** G1494; pret. 3pl. **stigon** G1375. [Ger. *steigen*]

stigwita, wk.m., *overseer, officer of a household*; dpl. **-witum** G2079. [**stīg**, n., Eng. *sty*]

stilness, f., *stillness, tranquility*; ds. **-e** C119.

stincan, st.v.3, *spring, move*; *rise*; pret. 3s. **stonc** R29:12.

stīðe, adv., *severely, bitterly*.

stīðferhð, adj., *strong (severe)-minded, determined, stern*; nsm. G1406.

stōd, stondað, see **standan**.

stonc, see **stincan**.

stōp, see **stæppan**.

storm, m., *storm*; ds. **-e** WL48.

stōw, f., *place*; ds. **-e** AI 47; as. **-e** C96, G1466.

stræc, adj., *violent*; aplm. **strece** W33. [rel. **streccan**, wk.v.I, *stretch*]

strǣt, f., *street, way*; as. **-e** Y.

strang, adj., *strong, powerful, firm*; nsm. G1376; gsm.wk. **-an** R47:5.

stranglic, adj., *strong, robust*; nsm. AII 7.

strēam, m., *stream*; *sea(s), ocean*; dis. **-e** Wh18; dpl. **-um** G1406, 1459.

strēamstæð, n., *sea-bank, shore*; ds. **-staðe** G1434.

strēamweall, m., *sea-wall (boundary), shore*; as. G1494.

strece, see **stræc**.

strūdan, st.v.2, *ravage, plunder, pillage*; pret. 3pl. **strūdon** G2006.

stȳpel, m., *tower*; as. W6. [Eng. *steeple*; rel. **stēap**, *high*]

styrian, wk.v.II, *stir (up)*, *induce*; pres. 3pl. **styriað** AI 21; pret. 3s. **styrede** W54.

suhtriga, wk.m., *brother's son*, *nephew*; ns. G2029; ds. **-n** G2071.

sum, indef. pron. and adj., *(a certain) one*; *some*; nsm. AI 1, Cl, 27, V23, W60; nsn. W71; gsm. **-es** AII 56, 57, R47:3; dsf. **-ere** AI 47, **-re** C24; dsn. **-um** AI 2; asm. **-ne** AII 6; asn. C57, Wh12; nplm. **-e** W17, 19, 20, 20, 67; dplm. **-um** W52; aplm. **-e** Wh(n30); apln. **-u** C100.

sumorlang, adj., *long as in summer, very long (in time)*; asm. **-ne** WL37, (n37).

sund, n., *sea, ocean*; *swimming*; gs. **-es** Wh15; ds. **-e** G1429; as. G1388. [Eng. *sound*]

sundhwæt, adj., *sea-quick*; *vigorous in swimming*; nplm. **-hwate** Wh57.

sundor, adv., *separately, each by himself.*

sundorcræft, m., *special skill, singular power*; as. R39:3.

sundorwundor, n., *special wonder, unique truth*; gpl. **-wundra** V2.

sundreced, n., *sea-house (hall), the ark*; as. G1335.

sunne, f., *sun*; ns. P(n17), 21; gs. **sunnan** P(n17); ds. P28; as. **sunnan** W15.

sun(n)eléome, wk.m. (? or f.), *sun-beam*; ns. P28, 32; as. P57.

sunu, m., *son*; ns. AII 86 (voc.), G1286, 1368, 1425, 1441, W48, 53, 68, 71, Y, **suna** W86; ds. P(n19); as. G1408; dpl. **-m** G1300.

sūð, adv., *south(wards), from the south.*

sūðan, adv., *from the south.*

sūðfolc, n., *people who dwell in (come from) the south*; dpl. **-um** G1996.

sūðmonn, m., *man living in the south*; gpl. **-a** G2017, 2090.

swā, adv., *so, in such manner, thus*; conj. *as, as if*; phrasals: **swā gelīce**, *similarly*; **swā hwæt swā**, *whatsoever*; **swā oft swā**, *whenever*; **swā same/some**, *in like manner, similarly*; **swā . . . swā**, *even as, just as.*

swāþēah, adv., *although, however.*

swaðu, f., *track*; ds. **swaþe** G2001, 2077. [Eng. *swath(e)*]

swealg, see **swelgan**.

sweart, adj., *black, dark*; nsm. G1414; gsf. **-an** R29(n9); dsm. **-um** G1449; asm. **-ne** G1441; nplm. **-e** G1326; npln. G1300; aplm. **-e** G1375. [Eng. *swart*, Ger. *Schwarz*]

sweartracu, f., *dark course of the sea*; ns. G1355.

swefan, st.v.5, *sleep*; inf. Y.

swefen, n., *sleep, dream*; as. **swefn** C27, 53.

swegl, n., *sky, the heavens*; gs. **-es** Wh(n85); ds. **-e** G1414.

swelce, see **swilce**.

swelgan, st.v.3, w. dat., *swallow, devour*; pres. 3pl. **swelgað** G1301; pret. 3s. **swealg** R47:6.

sweltan, st.v.3, *die*; inf. AI 25, 30.

swēora, wk.m., *neck, nape*; ns. P45.

sweord, n., *sword*; apl. G1992.

swēot, n., *troop, band (of men)*; dpl. **-um** G1975.

sweotol, adj., *clear, evident, manifest*; nsf. R39:3.

swerian, st.v.6, *swear, make an oath*; pret. 3s. **swōr** AII 99.

swēte, adj., *sweet*; nsm.wk. **swēta** Wh57; asm. **swētne** Wh65; superl. asn. **swēteste** C69.

swētness/-niss, f., *sweetness*; ds. **-e** C6, 79; as. **-e** Wh(n65).

swīcan, st.v.1, *turn from, fall away*; *move about, plot*; pres. 3s. **swīcað** W80; pret. 3pl. **swīcon** G1981.

swice, m., *departure, escape*; *outcome, result*; *treachery*; ns. V31; ds. V61; as. Wh78; see next word.

swice, adj., *deceptive, fraudulant*; *?deceptive in strength*; nplm. G1996. [rel. **swīcan**]

swicol, adj., *false, treacherous*; nsm. W61.

swilc/swylc, dem. pron., *such*; as noun, *such a one*; asn. G1383, W84.

swilce/swelce/swylc(e), conj. adv., *likewise*; *as if, like, as*; **swelce ēac**, *likewise also.*

swimman, st.v.3, *swim*; inf. Y; pres. 3pl. **swimmað** Wh57.

swinsung, f., *harmony, melody*; ds. **-e** C58. [**swin**, mn., *melody, song*]

swīðan, wk.v.I, *make strong, support*; inf. G1980.

swīðe/swȳðe, adv., *very much, exceedingly*; *severely*; comp. **swīðor**, *more, rather*; superl. **swīðost**, *most, exceedingly*; **for swīðe**, *very much.*

swīðmōd, adj., *strong-minded*; nsm. Y.

swīðre, comp. adj. (of **swīð**, *strong*), *right*; asf. **swīðran** AII 97, 100 (absol.).

swōgan, st.v.7, *sound, roar*; inf. G1375.

swōr, see **swerian**.

swylc(e), see **swilc**, **swilce**.

swyster, f., *sister*; ds. W43.

swȳðlic, adj., *very great*; dsf. **-um** W77.

sȳ, see **bēon**.

sybb, see **sibb**.

sylf/self/seolf, pron. and adj., *self*; nsm. AI 65, 74, AII 3, 68, 79, 100; nsm.wk. **selfa** G1390; gsm. **seolfes** C128, **sylfes** AII 27, V28; gsf. **sylfre** WL2; dsm. **sylfum** C56, WL45; asm. **seolfne** C126, **sylfne** AII 34, 90, V52; nplm. **seolfan** C70; gplm. **sylfra** V64; dplm. **sylfum** W82.

sylfwylle, adv., *own will*; **-wylles** AI 16, *of your own accord, voluntarily.*

syllan, see **sellan**.

sym(b)le/simble, adv., *ever, always*; see next word.

symbel, n., *feast, banquet*; ds. **symble** C23, V15.

symbelwlonc, adj., *feast-proud, ?fat with boasting*; nsm. V40.

synd/synden/syndon, see **bēon**.

syndrig, adj., *singular, special*; nsn. G1324. [Eng. *sundry*]

syndriglīce, adv., *specially, particularly.*

synlic, adj., *sinful*; dplm. **-um** AII 34.

synn, f., *sin, guilt*; gpl. **-a** AII 114, C82, Wh(n65); dpl. **-um** G 1293.

syrwiend, pres.p. adj. (of **syrwan**, wk.v.I), *plotting, scheming*; nsm. wk. **-a** W80.

syððan, see **siððan**.

syxhund, num. adj., *six-hundred*; acc. G1368.

T

tācen, n., *token, sign*; ds. **tācne** Y.

tæcan, wk.v.I, *appoint, prescribe, enjoin; instruct, teach*; pres. 3pl. **tæcaþ** [MS **tætaþ**] G(n1298); pret. 3s. **tæhte** AI 47 [MS **tæhta**], AII 22.

teala, adv., *well, good.*

tēar, m., *tear*; dpl. **-um** AII 95.

telga, m., *twig, branch*; dpl. **telgum** G1470.

tellan, wk.v.I, *believe, reckon*; pret. 3s. **tealde** G1443.

temian, wk.v.II, *tame, control*; pres. 3pl. **temiaþ** G(n1298) [MS **tennaþ**].

tēon, st.v.2, *draw, pull*; pres.p. nsm. **tēonde** AI 64.

tēon, wk.v.III, *make, create, ordain*; pret. 3s. **tēode** C44.

teosu, f., *hurt; destruction*; as. Wh34.

tīd, f., *time, period of time* (an hour, an age); ns. P(n13); gs. **-e** C117; ds. **-e** C24, 26, 89, 114; as. C92, V10, 52, Wh64, 86, **-e** C18; dipl. **miclum tīdum**, *?for much time/for many hours*, R39:2. [Eng. *tide*]

tihting, f., *inducement, enticement*; ds. **-e** AI 4. [rel. **tēon**, st.v.2]

til, adj., *good*; gplf. **-ra** Wh34.

tintreglic, adj., *hell-tormenting, torturing*; gsn. **-an** C79.

tīr, m., *glory*; gs. **-es** Y.

tō/to, prep. w. dat., *to, for, at*; phrasals: **tō hwon**, *to that extent; to what* (*end*, etc.); **tō þām**, *to that extent*; **tō þæs**, *to that extent*; **tō þon**, *to that extent*; with gerund.

tō, adv., *too*.

tōcnāwan, st.v.7, *discern, distinguish*; inf. W22.

tōcyme, m., *coming, advent*; as. V(n34).

tōdæg, adv., *today*.

tōdǣlan, wk.v.I, *divide, part, separate*; pret. subj. 3pl. **tōdǣlden** WL12.

tōdrīfan, st.v.1, *drive away, disperse*; pret. 3s. **tōdrǣfþ** R29(n11).

tōfēran, wk.v.I, *go in different directions, disperse*; pret. 3pl. **tōfērdon** W8.

tōgæd(e)re, adv., *together*.

tōgēanes, adv., *opposite*; prep., *against, towards*.

tōgeþēodan, wk.v.I, *join*; pret. 3s. **-þēodde** C48.

torfian, wk.v.II, *throw dirt at, stone; strike*; pres. 3pl. **torfiað** AI 50. [rel. **turf**, f., *sod*]

torht, adj., *bright, splendid*; asm. **-ne** G1416 [MS **torht**]; dplm. **-um** G1470.

torn, n., *violent passion, anger*; as. G2037. [Ger. *Zorn*]

tōsamne/tōsomne, adv., *together*.

tōteran, st.v.4, *tear to pieces*; pret. 3s. **tōtær** AI 75.

tōweard, adj., *approaching, impending*; nsn. G1318; gsm. **-an** C78.

tredan, st.v.5, *tread, walk upon*; pret. 3s. **træd** Y.

trēow, f., *truth, (pledge of) fealty, loyalty*; as. **-e** G2046; apl. **-a** G2037. [Ger. *Treue*]

trēo(w), n., *tree*; ns. P15; gs. **-es** G1458, 1470; as. **trōw** P28.

trum, adj., *strong*; superl. nsm.wk. **-esta** R47(n5).

trūwa, wk.m., *trust, faith, belief*; ds. **-n** AII 23, 54.

tūd(d)or, n., *offspring, issue*; gs. **tūdres** G1313, 1440; ds. **tūdre** G1305; as. G1402; gpl. **tūdra** G1336.

tunge, f., *tongue*; ns. C124; as. **tungan** C16.

tūngerēfa, wk.m., *town-reeve, steward*; ds. **-n** C49.

twēgen, m., **twā**, f., **tū**, n. num. adj., *two*; nf. **twā** W45; nom.n. **twā** P31; gen. **twēga** R39:11; af. G2055; an. G1338.

twig, n., *twig, branch*; as. G1473.

twispǣc, f., *double talk, vilification*; as. **-e** P(n19). [**twi-**, prefix; *two, double*; Ger. *zwie-*]

tyhtan, wk.v.I, *draw (on), incite, persuade*; pres. 3pl. **tyhtað** Wh34. [cp. **tihting**]

Þ

þā, adv., *then, after that*; conj. *when*; **þā þā/þā ... þā**, *then when, when ... then.*

þā, see **sē**.

þā gȳt(a), adv., *still.*

þǣm, see **sē**.

þǣra, see **sē**.

þǣr(e), adv., *there, where*; conj. *where, there where.*

þǣre, see **sē**.

þǣrinne, adv., *therein.*

þæs, see **sē**.

þæs þe, conj., *as, since.*

þæt, conj., *that, so that, in order that*; *for, because*; **swā þæt(te)**, *so that*; see **sē**.

þafian, wk.v.II, *consent to, agree with*; pret. 3s. **þafode** C64.

þafung, f., *consent, permission*; ds. **-e** W26.

þām, see **sē**.

þancian, wk.v.II, w. dat. of person, *thank, give thanks*; pret. 3s. **þancode** AI 72; pret. 3pl. **þancodon** Y.

þanon, adv., *thence, from that place*.

þāra, see **sē**.

þās, see **þēs**.

þē, see **þū** and **sē**.

þe/þē, relative pronoun particle, indecl., *who, which, that*.

þe, conj., *when, while*.

þē(a)h, adv. *still, however, nevertheless, although*. [Eng. *though*]

þēah þe, conj. *(even) though*.

þeahte, see **þeccan**.

þearf, f., *need*; ns. C103, G1482, 2054. [Ger. *Bedarf*]

þearft, see **þurfan**.

þēaw, m., *custom, usage*; *manner, way*; ns. C93, Wh31; dpl. **-um** AII 9, 26, 28, 34; apl. **-as** AII 2. [Eng. *thew*]

þeccan, wk.v.I, *cover (over)*; pret. 3s. **þeahte** G1377; pp. nplm. **þeahte** G1989. [Eng. *thatch*]

þegn, m., *servant, retainer*; *thane*; ns. AI 1, C97; as. C95, V45, 79; gpl. **-a** Y.

þegnian, wk.v.II, w. dat., *serve, minister to*; inf. C95.

þēh, see **þēah**.

þellfæsten, n., *fastness made of planks, the ark*; ds. **-ne** G1482.

þencan, wk.v.I, *think, consider*; pres. 3s. **þenceð** V30; pret. 3pl. **þōhton** V61.

þenden, conj., *while*.

þēnung (= **þegnung**), f., *service, ministration*; apl. **-a** AII 52. [rel. **þegnian**]

þēod, f., *people*; *nation*; ds. **-e** V79; gpl. **-a** X1023; dpl. **-um** G1318, W52.

þēodcyning, m., *king (of a tribe, a nation)*; npl. **-as** G1965.

þēode, see **þēow(i)an**.

þēoden, m., *chief, lord*; ns. (voc.) Y; gs. **þēodnes** Y.

þēodenhold, adj., *faithful to a lord, loyal*; gplm. **-ra** G2042 [MS **þeonden-**].

þēodenstōl, m., *lord's throne*; *high throne*; gs. **-es** V62.

þēodscipe, m., *fellowship, association*; dpl. **-scipum** C85.

þēof, m., *thief*; ns. R47:4.

þēostru/þȳstro, f., *darkness, shadow*; ds. R47:4; apl. R29(n9). [Ger. *düster*]

þēow, m., *servant*; gpl. **-a** C66.

þēowdōm, m., *service*; ds. **-e** AI 2, AII 110.

þēow(i)an, wk.v.I (and II), w. dat., *serve*; pret. 3s. **þēode** C122.

þēownȳd, f., *necessity that enslaves, enslavement*; as. G2030.

þēs/þes, **þēos**, **þis**, dem. adj., and pron., *this*; nsm. **þes** W65, WL29; nsn. **þis** C36; gsf. **ðēosse** C1, **þissere** AII 14 (? or dsf.); dsm. **þēossum** C30, **þissen** P21, **þissum** W57, WL16; dsf. **þisse** P19, V72, **þissere** AII 55; dsn. **þissum** WL41; asm. **þisne** AII 12, 87, R39:19, **þysne** W55; asf. **þās** AI 73, C34, R39:17, 26, Wh64; asn. **þis** AI 74, WL 1; nplm. **þās** W22, 46, 78; dplm. **þissum** R47(n5); dipln. **þissum** V46, 77; aplf. **þās** P(n19); apln. **þās** AII 91, 93, W22, WL36.

þicce, adv., *thickly, closely*.

þīn, poss. pron. adj., *thy, thine*; dsf. **-re** AI 24, AII 12, 89, 91, C104; dsn. **-um** AI 17; asm. **-ne** AI 17, AII 86; gplm. **-ra** Y; dplm. **-um** G1300; aplm. **-e** G1333; see pers. pron. **þū**.

þinc-, see **þync-**.

þing, n., *thing*; *affair*; ns. G1318, R39:24; as. W25; gpl. **-a** W1; dpl. **-um** P(n19); apl. AII 52, C100, W21, 22, 25, 28, 85.

þingian, wk.v.II, *intercede, ask favor for*; inf. AI 61.

þis(-), see **þēs**.

þiwracu, f., *threat*; apl. **-wracan** AI 56.

þōhton, see **þencan**.

þolian, wk.v.II, *suffer, endure*; pret. (?subj.) 3s. **þolode** G2030.

þon, see **sē**; see also **ēac**.

þonan, adv., *thence*.

þone, see **sē**.

þon(n)e, adv., *then*; conj. *when, than*; **þonne ... þonne**, *when ... then/then ... when*.

þoterung, f., *wailing*; ds. **-e** AII 95.

þræcrōf, adj., *brave under attack, valiant*; aplm. **-e** G2030. [**þræc**, n., *force, violence*; **rōf**, adj., *strong, brave*]

þræft, n., *incontinent, contentious speech* (or *behavior*); dis. **-e** V42.

þrāg, f., *time, space of time*; gs. **-e** G1420; as. **-e** G1426.

þrēalic, adj., *terrible*; nsn. G1318. [Eng. *throe*]

þrēan, wk.v.III, *chasten, discipline, punish*; pres. 3s. **þrēað** X1023.

þrēohund, n., *three hundred*; gen. G1308.

þridda, num. adj., *third*; dsm. **-n** P59; asm. **-n** G1492 [MS þridda], 2027; asf. **-n** G1477.

þringan, st.v.3, *press (on), advance, crowd upon*; inf. G1373, V42; pres. 3s. **þringeð** V24 [MS þringe]. [Ger. *dringan*]

þrittig, num. adj., *thirty*; gen. **-es** G1308.

þrintan, st.v.3, *swell, puff up*; pres. 3s. **þrinteð** V24.

þrīð, f., *strength*; dipl. **-um** (adv., *forcefully, mightily*) V(n24).

þrōwung, f., *suffering, passion*; ds. **-e** C76. [Eng. *throw, throe*]

þrȳ, num., *three*; nm. G2033, 2045; dm. **-m** W86; am. AI 47, G1334, W87.

þryccan, wk.v.I, *press, afflict*; pp. nsm. **þrycced** C91.

þrymcyning, m., *glory-king, God*; as. V62.

þrymfæst, adj., *glory-fast, glorious*; asm. **-ne** R47:4.

þrymm, m., *troop, host; force, power*; dis. **-e** G1492, 1965; as. X1023.

þrymme, adv., *violently*; V24 [MS þrȳme].

þrȳðig, adj., *powerful, strong*; nplm. **þrȳðge** G1986 [MS þrydge].

þrȳðlic, adj., *mighty, splendid*; nsm. Y.

þū, pers. pron. 2s., *thou*; ns. **þū**, gs. **þīn**, ds. **þē**, as. **þē**; see **gē**, and the poss. prons. **þīn**, **ēower**.

þūhte, see **þyncan**.

þurfan, pret.-pres.v. *need*; pres. 3s. **þearft** Y. [Ger. *bedürfan*]

þurh, prep. w. acc., *through, by means of, because of*.

þurhwunian, wk.v.II, *continue*; inf. AII 26.

þus(s), adv., *thus, so*.

þūsend, num., *thousand*; acc. P(n16), 54, 62.

þȳ, see **sē**.

þyncan, wk.v.I, impers. w. dat. of person, *seem, appear*; pres. 3s. **þynceð** P54; pres. subj. 3s. **þince** V30; pret. 3s. **þūhte** AII 42, C98, R47:1.

þyslic (= **þyllic**), pron. *such (a)*; asm. **-ne** V45.

þȳstro, f., *darkness*; ds. R47:4. [Ger. *düster*]

U

ufan/ufene/ufon, adv., *above, from above; over, on high.*

ūhtcearu, f., *early-morning (pre-dawn) care, anxiety;* as. **-ceare** WL7.

ūhte, f., *the twilight period before dawn;* ds. **ūhtan** WL35; gpl. **ūhtna** WL(n7).

ūhtsong, m., *morning-song, matins;* as. C115.

unc, uncer, see **wit**.

unclǣne, adj., *unclean, impure;* nsf. X1016.

unclǣnness, f., *impurity, uncleanness;* ds. **-e** W83.

under, prep. w. dat., *beneath, under.*

underbæc, adv., *back, behind.*

underfōn, contr.v.7, *receive; undertake;* inf. AI 45; pres. 3s. **-fēhþ** AI 16; pret. 3s. **-fēng** AII 15, 21, 57; pp. nsm. **-fangen** AII 41.

underþēodan, wk.v.I, *subject (to), subjugate, reduce;* pp. nsm. **-þēod** AII 44; **-þēoded** C85.

unēaðe, adv., *scarcely, only just.*

unfæderlīce, adv., *in an unfatherly manner.*

unfæg(e)re, adv., *unpleasantly, terribly.*

unfeor, adv., *not far off.*

unforcūð, adj., *reputable, brave;* nfs. V31.

ungelīc, adj., *unlike, dissimilar;* nplm. **-e** V23.

ungelīce, adv., *unlike, dissimilar.*

ungemedemad, pp. adj. (of **medemian**, wk. v. II), *immoderate, unmeasured;* V25.

ungemetegod, adj., *immoderate, inordinate;* asf.wk. **-an** AI 5.

ungemīdlod, adj., *unbridled;* nsn. AII 37.

ungerīped, adj., *immature, premature;* dsm. **-um** AII 27.

ungetrēow, adj., *untrue, unfaithful, faithless;* nplm.wk. **-a** AI 13.

ungewǣpnod, pp. adj. (of **gewǣpnian** II), *unarmed;* asm.wk. **-an** AII 87 [MS **-e**].

unlond, n., *non-land, seeming land;* ds. **-e** Wh14.

unrǣd, m., *evil counsel, folly;* as. Wh70.

unrǣdlīce, adv., *unadvisedly, inconsiderately.*

unriht, n., *unrighteousness, wickedness;* ds. **-e** G1292.

unrihtgitsung, f., *wicked greed*; as. P(n19).

unrihthǣmed, n., *wicked adultery*; as. **-u** P(n19).

unrīm, ?adj., *countless*; nsn. (or f.) P19.

unrīm, n., *countless number, great host*; ns. P22.

unsofte, adv., *with difficulty*.

unstæððig, adj., *unstable, inconstant*; dplm. **unstaððigum** AII 27.

untrum, adj., *weak, infirm*; gplm. **-ra** C92; aplm. (absol.) **-an** C93.

untrymness, f., *infirmity, illness, weakness*; ds. **-e** C90.

unþēaw, m., *evil habit, vice*; apl. **-as** (? for **-a**, gpl. after **fela**) AII 29.

unwær, adj., *unwary*; disn. **unware** Wh59; asm.wk. **-waran** Wh(n59, 65); aplm. **-e** Wh(n59).

unwærlīce, adv., *unwarily*.

unwillum, adv., *unwillingly*.

ūp/upp, adv., *up, upwards*.

ūpāhafen, adj., *uplifted*; dplf. **-um** AI 68, 69.

ūpāstigness, f., *ascension*; ds. **-e** C77.

ūphēah, adj., *towering*; nplf. **ūphēa** WL30.

uppan, prep., *upon, on*.

ūppārīsan, st.v.1, *rise*; pres. 3s. **-rīseð** P63.

uppe, adv., *above, up*.

ūppriht, adj., *upright, straight up*; nsm. **-e** P19.

ūre, poss. pron., *our*; nsm. AI 44, R47(n5); gsm. **ūres** W26; asm. **ūrne** P(n19); see pers. pron. **wē**.

ūs, see **wē**.

ūs(s)er, poss. pron. *our*; nsm. G1295, 1327, 1367, 1391, 1483; see pers. pron. **wē**.

ūt, adv., *out*.

ūtan, adv., *on the outside; from without*.

ūtbrecan, st.v.4, *break out, escape*; inf. V(n34).

ūtgān, anom.v., *go out, withdraw*; pret. 1s. **ūtēode** C30.

ūtgong, m., *going out, exodus*; ds. **-e** C73.

uton, pres. subj. 1 pl. of **wītan** (st.v.3, *go*), with infinitive, *let us*; W85; see **wuton**.

ūtsīð, m., *journey out, departure*; as. Wh79.

W

wā, interj., *woe!*; WL52.

wāc, adj., *weak*; comp. asm. **-ran** (absol.) V7.

wacian, wk.v.II, *watch, wake*; inf. AI 61.

wāclic, adj., *base, mean, lowly*; nsn. AII 42.

wæd, n., *shallow water*; *sea*; gs. **-es** Wh9.

wǣg, m., *wave, sea*; dis. **-e** G1379; as. G1462, Wh27. [rel. **wegan**]

wǣgbord, n., *wave-board*; *the ark*; as. G1340.

wǣgliðend, m., *sea-farer, sailor*; npl. **-e** G1432, Wh11; dpl. **-um** G1395.

wægon, see **wegan**.

wǣgðel, n., *wave-board*; *the ark*; ds. **-e** G1446, 1496; as. G1358. [ðel, Ger. *Diele*]

wǣgþrēa, ?m. ?n., *wave-attack*; ds. G1490.

wǣgþrēat, m., *wave-press, wave-disaster*; *deluge*; ds. **-e** G1352.

wæl, n., *slaughter* (field, place); as. G2038.

wældrēor, m., *slaughter-gore, corpse-blood*; ds. **-e** Y. [drēor, rel. drēosan, st.v.2, *fall*]

wælgār, m., *slaughter-spear, deadly weapon*; gpl. **-a** G1990.

wælhere, m., *slaughter-army, fierce host of men*; npl. **-herigas** G 1983.

wælhrēow, adj., *slaughter-fierce, cruel*; nsm. W37; nsm.wk. **wælrēowa** AI 63.

wæl(l)grim, adj., *slaughter-grim, violent, cruel*; nsm. G1384.

wæl(l)regn, m., *slaughter-rain*; *deluge*; as. G1350.

wælsteng, m., *slaughter-shaft, spear-shaft*; ds. **-e** Y.

wælstōw, f., *slaughter-place, battlefield*; as. **-e** G2005.

wælstrēam, m., *slaughter-stream, deadly flood*; npl. **-as** G1301.

wǣmn, n. (LWS var. of **wǣpen**), *weapon*; apl. **-a** AII 94.

wǣpen, n., *weapon*; ns. Y; dis. **wǣpne** Y; gpl. **wǣpna** G2005, 2040.

wǣr, f., *promise, vow, word of honor*; as. G1329.

wǣre, see **bēon**.

wǣren, see **bēon**.

wǣrfæst, adj., *honor-bound, faithful*; nsm. G1320, 2026.

wǣrlīce, adv., *faithfully*, *truly*.

wǣrloga, wk.m., *faith-breaker*; *perfidious person*; ds. **-n** Wh37. [**-loga**, rel. **lēogan**, st.v.2, *lie*, *betray*]

wǣron, see **bēon**.

wæs, see **bēon**.

wæstm, m., f., *growth*, *plant*, *fruit*; *fullness*; ds. **-e** AII 7; as. **-a** P(n13); dpl. **-um** G1339. [Ger. *Wachstum*]

wæter, n., *water*; ns. Y; gs. **wætres** G1395; ds. **wætre** G1409, WL49, **wætere** Y; as. G1331, 1445, 1451, W20; npl. G1300, 1325; dpl. **wætrum** G1377, 1460.

wæterþīsa, wk.m., *water-rusher*; *the whale*; ns. Wh50.

wāfian, wk.v.II, *waver*, *be agitated*; *be amazed*; pres. 3s. (or pl.) **wāfigeð** P39; pret. 3s. **wāfode** AII 59.

wāg, m., *wall*; ds. **-e** Y.

waldan, st.v.7, rd.v., *rule*; pres.p. nsm. **waldende** X1010; cp. **wealdan**.

walde, see **willan**.

waldend, m., *ruler*, *leader*; *the Lord*; ns. G1294, 1365, 1408, W86, Y; as. V84.

wann/wonn, adj., *dark*, *dusky*; nsm.wk. **-a** G1983; dsm.wk. **-an** G1379; asm. **-e** G1462; nplm. **-e** G1301; nplf. **-e** G1430. [Eng. *wan*]

wāt, see **witan**.

wē, pers. pron. 1pl., *we*; nom.pl. **wē**, gpl. **ūre**, **us(s)er**; dpl. **ūs**, apl. **ūs**; see **ic**, **wit**, and the pers. prons. **ūre**, **us(s)er**.

wealdan, st.v.7, rd.v., *rule*, *command*, *govern*; pret. 3s. **wēold** G1377, 2005.

wealdgenga, wk.m., *forest-goer*, *robber*; ns. AII 92; ds. **-n** AII 67; dpl. **-gengum** AII 46. [Ger. *Wald*]

wealdleðer, n., *bridle-leather*, *rein*; as. AII 77.

weall, m., *wall*; *hill* (in the aspect of a wall); gs. **-es** R29:7.

weard, adv., *-ward*: **wið . . . weard**, *toward*.

weard, m., *guardian*, *lord*; *God*; ns. C43, G1363, 1426, 1484, 2073; as. C37. [Eng. *ward*; Ger. *Wart*]

weardian, wk.v.II, *inhabit*, *occupy*, *hold*; pres. 3pl. **weardiað** Wh26, WL34.

weardmann, m., *watchman, guard*; npl. **-men** AII 77; dpl. **-um** AII 76.

wearð, see **weorðan**.

wēaþearf, f., *grievous need*; *woeful necessity*; ds. **-e** WL10.

weaxan, st.v.7, *grow, increase*; pres. 3pl. **wexeð** P61; pret. 3s. **wēox** W9, WL3 [?read **āwēox**].

weccan, wk.v.I, *kindle*; pres. 3pl. **weccað** Wh21.

wedd, n., *pledge*; *what is given as security*; ds. **-e** G2070. [Eng. *wed*]

weder, n. (good) *weather*; gs. **wedres** Wh26.

weg, m., *way, path, road*; gs. **-es** AII 73; as. G1329, **on weg** (*away*) R39:6; gpl. **-a** W63.

wegan, st.v.5, *bear, carry*; inf. G2044; pret. 3pl. **wægon** G2049. [Ger. *bewegen*]

wegnest, n., *provisions for a journey, viaticum*; ds. **-e** C113.

wel, adv., *well, fully.*

wela, wk.m., *wealth*; pl. *riches, bounties*; gpl. **welena** P18. [Eng. *weal*]

weler, m., *lip*; apl. **-as** Wh54.

welhwā, pron., *each (one), every (one)*; ds. **-hwām** V30.

welle, f., *well, spring*; ns. P10, 11, 14; ds. P27, 60.

welm/wylm, m., *surge*; *stream*; *a surging place* (hell); *fervor*; ds. **-e** C86; as. Wh46.

welwyllende, adj., *of good will, benevolent*; nsm. AI 44.

wēman, wk.v.I, *persuade, entice*; pres. 3pl. **wēmað** Wh35.

wēn, f., *expectation, hope*; ns. G1446.

wēna, wk.m., *expectation*; ds. **-n** G1985.

wēnan, wk.v.I, w. gen. or acc., *believe, suppose*; *expect*; pres. 3pl. **wēnað** Wh11, 20; pret. 3s. **wēnde** AII 25, 56. [Eng. *ween*]

wēnlic, adj., *fair, handsome*; nsm. AII 6.

wēold, see **wealdan**.

wēop, see **wēpan**.

weorc, n., *work, deed, act*; *labor, pain*; ns. Wh(n35); dis. **wæs** ... **weorce**, *was painful* G2028; as. C39, Y; gpl. **-a** X1037; dipl. **-um** Wh84, Y.

weorðan, st.v.3, *become*; *be* (auxiliary in forming the passive w. past. part.); *happen*; pres. 3s. **weorþeð** Wh42, X1022, 1028, **wurð**

P58, **wyrðeþ** P(n17); pres. 3pl. **weorðaþ** Wh56; pret. 3s.
WEARð AI 3 etc.; pret. subj. 3s. **wurde** AII 107, G2032; pret.
3pl. **wurdon** G1996, 2073, W9, **wurdan** W33; see next verb.

weorðian, wk.v.II, *honor, show honor to*; *worship*; inf. W19; pres. 3s.
weorðað W85; pres. 1pl. **wurðiaþ** W28; pres. 3pl. **weorðiaþ**
W53, **wurðiað** W74; pret. 3pl. **wurðedon** W14, **wurðodon** W47,
55; ger. **tō wurðienne** W32.

weorðmynt/wyrðment, f., *honor, respect, esteem*; ns. W88; ds. **-e** W77.

weorðung, f., *worship*; ds. **-e** W57.

weorud, see **werod**.

w(e)oruldhād, m., *world(ly) condition, secular life* (as opposed to
religious or monastic life); ds. **-e** C18; as. C63.

wēox, see **weaxan**.

wēpan, st.v.7, *weep (for)*; inf. WL38; pret. 3s. **wēop** AI 26, AII 94;
pres. p. asm. **wēpende** AII 102.

wer, m., *man; male*; ns. AI 38, 43, 67, G1476, 2053; gs. **-es** P(n18);
ds. **-e** AI 55; npl. **-as** P(n13), Y; gpl. **-a** G1379, 1968, 2007, 2069,
R29:14, R47:3; dpl. **-um** G1291, 1384, 2064, V18; apl. **-as**
G1352, 1358. [as in Eng. *werewolf*]

wergend, m., *defender, protector*; npl. G1971.

werian/wergan, wk.v.I, *hinder; defend, protect*; inf. G1976, V39.

wērig, adj., *weary, exhausted*; nsm. G1462; nsf. G1469.

wērigferhð, adj., *weary-hearted (minded)*; nplm. **-ferðe** Wh19.

wērigmōd, adj., *weary-minded; disconsolate*; nsm. WL49.

werod/weorud, n., *throng, host, company (of men)*; ds. **-e** G1346, 1963
[MS **worulde**]; dis. **werede** G2093, **weorude** Wh59; gpl. **-a**
G1362, 1411; dpl. **-um** G1301, 1340, **weredum** X1010.

?wertācen, n., *?people-sign, ?an emblem for men*; ns. P(n16).

wesan, see **bēon**.

west, adv., *west(ward)*.

wex, n. (= **weax**), *wax*; ds. **-e** P42.

wexeð, see **weaxan**.

wīc, n., *abode, dwelling; camp*; ns. WL32; as. Wh26, 37, WL52; dpl.
-um G2061, V7, 46. [Eng. *wick*, as in place-names]

wīd, adj., *wide, vast, great*; nsm.wk. **-a** Wh59; gsf. **-re** G1350; dsn.
wk. **-an** Wh88; asn. G1307; aplm. **-e** Wh54.

wīde, adv., *widely, far and wide*; WL46.

wīdeferh, adv. (= **-ferhð**, *long life*), *always, forever*; R39:8, 21.

wīdgil, adj., *wide-spreading*; dplf. **-lum** AII 47.

wīdl, m. and n., *impurity, filth*; dpl. **-um** G1294.

wīdland, n., *wide land, extensive country*; as. G1412.

wīdlian, wk.v.II, *pollute, profane*; pret. 3pl. **-ledan** V60 [MS **wid lædan**].

wīdmǣre, adj., *widely famous, well known*; nsn. V59.

wīf, n., *woman*; *wife*; ns. AI 39, W71; ds. **-e** AI 7, 35; npl. 1432, 2087; apl. G1334, 1358.

wīfhād, m., *woman-nature, female sex*; gs. **-es** P(n18).

wīg, n., *fight, battle, war*; ds. **-ge** Y; dis. **-e** V65; as. G2070.

wiga, wk.m., *warrior*; gpl. **wigena** G2040.

wīgcyrm, m., *battle-din, noise of men and weapons in combat*; ns. G1990.

wīgend, m., *warrior, fighter*; apl. G1411.

wīgrōd, f., *warpath, road to (of) battle*; as. **-e** G2084.

wīgsigor, m., *battle-victory*; as. G2003.

wīgsīð, m., *war-journey*; as. G2094.

wīgsmið, m., *war-smith, craftsman of battle-deeds*; npl. **-as** V14.

wīgsteal, n., *war-place, fortification against attack, bulwark*; as. V39.

wiht/wuht, f. and n., *creature*; *thing*; ns. R29:7, R39:1; gs. **-e** R29:14; as. R29:1, R39:26, Y; gpl. **-a** G1297, R39:14.

wihte, adv., *at all*; **ne ... wihte**, *not at all, not a whit*, R47:6.

wiites, see **wīte**.

wilde, adj., *wild*; nsm.wk. **-a** G1460; nsf. G1465; asf. G1477.

wilgest, m., *willing guest* (Christ); as. V7.

willa/wylla, wk.m., *faculty of the will*; *mind*; *desire*; *joy*; gs. **-n** Wh66; ds. ?**wille** AII 25, **-n** Wh(n35); as. **-n** AI 31, G1455, 2087, R29:10, Wh(n35), 43, **willa** Wh(n35), **wille** P67; ?as./apl. **-n** Wh35; dipl. **willum** (adv., *willfully*) V72.

willan, anom.v., *be willing, wish, desire*; pres. 1s. **wille/wylle** AI 41, 42, AII 12, 88, 89, G1296, 1344, 1351, Wh2; pres. 2s. **wylt** AI 40; pres. 3s. **wile/wyle** AI 44, R39:5, Wh(n35, 65); neg. pres. 3s. **nele** AII 37; pret. 1s. **wolde** AI 27; pret. 3s. **wolde** AI 1, 9, 12, 26, 63, AII 15, 42, 45, 99, G1291, 1360, 2047, W42, **walde**

R29:5; pret. subj. 3s. **wolde** G1445; neg. pret. 3s. **nolde** AI 31, 33, AII 58, 78, G1448, 1480; pret. 3pl. **woldon** C86, G1975, 1979, W57; neg. pret. 3pl. **noldon** W31.

willeburne, f., *spring (of water)*; apl. **-burnan** G1373. [**wille**, m., *well, spring*; **burn(e)**, f., *stream*]

willflōd, m., *water-flood, deluge*; ns. G1412.

willgesīð, m., *willing (trustworthy) companion*; npl. **-ðas** G2003.

willgeþofta, wk.m., *beloved companion*; apl. **-n** G2026.

wilnian, wk.v.II, w. gen., *desire, ask for*; pres. 2s. **wilnast** AI 29.

wilsum, adj., *wilsome, lovely*; nsn. V81.

wilsumness, f., *devotion*; dis. **-e** C122.

wīn, n., *wine*; ns. V18; dis. **-e** V41.

wīnburg, f., *festive fortification, wine-filled bulwark*; dpl. **-um** V14.

windan, st.v.3, *wind; fly around*; pret. 3pl. **wundon** G(n1983); see also **wundene**.

wine, m., *friend; lover*; ns. WL49, 50; gpl. **winigea** Y.

winelēas, adj., *friendless, companionless*; nsm. WL10.

winnan, st.v.3, *suffer*; pret. 1s. **wonn** WL5.

winter, m., *winter*; pl. *years*; gpl. **wintra** G1320, 1368, 1976, **wintren** P54, 62.

wīsa, wk.m., *leader*; ns. G2004.

wīsdōm, m., *wisdom*; ds. **-e** W13.

wīse, wk.f., *manner, way, custom; matter*; ns. V30, Wh32, Wh(n65); ds. **wīsan** C86, W67, **wīsen** P38; as. **wȳsan** AI 56, **wīsan** C59; npl. **wīsan** P(n18). [as in Eng. *likewise*]

wīshȳdig, adj., *wise-minded*; nsm. G2053.

wīsian, wk.v.II, *guide*; pret. 3s. **wīsode** Y.

wīslīce, adv., *wisely*.

wissian, wk.v.II, *instruct, guide*; inf. AII 55.

wist, f., *food*; as. **-e** G1340.

wit, dual pron., *we two*; nom. WL13, 21; gen. **uncer** WL25; acc. **unc** WL12, 22.

wita, wk.m., *wise man, teacher*; ns. V1.

witan, pret.-pres.v., *know*; inf. V8 [MS **witon**], 16; pres. 1s. **wāt** G1346; pres. 3s. **wāt** P(n18), 64, V35; pres. subj. 1pl. **witon** P(n19); pres. subj. 3pl. **witen** R39:4; pret. 3s. **wiste** G1287,

2043; neg. pret. 3s. **nyste** AI 33; pret. 3pl. **wiston** C108; imper. 2s. **wite** AII 11, V46, 77.

wīte, n., *punishment, torment, torture*; ns. G1319; gs. **wiites** C79, as. WL5; dipl. **wītum** V56.

wīt(e)ga, wk.m., *wise man, prophet*; ns. V50, 81.

wītig, adj., *wise, learned*; diplf. wk. **wītgan** V3.

witodlīce, adv., *certainly, truly*.

wið, prep., w. dat. and acc., *against*; **wið þām þe**, conj. *when, at the time when*.

wiðersæc, n., *denial, apostasy*; as. AI 37. [**sæc(c)**, f., *struggle, strife*; rel. **sacan**, st.v.6, *dispute, fight*]

wiðertrod, n., *return, retreat*; as. G2084. [**trod**. n., *track*; rel. **tredan**. st.v.5, *tread, traverse*]

wiðinnan, adv., *from within, inwardly*.

wiðsacan, st.v.6, w. dat., *gainsay, deny, reject, resist*; inf. AI 12, -**sacen** AI 9; pres. 2s. **wiðsaca** AI 17; pres. subj. 3s. **wiðsace** Wh83; pres. 2pl. -**sacað** AI 14; pret. 1s. -**sōc** AI 42.

wlītan, st.v.1, *look, gaze*; pres. subj. 3pl. **wlīten** Wh12.

wlite, m., *beauty; countenance*; ns. X1037; as. P(n13).

wlitesēon, f., *marvelous sight, spectacle*; ns. Y.

wlitig, adj., *lovely, bright*; nsm. P(n16), 66; nsn. (or f.) P18; asn. Y.

wlonc, adj., *proud*; nsm. Wh50; nplm. -**e** V14; dplm. -**um** Wh43.

wōcor, f., *offspring, progeny*; ns. G1312; as. **wōcre** G1342, 1409, 1490.

wōdlic, adj., *mad, frantic*; dsf.wk. -**an** AI 30.

wōdlīce, adv., *madly; blasphemously*.

wōh, adj., *twisted, woven; perverse*; npln. R39 : 24.

wolcen, m. or n., *cloud; sky, heaven*; dpl. **wolcnum** G1392, 1438, Y. [Eng. *welkin*]

wolde, woldon, see **willan**.

wōlic, adj. (= **wōh**-), *wrong, perverse*; dpln. -**um** AII 30 [MS **woc**-].

wōlīce, adv. (= **wōh**-), *wrongly, perversely*.

womb, f., *womb*; ns. V(n24).

wonn, see **winnan**; see also **wann**.

wōp, m., *weeping*; ds. -**e** AI 39, AII 63. [cp. **wēpan**]

word, n., *word, speech, sentence; command*; ns. Wh(n35); ds. -**e** G1412; as. AI 34, AII 17, C57, G1362; gpl. -**a** AI 29, X1037; dpl. -**um**

C47, G2035, 2053, R47:6; dipl. **-um** P(n13, 16), R39:26, 29, V16, Wh2, 84, **-en** P53; apl. AII 91, 93, C35, 47, 124, 125, R47:1, V41.

wordhord, n., *word-hoard*, (great) *store of words*; as. V3.

worhton, see **wyrcan**.

wōrian, wk.v.I, *wander about, toss about*; pres. subj. 3s. **wōrie** Wh9.

worn, m., *a great number, multitude*; as. (w. partitive gen.) G1320, 1331, 1438, V33.

woruld/world/wurld, f., *world*; gs. **-e** C8, WL46; ds. **-e** C96, P(n16), 19, V72, 81, W4, 79, X1022; as. G1373, W89; gpl. **-a** W89.

woruldafol, n., *worldly power*; dpl. **-afelum** W33.

woruldhād, see **w(e)oruld-**.

woruldmonn, m., *human being, mortal man*; gpl. **-monna** X1015; apl. **-men** W33.

woruldrīce, n., *realm of the world, the whole world*; ds. WL13.

wōðcræft, m., *poetic skill*; dis. **-e** Wh2. [**wōð**, f., *sound, voice, poetry*]

wracu, f., *pain, suffering*; apl. **wraca** W54. [rel. **wrecan**]

wræc (wræcon), see **wrecan**.

wræcca/wrecca, wk.m., *exile*; *a wanderer in foreign lands*; ns. WL10; gs. **-n** R39:8, as. **-n** R29:10. [Eng. *wretch*; rel. **wrecan**]

wræcsīð, m., *exile journey*; *miserable course*; *privation*; gpl. **-a** WL5; apl. **-as** WL38.

wrǣtlic, adj., *marvelous, wondrous, curious*; nsf. **-u** R47:2, Y; nsn. R39:24; comp. asf. **-ran** Wh50. [**wrǣt(t)**, f., *work of art, ornament, precious object*]

wrāð, adj., *wroth, angry*; as noun, *hostile one, enemy*; nplm. **-e** G1983; gpl. **-ra** G1496; dpl. **-um** G1976, 2038.

wrāðe, adv., *wrathfully, fiercely*.

wrāðu, f., *support, help*; as. **wraþe** Wh35.

wrēah, see **wrēon**.

wrecan, st.v.5, *drive out*; *punish*; *avenge*; pret. 1s. **wræc** Y; pret. 3s. **wræc** G1380; pret. 3pl. **wræcon** G1385; *utter, tell*; pres. 1s. **wrece** WL1; pres. 3pl. **wrecað** V15.

wrecca, see **wræcca**.

wrencan, wk.v.I, *wrench, twist*; *plot*; pres. 3s. **wrenceþ** V33.

wrēon, contr.v.1, *cover, envelop*; pret. 3s. **wrēah** G1377, 1386.

wrītan, st.v.1, *write, inscribe*; pres. 3pl. **wrīteð** P42; imper. 2s. **wrȳt** AI 16; pret. 3pl. **wrēoton** C71.

writian, wk.v.II, *chirp*; pres. 3pl. **writigeð** P37.

wrixendlice, adv., *in turn*.

wrixl, f., *exchange*; ns. G1990.

wrixlan, wk.v.I, *vary, exchange*; pres. 3pl. **wrixlað** V16.

wrōht, f., *crime, strife*; as. V59, **-e** W54. [rel. **wrēgan**, wk.v.I, *stir up*]

wrȳt, see **wrītan**.

wucu, f., *week*; ds. **wuca** P26, as. **wucan** G1465, 1477; apl. **wucan** P35, 49.

wudeholt, n., *forest, grove*; ns. P15.

wudu, m., *wood; tree*; gpl. **wuda** WL27.

wudufæsten, n., *wooden fastness; the ark*; as. G1312.

wuduwe, f., *widow*; npl. **wuduwan** G2010.

wuhta, see **wiht**.

wuldor, n., *glory*; gs. **wuldres** V65, 72, Wh88.

wuldorcyning, m., *king of glory, God*; ns. X1022; gs. **-es** G1384, R39:21 [MS **-cyninge**]; ds. **-e** V50, **-cyning** V77 (?read **-e**); as. Wh67, 84.

wuldorfæder, m., *father of glory, God*; gs. C39.

wuldorlic, adj., *glorious*; nsm. X1010.

wunden, pp. adj. (of **windan**, st.v.3), *twisted, wound* (in ornamentation); asn. G2070.

wundon, see **windan**.

wundor, n., *wonder; glory*; ns. X1015; as. R47:2; gpl. **wundra** C39.

wundorlic, adj., *wondrous*; nsm. P(n16); nsf. **-u** R29:7; asm.wk. **-an** W6; asf. **-e** R29:1; nplf. **-e** P(n18).

wundorlīce/wunder-, adv., *wonderfully, wondrously*.

wundorworuld, f., *world of wonders, wondrous world*; as. R39:17.

wundrian, wk.v.I, *wonder at, be astonished, be amazed*; pres. 3s. (or pl.) **wundrigeð** P39; pres. 3pl. **wundriað** P(n13); pret. 3s. **wundrode** C97.

wunian, wk.v.II, *inhabit, dwell, live*; inf. P(n19), V46, 56, WL27, **wunigen** P68; pres. 3s. **wunað** AII 68, **wuneð on** P22, 24,

wuneð P34; pres. subj. 3s. **wunige** V18; pres. 3pl. **wuniað** Wh25; pret. 3s. **wunode** AII 24. [Ger. *wohnen*]

wunung, f., *dwelling*; ds. **-e** AII 17.

wurld, see **woruld**.

wurde, wurdon, wurð, see **weorðan**.

wurðiaþ, see **weorðian**.

wurðlicor, comp. adv. (of **wurðlice**), *worthier, more glorious*; with instr. **þon**, G2094.

wurðodon (wurðedon), see **weorðian**.

wuton, pres. subj. 1pl. of **wītan** (st.v.3, *go*), with infinitive, *let us*; C117.

wylcumian, wk.v.II, *welcome, greet*; pres. 3s. (or pl.) **-cumigeð** P39.

wyle, wylt, see **willan**; **wylla**, see **willa**.

wylm, see **welm**.

wynlic, adj., *joyful*; comp. asn. **-ran** WL52.

wyn(n), f., *joy, pleasure, delight*; ns. WL46; ds. **-e** P68, (n19); as. **-e** Wh69; gpl. **-a** WL32; dpl. **-um** Wh22. [Eng., as in *winsome*; Ger. *Wonne*]

wynlond, n., *land of joy; a paradise*; as. V65.

wynsum, adj., *winsome, pleasant*; nsm. P66, Wh54; nsn. (or f.) P18; npln. **-u** C70.

wyrcan, wk.v.I, *form, make, prepare*; inf. C3, 11, 15, G1302, 1316; pres. 3pl. **wyreceð** P42; pret. 3pl. **worhton** W6, 11.

wyrd, f., *fate, destiny; event*; ns. G1399, R47:2; gpl. **-a** R39:24. [rel. **weorðan**]

wyrhta, wk.m., *builder, maker, worker; the Creator*; ns. W88, **wyrhte** P54; gpl. **wyrhtena** W8. [rel. Eng. *wright*]

wyrm, m., *worm*; ns. R47:3 (*bookworm*); dipl. **-um** V56.

wyrðe, adj., *worthy*; nsm. G1347; gsm. **-s** C48.

wyrðeþ, see **weorðan**.

wyrðment, see **weorð-**.

wȳsan, see **wīse**.

wyðersaca, wk.m., *rebel, apostate*; ns. AI 41. [**wiðer**, adv. prep., *against*; prefix, *counter, opposing*; **saca**, wk.m., *opponent*; rel. **sacan**, st.v.6, *struggle, dispute, contend*]

Y

yfel, adj., *evil, bad*; dsm.wk. **-an** AII 46; asf.wk. **-an** W74; nplm. **-e** Wh(n35); dplm. **-um** AII 45.

yfel, n., *evil*; ds. **-e** AII 44.

ylce, see **ilca**.

ylde, m. pl., *men*; gpl. **ylda** Y; see **yldu**.

yldest, superl. adj. (of **eald**), *eldest*; (absol.) *chief, leader*; nsm. AII 46.

yldu, f., *age, time of life*; gs. **ylde** AII 6, 85, C19.

ymb(e)/emb(e), prep. w. acc., *about, near, beside*; *concerning*; *with reference to*; *after*.

ymbsellan, wk.v.I, *surround*; pp. **ymbseald** Wh10.

ymbūtan, prep. w. acc., *round about*.

yrming, m. (= **earming**), *wretch, poor fool*; as. W55.

yrmþu, f., *hardship, pain*; gpl. **yrmþa** WL3.

ȳtmæsta, superl. adj., *uttermost, last*; apln. **-n** C125.

ȳð, f., *wave*; npl. **-a** G1385, 1430; ?gpl., ?apl. **-a** G1309, WL7.

ȳðhōf, n., *wave-house*; *the ark*; as. G1316.

ȳðmearh, m., *wave-steed, ship*; apl. **-mearas** Wh49. [**mearh**, m., *horse*; Eng. *mare*]

Proper Names

Abraham, m., nom. G2024, 2045, 2069, 2083, 2089; gen. G2012; dat. 2036; acc. 2020.

Adam, m., *Adam*; acc. W10.

Ægypte, m., *Egypt*; gen. **Ægypta** C74.

Ambrafel, m., nom. G1962.

Aner, m., acc. G2027.

Armenia, f., nom. G1423.

Basilius, m., *St. Basil*; nom. AI 46, 51, 59, 65, 75; dat. **Basilie** AI 37.

Crēata/Crēta, f., *the island Crete*; nom. W36, 42.

Cedmon, m., nom. (voc.) C28.

Crist, m., Christ; nom. P68, (n19); gen. **-es** AI 77, AII 13, 22, 83, C76, 118; dat. **-e** AI 2, 12, 15, 17, 27, 40, 42, AII 9, 89, 105; acc. P(n19).

Dāmascus, f., dat. **Dōmasco** G2082.

ebrisc, adj., Hebrew; dsm. **-an** G2021.
Egipteland, n., Egypt; dat. **-e** P35.
Elamitare, mpl., gen. **Elamitarna** G1960, 1980, 2004, 2081.
Ephesa, f., the city, Ephesus; ?dat./gen. **-n** AII 2; gen. **-n** AII 20.
Escol, m., acc. G2027.

Fenix, m., the mythical bird, Phoenix; nom. P24, 34, 40, 41, 48, 52, 58, 59, 65; dat. P55; acc. P37, 40, 42, 44.

Gomorra, f., acc. **-n** G1966, 2008.
Gomorre, mpl., nom. G1997; gen. **Gomorra** G2078.

Iohannes, m., St. John, the Apostle; nom. AII 6, 10, 17, 50, 58, 60, 64, 70, 84, P1, 53; dat. **Iohanne** AII 64; gen. AII 95.
Iouis, m., Jove (or Jupiter), son of Saturn; nom. W40, 43, 68, 70; gen. **Ioues** W72.
Israhēl, m., the (ancient) land of Israel; gen. **-hēla** C74.
Iuno, f., Juno, daughter of Saturn, sister and wife of Jove-Jupiter; nom. W44.

Jordan, dat. G1967.

Lamech, m., gen. **-es** G1286, 1368, 1408, 1425, 1441.
Loth, m., Lot; nom. G2085; gen. **-es** G2023, 2080; acc. G2016, 2048.

Manre, m., acc. G2027.
Mars, m., the god of war, Mars; nom. W53.
Mercurius, m., Mercury, god of eloquence and of thieves, keeper of roads; nom. W68; gen. **Mercuries** W68.
Minerua, f., the goddess Minerva; nom. W45.

Nembroð, m., Nimrod; nom. W6.

Noe, m., Noah; nom. G1285, 1314, 1356, 1367, 1443; gen. **-s** G1323, 1423, P4, 6, W5, 7; dat. G1295, 1327, 1483.

Orlahomar, m., acc. G1962.

Oðon, m., Odin, the Scandic god (the Anglo-Saxon Woden); nom. W66, 69.

Radionsaltus, m., a glen in Paradise; nom. P15.

Saturnus, m., Saturn, the god of Latium; nom. W36; gen. **Saturnes** W71.

Sennar, m., dat. G1963.

Sodoma, mpl., gen. G2013, 2022; acc. G2077.

Sodom(e), f., gen. G1975; acc. **Sodoman** G1966, 2008.

Sodomware, mpl., inhabitants of Sodom; npl. G1996.

Þare, m., gen. **-s** G2054.

Þor, m., the god Thor (Anglo Saxon Þunor); nom. W51, 68.

Uenus, f., Venus, the goddess of love; nom. W46, 71.

Bibliography

I. BIBLIOGRAPHIES

Annual Bibliography: The Modern Language Association, Old English Group. Mimeograph. Prepared by A. K. Brown, and distributed by the Center for Medieval and Renaissance Studies, The Ohio State University.

Annual Bibliography: *PMLA* (issued in June of each year; as of 1969 the OE Bibliography appears in vol. I).

W. Bonser, ed., *An Anglo-Saxon and Celtic Bibliography, 450–1087*, 2 vols. (Berkeley, 1957). Historical and cultural subjects, through 1953.

The Cambridge Bibliography of English Literature, vols. I and V (Supplement, to 1954) (Cambridge, Eng., 1940, 1957).

A. G. Kennedy, ed., *A Bibliography of Writings on the English Language . . . to 1922* (Cambridge, Mass., 1927).

F. C. Robinson, ed., *Old English Literature: A Select Bibliography* (Toronto, 1970).

F. C. Robinson, "Old English Research in Progress," annually in *Neuphilologische Mitteilungen* (Helsinki).

(An exhaustive bibliography of literary and textual studies is being prepared by F. C. Robinson and S. B. Greenfield.)

The Year's Work in English Studies (London, 1921–).

II. GRAMMAR

K. Brunner, ed., *Altenglische Grammatik, nach der angelsächsischen Grammatik von Eduard Sievers* ["Sievers–Brunner"], 3rd ed. (Tübingen, 1965).

A. Campbell, *Old English Grammar* (Oxford, 1959).

R. Quirk and C. L. Wrenn, *An Old English Grammar*, 2nd ed. (London and New York, 1958).

J. and E. M. Wright, *Old English Grammar*, 3rd ed. (Oxford, 1925).

III. DICTIONARIES and VOCABULARY

J. Bosworth, *An Anglo-Saxon Dictionary*, ed. and enlarged by T. N. Toller; and Toller, *Supplement* ["Bosworth-Toller"], 2 vols. (Oxford, 1908–1921). In preparation are a new Supplement edited by A. Campbell, and a new dictionary of Old English, sponsored by Oxford University and the University of Toronto.

J. R. Clark Hall, *A Concise Anglo-Saxon Dictionary*, 4th ed., with a Supplement by H. D. Meritt (Cambridge, Eng., 1960).

H. Gneuss, *Lehnbildungen und Lehnbedeutungen im Altenglischen* (Berlin, 1955).

C. W. M. Grein, *Sprachschatz der angelsächsischen Dichter*, revised by J. J. Köhler and F. Holthausen (Heidelberg, 1912–1914). A partial concordance of the poetry.

F. Holthausen, *Altenglisches etymologisches Wörterbuch*, 2nd ed. (Heidelberg, 1963).

H. Kurath and S. M. Kuhn, eds., *Middle English Dictionary* (Ann Arbor, 1952–).

H. D. Meritt, *Fact and Lore About Old English Words* (Stanford, 1954).
———, *Some of the Hardest Glosses in Old English* (Stanford, 1968).

W. G. Searle, *Onomasticon Anglo-Saxonicum* (Cambridge, Eng., 1897).

(An exhaustive, computer-produced concordance of the poetry, based on the Krapp-Dobbie *Anglo-Saxon Poetic Records* [see V below], is in preparation by J. B. Bessinger, Jr., and P. H. Smith, Jr.; an initial volume, published by Cornell University Press [1969] contains *Beowulf*.)

IV. MANUSCRIPTS and PALEOGRAPHY

A. Cappelli, *Dizionario di abbreviature latine ed italiane*, 5th ed. (Milan, 1954).

W. Keller, *Angelsächsische Paleographie*, 2 vols. (*Palaestra*, xliii, 1906).

N. R. Ker, *Catalogue of Manuscripts Containing Anglo-Saxon* (Oxford, 1957).
———, *Medieval Manuscripts in British Libraries*, vol. I: *London* (London, 1969).

E. M. Thompson, *An Introduction to Greek and Latin Paleography* (Oxford, 1912).

(See also IX below.)

V. COLLECTIONS of TEXTS

W. F. Bolton, ed., *An Old English Anthology* (London, 1963).

G. L. Brook, gen. ed., Old and Middle English Texts (Manchester, Eng.):
Three Old English Elegies, ed. R. F. Leslie (1961).
The Phoenix, ed. N. R. Blake (1964).
The Wanderer, ed. R. F. Leslie (1966).

J. J. Campbell and J. L. Rosier, eds., *Poems in Old English* (New York, 1962).

G. P. Krapp and E. V. K. Dobbie, eds., *The Anglo-Saxon Poetic Records* [ASPR] (New York):

    Vol.   I. The Junius Manuscript, ed. Krapp (1931).

    Vol. II. The Vercelli Book, ed. Krapp (1932).

    Vol. III. The Exeter Book, ed. Krapp and Dobbie (1936).

    Vol. IV. Beowulf and Judith, ed. Dobbie (1953).

    Vol. V. The Paris Psalter and the Meters of Boethius, ed. Krapp (1933).

    Vol. VI. The Anglo-Saxon Minor Poems, ed. Dobbie (1942).

J. C. Pope, ed., *Seven Old English Poems* (New York, 1966).

A. H. Smith and F. Norman, general eds., Methuen's Old English Library [MOEL] (London and New York):

    The Dream of the Rood, ed. B. Dickens and A. S. C. Ross.

    The Battle of Maldon, ed. E. V. Gordon.

    Deor, ed. K. Malone.

    Juliana, ed. Rosemary Woolf.

    Cynewulf's Elene, ed. P. O. E. Gradon.

    The Seafarer, ed. I. L. Gordon.

    The Wanderer, ed. T. P. Dunning and A. J. Bliss.

    The Parker Chronicle: 832–900, ed. A. H. Smith.

    Ælfric's Colloquy, ed. G. N. Garmonsway.

    Sermo Lupi ad Anglos, ed. D. Whitelock.

    Lives of Three English Saints, ed. G. I. Needham.

Dorothy Whitelock, rev. ed. of *Sweet's Anglo-Saxon Reader in Prose and Verse* (Oxford, 1967).

VI. LITERARY HISTORY

S. B. Greenfield, *A Critical History of Old English Literature* (New York, 1965).

K. Malone, "The Old English Period (to 1100)," in *The Middle Ages*, vol. I of *A Literary History of England*, ed. A. C. Baugh, 2nd ed. (New York, 1967).

J. C. Pope, *English Literature before the Norman Conquest* (Oxford, forthcoming).

E. G. Stanley, ed., *Continuations and Beginnings* (London, 1966).

C. L. Wrenn, *A Study of Old English Literature* (New York, 1967).

R. P. Wülcker, *Grundriss zur Geschichte der angelsächsischen Litteratur* (Leipzig, 1885).

VII. POETIC METER

A. J. Bliss, *The Metre of Beowulf* (Oxford: Basil Blackwell, 1958).

A. Heusler, *Deutsche Versgeschichte, mit Einschluss des altenglischen und altnordischen Stabreimverses* (Paul's *Grundriss der Germanischen Philologie*, 8: Berlin and Leipzig, 1925–1929).

W. P. Lehmann, *The Development of Germanic Verse-Form* (Austin, Tex., 1958).

J. C. Pope, "Old English Versification," in *Seven Old English Poems* (see under V above).

J. C. Pope, *The Rhythm of Beowulf*, rev. ed. (New Haven, Conn., 1966).

E. Sievers, *Altgermanische Metrik* (Halle, 1893).

VIII.   RELATED TOPICS

A. C. Bartlett, *The Larger Rhetorical Patterns in Anglo-Saxon Poetry* (New York, 1966).

P. H. Blair, *An Introduction to Anglo-Saxon England* (Cambridge, Eng., 1956).

W. F. Bolton, *A History of Anglo-Latin Literature*, 2 vols. (Princeton, 1967–).

R. W. V. Elliott, *Runes* (Manchester, 1959).

R. H. Hodgkin, *A History of the Anglo-Saxons*, 2 vols., 3rd ed., with an appendix on the Sutton Hoo Ship Burial by R. L. S. Bruce-Mitford (London, 1953).

K. Jackson, *Language and History in Early Britain* (Edinburgh, 1953).

W. Levison, *England and the Continent in the Eighth Century* (Oxford, 1946).

M. Manitius, *Geschichte der Lateinischen Literatur des Mittelalters*, 3 vols. (Munich, 1911–1931).

M. C. Morrell, *A Manual of Old English Biblical Materials* (Knoxville, Tenn., 1965).

J. D. A. Ogilvy, *Books Known to the English, 597–1066* (Cambridge, Mass., 1967).

K. Sisam, *Studies in the History of Old English Literature* (Oxford, 1962).

K. Strecker, *Introduction to Medieval Latin*, rev. and trans. R. B. Palmer, (Berlin, 1957).

D. Whitelock, *The Beginnings of English Society* (Baltimore, Md., 1952).

C. E. Wright, *The Cultivation of Saga in Anglo-Saxon England* (Edinburgh, 1939).

IX.   FACSIMILES of MANUSCRIPTS CONTAINING ANGLO-SAXON
(*EEMF = Early English Manuscripts in Facsimile* [Copenhagen]. The number in brackets which follows each entry is the item-number in N. R. Ker's *Catalogue of Manuscripts Containing Anglo-Saxon*.)

Brussels Glosses to Aldhelm's prose *De laude virginitatis*, ed. G. van Langenhove (Ghent, 1941), [8].

The Parker Chronicle and Laws, ed. R. Flower and H. Smith (Oxford, 1941), [39].

The Canterbury, or Eadwine's, Psalter, ed. M. R. James (London, 1935), [91].

The Durham Ritual, ed. F. Wormald *et al.*, *EEMF*, XVI (1969), [106].

The Épinal Glossary, ed. O. B. Schlutter (Hamburg, 1912), [114].

The Exeter Book of Old English Poetry, ed. R. W. Chambers *et al.* (London, 1933), [116].

The Tollemache Orosius, ed. A. Campbell, *EEMF*, III (1953), [133].

The Lindisfarne Gospels, ed. T. J. Brown *et al.* (Olten, Lausanne, 1956–60), [165].

Marvels of the East, ed. M. R. James (Oxford, 1929), [193.b, 216.2].

The Vespasian Psalter, ed. D. H. Wright, *EEMF*, XIV (1967), [203].

The Beowulf Manuscript, or Nowell Codex, ed. K. Malone, *EEMF*, XII (1963); of *Beowulf* alone, ed. N. Davis, with the original transcription and notes of J. Zupitza (EETS, 245 [London, 1959]), [216].

Ælfric, First Series of Catholic Homilies, ed. N. E. Eliason and P. Clemoes, *EEMF*, XIII (1966), [257].

Bald's Leechbook, ed. C. E. Wright, *EEMF*, V (1955), [264].

The Pastoral Care, ed. N. R. Ker, *EEMF*, VI (1956), [324].

The Caedmon Manuscript of Old English Poetry, ed. I. Gollancz (Oxford, 1927), [334].

The Peterborough Chronicle, ed. D. Whitelock, *EEMF*, IV (1954), [346].

The Paris Psalter, ed. B. Colgrave *et al.*, *EEMF*, VIII (1958), [367].

Textus Roffensis, ed. P. Sawyer, *EEMF*, XI (1962), [373].

The Blickling Homilies, ed. R. Willard, *EEMF*, X (1960), [382].

The Vercelli Book of Old English Poetry, ed. M. Förster (Rome, 1913), [394]. A new facsimile will appear in *EEMF*.

X. SOME ESSAYS *in* LITERARY THEORY *and* METHOD

L. D. Benson, "The Literary Character of Anglo-Saxon Formulaic Poetry," *PMLA*, 81 (1966), 334–41.

M. W. Bloomfield, "Understanding Old English Poetry," *Annuale Mediaevale*, 9 (1968), 5–25.

A. G. Brodeur, "The Diction of *Beowulf*," chapter I of *The Art of Beowulf* (Berkeley, 1960), pp. 1–38.

A. Campbell, "Verse Influences in Old English Prose," in J. L. Rosier, ed., *Philological Essays* (The Hague, 1970), pp. 93–98.

J. J. Campbell, "Learned Rhetoric in Old English Poetry," *MP*, 63 (1966), 189–201.

P. Clemoes, *Rhythm and Cosmic Order in Old English Christian Literature* (Cambridge, Eng., 1970).

R. Derolez, "Anglo-Saxon Literature: 'Attic' or 'Asiatic'? Old English

Poetry and Its Latin Background," in *English Studies Today*, ed. G. A. Bonnard (Bern, 1961), pp. 93–105.

S. B. Greenfield, "Grammar and Meaning in Poetry," *PMLA*, 82 (1967), 377–87.

F. Norman, "The Early Germanic Background of Old English Verse," in D. Pearsall and R. A. Waldron, eds., *Medieval Literature and Civilization* (London, 1969), pp. 3–27.

R. Quirk, "Poetic Language and Old English Metre," in A. Brown and P. Foote, eds., *Early English and Norse Studies* (London, 1963), pp. 150–171.

F. C. Robinson, "The Significance of Names in Old English Literature," *Anglia*, 86 (1968), 14–58.

————, "Lexicography and Literary Criticism: A Caveat," in J. L. Rosier, ed., *Philological Essays* (The Hague, 1970), pp. 99–110.

J. L. Rosier, "Hands and Feasts in *Beowulf*," *PMLA*, 78 (1963), 8–14.

E. G. Stanley, "Old English Poetic Diction and the Interpretation of *The Wanderer, The Seafarer* and *The Penitent's Prayer*," *Anglia*, 73 (1956), 413–66.

D. Whitelock, *Changing Currents in Anglo-Saxon Studies* (Cambridge, Eng., 1958).

C. L. Wrenn, "On the Continuity of English Poetry," *Anglia*, 76 (1958), 41–59.